Introduction to UNIX®

Mark Schulman

Library of Congress Catalog No.: 91-61972

ISBN: 0-88022-745-1

94   93   92   4   3   2

Interpretation of the printing code: the rightmost double-digit number is the year of the book's printing; the rightmost single-digit number, the number of the book's printing. For example, a printing code of 92-1 shows that the first printing of the book occurred in 1992.

Introduction to UNIX is based on all releases of UNIX System V.

Publisher: Lloyd J. Short

Acquisitions Manager: Rick Ranucci

Product Development Manager: Thomas H. Bennett

Managing Editor: Paul Boger

Book Designer: Scott Cook

Production Team: Michelle Cleary, Mark Enochs, Brook Farling, Sandy Grieshop, Juli Pavey, Linda Seifert, Louise Shinault, Kevin Spear, Bruce Steed, Susan VandeWalle, Allan Wimmer, Phil Worthington

For my grandfather, Sam Schulman, who will always be with me.

Product Director
Mary Bednarek

Production Editor
Barbara K. Koenig

Editors
Sara Allaei
Sharon Boller
Dennis G. Frazier

Technical Editor
David W. Solomon

*Composed in Garamond and MCP Digital
by Que Corporation*

Mark Schulman

Mark Schulman is a computer programmer and instructor with Cincinnati Bell Information Systems (CBIS). He has worked with a wide range of computer hardware and operating systems, from micros to mainframes. Since 1983, most of his work has been in UNIX and XENIX, writing software for a variety of applications and teaching classes in UNIX and the C and C++ programming languages.

He has taught as a visiting instructor at a number of major UNIX companies, including AT&T Bell Labs. He lives in Orlando, Florida with his wife Diedre, children Douglass and Belinda, and assorted animals.

TRADEMARK ACKNOWLEDGMENTS

Que Corporation has made every effort to supply trademark information about company names, products, and services mentioned in this book. Trademarks indicated below were derived from various sources. Que Corporation cannot attest to the accuracy of this information.

1-2-3 and Lotus are registered trademarks of Lotus Development Corporation.

A/UX and Macintosh are registered trademarks of Apple Computer, Inc.

AT&T and UNIX are registered trademarks of AT&T.

COBOL is a trademark of Micro Focus, Inc.

Cray-II is a trademark, and UNICOS is a registered trademark of Cray Research, Inc.

dBASE is a registered trademark of Ashton-Tate Corporation.

HP is a registered trademark of Hewlett-Packard Company.

Mach is a trademark, and Microsoft, MS-DOS, and XENIX are registered trademarks of Microsoft Corporation.

NFS is a trademark of Sun Microsystems, Inc.

PC/AT and Presentation Manager are trademarks, and AIX, IBM, and OS/2 are registered trademarks of International Business Machines Corporation.

PDP-7, PDP-10, PDP-11, and VAX are trademarks, and DEC is a registered trademark of Digital Equipment Corporation.

Post-it is a trademark of 3M Company.

UNiSYS is a trademark of UNiSYS Corporation.

WordPerfect is a registered trademark of WordPerfect Corporation.

WordStar is a registered trademark of MicroPro International Corporation.

ACKNOWLEDGMENTS

My heartfelt thanks to everyone at Que Corporation who applied the consistent and firm pressure I needed to get this job done.

Special thanks to Mary Bednarek, who kept me in line and didn't laugh when I said something stupid.

Thanks to Barbara Koenig, who fixed all my mistakes.

Thanks to David Solomon, who never failed to have a helpful suggestion.

Ralph Barkor and Jordan Gold at UniForum provided me with a wealth of information about UniForum and its activities.

Thanks to the folks at USENIX, who supplied stacks of material about USENIX.

Thanks to Dan Cunningham, Anne Spalding, and Greg Allender at CBIS, who were never too busy to lend an ear or a manual, reboot a machine, patch a panel, or reset a balky modem.

Thanks to all the hundreds of friends on Usenet who taught me so much. If you read nothing else in this book, read about the great folks on Usenet, in Chapter 11.

And finally, thanks to my father, Charles Schulman, who encouraged me; my mother, Edith, who set the example; my wife, Diedre, who always understood why I had to work on the book; and my children, Douglass and Belinda, who did without a dad more often than they'd have liked.

—M.S.

CONTENTS AT A GLANCE

TABLE OF CONTENTS

Introduction

By the early 1980s, UNIX was still in its infancy, even though it was nearly a teenager. UNIX ran on a smattering of computers at universities commercial sites, as well as within AT&T Bell Labs where it was born. A Bell Labs manual of the time (*UNIX Programmer's Manual*) admitted that UNIX "…delivered with no support and with an amateurishly published manual…has earned worldwide respect, sometimes bordering on adulation." A few years before, a 1978 edition of *Bell System Technical Journal* had boasted that UNIX was running on several hundred computers, a number that pales next to today's figures.

UNIX in the 1980s was just beginning to make its presence felt. Largely unknown outside the computer research community, UNIX had made no impact at all on the small businesses where PCs soon would thrive, beginning in 1981. Compared to other operating systems, such as MS-DOS, which overnight became the most popular operating system ever, UNIX was a slow starter indeed.

In recent years, however, UNIX has made up for lost time. It no longer is relegated to research facilities, but has become common in areas ranging from business to defense-related industries. Market analysts predict that nearly one million UNIX systems will be shipped worldwide in 1991, bringing the total number of UNIX systems worldwide to about 3.5 million.

UNIX is now the de facto standard for minicomputer operating systems, and very few minicomputer manufacturers today would think of marketing a new computer that cannot use UNIX. Most major computer manufacturers have embraced UNIX, although some only grudgingly because the market demanded it. UNIX now runs on PCs and mainframes, spreading throughout the computer industry like a benevolent virus. In any large bookstore, where once only a few UNIX books were available—or perhaps none at all—many shelves are now devoted to UNIX.

From its meager beginnings, the UNIX market has exploded. UNIX has become many things to many people. To some it is merely a tool for getting work done; for others it is an elegant expression of how a computer should be organized; for still others it forms a community of fellowship and common interests.

Introduction to UNIX explores the unique environment that UNIX provides. You discover how and why it works the way it does, and perhaps you will begin to understand the popularity of the license plates, distributed by a manufacturer at a UNIX convention, that so elegantly capture the spirit of many UNIX users: "Live Free or Die: UNIX."

Who Should Use This Book?

If you are a new UNIX user, you will find that *Introduction to UNIX* will help you understand the important concepts around which UNIX is built. You will find this book a valuable supplement to your computer's documentation. Too often, computer manuals are filled with the details of the day-to-day operations you need to perform, but may barely touch upon the broad concepts that unify the UNIX environment and make it understandable.

Unlike most introductory books, *Introduction to UNIX* does not concentrate as much on how to accomplish specific tasks, but instead strives to give you a solid foundation in the concepts of UNIX. You will come to understand the ideas of the original designers of UNIX, and you will learn why they organized UNIX the way they did.

If you are an experienced PC user who is now turning to UNIX as a new way to do your work, you will find many similarities between UNIX and the standard PC operating system, MS-DOS. The designers of MS-DOS at Microsoft Corporation were familiar with UNIX and borrowed many of UNIX's concepts in constructing and improving MS-DOS.

If you are a system administrator for UNIX computers, you will find in *Introduction to UNIX* the important concepts you need to fully understand your job and competently assist your users.

If you are a manager who will be managing UNIX users, programmers, and administrators, you will acquire the understanding of UNIX that you need to interact intelligently with your personnel.

How To Use This Book

You will find *Introduction to UNIX* most useful in conjunction with a more traditional how-to book or with your computer's documentation. This book will help you understand the underlying concepts; your computer's documentation or a good command reference will give you the details to fully exploit the power of the various commands.

Asides

Throughout this book, certain discussions are expanded with asides—shaded boxes containing interesting facts, bits of history, or peripheral topics. The information in an aside may be of a somewhat technical nature, or perhaps serves as an elaboration of some element being discussed. This elaboration might be somewhat "out of context" if included in-line with the rest of the text, but used as an aside, it can provide you with additional information and interesting tidbits. Asides help you obtain an even deeper understanding of UNIX's design and features.

How This Book Is Organized

Introduction to UNIX is organized into 12 chapters, each of which presents the concepts for a particular aspect of UNIX.

Chapter 1, "Introducing the UNIX Operating System," explains the function of an operating system in a modern computer and how UNIX accomplishes these functions. Chapter 1 also presents a history of UNIX and discusses the versions available from various manufacturers. If you are new to computers,

Chapter 1 will be especially useful for helping you understand the concepts of an operating system and comparing UNIX with other popular operating systems.

Chapter 2, "Understanding UNIX Basics," will help you understand the major parts of UNIX and how they interact. Chapter 2 also includes a discussion on the documentation that comes with most UNIX computers.

Chapter 3, "Understanding Files and Directories," explains the organization of the files on a UNIX system and the security issues associated with a multiuser system such as UNIX. If you are new to UNIX and unfamiliar with any other operating system that uses a hierarchical file system, such as MS-DOS or VMS, Chapter 3 is especially important, because the organization of the UNIX file system has a great impact on how you plan and execute your work.

Chapter 4, "Understanding the UNIX Shell," teaches you about the UNIX command interpreter—the shell—and the various alternative shells. Chapter 4 also looks at alternatives to the shell, such as the graphical user interfaces.

Chapter 5, "UNIX Tools," teaches you about the most popular UNIX tools, including batch processing tools such as `batch`, `at`, and `cron`. You also learn about commands you use with the UNIX print spooling system.

Chapter 6, "Text Processing in the UNIX Environment," covers the UNIX text editors and the formatting tools `nroff` and `troff`. Chapter 6 also presents numerous tools that assist you in preparing documents.

Chapter 7, "Understanding Communications and Networking," teaches you about the methods of communicating and sharing information between users, including electronic mail and networking.

Chapter 8, "Programming Languages and UNIX Software Development," describes the UNIX software development environment. If you are a programmer—or want to become more proficient at programming—Chapter 8 will be of particular interest to you. Chapter 8 presents the important UNIX programming languages, such as C, C++, BASIC, FORTRAN, COBOL, Pascal, LISP, and many others, and discusses important software development tools, such as debuggers, profilers, builders (`make`), and the source code control systems.

Chapter 9, "UNIX System Administration," presents the concepts that will be most important to you if you will be administering a UNIX system. You learn about the duties of a system administrator, common commands, and security issues. Even if you do not plan to administer a UNIX system, this chapter gives you insight into the duties of your system administrator and helps you work with him or her (or them) more effectively.

Chapter 10, "Understanding the Internal Structure of UNIX," explores the internal workings of UNIX. You will learn about the more advanced concepts that concerned the designers of UNIX. You will find out how information is *really* stored on-disk, learn about the tables of data UNIX maintains internally, and understand how UNIX, through swapping and paging, simulates more memory than is actually available. You will even find a discussion of zombies.

Chapter 11, "Introducing the UNIX Community," discusses the organizations, publications, and conventions available to bring you together with other UNIX professionals, present new ideas and products, and deepen your understanding of UNIX. Chapter 11 also describes Usenet, a massive worldwide network of UNIX users who trade ideas, offer assistance, and exchange software.

Finally, Chapter 12, "UNIX and the Market," describes the worldwide UNIX market, the vendors competing for a piece of the market, and the other operating systems with which UNIX competes. Chapter 12 also describes the organizations working to standardize UNIX. Chapter 12 offers a glimpse at the future of UNIX and the research underway today to improve UNIX and even to develop a successor to UNIX.

UNIX Versions and Releases

As you will discover, many different versions of UNIX exist, and many of these are not even called "UNIX." Chapter 1 describes the early days of UNIX in AT&T's Bell Telephone Laboratories, and how UNIX eventually spread to other organizations. The University of California at Berkeley adopted UNIX in the mid-1970s and released its own version of UNIX, greatly modified, soon after. Many manufacturers today sell versions of UNIX that are based on the Berkeley modifications. In addition, many manufacturers wrote operating systems identical to UNIX, but with names other than UNIX, to avoid paying licensing fees to AT&T. These UNIX look-alikes include Ultrix, HP-UX, XENIX, AIX, and many others. In most cases these manufacturers added new features to take advantage of the capabilities of their computers.

The primary focus of this book is AT&T's version of UNIX, known as System V (five); however, where differences exist between AT&T's UNIX System V and other versions, this book attempts to explain the differences.

Where To Find More Help

You can become more proficient in UNIX if you supplement this book with a good command reference. If you plan to use only a single make and model of computer with a single version of UNIX, your most complete reference is the manufacturer's documentation. Among the various books delivered with your system, most likely you will find a book with a title such as *User Reference Guide* or *Command Reference Guide*, which will contain detailed information about your computer.

Alternatively, consider a how-to book that contains a good command reference, such as Que's *Using UNIX*, which dovetails well with this book.

If you want to become a more serious UNIX user, pay special attention to Chapter 11, which discusses the available UNIX organizations and publications. Magazines such as *UNIXWorld*, *UNIX Today!*, and *UNIX Review* and organizations such as UniForum and USENIX are your best sources for the most current UNIX developments.

If you want a more structured, formal-education approach to UNIX, consider taking a college course on UNIX. Most colleges and universities offer courses on UNIX—both for credit and as continuing education. You also will find that many private companies offer a variety of UNIX-oriented classes to the public; other companies have internal employee education programs that provide UNIX classes. The opportunities for taking a more formal approach to learning UNIX are easy to find.

Conventions Used in This Book

Introduction to UNIX uses certain conventions to help you more easily understand its discussions. The conventions are explained again at appropriate places in the book.

Special Typefaces

This section describes the special typefaces used in *Introduction to UNIX*. Note that UNIX is case-sensitive, which means that it is responsive to the difference between uppercase and lowercase letters. In many cases, commands and options are interpreted by UNIX in a certain manner, depending on case.

Typeface	Meaning
`Special font`	This font represents UNIX commands, the names of files and directories, and system output, such as prompt signs and screen messages.
`Special font bold`	This font represents user input, such as commands, options to commands, and names of directories and files used as arguments.
`Special font italic`	This font represents the names of variable elements, such as file names or arguments, which users substitute with their own information.
<Input>	Angle brackets enclose user input that does not appear on-screen when it is typed. Such input can be <password>, special keys such as <Return> and <Delete>, or control-key characters such as <Ctrl-D>.

Prompts

The UNIX system prompts appear in the special typeface. In many sample commands, you will see a dollar sign ($), which the Bourne Shell uses by default, at the beginning of the command. Your prompt may be different. In addition, # and % are also used as prompts under various circumstances. You do *not* type the prompt.

Keyboard Keys

Most keys are represented as they typically appear on keyboards and are shown enclosed within angle brackets. Such keys include <Return>, <Delete>, <Break>, and so on. Your keyboard may have different names for these keys. You do *not* type the angle brackets.

Control-Key Combinations

In text, control-key combinations are enclosed in angle brackets. To enter a control-key combination, you press the Ctrl key, hold it down, and then press the specified key. For example, to enter <Ctrl-D>, you hold down the key marked Ctrl on your keyboard and press the D key. You do *not* type the angle brackets. On-screen, the Ctrl key is represented by a caret (^), and the control-key combination is enclosed in angle brackets, such as <^D>. Again, do not type the angle brackets.

A Final Note

If you are new to UNIX, becoming familiar with UNIX will be a challenging but rewarding experience. If you are already familiar with PCs, you will enjoy the new capabilities that UNIX offers. If you are already a "mainframer," used to working on large mainframes, you will enjoy the freedom and additional latitude that UNIX offers. If you are new to computers entirely, you will be pleasantly surprised with all the ways in which computers can help you in your everyday work.

Introduction to UNIX will find a useful place in your UNIX library as it conveys to you the excitement that UNIX holds for so many of its devotees.

Introducing the UNIX Operating System

This chapter will help you understand the vital functions that an operating system performs for a computer, and how UNIX accomplishes these functions. The chapter also presents a brief history of the origin of UNIX, which is invaluable for understanding why UNIX is built as it is. Finally, you learn to recognize the variety of manufacturers and computers associated with UNIX.

What Is An Operating System?

Other than users such as hobbyists, hackers, and students, most people who use an operating system consider the system itself secondary. The goal of computing usually is to accomplish some task by using *application programs*—software written to perform some type of real-world task, such as word processing or accounting. The operating system is a necessary tool for using the computer to run application programs. The following sections discuss the ways in which an operating system can help you perform these real-world tasks, and present some of the features that UNIX offers.

A computer without software—what might be called a "bare-metal" computer—is amazingly incapable of performing many common tasks without a lot of assistance. Tasks such as printing information on-screen and transferring data to disk require complex sequences of instructions. In days gone by, application programs had the responsibility of controlling every minute detail of such operations, and the programs consequently were far more complicated than their counterparts today. Similarly, communication between the user and the computer was much more tedious; users often entered commands by flipping toggle switches, and received responses on rows of lights.

People expect more from computers now, and using computers today is relatively easy, due to improvements in operating systems. An *operating system* is the software that supervises and assists you and the application programs you run on your computer. A computer's operating system handles the details of common operations so you and your programs can concentrate on less-technical concerns—the concerns for which you bought the computer—such as balancing your books, finishing your letter to Aunt Peggy, or selling more cars.

Many different operating systems are available, but all perform similar kinds of tasks, including the following:

- *Provide system services.* On today's computers, application programs do not have to directly control operations such as printing data, displaying characters on-screen, and transferring information to and from disk. The operating system contains the software to perform these tasks, and application programs simply ask the operating system to perform certain tasks for them. The operating system then supervises the details of getting the task done. The mechanism by which an application program asks the operating system to perform a task is called a *system call.*

- *Provide a user interface.* The operating system provides a means for you to tell the computer which programs to run.

- *Coordinate the sequence of events.* Especially on large computers, many users may try to do work simultaneously. The operating system ensures that each user gets a fair share of the computer's attention.

- *Control resources.* The term *resource* refers to any component or service provided by the computer that is in limited supply, including memory, disk space, and various pieces of hardware. The operating system ensures that all users share resources, and that no two users use the same resource at the same time.

- *Enforce security.* The operating system enables you to protect your data so that outsiders—or even other users who are not authorized for that particular data—cannot access restricted information.

- *Provide tools.* An operating system includes a collection of programs to accomplish common tasks, such as copying files or printing reports. Among UNIX users, these programs are known as *tools* because they are an important means of accomplishing their work, just as a carpenter uses his tools to perform his job.

The Features of UNIX

UNIX is an operating system rich with features for the programmer and computer, features unique among the available operating systems. Its multiuser and multitasking capabilities, device independence, and what is known as the *tools approach* mean that UNIX users can produce more than is possible on systems that lack these features. The portability of UNIX provides users, managers, customers, and business planners with a greater range of choices than is available with any other operating system. This section will help you understand these features and compare them to other operating systems, such as MS-DOS, MVS, VMS, and OS/2.

Multiuser Capabilities

UNIX is a multiuser operating system. Unlike other operating systems such as MS-DOS and OS/2, but like Pick, VMS, and MVS, UNIX enables more than one person to use the computer at the same time. Each of the computer's users can be involved in completely unrelated tasks while seemingly holding the computer's undivided attention.

UNIX perpetrates this illusion through a process known as *time-sharing*. Although the computer seems to be devoting its full time to each user, it actually spends only a few milliseconds at a time with any user, rapidly switching its attention from one user to the next. As one of its many tasks, UNIX continuously decides who to work with next, and how long to spend with each user. The process occurs so quickly that it is transparent to the user, who may not realize that UNIX actually abandons him or her for a short time before quickly returning.

Each user works at a *terminal*, which is merely a keyboard and screen connected to the computer by a cable. Terminals look somewhat like PCs, but in most cases, the terminal does not contain its own processor. Terminals therefore sometimes are burdened with a more descriptive but somewhat derisive name: *dumb terminal*. The only purpose of the terminal is to send characters from the keyboard to the computer, and then receive characters from the computer and display them on-screen. (Refer to the following chapter, "Understanding UNIX Basics," for a more detailed discussion of terminals.)

Some terminals may include processors to aid them in the task of transferring data—for example, graphics processors are a common component for helping with the display of graphics—but these processors are an internal detail that ordinarily does not concern the user.

On most machines, especially small systems, each terminal connects to the computer through a *serial port*, a connector that provides access to the computer's communication circuitry. PCs have only a few serial ports, although you also can use the computer's built-in monitor and keyboard as a terminal. Minicomputers may have dozens of serial ports. On large mainframes, *controllers*—small computers in their own right—coordinate the input from groups of terminals, taking some of the load off the main computer.

A multiuser operating system such as UNIX offers several advantages over single-user systems:

- *Cost per user.* On a multiuser system such as UNIX, each user needs only a dumb terminal, which usually costs only a few hundred dollars. These terminals are connected to a single computer. If single-user PCs are used instead, each user is provided with a "personal computer," costing thousands of dollars. Although the UNIX computer is more expensive than a single PC, the UNIX computer often costs less per person than the PC. UNIX provides an extremely cost-effective method for providing computer access for many people.

- *Central Administration.* Because each user does not have his or her own computer, large companies can employ a much smaller staff to perform routine computer chores, such as backups and maintenance, because these tasks can be performed from a central location, with no need to visit the workers' terminals.

- *Shared resources.* Users on multiuser systems can share information and interact with each other in a way not possible on single-user systems. Electronic mail messages can be sent and received easily, data can be exchanged, and modems, printers, faxes, tape drives, and other equipment can be shared.

Gauging the Number of Users

Beware of sales figures suggesting the number of terminals a UNIX system—or any multiuser system—can support. Loading up a computer with far more terminals than it reasonably can handle is possible.

An IBM PC/AT, for example, can have enough installed serial ports to connect with as many as four terminals—and even more with third-party add-on boards—but that does not mean that the AT has the raw computing power to support four or five users working at the same time. In such a small system, UNIX would be unable to accomplish much work as it rushes from one user to the next; in fact, it would spend more of its resources moving from user to user than it would actually doing useful work for any of the users. The users would perceive a very slow computer.

Most reputable manufacturers publish the number of users that reasonably can work on the computer at the same time, not just the number of terminals that can be connected.

Multitasking Capabilities

In addition to its capability of working with more than one user at a time, UNIX can perform more than one task at a time for each user, a capability known as *multitasking*. Multitasking can take several different forms:

- *Background processing.* You can place tasks that require no human interaction, such as formatting a disk or sorting a data file, in the background. Background tasks receive a share of the computer's attention, but do not use the keyboard, thus freeing the keyboard for use with another task.

- *Windowing capability.* Some sophisticated terminals, such as X Windows or AT&T's Blit, enable you to divide the screen area (charmingly known as *real estate*) into windows to display a different activity in each. You can watch results simultaneously produced by several tasks and can send keyboard input to any task desired. (Refer to Chapter 4, "Understanding the UNIX Shell," for more details.)

- *Task-switching.* Using a UNIX variant such as XENIX on your PC, you can begin several tasks and then press a combination of keystrokes to switch between them.

Multitasking greatly increases your productivity. You do not need to perform tasks one by one, waiting for each to finish before beginning the next. You simultaneously can undertake many tasks, focusing your attention on individual tasks as necessary. UNIX's multitasking capabilities usually are limited only by the user's ability to think of different tasks to perform simultaneously.

Device Independence

Most computer operations involve moving data to and from files or devices, and UNIX attempts to handle these operations in a device-independent manner. UNIX enables you to use files and devices interchangeably. You can tell a program that normally sends its results to the screen to use the printer instead; similarly, you can tell a tool that usually reads information from a disk file to use a tape drive instead.

UNIX provides names for all the devices connected to the computer, and you can use those names in many contexts in which a file name usually appears. The device drivers enable UNIX to treat all types of input and output consistently. (Refer to Chapter 2, "Understanding UNIX Basics," for a detailed discussion of device drivers.)

Device independence does not mean that you can perform any operation on any file or device; some operations don't make sense in some contexts. For example, you can use printers only for output—not input. Thus, an attempt to read data from a printer would fail.

Most devices also have unique capabilities. You can format disks, rewind tape drives, and adjust various terminal settings. UNIX provides special commands and programming functions for performing these operations.

Portability and Open Systems

Perhaps the most notable feature of UNIX is its *portability*—its capability to run on a wide range of different computer makes and models.

Most other operating systems are *proprietary*—that is, written by a computer manufacturer and specifically designed for use on a single make (and often a single model) of computer. VMS was designed exclusively for the DEC (Digital Equipment Corporation) VAX; MVS was designed to run on IBM mainframes. Before the advent of UNIX, each computer had its own operating system, and the application programs—word processors, accounting programs, and so on—had to be written specifically for that operating system.

Switching from one proprietary operating system to another entails these expenses:

- *Retraining.* Programmers and computer users have to be retrained to be able to use the new operating system.

- *Replacement and modification.* Application programs designed for the old operating system have to be replaced or modified to work with the new operating system. Likewise, data files have to be modified to work with the new application programs.

Historically, the large computer manufacturers encouraged the use of proprietary operating systems. If a company bought a computer from Vendor A, the company had a strong incentive to buy its next computer from the same source because any other decision would mean an additional investment in mastering a new operating system, new applications, and data conversion. Vendor A, of course, would encourage such a trend.

UNIX changed the course of computing, leading many manufacturers and buyers away from proprietary systems to what became known as *open systems.* UNIX systems today run on a wide variety of computers built by scores of manufacturers. Computers running UNIX cover almost the entire range of computer capabilities, from all but the smallest microcomputers to mainframes and supercomputers. XENIX, Microsoft's version of UNIX, runs on machines as small as an IBM PC/AT, whereas UTS, Amdahl's version of UNIX, runs on the largest mainframes. The Cray-II supercomputers use UNIX as their operating system. No other operating system even approaches this level of portability.

Open systems such as UNIX provide a number of benefits to the computer buyer. A company using proprietary systems carefully must weigh the benefits of growth or change against the cost of converting to a new system; however, a company using UNIX is largely immune to the pitfalls of converting to a different make or size of computer. The company's workers need little or no additional training, and exercise minimal effort to convert data and software to the new system.

UNIX also improves the interoperability between systems. Computers running UNIX stand a greater chance of being compatible with one another than computers that run proprietary operating systems. A company might start with a few IBM PCs on its workers' desks. Later the company might make these computers part of a network connected to minicomputers from AT&T, Hewlett-Packard, IBM, or DEC. It could upgrade the system to larger minis from Sequent and update the PCs to larger workstations from Sun Microsystems. Finally, the company could purchase a mainframe from UNiSYS to work side-by-side with the minis. Throughout the process, all machines could use UNIX, and users on all computers could work together, sharing information. With careful planning, application programs can be written once and versions made available for each machine.

While UNIX and MS-DOS share many common features (which MS-DOS inherited from UNIX), the portability of UNIX is of a different order than that available from MS-DOS. Many PC users think of MS-DOS as highly portable, because you can use it not only with the IBM PC for which it was designed, but also with PCs from many other vendors. Any claim to UNIX-style portability, however, is an illusion. Although MS-DOS does indeed run on machines from many different manufacturers, it does so only because AT&T, Goldstar, DEC, Zeos, Toshiba, PC Factory, and all the rest design their PCs to be internally indistinguishable from an IBM PC. Further, MS-DOS is restricted to single-user PCs and cannot be used with machines larger than a PC. Conversely, UNIX can work on almost the entire range of computers, from PCs to mainframes.

The Tools Approach

From its earliest days, UNIX has relied on what is known as "the tools approach" to solving problems. This approach to solving problems encourages a user to break down a task into small pieces and solve each piece by assembling UNIX tools—building-block style.

Rather than using narrowly focused programs that solve a large, complex task, UNIX encourages programmers to write small programs that accomplish a small task in a very general way. Today UNIX has hundreds of small, built-in programs called *tools*, each of which accomplishes a common, simple task. You can accomplish complex tasks by combining tools in various ways.

Tools are connected through a feature called a *pipe*. Pipes enable data to pass from one program to another; each program can modify the data in some way. When you include a *vertical bar* (¦), or pipe, within a UNIX command, the vertical bar indicates that data is passed from one program to another.

For example, suppose a user named Mary maintains a file called `clients`. Each line of the file contains information—such as name, address, company, phone, and more—about a business associate. Using various combinations of tools, she can extract many different selections of information from this file. For example, perhaps she needs to call her buyers who work for Ace Trucking, and she wants to display names and telephone numbers for clients working for Ace. Being an organized person, she also wants the list in alphabetical order. After considering the tools available, she might use `grep` to find the lines in her `clients` file that contain the phrase *Ace Trucking*, `cut` to pick out just the names and telephone numbers, and `sort` to arrange the information in alphabetical or numerical order. Using pipes, Mary can type a single command to invoke all of these tools in concert.

Each of these tools accomplishes a single, simple task; by combining tools, Mary can perform larger, more complex tasks than she can with a single tool.

The tools approach provides several advantages over collections of more complex programs:

- *Flexibility.* Because so many general-purpose tools come built in with UNIX, you can accomplish most complex tasks by combining the available tools.

- *Speed.* You quickly can accomplish tasks because all the building blocks already are available.

- *Structured approach.* Because all UNIX users start with the same building blocks, the tools approach encourages all users to solve problems in similar ways.

UNIX Compared with Other Operating Systems

How does UNIX compare with other widely available operating systems? In Table 1.1, you can see how UNIX's features compare with the features of other operating systems.

Table 1.1
UNIX Compared with Other Operating Systems

	Different Manufacturers	Hardware Required	Multi- User	Multi- Tasking	Primary Market
MS-DOS	Yes	IBM PC or compatible	No	No	PCs
OS/2	Yes	IBM PC or compatible	No	Yes	PCs
PICK	Yes	Various	Yes	Yes	Small business systems
VMS	No, only DEC	Only DEC VAX architecture	Yes	Yes	Minis and superminis
MVS	Yes, mostly IBM	IBM mainframe architecture	Yes	Yes	Mainframes
UNIX	Yes	Various	Yes	Yes	Micros to mainframes

The History of UNIX

The history of UNIX not only is entertaining (as histories of operating systems go), but also helpful in understanding why various components work the way they do in a UNIX environment. So many operating systems begin the story of their history with "Manufacturer X got together a large team of designers...." With UNIX, however, just the opposite is true.

The story indeed does begin with a team of operating system designers, but the product under development was not UNIX. In the 1960s, most operating systems were oriented toward *batch processing*—users provided programs and data to the computer, the computer processed the data, and results were printed. Very little human interaction with the computer was required, or even possible.

By the late 1960s, however, AT&T Bell Labs in Murray Hill, New Jersey, was undertaking the development of a new operating system called *Multics*. Multics was a joint effort with General Electric and Massachusetts Institute of Technology. Multics was an *interactive* operating system, in which the computer and user essentially carried on a conversation with each other. Such an environment had a much greater potential than older batch systems, and the developers at Bell Labs were becoming accustomed to the capabilities Multics offered on the Labs' General Electric GE 645 computer; however, Multics was proving to be very expensive, and by 1969, Bell Labs decided to extricate itself from the project. By March 1969, the GE 645 was gone.

Involved in the ill-fated Multics project were a handful of programmers who found that they liked the interactive environment Multics offered. Two programmers in particular—Ken Thompson and Dennis Ritchie—later became the primary players in developing UNIX. The group suddenly found themselves without a computer, and attempts to requisition one were rejected as too expensive.

Thompson's immediate impetus for finding a new computing environment was the continuing development of a game called "Space Travel." Written in FORTRAN, it was a simulation of the movements of the planets and major moons in which the player guided a spacecraft around the objects of the solar system. Thompson found a disused DEC PDP-7, and because it lacked a viable operating system, he split his attentions toward the development of a new operating system. Thompson and Ritchie sketched the beginnings of a new file system, a crucial component of what was to become UNIX. As the 1960s came to a close, with input from Rudd Canaday, they implemented a very basic version of the new operating system on the PDP-7.

This original operating system barely is recognizable when compared with today's UNIX. The file system was primitive and unwieldy by today's standards, and it was a single-user system with no timesharing capabilities. Brian Kernighan, another Bell Labs researcher, suggested the name UNIX in 1970 in what Ritchie described as "a somewhat treacherous pun on Multics."

In 1970, DEC introduced its new PDP-11 computer, and Thompson and crew managed to obtain one. They moved UNIX to the PDP-11 and, the following year, applied the system for the first time in the Bell Labs Patent Department. In addition to providing Thompson and Ritchie with a computer on which to continue their work, the system provided text processing (known today as *word processing*) facilities for three typists who prepared patent applications. This first version of UNIX was known as UNIX First Edition.

In the early 1970s, UNIX was written in *assembly language*, as were all operating systems. On any machine, assembly language is the most efficient language in which any program can be written, and efficiency is particularly important for an operating system. Each machine, however, has its own assembly language, and transferring assembly programs from one type of computer to another is difficult and expensive. Thus UNIX, written in assembly language for the PDP-11 computer, was confined to the PDP-11.

In 1971, however, in an initially unrelated project, Brian Kernighan and Dennis Ritchie began developing a new programming language called C. It was derived from an older language—B—which, in turn, was derived from BCPL. C was notable because it not only produced very efficient programs—often as much as 90 percent as efficient as assembly language—but C programs could run on a wide range of computers with little or no modification. In 1973, Thompson, Ritchie, and others at Bell Labs rewrote UNIX almost entirely in C.

Though not immediately apparent, this step became a crucial milestone for UNIX. Because UNIX was rewritten in C, the vast majority of it could run without modification on any machine for which C was available. Since that time, UNIX has spread to many different makes and models of computers largely because so few changes were necessary to move it to a new computer. To this day, all versions of UNIX are written in C.

Throughout much of the 1970s, UNIX primarily was considered by AT&T as a tool for internal use. The Sixth Edition, released in May 1975, was the first version of UNIX widely available outside Bell Labs.

UNIX soon found a comfortable niche among educational institutions. UNIX quickly was recognized as an ideal teaching environment, and today 80 percent of universities have UNIX systems. As AT&T began to license UNIX to universities, the history of UNIX branched. Development continued within AT&T at Bell Labs and also took off outside AT&T at the University of California at Berkeley.

The AT&T Versions of UNIX

In 1973, Thompson's team released PWB/UNIX (Programmer's Workbench) for use within Bell Labs. It later was released outside Bell Labs. PWB/UNIX included many of the programming tools that later earned UNIX a reputation as a powerful program development environment. In 1981, AT&T released UNIX System III, which included features from PWB/UNIX.

In 1983, AT&T released System V (five), which it intended to market as its standard commercial version of UNIX. (AT&T developed a system called System IV, but never released it outside Bell Labs.) No longer just a pleasant environment for programmers and researchers, System V was a true commercial operating system that included features required by business computing systems. AT&T claimed that System V would be the version under which all future development would occur and that all enhancements to UNIX from that point would be compatible with earlier System V releases. As expected, AT&T released enhancements, such as System V Release 4 (abbreviated SVR4), released in 1990.

If System V was to be AT&T's standard version of UNIX, the company needed a formal definition of that standard, which it released as the System V Interface Definition (SVID). SVID was a document that spelled out the way in which UNIX System V and user software should interact. Any version of UNIX that acted the way SVID described was compatible with AT&T's UNIX System V; otherwise, it was not. SVID served not only to guide other UNIX suppliers in making their systems compatible with System V, but it also spelled out for the UNIX programmer the features that AT&T considered standard parts of UNIX and, therefore, guaranteed not to change in the future. Programmers could be confident that if they used the features spelled out in SVID—and no others—their software would run correctly on any future version of UNIX System V.

Technically, a non-UNIX operating system—quite different from UNIX in structure, outward appearance, and internal workings—could be compatible, nonetheless, with SVID. SVID merely specifies the manner in which the operating system and user software interact; it says nothing of the internal workings. The government put out Requests for Proposals for several projects that did not (and in some cases could not) specifically require AT&T UNIX System V, but that did require the operating system to be SVID compatible. Not surprisingly, other manufacturers cried foul.

As AT&T produced new releases of System V, they added new features to SVID. But they always *added* features, never changed or removed them. Although programmers could not use newly added features with earlier releases of System V, AT&T guaranteed that the features would continue to work for all future versions.

Along with SVID, AT&T also released the System V Verification Suite (SVVS). SVVS consisted of a series of programs designed to test an operating system for compliance with SVID. As AT&T added new features to UNIX, they expanded SVVS to verify the new features.

With the rapid growth of UNIX in recent years, AT&T formed a separate department, the UNIX Software Operation, later renamed UNIX System Labs, charged with all future UNIX System V development.

The Berkeley Versions of UNIX

In the mid-1970s, the University of California at Berkeley acquired UNIX and began a constant program of development that had a major impact on the future of UNIX. Many of the programs developed at Berkeley, such as the `vi` text editor, now are standard UNIX tools.

Berkeley went on to develop its own versions of UNIX. In 1981, Berkeley released 4.1 BSD (Berkeley Software Distribution), an enhanced version of UNIX with added tools and capabilities. They released 4.2 BSD in 1984, and 4.3 BSD is with us today. Many versions of UNIX released by hardware manufacturers, such as DEC's Ultrix, were based on the Berkeley version of UNIX.

Microsoft's XENIX

Long before anyone had heard of MS-DOS, a small company in Bellevue, Washington, was working on a new version of UNIX, called XENIX. Although their enormous success later was predicated on MS-DOS and other products for the IBM PC, Microsoft was the company that set out to create the first commercially usable UNIX implementation. At that time, UNIX had a reputation as a wonderful system for development and research, but it lacked many of the features necessary in a commercial operating system. Most obvious, the documentation available from AT&T was notoriously poor (UNIX experts of the era seemed to derive a perverse pleasure from being able to use the sparse manuals), and customer support from Bell Labs was nonexistent.

Originally based on AT&T's System III, XENIX became the de facto standard, small-system version of UNIX. Machines from Tandy and Altos were the first to run XENIX. Later, XENIX was available on any 80286-based machine (that is, any IBM AT clone). Today XENIX is System-V compatible and available on 80386- and 80486-based machines. Because the proportion of small machines is so great, more computers run XENIX than all other versions of UNIX.

The UNIX Heritage

The history of UNIX is the key to understanding much about UNIX, its strengths, and why it works the way it does today. By examining the environment in which UNIX began, you often can answer questions that begin, "Why does UNIX...?"

For example, note that UNIX was not written by a development team as a commercial product, but rather by a handful of programmers as a means to accomplish their work. Consequently UNIX remains to this day one of the foremost program development environments, rich in the kinds of tools programmers need.

Because UNIX was born among a close-knit group that worked together on common projects, they emphasized sharing rather than keeping secrets. This heritage is evidenced in UNIX today by the variety of methods available to share data between users and machines. This openness and ability to share mail, programs, and data is one of UNIX's most attractive features, culminating in the creation of Usenet (see Chapter 11, "Introducing the UNIX Community," for more information), a phenomenon that probably could not have developed in any other environment. Conversely, the lack of concern about keeping information private has come back to haunt the current keepers of UNIX. As UNIX becomes more common in areas in which everyone cannot be trusted fully, the Department of Defense and many commercial companies are demanding stricter security.

Because UNIX's developers first applied the system in the Bell Labs Patent Department, early emphasis was placed on text processing, and UNIX quickly came to include a large collection of text processing tools. One of the great strengths of UNIX even today is that you easily can perform complex and powerful text manipulation by using standard UNIX tools, either individually or in various combinations. Moreover, nonprogrammers using UNIX can perform text processing tasks that in other environments would require a programmer's talents.

The programmers at Bell Labs who developed UNIX, and the graduate students at Berkeley who later began development, were computer experts who knew what they needed to do and didn't want an operating system to get in their way. Consequently most UNIX commands seem to have been written with the philosophy that if you issue a command, and do so correctly, the operating system should do it without trying to second-guess the appropriateness of the action. Thus when you issue the UNIX command rm * to delete all files, the deletions begin the instant you press <Return>. In contrast, the equivalent MS-DOS command, DEL *.*, requires confirmation and responds, "Are you sure?" Experienced users find the UNIX philosophy more palatable because the operating system is not constantly questioning their intentions; beginning users often find this same philosophy hostile because a single command can cause great loss of data.

UNIX has a reputation for being terse. The developers of UNIX seemingly frowned on excessive typing; most commands have short, often obtuse names (`grep` and `awk` being the two most famous), and you usually specify options with single letters. For example, consider the following command:

```
lp -n3 -m -dsneezy clients
```

You can type this command quickly, but its purpose is not immediately apparent to the beginner. (This command prints three copies of the file named `clients` on a printer called `sneezy` and sends the user mail when it is finished.) To help you find rarely used UNIX commands and options, you may find that a book (such as Que's *Using UNIX*) containing a command reference is useful.

UNIX Computer and Printer Names

All UNIX computers and printers have names, and UNIX users love to choose clever and cutesy names, with much the same enthusiasm as truckers pick their CB handles. Often computers owned by a single group have related names, such as `kandu`, `namu`, and `shamu`, owned by an AT&T group and named after the Sea World whales. Cartoon and comic strip characters are popular, such as `booboo`, `garfield`, `gumby`, `opus`, `thumper`, and `zonker`, all of which are genuine names of real UNIX computers. Also common are science fiction names (`scotty`, `trantor`, and `xanth`) and classic heros (`porthos` and `sherlock`). Other names provide an interesting insight into their owners' interests in life, such as `bikini`, `doorknob`, `spam`, and `yenta`.

Among UNIX users, this disdain of typing seems to have reached a pitch in the `vi` text editor; the developers seem to have taken the attitude that whenever they encounter a common operation that requires two or more keystrokes, they should invent a new command that requires only one.

Just as UNIX requires that you type few characters to enter commands, UNIX is equally terse in its responses. Early UNIX systems made use of printing terminals that, by today's standards, seem unbearably slow, and users lacked the patience to sit through verbose messages. At 110 baud (common in those days), the message `Operation successfully completed` required three seconds to print. Consequently UNIX adopted the policy that no news is good news, and most commands produce no response when successful.

Although portability was not one of the design goals of UNIX from the start, it is one of its most important attributes today. You can understand some UNIX features fully (most notably the vi editor) only in light of its portability. A particular program written to be able to run on any UNIX computer may behave in ways that seem unusual. The program may not take advantage of features present on your computer because not all UNIX computers have those features.

UNIX Today

With the advent of the Intel 80386 and 80486 chips, PCs attained a level of power only mainframes could rival just a few years ago. Such computing capacity almost was unimaginable when MS-DOS was developed in the early 1980s. 80386- and 80486-based computers have the power to perform complex graphics and multitasking functions, but MS-DOS was not designed to take advantage of these capabilities.

UNIX is in a position to make excellent use of these machines. Versions of UNIX from AT&T, Esix Computer, Mark Williams, SCO, Microport, and others are available at very reasonable prices; Coherent from Mark Williams, although based on the older 7th Edition, is less than $100 as of this writing.

UNIX's greatest competition in the large PC market comes from OS/2—a powerful multitasking operating system with a sophisticated graphical user interface—originally developed jointly by Microsoft and IBM.

UNIX has long been a powerful force in the workstation market. *Workstations* are desktop computers, often with massive processing capacities, that are connected by networks to larger computers. In a scheme that mixes the best advantages of PCs and large computers, workstations can exchange files with the larger computers and share processing of complex tasks.

Machines and Manufacturers Using UNIX

As UNIX has matured, its most notable feature is the wide spectrum of machines with which it is used, matched by no other operating system. UNIX is available under many different brand names from many different manufacturers, and on many different types of computers.

Types of UNIX Computers

UNIX is the only major operating system available today that covers almost the entire spectrum of computer classes—only the smallest computers, such as 8086 PCs, cannot run UNIX. The classes of UNIX computers include microcomputers, minicomputers, mainframes, RISC systems, fault-tolerant computers, and parallel processors.

UNIX runs under the most popular microchips in today's *microcomputers*. Most popular, of course, is the Intel line of chips—the 80286, 80386, and 80486. Machines based on these chips can use UNIX from many sources. Altos, Convergent Technologies, Fortune, NCR, Tandy, and Sun are among the manufacturers of machines based on the Motorola 68000 series of chips, with the Sun machines making up the most popular workstations. One of Convergent Technologies' machines was repackaged by AT&T and sold as the UNIX PC, a machine that unfortunately never found its market but remains popular today among UNIX enthusiasts. AT&T's line of supermicros—the 3B2 series—is based on AT&T's proprietary WE32000 series of chips, and of course they all run UNIX. The larger Apple computers also run Apple's version of UNIX—A/UX.

Minicomputers from DEC, IBM, Perkin Elmer, Gould, AT&T, Sequoia, and Sequent run UNIX.

Mainframe computers from IBM, Amdahl, and UNiSYS run UNIX (although UNIX remains a minor player for IBM, and to a lesser extent, Amdahl).

Many *Reduced Instruction Set Computers* (RISC) run UNIX, including IBM's new RS/6000, which uses IBM's version of UNIX—AIX. Machines from Pyramid, Hewlett-Packard, and Ridge also run UNIX.

Parallel processors, which make use of multiple processors on a single computer, are available from AT&T and Cray, and they run UNIX.

Fault-tolerant computers are designed to continue working after any single part fails. Many such computers, including machines from Tolerant Systems, Stratus, Sequent, and Tandem, run UNIX.

The Manufacturers

UNIX has been widely adopted by a large number of computer manufacturers. Table 1.2 lists some of the major computer vendors that have a large stake in the UNIX hardware market.

Table 1.2
Major UNIX Hardware Manufacturers

Altos	Perkin Elmer
Amdahl	Phillips
Apple	Plexus
AT&T	Prime
Bull HN Information Systems	Pyramid
Convergent Technology	Ridge
Cray	Sequent
Data General	Sequoia
Digital Equipment Corporation	Siemens
Fortune	Sony
Gould	Stratus
Hewlett-Packard	Sun Microsystems
IBM	SunRiver
Motorola	Tandem
NCR	Tandy (Radio Shack)
Next	Tolerant Systems
Nixdorf	Toshiba
Olivetti	UNiSYS
Onyx	Wang

Some manufacturers, such as AT&T, Sun, and Next, make almost nothing but UNIX computers and workstations. Others, such as DEC and IBM, sell computers that run UNIX but also sell computers that run their own proprietary operating systems.

UNIX Look-Alikes

Although UNIX is widely available on a variety of machines from many different hardware manufacturers and software developers, it is not always called UNIX. In some cases a UNIX look-alike may be a direct port of AT&T's

UNIX but carries a different name because AT&T reserves the rights to the UNIX name; in other cases, the operating system may have been written from the ground up by the vendor, but is functionally identical to UNIX.

Some of the common UNIX look-alikes include the systems listed in Table 1.3.

Table 1.3
UNIX Look-Alikes

Operating System	Manufacturer
HP-UX	Hewlett-Packard
Venix	Venturecom
XENIX	Microsoft
Uniplus	Unisoft
UTS	Amdahl
Ultrix	DEC
AIX	IBM
Coherent	Mark Williams Co.
OSF/1	Open Software Foundation
NonStop-UX	Tandem
ESIX	Esix Computer

As a rule of thumb, any operating system name that begins with the letter U or ends with an X is likely to be UNIX.

Chapter Summary

In this chapter you have explored some of the basic UNIX features and a little of the environment in which UNIX was developed and matured. Born in AT&T's Bell Labs, UNIX is a popular operating system today, available on a wide range of computers and from most computer manufacturers. UNIX includes powerful multiuser, multitasking capabilities.

2

Understanding
UNIX Basics

I n this chapter, you learn the basics of how UNIX is built and how it is used. Compared to PC operating systems like MS-DOS, UNIX is complex. Unlike DOS, UNIX must be able to juggle many balls at the same time, because many users may be using the computer simultaneously and because each of them may be working on several things at the same time. In addition, UNIX must be concerned with security, record locking, and other issues that arise only on a multiuser system.

If you want to understand how UNIX works, you need to understand how UNIX is built. This chapter gives you a basic blueprint for the organization of a UNIX system—both the hardware on which UNIX runs and the UNIX software itself.

You also learn about the basics of accessing a UNIX system. Most importantly, using UNIX requires knowing how to log in; without this procedure, UNIX stubbornly refuses to talk. This chapter presents the basic information to accomplish this first step.

Finally, to effectively use any computer system, you must be able to find information in the system's reference manuals. This chapter explains how UNIX manuals are organized and how you can use them to explore UNIX further.

Understanding the Parts of UNIX

This section discusses the components that make up a UNIX system, both hardware and software.

The Hardware

The *hardware* portion of a UNIX system is the equipment that makes up the physical computer. Configurations vary widely from one computer make and model to another, but most computers that use UNIX include a processor, a terminal or terminals, and assorted peripherals.

The Processor

The *processor unit* or *system unit* is the box that does the computing. This unit is the brain of the computer, where information is stored and processed. The processor may range in size anywhere from a few circuit boards and a small disk drive built into a Toshiba laptop to hundreds of square feet of cabinets for an Amdahl mainframe.

Included in the processor are

- *The central processing unit (CPU)*, which processes data according to instructions provided by software

- *Random-access memory (RAM)*, which provides temporary data storage for running programs and their associated data

- *Disk drives*, which provide mass storage facilities for large amounts of data for long periods of time

Terminals

Users communicate with the computer through a *terminal*, usually a unit consisting of a screen and keyboard (see fig. 2.1). A single UNIX system may have only one terminal, or it may have thousands of terminals located around the world. Although terminals by themselves superficially look like whole computers, most of them lack any kind of processor. Terminals merely serve as conduits for inputting and displaying characters; however, this is not true for all terminals. X Windows terminals, for example, include processors more powerful than many PCs. Chapter 4, "Understanding the UNIX Shell," discusses these specialized terminals in more detail.

Fig. 2.1. *A terminal.*

A *console* is a terminal directly connected to a special connector (called a *port*) on the computer. Although the terminal itself may be the same type as every other terminal connected to the computer, you can use the console in special ways, by virtue of being connected to the special port. If a severe error occurs, UNIX displays the appropriate message on the console, and some activities, such as shutting down the system or performing maintenance, can be performed only at the console. When not performing these special functions, you can use the console like you do any other terminal on the system. Some UNIX computers, especially PCs, have no terminals other than the console.

Peripherals

Peripherals include other equipment you can hook up to the computer. The list of peripherals grows daily: disk drives, tape drives, floppy disks, optical disks, scanners, printers, modems, voice synthesizers, fax boards, automatic equipment controllers, and dozens of other types of equipment (see fig. 2.2 for an example of a disk drive and a tape drive).

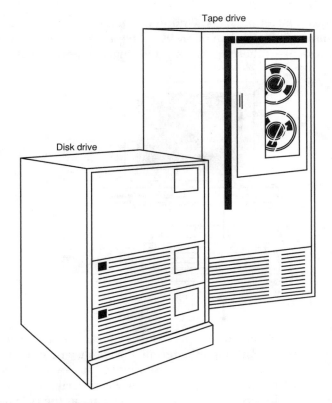

Fig. 2.2. Samples of peripherals.

Not all UNIX computers fit neatly into this configuration—processor, terminals, and peripherals. Many computers are part of networks, in which determining precisely where one computer ends and another begins becomes difficult (see Chapter 7, "Understanding Communications and Networking," for more information about networks). Also, many terminals are being replaced by *workstations*, which often include powerful processors of their own. You can do much of the actual computing work at your workstation, which relieves the main computer of some of its burden.

The Software

The hardware is the tangible part of a computer system—in a sense, the physical body of the computer. *Software* is the intangible portion—instructions that tell the computer what to do to accomplish useful work. By this definition, UNIX itself is software—a large sequence of millions of instructions that control the hardware and guide it in performing tasks. You can think of the software on a UNIX computer as consisting of several parts working together: the kernel, shell, tools, and applications.

The Kernel

Figure 2.3 illustrates the relationship between the parts of a UNIX system— the hardware and the software. The goal of all computing is to control the hardware in such a way as to make it do something useful. The hardware is shown at the center of figure 2.3; surrounding it is the UNIX *kernel*.

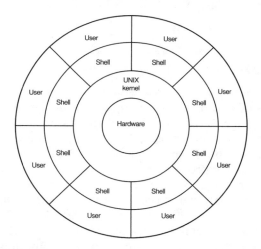

Fig. 2.3. *Parts of a UNIX system.*

The kernel is the central core of UNIX and gets its name from the inner seed of a plant. The kernel is "action central" for UNIX—the place where the computer's activities are coordinated and controlled. After you *boot* (start up) a UNIX computer, its first major job—after perhaps running some diagnostics on the machine—is to load the kernel. The kernel remains in the machine's memory until you shut down the computer. The kernel controls every facet of the hardware's operation and acts as a protective layer surrounding the hardware. Programs can communicate with the hardware only by using the kernel as intermediary.

The kernel is both servant and master for the programs running on the machine. Each running program is more correctly called a *process*. The kernel supervises the processes, but it also performs various tasks that the processes request.

Because the kernel works so intimately with the hardware, parts of the kernel often must be written especially for the machine on which it runs. The kernel is one of the few components of UNIX that cannot always be picked off one machine and slapped on another and still be expected to work correctly without modification. These portions of the kernel are *machine-dependent*.

Although the kernel essentially is one large program, it contains several components, which you can identify according to the kinds of tasks they perform.

The Scheduler

Perhaps the most complex portion of the kernel is the *scheduler*, which handles the task of starting and stopping the various processes running on the machine. Most UNIX computers use a timesharing technique to enable many processes to run simultaneously. Each process uses the computer's processor for a very brief time, after which UNIX temporarily stops the process so that another process can take its turn. The scheduler maintains a list (called the *process table*) of all processes currently running. The scheduler uses information in this list to make decisions concerning which processes are executed, in what order, and for how long. To ensure that all processes get a fair share of the computer's time, the scheduler must weigh many factors about the processes running on the computer when making these decisions.

The Memory Manager

Closely tied with the scheduler is the *memory manager*, which controls the allocation of sections of memory to each process. All processes on the computer require main memory (RAM). The memory manager keeps track of which parts of memory are unused, allocates memory to new processes, and marks memory as unused when that memory is no longer needed by processes. The memory manager must also ensure that one process does not inadvertently use memory that has been allocated to another process.

Most UNIX systems today employ a technique called *virtual memory management*, an arrangement that makes the computer seem to have much more memory than it really does. This technique (explained in more detail in Chapter 10, "Understanding the Internal Structure of UNIX") enables the computer to use disk space in place of RAM when necessary. The result is the illusion that all programs have all the memory they need, when in reality the amount of memory required by all programs separately far exceeds the amount of memory actually present in the computer.

Device Drivers

Device drivers are modules that directly control terminals, disk drives, tape drives, and other peripheral hardware. A device driver is included for each type of hardware on the system and contains the instructions necessary to perform operations such as reading and writing data.

When other parts of the kernel need to access a device, the kernel calls upon the appropriate device driver to handle the details. For example, if part of the kernel needs to read block number 489 from disk drive 2, that part of the kernel sends a request to the device driver responsible for the appropriate disk. The device driver understands how the disk is divided into tracks, cylinders, and platters, and supervises the reading operation.

More than any other part of UNIX, the device drivers are specific to a particular configuration of hardware. As vendors build new computers and peripherals, or as you connect new device drivers to your existing computer, you may have to provide the computer with new device drivers to control the new equipment. Usually these are available from the manufacturer that provides the equipment or from third-party vendors. In rare cases you may want your computer to control equipment for which no device driver is available; in these cases, a knowledgeable programmer must write a device driver.

Device drivers do not always control actual pieces of input/output equipment; some, called *pseudo-device drivers*, deal with concepts rather than reality. For example, one pseudo-device is called null. In effect, the device driver discards the output you send to null. This function can be useful with programs that both produce output and perform a task. If you do not want the output, send it to null; the program still performs its other task. (Chapter 10 presents a more detailed discussion of device drivers.)

System Calls

System calls provide a way for the programs running on the computer to communicate with the kernel. When a program needs to create a file, write to a printer, communicate with another program, or perform any of dozens of other possible operations, the program uses a system call to ask the kernel to take the appropriate action. The system call then either performs the operation or calls upon some other portion of the kernel to perform the operation.

System calls offer programs a standardized mechanism for communicating with the UNIX kernel. System calls themselves are identical from one computer to another, regardless of the version of UNIX or the computer on which UNIX is running. The internal details of how the kernel accomplishes a system call's task may vary from one UNIX system to another, but the way in which the programs use the system calls remains the same. The uniformity of system calls on all UNIX systems hides the underlying details from programmers writing programs for UNIX computers.

UNIX security is enforced within the system calls. When a program asks the kernel to perform an operation on its behalf, the system call must determine whether that program has the proper permissions. If the program attempts to access a protected file or perform an operation restricted to the system administrator, the system call signals the program to let it know that the system call will not complete the operation.

The concept of system calls is not unique to UNIX; most operating systems have them. The more complex the operating system is, the more dependent the programs are on system calls. PC operating systems such as MS-DOS also have system calls, although an important benefit of standardization is missing. Many MS-DOS application programs bypass the system calls, handling operations such as screen access and keyboard input by directly controlling the hardware. Although this direct control often is more efficient, clone PCs must completely duplicate the internal structure of an IBM PC; otherwise, software written for one MS-DOS machine may not run on another. In UNIX, however, the standard UNIX system calls are sufficient for any operation to be performed with acceptable efficiency.

Because these subsystems—scheduler, memory manager, device drivers, and system calls—all must closely work together, identifying where one ends and another begins is not always easy. Experts even disagree on how many distinct subsystems exist and how the responsibility is divided.

The Shell

Included in the UNIX software package is the *shell*, a program that provides an interface, or a link, between the user and the kernel, communicating with each in a compatible way. The shell gets its name from its function as an outer layer for the UNIX kernel (again see fig. 2.3).

The shell serves two major functions:

- *Command interpreter*. The shell accepts commands you type at the keyboard, interprets them, and takes appropriate action—usually by system calls to the kernel.

- *Programming language*. The shell includes a built-in programming language. By writing *shell programs*, sometimes called *shell scripts*, you can create customized commands to handle complex or repetitious tasks. Shell programs can range from very simple to very complex. Professional programmers find that the shell provides a full-featured language, and users with little or no programming experience find that they easily can write small programs to simplify their daily work.

In many respects the shell gives UNIX its personality because the shell is the part of UNIX with which most users directly interact. The shell provides the prompt you receive, inviting you to enter a command. When users say that UNIX is "easy to use," "difficult to use," "powerful," or express other opinions, they usually are making comments about the shell, rather than UNIX as a whole. Yet the shell is not an integral, built-in part of UNIX. Rather, it simply is a program (albeit a complex one), written in a programming language called C, that accepts commands from the keyboard, interprets them, and takes action. When necessary, the shell communicates with the kernel by system calls, just as all programs under UNIX do.

Technically, talking about "the" shell is incorrect, because any program that acts as a go-between for the user and the kernel can properly be called a shell. In fact, many times throughout the history of UNIX, programmers have written other shells. Chapter 4, "Understanding the UNIX Shell," discusses the various shells that are widely available and the differences between them. When UNIX documentation refers to "the" shell, it usually refers to the Bourne Shell. Named after its author, Steve Bourne, the Bourne Shell is the original UNIX shell and comes with all UNIX systems.

Note that a UNIX computer has only a single kernel, which is constantly loaded into the computer's memory; however, many copies of the shell can run simultaneously. Typically a new shell starts each time a user logs in and terminates when the user logs off. Thus, the computer is always running one kernel, but the number of shells varies as users log in and log off. In a sense, the kernel handles "the big picture" for the computer; each shell handles the details associated with a user.

Tools

UNIX includes a wide variety of utility programs, often called *tools* or *commands*. Most tools are small and relatively simple, and each accomplishes a single task or group of related tasks. These tasks, such as copying files or making backups, usually are secondary to the computer's work. You did not purchase your computer to perform these tasks, but they are necessary activities.

Some tools, such as cp, which copies a file, were available almost from the first days of UNIX at Bell Labs. Others are more recent additions, added in the latest versions of UNIX. Most tools, other than those tools introduced very recently, have undergone some evolution since their introduction. The programmers who maintain versions of UNIX for various vendors have added options from time to time to increase the usefulness of tools in a variety of situations.

Applications

People purchase computers not to communicate with the operating system or to use UNIX tools, but to run *application programs*. Application programs earn the computer's keep by balancing budgets, storing and retrieving customer lists, helping in the composition of documents, and carrying out many other useful functions.

Most versions of UNIX do not come with applications, although older versions of UNIX included text processing software. Applications usually must be purchased, either from the computer manufacturer or from third-party vendors.

Thousands of UNIX packages are available. Text processing, business software, computer-aided design (CAD), and research are a few of the areas in which a particularly rich assortment of application software has been developed. In addition, as the UNIX market grows, many software developers who started in other environments now are attracted to UNIX. Many manufacturers have converted their PC applications in particular to UNIX. Word processing software such as Microsoft Word and WordPerfect, spreadsheets such as Lotus 1-2-3, and databases such as dBASE now are available on many UNIX machines. Other software, developed especially for UNIX, takes advantage of its powerful multiprocessing capabilities. Examples include general applications—such as business accounting software and drafting and design software—and specialized applications, such as medical and legal software.

Accessing UNIX

Multiuser systems such as UNIX must be concerned with security. Terminals connected to a large UNIX system may be numerous and spread throughout a large building. Not just anyone can walk up to a terminal and access sensitive data on the computer. Moreover, most UNIX systems are connected by modems to telephone lines, and companies dare not risk their confidential data by making their systems available to anyone who happens to know the telephone number.

UNIX's first line of defense is the *login* procedure. Before being granted access to UNIX, a user must be positively identified. This identification not only verifies that the person may use the computer but also determines exactly what the user may do. For each user (except the system administrator), certain programs and data are off-limits. Some users may be so restricted that they can do only one thing on the computer. (See Chapter 3, "Understanding Files and Directories," for more information about how to use UNIX security to protect your data, and refer to Chapter 9, "UNIX System Administration," for more details about the login procedure.)

Accessing the Computer

Before you can communicate with UNIX, you must connect your terminal to the computer. This connection is made in any of several ways.

- For small computers, such as PCs, the terminal actually is the keyboard and monitor built into the computer. No communication setup is necessary beyond connecting the keyboard and monitor cables.

- For other kinds of computers, terminals usually are connected by some type of cable. Most often this cable is an RS-232 serial cable, but coaxial network cables are becoming more common. At a large company, the proper cables are usually installed for you.

- Computers often have modems, which enable access by telephone. With a terminal and a modem, you can command the modem to dial the proper telephone number to connect the terminal to the computer.

- In large companies, many terminals and computers are connected to a central data switching unit. Connecting a particular terminal to a particular computer is like placing a telephone call—by dialing numbers, you instruct the telephone switching office to connect your telephone to the telephone being called. Any telephone can call another telephone. Similarly, if you use a terminal on a central data switching unit, you type commands to instruct the data switching unit to connect your terminal to a specific computer.

In addition to establishing a physical connection, you must make sure that a number of settings match between your terminal and the computer, especially when modems or serial cables are involved:

- The terminal and computer must agree on the speed at which information is transmitted back and forth. The *baud rate* is, roughly, the number of bits per second that are exchanged. Common settings are 1200 or 2400 when you use a modem and 9600 or 19200 when you use other types of connections.

- UNIX supports *full duplex* operation, which means the computer and terminal exchange data in both directions at the same time. This mode is similar to the way in which telephones enable two parties to talk at the same time. Although two parties sending data simultaneously can be confusing, the hardware enables you to do it. Other types of operating systems, most notably IBM midrange and mainframe computers, enable communication in only one direction at a time, referred to as *half duplex*. If your terminal can operate in either full duplex or half duplex, use the setting for full duplex operation.

- *Parity* is an error-checking mechanism that sometimes can detect characters that were not received correctly by the computer or terminal. Possible settings include *even*, *odd*, and *none*. Which setting you use is probably not important, as long as the computer and terminal use the same setting. You often have no control over the setting of the computer, so you must set your terminal to match the computer.

- You can set the number of bits in each character to either 7 or 8 on most terminals. Seven is the usual setting when parity (either even or odd) is on; eight is more common when parity is off. As with the parity setting, the most important factor is making sure the terminal and computer settings agree.

For some terminals, other settings also may be important. For example, all terminals respond to a set of special codes that enable the computer to control the terminal's behavior. In effect, these control codes make up the language that the terminal speaks. Some terminals are multilingual—that is, you can set them to recognize several different sets of control codes—and as with most other settings, you must make sure that the terminal and the computer are set to exchange the proper set of codes. Other important settings include colors, screen size, and the human language (such as English, Danish, or German) that the terminal keys generate.

Logging In

Before you can use a UNIX computer, the system administrator must tell the computer that you are authorized to do so (see Chapter 9, "UNIX System Administration," for more information on the system administrator). Each authorized user on a UNIX system chooses or is assigned a unique *login name*, which is used as a means of identifying the user, much as a bank uses account numbers to identify its depositors. The login name can be any combination of letters and digits, from two to eight characters in length, and on most machines, it must begin with a lowercase letter. The login name usually is the user's first name, last name, initials, or some combination of name and initials, depending on local custom. For example, Jamie Smith might be assigned the login name `jamie`, `smith`, `jfs`, or `jsmith`.

When you first connect with a UNIX system, the system prompts with the following simple message:

```
login:
```

In effect, UNIX is asking you to identify yourself by typing a valid login name. After you enter your login name, the system prompts:

```
Password:
```

Your *password* is a combination of characters that serves to prove your identity. Although your login name is public knowledge among the users on the computer, your password is kept secret. Thus, only Mary can successfully identify herself to the computer as Mary, because (presumably) only she knows her password. As Mary types her password, no characters appear on-screen, so that someone looking over her shoulder cannot discover her password.

Your login name and initial password usually are assigned by the system administrator. Your login name never changes, but you can change your password at any time.

The Special Login Name root

All UNIX systems have a special login name, `root`, which the system administrator uses. When logged in as `root`, the system administrator bypasses all system security; `root` can perform many functions that are denied to all other users.

The Special Login Name root *(continued)*

The login name root affords the system administrator a great deal of
power. root often single-handedly can accomplish complex tasks
that normally require coordination of several users because in many
cases no one user has security permissions to execute all parts of the
task. Using root also carries great risk; with a single command, root
can wipe out a disk or crash the system. Because of the power that
root can wield, it often is referred to as the *superuser*.

If you supply a valid login name and password, UNIX grants you access to
the system. A typical login procedure looks like the following example:

```
login: stacy
Password: <password> (Passwords do not appear on-screen.)
UNIX System V Release 3.2.1 AT&T 3B2
calvin
Copyright (c) 1984, 1986, 1987, 1988 AT&T
All Rights Reserved
Login last used: Wed Mar  6 23:24:39 1991

*********************************************
*                                           *
*      Welcome to Acme Trucking Corp.       *
*                                           *
* Please note:  System will be down after   *
* 5:00 PM Friday for maintenance.           *
*********************************************

You have mail
$
```

The exact wording of UNIX's welcoming message varies from one version
of UNIX to another, but most have the following features in common:

- All UNIX systems have names, and most systems identify themselves
  when a user logs in. This step is becoming more important because
  many companies now own multiple UNIX computers interconnected through networks; knowing the computer to which your
  terminal is connected often is not easy. In the preceding example,
  the computer's name is calvin.

- Most computers provide a daily message that contains any informa-tion the system administrator wants users to see when they log in. As shown in the preceding example, administrators often surround the message with asterisks or other special symbols to emphasize the message.

- If you have electronic mail waiting, as in the example, UNIX usually alerts you with a message.

- After the login process is complete, the shell prints a prompt to indicate that it is ready to accept a command. By default, the shell uses a dollar sign ($) as the prompt.

UNIX Internals: The User ID

In addition to your login name, you are assigned a unique *user ID*, which is a number between 0 and 32,767. (A user ID of 0 carries special meaning and is reserved for root.) Like your login name, your user ID uniquely identifies you, but it is used almost exclusively by UNIX for internal accounting purposes. For example, the kernel uses user ID numbers within tables that identify which users are running programs on the system. The system administrator main-tains a file (/etc/passwd) that UNIX uses to correlate your user ID with your login name. (Chapter 9, "UNIX System Administration," discusses the passwd file in detail.)

Logging Off

Just as you must identify yourself by logging in when you want to use the computer, you must notify the computer when you are finished, a process known as *logging off*.

Throughout UNIX, pressing <Ctrl-D> from the keyboard indicates "The End." For example, you use <Ctrl-D> to signal that you are finished entering data from the keyboard. When the shell is expecting a command, pressing <Ctrl-D> signals that you have no more commands, and the shell logs you off.

Looking at the UNIX Documentation

When UNIX was still a research tool in its first few years at Bell Labs, the programmers that used it already knew the basics. They did not need manuals to teach them how to use UNIX; instead, they needed notes to remind them how to use various features when they couldn't remember the details. Because of this, the programmers who wrote the first UNIX manuals did not organize it in a fashion that lent itself to learning new topics; rather, they listed individual commands and programming features in alphabetical order for quick reference. The manual consisted of hundreds of entries, most a few pages long, each describing a single command or feature.

Today the situation is quite different; the set of manuals that comes with UNIX reflects the power and wealth of features in the operating system. Even PC versions now come with half a dozen or more books; large systems may include dozens. Although the contents of the manuals varies from one version of UNIX to another, tutorials and guides are often included. Some manufacturers also provide on-line manuals and tutorials, such as IBM's Info Trainer for AIX on its RS/6000.

Although the UNIX documentation continues to get more sophisticated, the original alphabetical reference—expanded and updated—usually is still provided with UNIX, often titled *User Reference Guide*. As the size of the reference guide has increased over the years, most manufacturers have split it into at least two volumes. It still is the handiest reference for people who are reasonably familiar with UNIX and need only occasional help filling in the gaps.

Chapter Summary

In this chapter, you learned some of the basics of working with a UNIX system. You saw that a UNIX system consists of two parts: the tangible equipment, or hardware, and the instructions that control its operation, or software. The software, in turn, is made up of the kernel, the shell, the tools, and the application software.

With an understanding of the internal structure of UNIX, you are ready to learn how to use UNIX. In this chapter you learned the basics of accessing a UNIX system, and you learned about the login and logoff procedures.

Finally, you learned important ways to get further help. The system administrator and the *User Reference Guide* are valuable sources of information when you are learning about UNIX.

3

Understanding Files
and Directories

O n most computers today, the computer stores data on some kind of
spinning disk. Commonly, the disk provides a recording surface that
is divided into hundreds of millions of microscopic sections, each of which
can be magnetized. The disk hardware records data on the disk by magne-
tizing a combination of sections in a particular way. Later the disk drive
retrieves data—on command from the computer—by reading the way in
which these sections were magnetized earlier. In a recent variation on this
theme, optical disks record data by burning tiny pits into a plastic disk with
a laser, and later read the data by using a weaker laser to detect where pits
have been burned and where they have not.

Consider a book containing blank pages, which you can purchase in any
bookstore. You could use such a book to write down various bits of useful
information you come across in your daily life, making that information
available for future reference. You may write the first interesting fact on page
1, and then proceed to page 2 with the next nugget of data. At first, retrieving
information from the book would be easy, but as you fill the book with more
and more items, finding a specific piece of data becomes increasingly more
difficult. Numbering the pages could help, but then you have to remember
which page contains what—such as remembering that the recipe for key
lime pie is on page 118. Eventually, if you don't come up with a scheme to
organize the material—such as a table of contents or an index—finding
anything in the book becomes hopeless.

An identical situation awaits the computer when it stores information on a
disk. To the equipment that does the reading and writing, the disk is one

huge, empty book in which information can be recorded almost anywhere. The disk hardware and software divide the disk recording area into cylinders that, in turn, are divided into tracks. Like the pages of a book, the tracks and cylinders of a disk are numbered. The disk equipment, however, provides no help in remembering that the March sales report is stored on cylinder 283, head 3, track 4.

One of the most important functions an operating system performs is imposing organization on the data stored on the disk. Almost all operating systems use a scheme that involves some kind of "table of contents," which is recorded in a specific area of the disk. The operating system uses this table of contents to keep track of what parts of the disk are used and what information is stored where.

Early in its history, UNIX developed an elegant scheme for organizing the data on disk. This scheme relieved the user from worrying about tracks, cylinders, and other internal details and provided a powerful means for classifying data into groups for faster reference. The UNIX scheme was so effective that it served as the model for other operating systems, such as MS-DOS, OS/2, and DEC's VMS. That classification scheme—into *files* and *directories*—is the subject of this chapter.

Introducing the UNIX File System

A *file* is a collection of data stored on disk. Each file usually contains related information, such as a list of delinquent customer accounts, or contains information that makes up a single logical entity, such as a letter to a state representative. A typical UNIX system contains thousands of files, which include the following types of files:

- *System files*. UNIX uses system files to store important information about the computer.

- *System programs*. These programs enable you to perform common tasks.

- *Application programs*. Application programs enable you to do useful work on the computer. Word processors, databases, and accounting systems are examples of this type of program.

- *User data files*. These files contain the information being processed on the computer, such as reports, correspondence, or the design of the next American sports car.

In the early days of computing, you frequently had to worry about the intricate details of storing information on disk. Even unsophisticated computers were expensive, and computer time was precious. If the computer's job could be made easier at the expense of the user's time and trouble, the trade-off was considered a good one. You had to know what kind of disk drives were being used, how many cylinders were on each disk, and how many tracks were on each cylinder. You worked out many of the details of working with a disk so that the computer could attend to other duties.

The designers of UNIX believed that fiddling with the details of how files were stored on disk was a computer's job. UNIX's file scheme eliminates the need for you to worry about the details of the disk equipment being used. In most cases, you don't need to know the figures for tracks, platters, cylinders, or sectors.

UNIX also keeps track of which parts of the disk are used and which parts are available for new files. When you create a new file, UNIX decides where to put it on the disk and keeps track of where the file's data is kept. UNIX stores this information in a special bookkeeping area that you never see. Some users don't even know such an area exists.

Finally, you do not need to know ahead of time how big the file will be. A file at first may be small, but if you add more data later, UNIX automatically locates unused disk space and enables the file to grow into that space. As long as the disk contains unused space, the file can continue to grow.

With the development of these features, UNIX designers anticipated a trend in which the computer's time becomes much more plentiful, and your time becomes more valuable; however, you pay a price for having UNIX attend to these details. UNIX has no knowledge of how you will use the file or how the file fits into the larger scheme with the other files on the computer. Will you use this file often or infrequently? Will it eventually grow to a large file or stay small? Will you usually use the file in conjunction with other files or by itself? Because UNIX lacks this kind of information, UNIX sometimes does not organize the disk as efficiently as a knowledgeable user can. Computers, however, are becoming more powerful and less expensive, and your time is becoming more valuable. By having UNIX attend to the details of managing the disk, you pay a very slight efficiency penalty in exchange for being able to concentrate on more important matters.

Introducing UNIX File Names

When you create a new file, you must assign it a name that you can use to identify the file. UNIX maintains a bookkeeping area—a kind of table of contents—that relates the name you select with an area of disk storage.

The name of a file can be anything you select, within the following guidelines:

- The name must be no longer than 14 characters. (Some versions of UNIX enable you to create longer names.)

- The name should be made up of some combination of alphabetic letters, digits, periods (.), underscores (_), dashes (-), and pluses (+).

- The name should *not* start with a dash (-) or plus (+).

- Unlike many other operating systems, UNIX is case-sensitive. Upper- and lowercase letters are distinct; thus, Letter.to.Jim is not the same name as letter.to.jim as far as UNIX is concerned.

- To be most useful, the file name should describe the contents of the file. june.sales.rpt is a good name; x is not (although technically x meets all the requirements, and UNIX accepts this name).

Unusual File Name Characters

Although letters, digits, periods, underscores, dashes, and pluses are the only characters you should use in a file name, other characters—dollar signs, percent signs, exclamation marks, and even control characters such as a backspace or carriage return—can be part of a file name if you are clever enough. Using these unusual characters, however, is almost always a bad idea. All of these characters, often known as *special characters*, have a specific meaning to UNIX when you use them in a command. If you use these characters as part of a file name, UNIX may perform an operation that you did not intend. Chapter 4, "Understanding the UNIX Shell," explains the exact meaning of many of these special characters.

With a few minor exceptions, UNIX doesn't attach specific meanings to any particular form of file name; to name a file, you can use any name that follows the rules previously listed. Although other operating systems use special file name endings to indicate the contents of certain files (for example, MS-DOS uses the endings EXE or COM to indicate executable files), the UNIX operating system doesn't.

Many of the programs and utilities provided with UNIX, however, do examine the last few characters of a file name to determine how you should use a file. For example, the C compiler expects all files containing C source code to have names ending in `.c`. The linker expects the names of object files to end in `.o` and libraries to end in `.a`. These special endings are known as *extensions* (see table 3.1 for common extensions used by important UNIX programs and commands). Some of the commonly used extensions have no special meaning to UNIX or any UNIX utility, but simply are handy because they enable you to classify your files easily (such extensions are marked *Traditional* in table 3.1).

Table 3.1
Common UNIX Extensions

Extension	Type of File	Associated UNIX Program
`.a`	Library (archive)	Linker
`.awk`	`awk` script	(Traditional)
`.c`	C source program	C compiler
`.C`	C++ source program	C++ compiler
`.doc`	Word processor document	Various word processors
`.f`	FORTRAN source program	FORTRAN compiler
`.h`	C header file	(Traditional)
`.mk`	`makefile`	(Traditional)
`.nr`	`nroff` source document	(Traditional)
`.o`	Compiled object file	Various compilers
`.pic`	Picture file	(Traditional)
`.s`	Assembler source file	Assembler
`.sh`	Shell program	(Traditional)
`.tbl`	Table file	(Traditional)
`.tr`	`troff` source document	(Traditional)
`.Z`	Compressed file	Compress and uncompress tools
`.z`	Packed file	Pack and unpack tools

The Use of Periods in UNIX File Names

The period has a special meaning within file names in many operating systems. Some systems use it to *delimit*, or separate, parts of a file name. In MS-DOS, for example, a period separates the base name from the extension, and each file name can have only one period. In contrast, UNIX does not treat the period differently from any other character; a UNIX file name can contain several periods. Multiple periods often make a name more readable, such as `feb.late.fees`. On most UNIX systems, file names can contain up to 14 characters, and each period counts as one of these characters.

In many ways, UNIX gives you more flexibility in selecting names than any other major operating system. This flexibility can cause some problems when several operating systems are interconnected and share a common disk, as sometimes happens on a *local area network* (LAN). File names that are valid in UNIX may be too long or contain too many periods for MS-DOS, OS/2, or other operating systems.

Understanding the Format of a UNIX File

You can use UNIX files to store any kind of data. Some of the types of data you can store in a file include the following:

- Text (letters, memos, reports)

- Binary data (perhaps a chart of customer or account information)

- Program source code

- Executable programs, such as system programs and word processors

- Application data, such as databases and spreadsheets

UNIX has a simplistic view of files. With the exception of device files, discussed further in this chapter, UNIX views all files as a sequence of bytes. Programs and applications use the data within these bytes to represent the information stored in the file. UNIX does not attempt to impose further organization on the data with the file. UNIX has no knowledge of how programs will interpret these bytes, or of how the various items of data within the file interrelate. UNIX simply knows that a particular file contains, for example, 4,189 bytes of data.

UNIX does not recognize different types of data files. Except for special system files such as directories and device files, UNIX does not categorize data files in any way. Many operating systems classify each file as one of several kinds, such as an executable program, or text, or some type of database. UNIX does not. All files, no matter what type of data they contain or how they are used, are considered *regular files,* or *ordinary files,* and are treated alike by UNIX.

UNIX does not divide data into records. Many operating systems can divide the data within a file into discrete pieces, called *records*. Each record contains all the data associated with a specific person, event, thing, or whatever is appropriate. For example, in a customer file, the first record could contain the data for Ace Trucking, the next record for Acme Investments, and so on. By comparison, UNIX treats a file as an undivided string of bytes.

This uniform approach has many advantages. Most importantly, you can use the same programs and commands to manipulate all data files, because all files have the same characteristics.

You should understand that although UNIX does not care about the organization of the data in a file, the utilities and application programs that use the file almost always require a specific organization. The C compiler, for example, expects C source files to contain lines of text, each representing valid C statements. The WordPerfect word processing program expects a document to contain text and special formatting codes that are meaningful to WordPerfect. These programs "complain" if the data files with which they are asked to work are not organized correctly.

One particular type of file is distinguished by the kind of data it contains. Many—perhaps most—UNIX files consist almost exclusively of printable characters (letters, digits, and punctuation) and are known as *text files*. Text files contain lines of legible data, such as English text or a list of names. Each line in a text file ends with a special nonprintable (invisible) character called a *newline*, which UNIX uses to determine where one line ends and the next begins. UNIX includes a large collection of programs that enable you to manipulate text files in a variety of useful ways (refer to Chapter 6, "Text Processing in the UNIX Environment").

Introducing the Elements of UNIX Commands

Like any operating system, UNIX provides facilities that enable you to perform common operations on files. UNIX comes with dozens of programs, most of them fairly small, often know as *tools*, that enable you to manipulate files in useful ways. You use the keyboard to type commands that invoke these programs.

Most important among these programs are the text editors, which enable you to easily create new text files and modify existing text files. (The text editors are discussed in Chapter 6, "Text Processing in the UNIX Environment.") Other important programs enable you to copy, rename, list, and locate files.

The *shell* is the program responsible for accepting the commands you type at the keyboard, analyzing them, and causing an appropriate action to occur. Chapter 4, "Understanding the UNIX Shell," explains in detail how the shell operates; for now, you should understand that the shell is the portion of UNIX that communicates with you and accepts your commands.

When the shell is ready to accept a command, the shell displays a prompt (by default, a dollar sign $). You then can type a command and press <Return>, and the shell performs the requested operation. In the case of a few types of commands, the shell knows how to accomplish the task and performs the operation you requested. In most cases, however, the shell does not directly understand what the command is trying to accomplish and must invoke another program to do the work. The shell searches for a program whose name is the same as the command you typed, and executes that program. For example, when you type **cp** (the command to copy a file), the shell has no understanding of what you want to do. The shell locates and runs the program called cp. The cp program then does the work to copy the file.

Note that as you type a command, the shell does not take action until you press <Return>. Pressing <Return> is your signal to the shell that you are finished typing the entire command and that the shell now can proceed in carrying out your command. You must press <Return> after each command for the associate operation to take place.

With a few exceptions, most UNIX commands have the following format:

commandname [*options*] [*arguments*]

This notation indicates that you first type the name of the command, followed by *options* and then *arguments*, which are defined in the following sections. You do not actually type the square brackets shown here surrounding the options and arguments; rather, they serve to indicate that you usually can omit these elements (in this case, options and arguments), because they are optional.

The *command name* is a single word that identifies the operation you want to perform. In most cases the command name is also the name of the program that the shell executes in response to the command. The command name is all that is required to perform some operation. Consider the following example:

```
passwd
```

This command causes the shell to run a program called passwd, which enables you to change your password.

Following the command name, a command can contain one or more options or arguments, or both. Options and arguments are discussed in the following sections.

UNIX File Name Arguments

You use *arguments* to provide a command with data for it to process. Most often arguments are the names of files that contain the information with which the command will work. For example, the lp command prints data to the printer. Consider this command:

```
lp daily.report
```

lp is the name of the command, and daily.report is the argument, representing the name of the file which contains the data to be printed. Most commands enable you to use several arguments, in which case the command works with each file in turn. Consider this example:

```
lp daily.report sales.memo note.to.jim
```

This command prints three files to the printer, one after another.

For some commands, the arguments represent something other than file names. The mail command, for example, expects the names of one or more users to be given as arguments, representing the people to whom you are sending mail. For example, if you type

```
mail sue jim belinda
```

mail is sent to the users named Sue, Jim, and Belinda.

UNIX Command Options

Options in a UNIX command line usually are represented by a dash followed by a letter, such as -a or -R. (A few commands have options that start with a plus rather than a dash.) In general, an option tells a command to perform its function in a slightly different way than usual, although the option does not change the fundamental purpose of the command. Various options can tell a command to produce its output in a slightly different format, or to follow slightly different rules in performing some task.

For example, the spell command enables you to check data for spelling mistakes. An example of a spell command with no options follows:

```
spell sales.memo
```

This command causes spell to produce a list of all the misspelled words in the file sales.memo. In this example, the command takes no options, but a single argument—the file name sales.memo.

If, however, you are preparing this sales memo for a client in London, you can apply the -b option of the spell command, as follows:

```
spell -b sales.memo
```

Like any option, the -b option does not change the fundamental purpose of the command (to list misspelled words), but the option alters some facet of the way the command does its work. In this case, the -b option causes the spell command to apply British spelling rules rather than American rules. The command therefore lists color and aluminum as misspelled words, but not their British counterparts, colour and aluminium. Option letters usually are abbreviations for a word describing the option; in this case -b stands for *British*.

Some commands have only a few possible options; others have many; a few have none. Most users don't even attempt to learn them all, but memorize only a few useful options for commonly used commands. For less commonly used options, experienced users keep handy a copy of the manufacturer's reference manual, an AT&T UNIX reference manual, or a book with a good command reference, such as Que's *Using UNIX*.

You will find that many commands use identical options, but that the options have different meanings for different commands. For example, the -b option tells the spell command to use British spelling rules rather than American. The same -b option, however, tells the diff command to ignore blanks (that is, spaces and tabs) when processing its data. This use of the same letter is often a source of confusion. Unfortunately, hundreds of options exist for all the UNIX commands, but only 52 different upper- and lowercase letters exist to represent these options.

Options and Arguments Combined in Commands

Three points should be made about options and arguments. First, some commands enable you to use options, some enable you to use arguments, some both, and some neither. A reference manual is the handiest way to find out about unfamiliar commands.

Second, some commands enable you to combine multiple options behind a single dash as a typing saver. For example, the `ls` command, which produces a list of files, enables you to type options separately—each with its own dash—or combined behind a single dash. Consider this example:

```
ls -a -C
```

This command lists all your files (`-a` for *all*) in columns (`-C` for *columns*); however, `ls` performs exactly the same operation if you instead type

```
ls -aC
```

The `ls` command is described in greater detail further in this chapter. Note that not all commands enable you to combine options in this way.

Third, most commands enable you to specify options in any order, and many even enable you to precede the options with arguments. For example, the `wc` (*word count*) command, which displays a count of lines, words, and characters in a file, can accept options in any order and also enables you to combine options. Thus to count words (`-w`) and lines (`-l`) in a file called `memo`, all of the following commands produce exactly the same result:

```
wc -w -l memo

wc -l -w memo

wc -lw memo

wc -wl memo
```

A flexible order of options, however, does not hold true for all commands. As an example, the order of options can be important for the `sort` command, which arranges data in some kind of order, such as alphabetical order. The following two `sort` commands, then, do not produce the same results:

```
sort +7 +2 datafile

sort +2 +7 datafile
```

The first command displays the data in `datafile` in order according to the seventh data field; however, in any lines in which the seventh fields are the same, the second field is used as a "tie breaker." The second command reverses the function of these fields—the second field is the primary field, and the seventh field becomes the tie breaker.

Introducing the Basic UNIX File Name Commands

UNIX provides a variety of commands that enable you to perform useful operations on files. Included are commands to display a list of file names, list the contents of files, print files, copy files, and manipulate files in other ways that help you accomplish your work. In this section, you learn about many of the commands that UNIX users find most useful.

Listing Files

The ls (*list files*) command lists the names of files. When issued with no options, ls lists the name of each file, one file per line, in alphabetical order:

```
$ ls <Return>
dog
management.doc
meeting_agenda
memo.to.jim
memo.to.rick
sales.report
test.c
$
```

A variety of options are available with ls. One, -C, tells ls to list the files in columns, rather than one per line. Consider this example:

```
$ ls -C <Return>
dog             management.doc      meeting_agenda
memo.to.jim     memo.to.rick        sales.report
test.c
$
```

The -l option is perhaps the most commonly used option; this option causes ls to produce a *long* listing, which provides additional information for each file listed. Following is typical output from an ls -l command:

```
$ ls -l <Return>
total 54
-rw-r--r--  1  mark      doc       1020  Jun 17 10:42  memo.to.jim
-rw-rw-r--  1  mark      doc      20432  May  8 15:01  sales.memo
-rwxrwx---  1  mark      doc      79802  Jun 18 08:44  testprog
$
```

Total — total 54

Mode — | Links | Owner | Group | Size | Last modification | File name

This listing contains a wealth of information about the file, including the following items:

- The *total* figure indicates the total number of disk blocks required to store the files. It provides information about how the files are stored on the disk. (More information can be found in Chapter 10, "Understanding the Internal Structure of UNIX.")

- The *owner* is the user who owns and controls the file.

- The *size* figures indicate the size, in bytes, of each file.

- The *last modification* time and date specify when the file was last changed in some way.

- The *file name*, of course, is the name of the file.

The mode, links, and group are explained further in this chapter.

If you specify arguments, they represent the files or directories for ls to list, rather than all files (a more detailed discussion of directories is found further in this chapter). This feature is especially useful with the –l option, which can otherwise produce a lengthy output. Look at this example:

```
$ ls -l memo.to.jim sales.memo <Return>
total 1
-rw-r--r--  1  mark      doc       1020  Jun 17 10:42  memo.to.jim
-rw-rw-r--  1  mark      doc      20432  May  8 15:01  sales.memo
$
```

Because the command line contains two file names, only those two files are listed in the output.

Copying Files

The cp (*copy*) command enables you to duplicate a file. With the cp command, you specify two arguments, which respectively represent the name of the file to copy and the name to call the copy. Consider the following example:

```
cp report report2
```

This command makes a copy of report and calls the copy report2. If a file called report2 already exists, cp deletes the old report2 and replaces it with a copy of report. Be sure to exercise caution so that you do not accidentally delete an important file by inadvertently using its name as the destination of a cp command.

Moving and Renaming a File

The mv (*move*) command moves the data in a file to another file and deletes the original file. Consider this example:

```
mv current.report 1991.report
```

This command moves the data in current.report to 1991.report, and deletes current.report. When the command is complete, current.report is gone, and 1991.report exists in its place. As with the cp command, if a file named 1991.report already exists, the new copy of current.report replaces it, and the old copy of 1991.report is lost.

The mv command often is thought of as "renaming" a file, because in cases such as the preceding example, file renaming is the effect of what the mv command does. In other circumstances, however, the mv command moves data from one place on disk to another.

Removing a File

The rm (*remove*) command removes a file you no longer want. You follow the rm command with a list of files you want to remove. After you invoke the command, the files are removed from disk and the data in these files is lost. Consider this example:

```
rm memo.to.pete sales.report inventory.1991
```

This command removes three files: memo.to.pete, sales.report, and inventory.1991.

Viewing the Contents of a File

Several methods are available for viewing a file. You can view short files with the cat command, as shown in this example:

```
cat shopping.list
```

This command displays the contents of `shopping.list` on-screen. Because the data is displayed as fast as the system can show it, unread data may scroll off-screen. Pressing <Ctrl-S> freezes the screen to give you a chance to catch up, and <Ctrl-Q> resumes the display. (`cat` gets its name from *concatenate*, which means to join together. One other use of `cat` is to join two or more files together.)

For longer files, the `pg` command is easier to use. `pg` displays one screenful of data at a time. When you are ready for the next screenful, you press <Return> to display the next batch of lines. While you are using the `pg` command to display a file, you can press q to quit `pg`. Consider this example:

    pg pool.rules

This command displays the first screen of data from `pool.rules` (23 lines on most terminals) and then pauses. Pressing q causes `pg` to quit; pressing <Return> causes it to continue with the next screenful. On UNIX systems based on the Berkeley version of UNIX, you use the `more` command in place of `pg`—the basic format is the same. Consider this example:

    more chart_of_accts

A public domain program called `less`, with additional capabilities, also is widely available. (The name is a pun on `more`.)

Printing Files to the Printer

You use the `lp` command to print files to the printer (on Berkeley systems, you use `lpr` instead). To print the file `superbowl.bets` to the printer, for example, you type

    lp superbowl.bets

On a Berkeley system, you type

    lpr superbowl.bets

The `lp` and `lpr` commands do not access the printer directly; instead they call upon a UNIX facility called the *print spooler*, which accepts requests to print on a printer, and controls the details of getting onto paper the data from the file you specify. This method has two advantages over accessing the printer directly:

- Printing a long file can take considerable time; however, because the `lp` (or `lpr`) command does not handle the details of printing, but merely makes requests of the spooler, the lp command seems to take only an instant, enabling you to continue with another command. While you continue with some other activity, the spooler is busy behind the scenes (or, in UNIX terminology, "in the background") taking care of the printing.

- If two people use the lp (or lpr) command at the same time, the spooler takes care of one first and then the other, avoiding a conflict in which the printer tries to print two files simultaneously.

See Chapter 5, "UNIX Tools," for more details on the print spooler system.

Classifying Files

Even though UNIX doesn't classify regular files into categories, you often need to know what kind of data a file contains. Sometimes the ending of the file name provides valuable clues: a .c ending indicates a C source program; a .doc ending usually indicates a word processing program. But often the name of a file offers no help—for example, sales.data.

The file command can help you determine the type and organization of a file. The file command examines a few hundred bytes at the beginning of the file for hints about the kind of data the file contains. Some of the possible conclusions that file may report include the following:

- If the file command notes that the file consists almost entirely of printable characters, it may identify that file as ascii text.

- If the file consists of printable characters, many of which happen to form words that file finds in the dictionary, it may report the file as English text.

- If the text contains formatting commands, the file may be identified as input text for the nroff or troff formatters, reporting [nt]roff, tbl, or eqn input text.

- If the file contains what seems to be programming constructs from C or FORTRAN, the file is identified as source code for those languages, reporting c program text.

In addition to the types listed here, file can recognize many other types of files.

Many files contain an important clue, which file often can use to accurately identify the type of a file. Some types of files, including executable programs, begin with a special two-byte number that identifies the type of file. This number is called a *magic number*. When trying to determine a file's type, file checks the first two bytes of the file against a table of magic numbers; if a match is found, file assumes that the file type matches the description in the table of magic numbers.

file can be fooled; it looks only at the first portion of the file rather than the entire contents. For example, if a technical paper on programming begins with a C programming example, the file command may errone-ously spot this fact and identify the file as a C program, even though the file is actually mostly English text. Also, magic numbers occasionally provide a false clue. For example, an ordinary data file may begin with two bytes of data that, by pure chance, happen to match one of the numbers in the magic number table. In this example, file will incorrectly identify the file as the type that matches the magic number.

The real power of UNIX derives not from its capability to manipulate files, but its capability to organize and group files in a simple, flexible way. UNIX accomplishes this organization with a special type of file, called a *directory*, which is the topic of the next section.

Pattern Searching

The word *grep* describes a family of related commands: grep, fgrep, and egrep. You can use these commands to search a set of files for one or more phrases or patterns. These commands can locate all files in which the phrase or pattern occurs, or can print all lines that contain a phrase or pattern. For example, to find and display all lines in the file cheeses that contain the word *cheddar*, type this command:

```
grep cheddar cheeses
```

The word immediately following grep is the search phrase, and all remain-ing words on the command line (cheeses in this example) specify the files to be searched.

If the search phrase contains any spaces or punctuation characters, you must enclose the phrase in quotation marks:

```
grep "Mary Smith" phonelist
```

grep also can search for patterns, more properly known as *regular expres-sions* (see Chapter 6, "Text Processing in the UNIX Environment," for a description of regular expressions). For example, if you want to search for all lines in the file customers that start with a digit, type

```
grep "^[0-9]" customers
```

As you learn in Chapter 6, the caret (^) means "beginning of line," and [0-9] means "any character 0 through 9." grep thus displays any line that starts with a digit.

Often in the world of computers, powerful programs run slowly. grep's relatives, fgrep and egrep, are a result of the desire of grep's designers to balance power with speed. fgrep (*fast grep*) performs a faster search than grep, but it is also the least powerful of the family. fgrep can search only for specific words or phrases, but not patterns. On the other end of the spectrum, egrep (*extended grep*) is the slowest of the group, but also the most powerful. It can search for more complex patterns and combinations of patterns than grep can.

Incidentally, the name grep, like so many UNIX command names, is actually an abbreviation. grep mimics the function of a command from the ed editor, which has the format g/*RE*/p, where *RE* is an abbreviation for *regular expression*.

Compressing Files

You can use any of several series of tools to compress files into a more compact form. In each case, these tools greatly reduce the size of a file by analyzing the data within the files and determining a way to represent the data in less space. Although compressed, you cannot use these files in any way—if you examine these compressed files, they seem to contain gibberish—but they contain enough information to recreate the original data. At a future time you can execute a command to uncompress the files and return them to their original form. You may want to use these tools for any of several reasons:

- You may want to compress files you probably will not need in the near future, yet don't want to erase. In their compressed format, these files occupy much less disk space than the originals, and if you should need the files at a future time, you can restore them to their original form.

- You can greatly reduce transmission time and long distance charges when sending data over telephone lines by compressing the data on the sending computer and uncompressing the data on the receiving computer.

Two sets of tools are widely used by UNIX users. The older set of tools is pack and unpack, which respectively compress and restore files. When you *pack* a file, pack renames the file to add .z to the end of the file name. Thus, if you type

```
pack memo
```

pack compresses memo and renames it memo.z. Typically pack can reduce the size of a file by approximately 25 percent.

Another set of tools, compress and uncompress, is widely available in the public domain and enables you to achieve a higher percentage of compression. A 45-percent reduction in size is not uncommon for compress, which may compress some files even more.

Understanding Directories

A typical UNIX system contains thousands of files; on large systems, the number may be tens of thousands, or more. Any operating system that deals with such large numbers of files must provide a means for organizing and categorizing files. UNIX provides a simple yet powerful scheme for organizing files by using a special type of file called a *directory*.

A directory is a table of contents, in a special format controlled by UNIX, that contains a list of files and important information you use to access the files. A directory serves a purpose much like an index in a book, which enables you to determine the proper page number for a specific topic. As you create new files and delete old files, UNIX adds and deletes entries in directories to keep track of the names and locations of files.

When you first begin using a UNIX computer, the system administrator provides a directory for you to use when creating files. This directory is known as your *home directory*. A directory is like a type of electronic filing cabinet in which you store new files. (This analogy is not completely accurate, but it will do for now.) Each time you create a new file, an entry is made in the directory. When you delete files, entries are removed. Later, when you want to retrieve information from the file, the directory entry provides important information that enables UNIX to access the data within the file.

By the time you have worked with a computer for a few months, you probably have created hundreds—perhaps thousands—of files as part of your daily work. Memos, reports, programs, and various data files soon litter the computer's disk. As large disks become less expensive, you have less incentive to delete old files; with plenty of disk space available, you may be tempted to keep all your files. But keeping all your old files causes your home directory to grow larger and larger. A listing of the names of the files becomes excessively long, and locating a file whose exact name has been forgotten becomes tedious. The human mind cannot confront such a large number of files, or a large number of anything for that matter, without experiencing a strong desire to organize.

Understanding Subdirectories

An important feature of directories enables you to impose order on such a collection of files. Directories can contain entries not only for regular files, but for other directories as well. Such a directory, listed inside another directory, is sometimes called a *subdirectory* (although *directory* and *subdirectory* are almost always synonymous terms). In effect, you can list a group of related files in a separate directory, which is listed in your home directory.

Consider a typical situation encountered by Karla, an assistant who spends her day performing various tasks on behalf of a small law firm. After a few months of experience, she notices that she can categorize most of her files— several hundreds of them—into several types of documents: pleadings, depositions, motions, correspondence, and deeds. Of course, she also has numerous miscellaneous documents that don't fit into these categories.

Instead of keeping all these documents listed in her home directory, Karla decides to create subdirectories called deeds, pleadings, motions, corre-spondence, depositions, and misc. Karla moves the appropriate documents from the home directory to the appropriate subdirectories. Karla now can locate documents quickly by looking for them in one of the subdirectories. Even if she doesn't remember the exact name of the letter she wrote to Acme Trucking, she knows the letter can be found in the correspondence subdirectory.

If Karla issues the ls command to display a listing of the files in her home directory, UNIX displays only the names of the subdirectories. If she uses ls to display a listing of the subdirectory pleadings, UNIX displays the file names of the small number of files containing pleadings, rather than the large number of files that previously resided in her home directory. Figure 3.1 shows a diagram of Karla's directories, including the six subdirectories she created.

Suppose that Karla eventually decides to further categorize her files. She notices that the correspondence directory is becoming large, and she has trouble finding the names of files she needs. To solve her problem, Karla creates subdirectories within the correspondence directory—jim, beth, fred, and fran—named after the four law partners for whom she works. She then moves each file to the appropriate subdirectory. Now letters written by Jim are located in the jim directory, which is in the correspondence directory. The correspondence directory, in turn, is located in Karla's home directory. Figure 3.2 shows the new organization of Karla's directories.

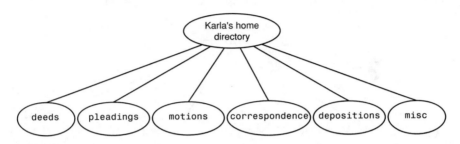

Fig. 3.1. A diagram of Karla's directories.

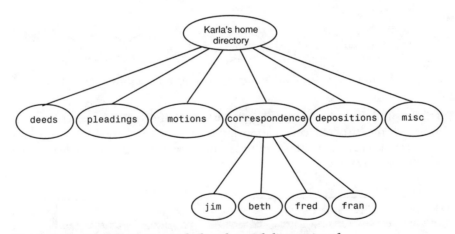

Fig. 3.2. Karla's directories, including four subdirectories of correspondence.

If necessary, Karla can subdivide the deeds, pleadings, motions, depositions, and misc directories. For example, if the deeds directory becomes large, Karla can subdivide it into the same directories she created for the correspondence directory, creating jim, beth, fred, and fran. This structure enables her to locate one of Fran's deeds in the fran directory, which is located in the deeds directory.

This solution is not the best one, however. Beth is the firm's real estate expert, and she handles almost all the deeds. Subdividing deeds by lawyer's name results in a large number of files in the beth subdirectory, and almost none in the others. In this case, Karla may want to subdivide deeds into directories named after the county in which the property is located. For example, all deeds for Seminole County would then be placed in the subdirectory seminole, regardless of which lawyer worked on the account. Figure 3.3 shows a diagram of this new directory organization.

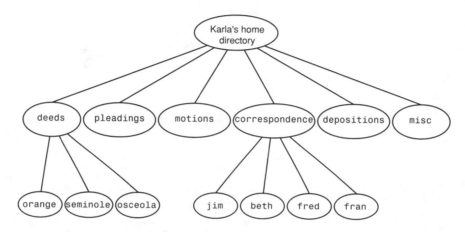

Fig. 3.3. Karla's directories, including subdirectories of deeds.

If these subdirectories become large, Karla can subdivide them also. You can continue the process of creating subdirectories to any level. You can organize files in an almost unlimited number of ways, and no single scheme is right for everyone.

Duplicate File Names

Although UNIX does not enable you to give the same name to two files in the same directory, files in different directories can share the same name. This name-sharing feature is possible because files are identified not only by name, but also by directory. In the example in this section, Karla created two subdirectories called fran, but no conflict results. One is fran in the deeds directory; the other is fran in the correspondence directory.

Understanding the File System

In the previous section, Karla divided her home directory into subdirectories, which she then divided into additional subdirectories. This arrangement often is referred to as a *hierarchical directory structure*, because a definite ranking (hierarchy) exists among the directories: each directory is subordinate to the directory in which it is listed.

In this same fashion, UNIX organizes all files into a single hierarchy of directories. The top directory—a kind of master directory—is the *root* directory, symbolized by a slash (/). A diagram of the directory organization looks like an upside-down tree, with the root directory located where the roots of the upside-down tree would be.

The root directory contains numerous subdirectories, many of which are found on all UNIX systems. These subdirectories form the major classifications of files on any UNIX system, just as Karla's subdirectories form the major classifications of her work. Some of UNIX's important subdirectories, which the installation software automatically creates, are listed as follows:

- bin

  The bin directory contains the executable programs that make up most of the important UNIX system commands. (bin is an abbreviation for *binary*, which is an old-fashioned name for executable programs. The bin directory is so named because it contains mostly executable system programs.)

- etc

  etc (often pronounced et-see) contains important system administration programs and data files.

- lib

  The lib directory contains some of the libraries that programming language compilers use (see Chapter 8, "Programming Languages and UNIX Software," for more details).

- dev

  This directory contains UNIX device files (explained in "Understanding Special Files and File Types," further in this chapter).

- tmp

  As the name implies, tmp is a directory in which you can create temporary files to hold data for a short period of time.

- usr

  usr contains files of general use to the users of a UNIX system.

Most of these directories have subdirectories. For example, usr contains many subdirectories, including bin (where application programs are stored) and lib (which contains more programming libraries and the terminfo library of terminal information).

A very important group of directories found within usr has names that match the names of the computer's users. These directories are the users' home directories; thus, returning to the example about Karla, the usr directory probably contains a directory called karla, which is her home directory.

Using Karla's directory system as an example, figure 3.4 shows a few of the directories that are part of most UNIX systems.

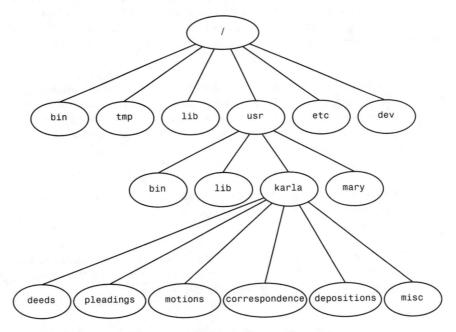

Fig. 3.4. UNIX system directories and sample user directories.

Understanding the Current Directory

At any given time while you are logged in to a computer, you have a *current directory*—also known as the *current working directory*—associated with your shell. As you perform operations such as creating, removing, copying, listing, and editing files, UNIX understands that file names refer to files in your current directory, unless you specify otherwise. UNIX provides commands that enable you at any time to select any directory as the current working directory (see "Changing the Current Directory," further in this chapter, for details).

Consider the following command:

```
rm kittens.4.sale
```

When you type this command, UNIX looks for a file called kittens.4.sale in the current directory and removes the file. Files in other directories may have the same name, but these files remain unaffected.

Understanding Path Names

Path names provide a mechanism for accessing files that are outside the current working directory. In effect, path names provide a roadmap for UNIX to use in locating files in other directories. UNIX recognizes two types of path names: *absolute* and *relative*.

Absolute Path Names

Absolute path names (also known as *full path names*) identify a specific file by providing a complete roadmap from the root directory to the file you want. An absolute path name begins with a slash (/), lists the complete chain of directories that UNIX must follow from the root directory, each separated by /, and finally ends in the name of the file you want. The root directory itself is symbolized by the slash that begins the path name.

Suppose that Sarah has a file system in UNIX that includes the directories shown in figure 3.5. She wants to print the file called daily.report. If her current working directory is reports, Sarah can type the simple command **lp daily.report**.

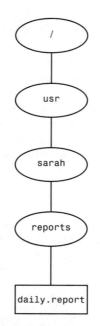

Fig. 3.5. *A variety of directories branching from the root.*

Sarah can use an absolute path name, however, regardless of the current directory. Listing all directories between the root directory and daily.report, Sarah uses the following command:

lp /usr/sarah/reports/daily.report

This command tells UNIX to access daily.report by starting in the root directory, then moving to the usr directory, then to usr's subdirectory sarah, then to sarah's subdirectory reports. The daily.report file is in the reports subdirectory.

You can specify directory names in the same way. To list all files in the reports directory, Sarah can type the following command:

ls /usr/sarah/reports

The absolute path name of files in the root directory is the file name prefixed by a slash. For example, the UNIX operating system is in the root directory, in a file called `unix`; its absolute path name is `/unix`. Note that you type **ls /** to list the names of the files in the root directory.

Relative Path Names

Relative path names provide a mechanism for specifying the location of a file within a directory, without referring to the root directory of the UNIX file system. Relative path names provide a roadmap from the current working directory rather than from the root directory. Absolute path names always begin with a slash to indicate that they start from the root directory; relative path names do not begin with a slash.

Using Sarah's directory structure as an example (again see fig. 3.5), suppose that Sarah's current working directory is her home directory, `sarah`. If she wants to access `daily.report`, the proper relative path name lists all the directories UNIX traverses between her current working directory and `daily.report`. Only the `reports` directory separates the two, so the relative path name is as follows:

```
reports/daily.report
```

On the other hand, if Sarah's current directory is `usr`, the relative path to access `daily.report` is as follows:

```
sarah/reports/daily.report
```

In this case, UNIX must cross two directories—`sarah` and `reports`—to get to `daily.report`.

Although a file has only one absolute path name, a file has many different relative path names—the proper path name for any particular file depends on your current working directory.

To summarize, an absolute path name begins with a slash, and its path starts with the root directory. By contrast, a relative path name does not begin with a slash, and its path moves from the current working directory.

MS-DOS and Directories

MS-DOS, like many operating systems, has a scheme of directories and subdirectories that is very similar to the scheme UNIX uses. Many people who are familiar with MS-DOS and then learn UNIX assume that UNIX got the idea from MS-DOS.

Actually, the reverse is true. UNIX had subdirectories more than ten years before anybody ever heard of MS-DOS. In fact, the original version of MS-DOS—Version 1.0—did not enable you to use subdirectories. The developers of MS-DOS at Microsoft, however, were familiar with UNIX's directory scheme and added the concept to subsequent versions of MS-DOS. Even before Microsoft developed MS-DOS, the company was involved in developing XENIX, a version of UNIX.

You may question why UNIX uses the slash in path names (such as /usr/bob/letters/delta), whereas MS-DOS uses backslashes (such as \BOB\LETTERS\DELTA). Unfortunately, when Version 1.0 of MS-DOS was developed, the idea that Microsoft might want to add subdirectory capabilities to MS-DOS didn't occur to its designers, and they commandeered the slash for other purposes: the slash serves to introduce an option (MS-DOS calls it a *switch*), much as the dash does for UNIX. Thus the MS-DOS command DIR /W executes the DIR command with the W switch (option). Rather than retroactively changing the syntax of existing commands, Microsoft looked around for some other suitable character to serve as the separator in path names and decided on the backslash. The resulting confusion and frustration among people who work in both UNIX and MS-DOS continues to this day.

Using Path Names with File Commands

Any of the UNIX commands that accept file names as arguments can accept path names as well. Almost without exception, none of the commands care whether the files are in the current directory or whether a path must be followed to find the file.

For example, the cp command can copy a file from one directory to another:

```
cp /usr/mark/time.report /usr/boss/mark.time.rpt
```

This command copies a file called `time.report` from the directory `/usr/mark` to the directory `/usr/boss`, and calls the copy `mark.time.rpt` in its new location.

The same name could have been used for the file in both directories:

```
cp /usr/mark/time.report /usr/boss/time.report
```

In this example, because the file is copied to a different directory, no conflict of names results. In fact, when you want the file name to remain the same, you do not need to specify the name—only the directory, as shown in this example:

```
cp /usr/mark/time.report /usr/boss
```

When the `cp` command sees that its second argument is a directory, the command understands that the file is to be copied into that directory under the same name the file had in the other directory.

You can mix and match absolute and relative path names, as shown in the following example:

```
cp memos/sales.memo /usr/fred/old.memos/sales.memo.90
```

This command finds the file `sales.memo`, which is in the `memos` subdirectory under the current working directory, and copies the file as `sales.memo.90` to the directory `/usr/fred/old.memos`.

Similarly, you can print files in other directories, as shown in the command

```
lp /etc/group
```

and you can view files contained in other directories:

```
pg /usr/bob/chili.recipe
```

The `ls` command can accept one or more path names as arguments. If an argument is a file, `ls` lists the name of the file; if an argument is a directory, `ls` lists all files in that directory. To get a listing of all the commands in the `/bin` directory, therefore, you type

```
ls /bin
```

Using Special Directory Names

Two special directory names are available for you to use in path names and for many commands. You can use the *dot* (.) to represent the current directory. This symbol primarily serves as a typing saver. For example, to copy a file called `employee_list` from `/usr/belinda` into the current directory, type

```
cp /usr/belinda/employee_list .
```

The `cp` command recognizes the second argument (.) as a directory (the current working directory) and copies the file as `employee_list` into that directory.

The second special directory name is the *dot-dot* (`..`). This symbol represents the directory one level up the tree, toward the root directory. This directory also is known as the *parent directory*. For example, if your current working directory is `/usr/roger/report/1991`, its parent directory is `/usr/roger/report`, the directory just above `1991`. To copy a file called `company.picnic` to this parent directory, you simply type

```
cp company.picnic ..
```

`cp` recognizes `..` as a directory (the directory one level up) and copies `company.picnic` to this directory, keeping the same file name. Alternatively, you can indicate that you want the file copied under a new name in the parent directory; for example, you can type

```
cp company.picnic ../new.picnic
```

Similarly, you can type the following command to list the files in the directory one level up:

```
ls ..
```

You can combine several dot-dots, separated by slashes, to specify a directory several levels up. For example, to list the directory two levels up (the parent of the parent directory), use this command:

```
ls ../..
```

The Parent of the Root Directory

The root directory is the master directory of a UNIX system and has no parent. Consider what happens if your current working directory is the root directory, and you invoke the following command to list the contents of root's parent directory:

```
ls ..
```

Because you're already at the top level of the directory system, UNIX handles the situation as a special case. In the root directory, `..` does not represent the parent directory, but rather the current directory (just as `.` does). Thus, typing `ls ..` from the root directory lists files in the root directory.

Introducing the Basic UNIX Directory Commands

UNIX provides commands for creating, removing, and navigating directories. These commands are discussed in this section.

Creating Directories

You follow the command `mkdir` (*make directory*) with one or more arguments, and UNIX creates subdirectories, using the specified arguments as the names of the subdirectories. Consider this example:

```
mkdir letters memos reports
```

This command creates directories called `letters`, `memos`, and `reports`, making them subdirectories of the current working directory.

Removing Directories

You can remove directories with the `rmdir` (*remove directory*) command. Like `mkdir`, its arguments list the directory or directories you want to remove. Consider this example:

```
rmdir memos
```

The `rmdir` command cannot remove a directory that contains files; if you do not remove the files first, an error message results. For example, if you type

```
rmdir oldstuff
```

`rmdir` displays the message

```
oldstuff: not empty
```

Using the `rm` command, you first must remove the files within `oldstuff`, and then you can remove the `oldstuff` directory.

Changing the Current Directory

The `cd` (*change directory*) command changes the current working directory. This command's single argument is the name of the directory you want to make the current working directory. Consider this example:

```
cd /usr/mark/letters
```

This command makes /usr/mark/letters the current working directory. You also can use relative path names, such as the following command:

cd reports

This command finds the reports directory—which must be a subdirectory of the current working directory—and makes it the new current working directory.

The following command makes the parent directory (the directory one level up) the current working directory:

cd ..

You also can use the cd command without specifying an argument, in which case the current working directory changes to your home directory. Thus, if Fred's home directory is /usr/fred, typing **cd** is equivalent to typing **cd /usr/fred**.

File Names Beginning with a Period

File names beginning with a period are treated a special way by UNIX. Many configuration files in your home directory have names that begin with a period, such as .profile (see Chapter 4, "Understanding the UNIX Shell") and .exrc (see Chapter 6, "Text Processing in the UNIX Environment"). Experienced users may have a dozen or more of these files in their home directories. To avoid cluttering up a directory listing with these file names, the ls command normally does not list the names of files beginning with a period; however, the -a (*all*) option tells ls to include these files.

In addition to showing names like .profile and .exrc, ls -a also displays the special directory names . and .., which are available in any directory.

Displaying the Current Working Directory

The pwd (*print working directory*) command displays the current working directory as an absolute path name. Consider this example:

```
$ pwd <Return>
/usr/lisa/reports/1991
$
```

In this example pwd prints the absolute path name of the current working directory: you are working in 1991, which is a subdirectory of reports, which in turn is a subdirectory of lisa, which is a subdirectory of usr, which is a subdirectory of the root directory.

Differences between UNIX and MS-DOS

Although MS-DOS adopted many features of UNIX's directory scheme, people who use both systems sometimes become frustrated by the minor differences that exist. The following items are the most important differences:

* cd

  In UNIX, typing cd with no argument changes the current working directory to your home directory. MS-DOS lacks the concept of a home directory. In MS-DOS, typing the cd command with no arguments displays the current working directory. UNIX uses the pwd command to display the current working directory.

* md and rd

  MS-DOS enables you to abbreviate the mkdir and rmdir commands as md and rd, respectively. UNIX does not. You can, however, use the alias features described in the following chapter to define any abbreviation for any command.

Understanding Special Files and File Types

In addition to regular files and directories, UNIX recognizes a class of files known as *special files*, or *device files*. These files have names, just like other files, and are displayed in directory listings, but these files do not represent a collection of data stored on disk. Rather, they represent (in most cases) pieces of hardware. You treat these files just like regular files, and all the commands for accessing regular files also work with special files. When you access these files, however, the equipment they represent is activated.

All UNIX systems come with a large number of special files in a directory called /dev (*device*). This directory is nothing special; it is merely a convenient collection place for UNIX's special files. An example of a special file is /dev/tty, which represents your terminal (tty is an abbreviation for *Teletype*, a terminal made by Teletype Corporation, used years ago, prior to CRT monitors). You access this file like you do any other file, but it represents a piece of equipment, not a disk file. For example, the command

```
cp sales.list /dev/tty
```

copies the file sales.list to /dev/tty, resulting in the contents of the file being printed on-screen.

Each terminal on a UNIX system has a unique name that identifies the terminal. For example, consider this command:

```
cp message /dev/tty47
```

This command copies the file named message to the terminal named tty47. (By the way, this action can severely annoy the person who happens to be working on that terminal at the time.)

Sometimes a single piece of equipment has several different special names, each with slightly different properties. For example, a UNIX system may contain these two special devices:

```
/dev/fd2s9s80t
```

```
/dev/fd2s18s80t
```

Both names represent the same piece of equipment—the system's floppy disk drive, as indicated by fd (*floppy disk*) at the beginning of both names. However, the drive accesses the diskette in the drive differently, depending on which name you use. If you use the first name, the drive—reading the letters in the name—accesses the diskette as a double-sided (2s) diskette with 9 sectors per track (9s) and 80 tracks (80t). If you use the second name, the drive instead accesses the diskette as having 18 sectors per track (18s). XENIX uses this scheme for naming the disk drive, and many other variations are possible.

Some special names represent logical devices that don't really exist, but are useful in some context. The best example is /dev/null, commonly known as *the bit bucket*. UNIX discards any data you send to /dev/null.

Consider this scenario: An accounting program posts transactions to a general ledger and produces a lengthy report detailing its activities. Before producing the report, the program prompts for a file name in which the report should be stored. Joan needs to post the transactions, but in this instance, she is not interested in the report. When the program prompts for a file name, she can specify /dev/null. The program still produces the report, but when the program sends the data to /dev/null, UNIX discards it.

Table 3.2 contains a list of some common UNIX device file names. Note that not all of them are found on all UNIX systems.

Table 3.2
Common UNIX Device File Names

Device File	Description
/dev/null	The bit bucket (all systems). UNIX discards all data sent here.
/dev/tty	The user's terminal (all systems)
/dev/tty21	Terminal #21 (terminal name varies)
/dev/console	The system console terminal (all systems)
/dev/diskette	The system diskette drive (drive name varies)
/dev/fd0	Common name for diskette drive #0 (drive name varies)
/dev/hd0	Common name for hard disk drive #0 (drive name varies)
/dev/lp	The system printer (all systems)
/dev/mem	The computer's random-access memory (all systems)
/dev/kmem	UNIX kernel memory; a special portion of the computer's memory (all systems)

Many names other than those listed in the preceding table usually are present on most UNIX systems.

Special files actually come in two types: *block* and *character*. The distinction indicates how the associated devices process data: in general, character devices represent equipment that processes data one character at a time, such as terminals and printers; block devices represent equipment that works with large chunks of data at a time, called *blocks*, such as tape drives and disk drives. This explanation is a tad simplistic, but until you start working with the internals of UNIX, it's sufficient.

> ### The Terminal /dev/tty
>
> UNIX treats /dev/tty somewhat differently than other device files. Although /dev/tty represents a piece of equipment, it does not always represent the *same* piece of equipment. /dev/tty represents the terminal on which you are logged in; thus, two users accessing /dev/tty at the same time access two different terminals because each user is logged in to a different terminal.
>
> Conversely, a device file name such as /dev/tty3a represents a specific terminal that never changes (unless you rewire the terminal connections).
>
> Another kind of file, first introduced under UNIX System V, is the *named pipe*, also known as a *FIFO (first in, first out)*. Unless you are a programmer, you never use these files; they are used strictly by programmers as a means of exchanging information in a cooperative way. On most systems, only a handful of these named pipes exist among the thousands of files on the system, and unless you look through some of the system directories, you never see them.

Determining File Type

Under UNIX System V, all files are classified as one of five types (see table 3.3). UNIX systems based on the Berkeley version of UNIX support two additional types, and other versions of UNIX may support still other types.

To identify a file type, you use the command ls -l. The first character in each line of the resulting list identifies the file type. Consider this example:

```
$ ls -l <Return>
total 1
-rw-r--r--  1  mark      doc      1020  Jun 17 10:42  memo.to.jim
drwxr-xr-x  2  mark      doc        64  Jun  3 12:02  reports
brw-r--r--  1  mark      dvlp     5, 6  Jan 31 17:82  special.file
$
```

The file type is identified by one of the characters in table 3.3.

Table 3.3
UNIX File Types

Character	File Type
–	Regular (ordinary) data file or program
d	Directory
b	Block device file
c	Character device file
p	Named pipe (FIFO)
l	Symbolic link (only Berkeley UNIX)
s	Socket (only Berkeley UNIX)

Sockets, which provide a flexible mechanism for two programs to communicate with each other, are used exclusively by programmers and not discussed in this book. Symbolic links are mentioned in "Understanding Multiple File Systems in UNIX," further in this chapter.

The last line of the output in the preceding example shows a special device file (which, in this case, happens to be a block device). Where ls normally displays the file size, it displays two numbers instead, 5 and 6 in this example. These numbers are the *major* and *minor device numbers*, which UNIX uses to identify the device internally. UNIX does not display the size because special files occupy no disk space.

Understanding File Links

In UNIX, a single file can have several different names, which you can use interchangeably to access the file. These different names for the same file more properly are called *links*. You may want to create multiple links (names) for a file for several reasons:

- You may be working with a file that has a very descriptive but long name, such as 1991.sales.rpt. While you are working with the file, you may want to give it a much shorter name, such as sr, which enables you to save time by using the file's shorter name to access it. Other users, however, can continue to use the longer name, with which they are familiar.

- If you need to access a file in another directory, you can create a link to that file in your current directory. This technique enables a file to be "in" two directories at the same time, enabling you to access the file easily from both directories without typing path names.

- Many application programs access data from files with specific names. If the data file does not have the name that the program expects, the program cannot access the data. Some day you may find yourself working with two such applications, both of which use different names to access the same data. For example, your general ledger program might expect the chart of accounts file to be called chart.accts, while your receivables program expects it to be called accounts. By using links, you can assign both names to the same data file, thus satisfying both applications at the same time.

You create a new name for an existing file with the ln (*link*) command. The ln command requires two arguments: an existing name for the file and a new name for the file. Consider this example:

ln salesfile salesfile.91

This command creates a new name, salesfile.91, that represents the same file as salesfile. The new file is not merely a copy of the other; rather, the two names represent the same identical file. UNIX does not differentiate between the original name and the new name; all existing names are equally valid, and you can use any link to access the file.

After you use the preceding command to create the link, invoking the command **ls -l** may generate the following output:

```
-rw-r--r--   2  sally      manager    43209   Aug 21   12:56   salesfile
-rw-r--r--   2  sally      manager    43209   Aug 21   12:56   salesfile.91
```

This listing does not specifically tell you that salesfile and salesfile.91 are two links to the same file; however, the number in the second column shows that both names refer to a file that has two names (links). Also, because both lines show identical information, they probably represent the same file.

A file can have links in different directories. Consider this example:

ln salesfile /usr/mark/oldfiles/salesfile.91

This command gives the file yet another name in the /usr/mark/oldfiles directory.

You may notice that when a directory appears in a listing produced by the `ls -l` command, the number of links is always at least two. At first this may puzzle you if you don't remember creating a second link for the directory; however, when you create a directory, UNIX automatically creates two names for the directory—the name you specified and the special name `.`, which you can use to refer to a particular directory when that directory is your current working directory.

Removing File Links

Strictly speaking, the command `rm` does not remove a file; rather, this command removes a link to a file. For example, if you issue an `rm` command such as `rm filename`, UNIX removes the name (link). If the file has more than one name when you issue the command `rm`, the name is removed, but the file is left untouched, enabling you to use all the other names for the file. Only when you remove the single remaining link to the file does UNIX remove the file's data. After you remove the last link to a file, the file is no longer accessible. Because the file has no name with which you can access it, retaining the data in the file makes no sense.

Understanding Multiple File Systems in UNIX

The PDP-7 and PDP-11 computers on which UNIX began had only a single disk drive, and many small computers today also get by with a single disk drive. On most UNIX computers, however—anything above the small PC level—a single computer may have access to several disk drives. Not only can UNIX use many different disk drives, but UNIX does so in such a way that the average user need never be concerned about what files are stored on which drives.

Each disk on a UNIX computer is called a *file system*. Each file system has a root directory and a directory tree that contain a collection of subdirectories and files, just like the overall UNIX system. A running UNIX computer, however, cannot have more than one root directory. One of the disks— usually referred to as *drive 0*, *partition 0*, or *hard disk 0*—is understood by

UNIX to be the "main" disk, and its root directory serves as the root directory of the entire UNIX system. When the system first starts up, but before anyone can log in, this disk is the only one available to UNIX.

UNIX cannot access the remaining disk drives until the system administrator performs on these disk drives an operation called *mounting*. The system administrator usually configures UNIX to perform this function automatically when the system starts up, but mounting also can be done manually with the `mount` command. The `mount` command superimposes the root directory of one of the disk drives with a directory on drive 0, called the *mount point*. After this task is done, any reference to the mount point directory actually references the root directory on the mounted disk drive.

Consider a system that has two disk drives, drive 0 and drive 1 (see fig. 3.6). When the system initially starts up, only drive 0 is available. Figure 3.6 shows the system's root directory (/) on drive 0 and three subdirectories: `bin` and `usr`, which contain other files and directories, and `usr2`, an empty directory. (Of course, many other files and directories are present on this drive, but this discussion focuses on the ones described here.) Drive 1 contains various directories that, by their names, seem to be home directories. These directories are as yet inaccessible.

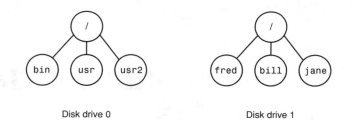

Disk drive 0   Disk drive 1

Fig. 3.6. Drive 0; drive 1, unmounted.

Drive 1 is inaccessible until a `mount` command is executed. Usually UNIX executes any necessary `mount` commands during system startup (see Chapter 9, "UNIX System Administration," for information on the startup process). In some cases, however, the system administrator may want to perform a `mount` manually, as in the case of a disk containing sensitive information that should not be accessible except when needed.

The `mount` command requires two arguments: the special file name that represents the disk drive you are mounting, and the mount point directory name. The special file name of the disk drive varies from one version of UNIX to another. If, on your system, drive 1 is called `/dev/hd1`, and you want to mount the disk on the `/usr2` directory, the command is

```
mount /dev/hd1 /usr2
```

This command tells UNIX that henceforth any reference to the /usr2 directory is a reference to the root directory on drive 1. The special name /dev/hd1 is the device name for *hard disk 1* on some systems. Figure 3.7 shows the system configuration after the mount command is executed.

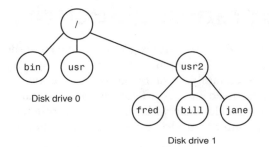

Fig. 3.7. Drive 0; drive 1, mounted on user2.

After this command is executed, referencing a file such as /usr2/bill /letters/jim.1 actually references /bill/letters/jim.1 on Drive 1.

All this activity is largely unseen by you. You are not likely to care that your home directory is on one disk drive and that files in some other directory are on a different drive. You access the files in the usr2 directory just like any other files, never knowing or caring that UNIX had to access a mounted disk drive.

You should know the following information about multiple file systems:

- A drive can be unmounted with the umount command; however, only the system administrator can unmount a hard disk on most systems.

- If you are interested, several UNIX commands, such as mount and df, can tell you which drives are mounted on which mount points.

- The mount point directory should be an empty directory. In the previous example, the system administrator probably created usr2 to serve specifically as a mount point, and therefore, no one uses usr2 for storing files. If usr2 contains any files or directories, they become inaccessible while usr2 serves as a mount point for drive 1.

- All links to a file must reside on the same file system as the data. In this example, the command ln /bin/date /usr2/bill/date would fail because the directories /bin and /usr2/bill are on different file systems (drives). UNIX systems based on the Berkeley version of UNIX, however, provide a type of link called a *symbolic link* that can link across file systems, but this feature is not standard on all UNIX systems.

Understanding Security

Every computer system contains programs and data that should not be made available to everyone. Company strategy memos, employee lists, and correspondence certainly must be kept confidential. Programs on the system may be licensed and proprietary and may contain trade secrets that cannot be made public. Even within a company, much of the information kept on the computer is not to be distributed to all employees.

UNIX provides several levels of security to ensure that people using the system's programs and data files are authorized to do so. These levels are the subject of the following sections.

Understanding System-Level Security

UNIX's first line of defense ensures that everyone using the computer is "allowed" to do so. As with almost every multiuser computer system, the *login* process accomplishes this task.

When you want to use the computer, you must *log in*. You have to enter a valid user *login name*, which has been set up by the system administrator, and a corresponding password. By doing so, you prove to UNIX that you have the right to use the machine.

The login process is especially important when modems are connected to the computer. Through the computer's modems, anyone with a modem, terminal, and phone service can dial into the computer and attempt to log in. If you know a valid login name and password, you can access the system.

Experts who study security believe that, for maximum security, you should change your password on a regular basis. Certainly you need to change your password if you suspect that someone has discovered your password. The passwd command enables you to change your password. This command first prompts for your old password, and then prompts for the new password. None of these passwords display on-screen as you type them. To ensure that you do not mistype the new password, passwd requires you to reenter the new password and makes sure the two new passwords are the same.

Consider this example:

```
$ passwd <Return>
Changing password for maggie
Enter old password: <password>
Enter new password: <new password>
Re-enter new password: <new password>
$
```

Understanding File-Level Security and Permissions

Being permitted access to the computer does not mean you are permitted to perform all functions and to access all data on the system. Almost all multiuser machines contain data that is not intended for all users. Managers may not want everyone on the computer rifling through their private memos and evaluations; likewise, a payroll department may have sensitive payroll information that must be protected.

Almost every operation performed on a UNIX computer involves accessing one or more files. Each time you attempt to run a program or access a file, UNIX file security comes into play to determine whether you are allowed to perform that operation.

All users on the computer are uniquely identified by the name with which they log in, called the *user login name*. In addition, each user is a member of one or more *groups*. The system administrator picks the names for the groups and decides which users should be members of which groups. The system administrator can organize users into groups according to any scheme that seems useful; most often users are grouped by company department, job function, or position within the company. If employees from several different companies share a large computer, the system administrator probably groups users by company. On small computers with only a few users, the system administrator probably would create a single group, perhaps simply called users, and make all users members of that group.

Every file and program under UNIX is owned by one of the system's users. The owner of a file is usually the person who created it, although the owner can transfer ownership to another user. The user who owns the file has control over determining who can access a file and what users with access are allowed to do.

In addition to having an owner, every file also belongs to one of the groups of users. The file's group is usually the group to which the user who created the file belongs; however, you later can change the group to which a file belongs.

You can determine the owner and group of a file from the output of the command ls -1. Consider this example:

```
$ ls -l memo.to.jim  <Return>
total 1
-rw-r--r--  1  mark         doc          1020  Jun 17 10:42  memo.to.jim
$
```

In this example, mark is the owner of the file, and the file belongs to the group doc (probably short for *documentation*).

Recall that the first character of each line of output in a file listing indicates the file type (see fig. 3.8). The remaining nine characters represent the security information, or *permissions*, which determines who can access the file and what they are allowed to do. These nine characters represent three sets of permissions:

- The first three characters represent the permissions for the owner of the file.

- The second three characters represent the permissions for every-one (except the file's owner) in the file's group.

- The final three characters represent the permissions for everyone else on the system.

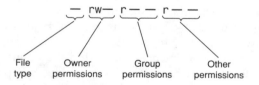

Fig. 3.8. File type and permissions characters.

These three sets of characters are known as the three classes of users: *owner*, *group*, and *other*. Whenever you attempt to access a file, UNIX first determines which of the three classes applies to you. If you are accessing one of your own files, UNIX classifies you as *owner*; if the file belongs to someone else in your group, UNIX classifies you as *group*; otherwise, you are classified as *other*. Every UNIX user is an owner of some files, a group member of other files, and an "other" of the rest.

After UNIX classifies you in relation to the file, UNIX looks for the proper set of permissions. For each set, three possible permissions may be turned on or off: r (*read*), w (*write*), or x (*execute*). In the file listing output, the presence of a letter indicates a permission that is turned on; a dash represents a permission that is off.

Permissions for Regular Files

For each of the three classes of users (owner, group, and other), the owner of the file can grant three permissions, each of which controls whether or not you are allowed to perform a specific type of operation:

- *Read permission* allows you to look at the data in a file, but not to modify it. Tasks such as printing the file, making a copy, or listing the contents of the file require this permission.

- *Write permission* allows you to modify the file. Tasks such as editing a file with vi, redirecting output to a file, or updating a database file require this permission.

- *Execute permission* applies only to an executable program and allows you to run the program. UNIX ignores this permission for files that are not executable programs.

Consider this line of output from the command ls -l:

```
-rw-r--r--  1  mark        doc        1020  Jun 17 10:42  memo.to.jim
```

In this example, Mark, the owner of the file, is allowed to look at (read) the file and modify (write to) the file, but not execute it, which doesn't matter because the file is not a program anyway. Users other than Mark who are in the doc group are allowed to read the file, but not write or execute it. Others also are allowed to read, but not write or execute.

The following file listing is another example:

```
-rw-------  1  leslie      clerk      1020  Jun 17 10:42  private.letter
```

For this file, which clearly is a private letter, the owner of the group (Leslie) is allowed to read and write the file, but all permissions are denied for users in the clerk group and for others.

Permissions and the System Administrator

You always should keep in mind that nothing is secure from the system administrator. When the system administrator—who typically logs in under the special name root—attempts to access a file, all security measures are bypassed. Regardless of the permission settings, files are secure only insofar as the system administrator can be trusted. Selecting reliable, trustworthy people for the job of system administrator is an important task in any company.

Permissions for Directories

UNIX interprets the permissions for directories somewhat differently than it does for regular files:

- Read permission enables you to list, using the ls command, the names of the files that are in the directory.

- Write permission enables you to create new files in the directory or to delete files from it. To make use of this permission, however, you also must have execute permission on the directory; write permission by itself is useless.

- Execute permission for directories is actually a misnomer. This permission enables you to access the files within the directory.

The way these permissions work for directories has several interesting implications:

- If you do not have execute permission on a directory, the directory is virtually useless to you. The only task you can perform in the absence of execute permission is to list the names of the files—if you have read permission on the directory.

- If you want to protect all files in a directory, you can effectively restrict other users from accessing those files by denying them execute permission on the directory. Without execute permission on the directory, users cannot access the files, regardless of the permissions on the files.

- If you have execute permission on a directory, but not read permission, you can access files if you know their names; however, you cannot obtain a listing of the files. In this case, someone has to tell you that a particular file exists in that directory; you have no way of discovering the file yourself.

- To delete a file, you need write permission on the directory. The permissions on the file make no difference. You probably should restrict write permission on your directories from all other users. Granting write permission on a directory to anyone else enables that person to delete files from that directory.

The following example is a typical line of output from the command `ls -l`:

```
drwxr-xr-x  2  mark        doc        320  Jun 17 12:18  memos
```

The d in the first position indicates that memos is a directory. The owner of the directory (Mark) has all permissions: read (he can list the names of files), write (he can create and delete files), and execute (he can access files). Users other than Mark who are in the doc group, and all others on the system, are allowed to list files and access files, assuming the permissions on the individual files permit this access.

Changing File Permissions

You can use the command chmod (*change mode*) to change the permissions on an existing file. The chmod command is so named because it changes a collection of information known as the *mode*. The permissions are only part of this collection. Only the owner of the file and the system administrator can change the permissions on a file.

The chmod command requires to sets of arguments. The first argument, immediately following the word chmod, specifies a set of permissions. The exact format of this argument is discussed in the following paragraphs. The remaining arguments represent the names of files to which you want to apply these permissions.

The chmod command provides two notations for specifying the permissions: *numerical* and *symbolic*. You can use whichever notation seems easier to you.

Specifying Permissions Numerically

You can specify permissions as a three-digit number, where the three digits respectively represent permissions for the owner, group, and others. Each digit is the sum of the permissions for that class of user; you add 4 to specify read, 2 to specify write, 1 to specify execute, and 0 to specify no permission.

For example, to allow the owner (you) to read and write a file, group members to read it, and deny all permissions to others, you type

```
chmod 640 myfile
```

The first digit (6) represents the owner permission, which is the sum of read (4) and write (2). The second digit (4) is the group permission, read only. The third digit (0) denies all permission to others.

Specifying Permissions Symbolically

Alternatively, you can use several mnemonic characters to specify the permissions. Many users find these characters easier to remember. You specify permissions symbolically as follows:

1. Using any combination of the following characters, you first specify the class of user to be affected: type **u** for *owner* (or *user*), **g** for *group*, **o** for *other*, and **a** for *all* (owner, group, and other).

2. Next, you specify whether permissions are to be added or taken away by typing **+** to add permissions or **-** to remove permissions.

3. Finally, you specify the permissions to be added or taken away by typing **r** for read, **w** for write, and **x** for execute, or any combination of r, w, and x.

For example, typing

```
chmod g+w sales.list
```

turns on write permission for group members. All other permissions remain the same.

To take away write and execute from group and other, you type

```
chmod go-wx sales.list
```

To add all permissions for all users, type

```
chmod a+rwx complaints
```

To take away write permission from yourself, type

```
chmod u-w phonelist
```

Two items should be noted. First, the owner is identified by the letter u (for *user*), because the letter o identifies *other*.

Second, to specify the user class, you can use the letter combinations in any order; for example, go is the same as og. This rule also applies when you specify permissions.

Changing a File's Owner and Group

You can use the command chown (*change owner*) to change a file's owner. Only the owner of a file can change ownership of a file; you can give away only your own files. After you give a file away, you are no longer the owner, and you no longer have control over the file.

The chown command requires two sets of arguments: the user name of the new owner and a list of one or more file names. For example, to transfer ownership of a file to Barry, you type this command:

```
chown barry oldfile
```

To change the group of a file, use chgrp (*change group*). This command has the same format as chown. For example, to transfer the file reorg.memo.nr to the group named manager, you type

```
chgrp manager reorg.memo.nr
```

Only the owner of the file can transfer the file to a different group. If you want to change both the owner and the group of a file, change the group first. After changing the owner, you no longer have control of the file and therefore cannot change the group.

File Encryption

For users who are "superconscious" about security (or "super-paranoid"), you can use the crypt command to encrypt files, providing the ultimate in security. Based on the Enigma encrypting machine used by the Germans in World War II, crypt uses a key that you provide—a word or phrase of up to eight characters—to transform the file into seeming garbage. When needed, you can return the file to its previous state by providing crypt with the same encryption key.

You should know a few facts before using this command. First, using crypt is the only way to protect data from the scrutiny of the system administrator. Although you cannot prevent the system administrator from looking at a file, he or she cannot see anything useful if the file is encrypted. The second fact you should know is that if you forget the key with which you encrypted the file, all is lost. You cannot recover the data from the encrypted file. Don't forget the key! Finally, you need to know that the crypt command is restricted by the U.S. Government and cannot be exported outside the United States.

Locating Files with `find`

The `find` command is a powerful file searching tool that enables you to locate all files that meet a certain set of criteria. Consider the following list of typical reasons to use `find`:

- *Locating lost files.* You know you wrote a memo to Jack, but you can't remember the directory in which you stored it.

- *Locating related files.* Your boss asks to see all the financial statements you worked on this week.

- *Locating recently modified files.* If you are performing an incremental backup, you may want to know which files have changed today (for more information about backups, refer to "Performing Backups" in Chapter 9).

- *Locating files not recently modified.* Your disk is getting full, and you want to delete files you haven't used in the past year.

- *Checking file organization or security.* The computer security department in your company is cracking down, and they don't want the computer to contain any files that can be modified by everyone—that is, files that have write permission for all users.

In each of these cases, you need to find files that have certain characteristics. The `find` command can perform these tasks and others. It has the following format:

find *directories criteria action*

In place of *directories*, you specify a list of one or more directories you want `find` to search. `find` searches these directories and all of their subdirectories. In place of *criteria*, you specify the characteristics of the files that interest you. In place of *action*, you specify what you want `find` to do with the files it finds that have those characteristics.

For example, suppose that John wants `find` to display the names of all files called `makefile` in his home directory or its subdirectories (refer to "The `make` Utility" in Chapter 8 for more information about makefiles, which are important to UNIX programmers). John types

find /usr/john -name makefile -print

This command tells `find` that the directory John wants to search is `/usr/john` (and all of its subdirectories); that John wants to find all files that share the characteristic of having the name `makefile`; and that when `find` finds these files, John wants `find` to display their names.

The following example shows the find command John uses and its output:

```
$ find /usr/john -name makefile -print <Return>
/usr/john/project/src/makefile
/usr/john/test/makefile
/usr/john/report/makefile
$
```

These lines of output represent the names of all files called makefile in John's subdirectories.

In Chapter 4, "Understanding the UNIX Shell," you learn about *wild cards*, which enable you to specify only part of the name of the files you want to find. Wild cards are especially handy when you cannot remember the exact name of the file you want. You can use wild cards with find if you enclose the wild card specification in quotation marks:

```
find /usr/fred -name "acme*" -print
```

This command tells find to search the /usr/fred directory and all of its subdirectories for a file whose name begins with acme, followed by any other characters, and to display the names of any files it finds.

The find command can find files that meet many useful criteria. For example, to find all files that have been modified within the past week, you type

```
find . -mtime -7 -print
```

This command finds and displays the names of all files in the current directory (.) and its subdirectories that have been modified within the past seven days. Conversely, to find all files that have not been modified in approximately six months, you type

```
find . -mtime +180 -print
```

This command finds and displays the names of all files that were last modified more than 180 days ago.

The find command can accept many options, too numerous to list here, but some of the criteria on which find can search include the following:

- Files that have or don't have specific permissions

- Files that are or are not regular files, directories, special files, or FIFOs

- Files that have more than, less than, or exactly a specific number of links

- Files that belong to or don't belong to a particular user or group

- Files that are less than, greater than, or exactly a specific size

On many systems other criteria also are available.

You also can tell find to use the files it finds as arguments to execute almost any UNIX command. For example, you can tell find to search for certain files and then print them to the printer, delete them, change their owner or group, change their permissions, move them from one directory to another, or perform almost any operation for which a UNIX command exists.

Finally, you can group criteria to find files that meet a combination of criteria. For example, you may want to find all files that are less than 1K bytes in size and that have not been modified in the past year.

Chapter Summary

This chapter presented many of the basic concepts you will need to understand and work effectively with UNIX. The chapter began by explaining the basic format of a typical UNIX command, including the three major components: command name, options, and arguments.

One of the most important contributions UNIX has made to the world of computers is its scheme for organizing files and directories. This chapter explained how you can use the UNIX directory scheme to organize files on a UNIX system. You first learned how to manipulate files with the file commands, such as rm, ls, cp, mv, and others. Later in the chapter you learned how to form path names, both absolute and relative, and how to use the directory commands to create directories (mkdir), remove directories (rmdir), change directories (cd), and display the path name of the current working directory (pwd).

You learned how to identify special files, which represent hardware devices, and you learned the concept of links in UNIX.

Finally, you explored the basics of UNIX security, both system level, which determines who is authorized to use the computer, and file level, which determines the operations that each user is allowed to perform on files and directories. You also learned basic commands for manipulating security, including chown, chgrp, and chmod.

Understanding the UNIX Shell

S ome UNIX users never use the shell. From the moment they log in, they enter an application program such as a spreadsheet or a word processing program, and there they remain until they log off. This setup is especially attractive for novices who use the computer exclusively for a single type of task and don't want to learn more than necessary about the computer. For most users, however, the UNIX shell provides a powerful means of telling the computer what tasks need to be done.

Chapter 2 explained that the *shell* provides an interface between the user and the internal portion of UNIX (the kernel). The shell accepts commands from the keyboard, interprets them, and takes action.

In this chapter, you learn more about the shell and its features. Most of the chapter focuses on the standard UNIX shell, or Bourne Shell, but you also find information about alternative shells, such as the C Shell and the Korn Shell. This chapter also explores more exotic ways in which you and the computer can communicate, such as graphical user interfaces.

The Login Process

Before you can issue commands to the shell, you must log in, and UNIX must start a shell to accept your commands. This process is not as simple as it seems; it requires at least four programs and several data files. Although the login process may vary slightly from one version of UNIX to another, the basic programs involved are always the same.

The `init` Program

When you first boot (start up) a UNIX computer, UNIX automatically executes, as one of its first tasks, a crucial program called `init`. Although relatively simple, `init` carries out many important functions without which UNIX cannot operate. The `init` program executes continuously until you shut down the system.

As one of its functions, `init` plays an important role in the login process. The system administrator configures a file that controls the actions of `init`. (See Chapter 10, "Understanding the Internal Stucture of UNIX," for a detailed description of the `/etc/inittab` and `/etc/ttys` files.) Among the information contained in the configuration file is a list of *terminal ports* at which you may log in. The terminal ports are connectors on the computer, attached to a terminal or perhaps to a modem for logins over telephone lines.

The `getty` Program

The `init` program constantly looks for a terminal port on which no program is running and no user is logged in. When `init` finds such a port, it starts up a program called `getty`. One `getty` exists per terminal port; on large systems, dozens of `getty`s can be running, each waiting for a user to begin the login procedure on that port.

The `getty` Program

`getty` is short for "get tty." The term *tty* is an abbreviation for Teletype, a terminal made by the Teletype Corporation (now owned by AT&T) that prints its output on paper rather than on-screen. Teletypes, or *teletypewriters*, commonly were used as computer terminals years ago, but now they have been almost completely replaced by CRT terminals (screens). History leaves its mark, however, and terminals today, regardless of their construction, are referred to as ttys in UNIX.

The getty program spends most of its time just waiting. On terminal ports with terminals directly connected, getty waits for the terminal to be turned on. On terminal ports with modems connected, getty (or a closely related program, uugetty—a version specifically designed to work with modems) waits for an incoming call. After you turn on the terminal or receive a call and establish communication, getty issues the prompt login: and waits for you to type a login name.

When you log in, getty determines certain characteristics of your terminal. This function is especially important for incoming modem lines, because you may receive calls at any of several different transmission speeds (baud rates). When the modem answers an incoming call, the modem automatically adjusts to the proper speed, but the modem has no way to indicate the correct speed to the computer. getty is responsible for getting the computer and the modem talking at the same speed, but does not automatically know what the correct speed is. getty can, however, find the correct speed by hunting for it, using the following procedure:

1. First, getty chooses a commonly used speed (such as 2400 baud), prints the message login: at that speed, and waits for a response. If getty has guessed the correct speed, you see the message and respond with a login name, which means that getty successfully has completed its job.

2. If getty's guess is incorrect, getty's login message appears as gibberish on-screen or may not appear at all. When this happens, getty expects you to press <Break>, after which getty surmises that the speed is wrong, selects another, and repeats the transmission at the new speed. For example, it might try 1200 baud next. This cycle continues until getty sees a correct response from you.

If you were to attempt a login to a UNIX computer by modem, you might see the message CONNECTED, which comes from your modem, indicating that your modem and the computer's modem are in contact. You may see gibberish such as g¦@x— getty's attempt to print login:—indicating that getty has not correctly guessed the speed. You would then press <Break>. If you see more gibberish, such as #~, getty still has the wrong speed; you press <Break> again. When you finally see the message login:, the computer, terminal, and modems are now communicating at the same speed. On most computers, if you press <Break> again, getty will try another speed, and you will have to press <Break> several more times until getty again finds the correct speed.

Exactly what appears on-screen depends on the computer and the transmission speeds involved.

The `login` Program

After `getty` correctly sets the speed and receives a valid login name, it passes control to a program called `login`. The `login` program prompts you for a password and verifies that the password is correct; an invalid password causes `login` to prompt again for the login name and password. (Notice that `getty` issues the initial `login:` prompt, but if another prompt for the login name is necessary, `login` handles the task without turning control back to `getty`. On some computers, you are allowed three attempts before being disconnected.)

If the login name and password are correct, `login` informs the kernel that you have logged in correctly. `login` then transfers control to the shell.

Before the shell is available to receive a command from you, however, it must perform two tasks:

1. The shell first locates and executes a shell program called `/etc/profile`. The system administrator uses this program to is- sue any administrative commands that should be executed every time you log in. Typical tasks that `/etc/profile` performs include displaying the message of the day and checking for mail. If you are using C Shell, the program may be `/etc/.login`, or C Shell may skip this step altogether, depending on the version of C Shell.

2. The shell then looks in your home directory for a shell program called `.profile`. If this program exists, the shell executes it. Thus, if you want a certain command performed automatically every time you log in, you simply add it to `.profile`. See "An Introduction to Shell Programming," further in this chapter, for more information on shell programs. Note that C Shell uses a file called `.login` in- stead of `.profile`.

Thus, `/etc/profile` contains commands for everybody; `.profile` con- tains commands for an individual user.

After these initial steps are complete, the shell begins its primary duty: accepting your commands. The shell prints its prompt, which by default is a dollar sign ($), and waits for you to enter a command.

When you want to log off, you press <Ctrl-D> or type **exit**. In most cases, you also can log off by disconnecting the modem or turning off the terminal. Logging off terminates the shell at that terminal. When `init` detects that no program is running on the terminal, it starts a new `getty`. The terminal port is then ready for a new login.

> **About `login` Programs**
>
> The `init` and `getty` programs are located in the `/etc` directory.
> The `login` and shell (`sh`) programs are in the `/bin` directory. The
> `uugetty` program, if present, is in `/usr/lib/uucp`.

Command Processing in the Shell

The standard shell on most UNIX systems is the Bourne Shell, so called because it was written by Steve Bourne at AT&T Bell Labs. Although other shells exist, such as the C Shell, someone referring to "the shell" usually is referring to the Bourne Shell.

The shell serves as the command processor for UNIX. You enter a command, and the shell interprets the command and performs a task. In most cases, the shell calls upon another program to carry out the command, but not always. In some cases the shell itself completes the command, without making use of any external program. Such commands are known as *internal commands* or *shell built-ins*. The `cd` command, for example, is a shell built-in.

Some commands require very little work on the part of the shell. For example, consider the following command:

```
cp oldfile newfile
```

This command requires the shell to do nothing more than execute the `cp` program, passing to it the arguments on the command line. On the other hand, many commands contain special characters that tell the shell to perform some action before running the program. Some of these special characters control the flow of input and output.

Input and Output

Most UNIX commands require input or produce output, or both. The shell plays an important part in setting up a command's input and output.

Before it starts a command, the shell sets up three default paths that the command can use for receiving input or sending output:

- *Standard input* is the default source for input. Most commands, unless told otherwise, look here to get the data they need. By default, standard input is the keyboard.

- *Standard output* is the default destination for output. Results produced by the command are sent here. By default, standard output is the screen.

- *Standard error* is the default destination for error messages. If a command produces errors, the errors are sent to standard error. By default, standard error also is the screen.

For example, consider the UNIX calculator bc. Most often you invoke the calculator simply by typing bc and nothing else. Unless told to do otherwise, bc reads input (equations) from standard input (the keyboard) and sends output (answers) to standard output (the screen).

But what if you want the input or output to go to a location other than the default? By using a process called *redirection*, you can redefine standard input, standard output, standard error, or some combination of the three as something other than the terminal—that is, as something other than the keyboard or screen.

Redirection

The Bourne Shell enables you to use many different techniques for describing the source of a command's input or the destination of a command's output. Most commonly, you will use the *less than* symbol (<) for input redirection and the *greater than* symbol (>) for output redirection. These symbols originated as a mathematical notation, but appear on your keyboard because programmers often use them while writing programs. When you use them as redirection symbols, think of them as arrows pointing in the direction that data is flowing.

Note that redirection changes the source of standard input and the destination of standard output or standard error only for a single command. When you enter the next command, input and output revert to the keyboard and screen, unless you specify otherwise.

Input Redirection

The input redirection symbol (<) tells the shell to redefine standard input as something other than the keyboard. Consider this example:

```
mail bob <msg
```

If you view the < symbol as an arrow, you can think of this command as graphically illustrating that the data is flowing from a file msg into the command for processing. The shell sees the < symbol and redefines the mail command's input as the file msg. Then the shell runs the command mail bob. When the mail command reads its standard input, UNIX supplies it with the data contained in the msg file, rather than accepting input from the keyboard. The mail command, like most UNIX commands, simply reads whatever data is available on its standard input, never caring whether that data is coming from the keyboard or a file.

For many UNIX commands, a second method exists for you to specify where the command should get its input: in addition to using redirection, many commands enable you simply to specify the name of the file on the command line, such as

```
sort phonelist
```

Although this command seems almost identical to the first, the mechanism used is actually quite different. The shell sees no redirection symbol, so it leaves the keyboard as standard input. When the sort command runs, it sees a file name provided as part of the command and gets its input from that file instead of from standard input.

Two practical differences exist between these two methods of specifying the location of input:

- The shell handles the redirection process; individual UNIX commands must handle command line file names. Redirection, therefore, works with almost any command, but you can use command line file names only with commands built to handle them. Some commands, such as mail and crypt, have no provisions for command line file names; these commands always get their input from standard input.

- Many commands accept several command line file names. The wc command, for instance, accepts any number of file names on its command line and displays word counts for each, followed by a grand total. However, using redirection, you can specify only one file name.

Output Redirection

A similar construct enables you to send the output from a command to a file instead of to the screen. The output redirection symbol (>) tells the shell to redefine standard output as a file, rather than the screen. Consider this example:

```
ls >listing
```

This command line causes the shell to send the output of the `ls` command to the file `listing`. You can visualize the command as indicating the flow of data from the command into the file. If the file doesn't exist, the shell creates it; if it does exist, the shell destroys its previous contents. As with input redirection, the `ls` command itself never knows that redirection has taken place; it produces the same output as always and sends the output to its standard output. Because all output now goes to the file, nothing appears on-screen.

The append redirection symbol (>>) also redirects standard output; however, the shell does not destroy the previous contents of the receiving file if the file exists. Instead, the new data is appended to the end of the file, after the existing data. If the file does not exist, the shell creates the file, as it does with >.

You can use both input and output redirection in the same command:

```
sort <list >sorted.list
```

This command reads lines from the file named `list` and writes them in sorted order to the file named `sorted.list`.

Redirection enables users to take full advantage of many commands. The `cat` command, for example, *concatenates*, or combines the data from a group of files into a single file. Concatenation is possible only with redirection.

Consider this command:

```
cat lastyear thisyear nextyear
```

This command displays three files—`lastyear`, `thisyear`, and `nextyear`—end to end on-screen.

The following command line is more useful:

```
cat lastyear thisyear nextyear >years
```

This command creates a new file, years, which contains the data from all three files.

The symbol > redirects output, but not error messages. The shell makes the very sensible assumption that you should not have to examine the contents of the output file to determine whether errors have occurred. Sometimes, however, you may want to redirect error messages, and for this purpose, a special notation is available.

The error redirection symbol (2>) tells the shell to define the command's standard error output as a file instead of the screen. Consider this example:

```
troff letter >output 2>errors
```

This command sends its output to the file named output and its error messages, if any, to the file named errors.

File Descriptors

It takes some knowledge of UNIX programming to understand why the *2* is used in 2> to indicate error redirection. Internally, the UNIX kernel keeps a list of files associated with each program and refers to each file by numbers, which programmers call *file descriptors*. Like most sets of numbers in the world of computers, the numbering starts at 0. Thus internally UNIX refers to standard input as file 0, standard output as file 1, and standard error as file 2. The *2* in 2> refers to this internal file number.

2>&1, a related (and somewhat cryptic) notation, redirects standard error to the same location as standard output. The following command is an example:

```
wc -l chapter >lines 2>&1
```

This command sends both its output and its error messages to the file named lines.

Some Exceptions to Redirection

A handful of commands actively defeat redirection. For example, the authors of the `passwd` command (with which you can change your password) thought it dangerous to allow a file to be used for input with this command, and therefore, the `passwd` command requires input from the keyboard, ignoring redirection. For various reasons, other commands, such as `crypt`, may insist upon input from the terminal.

Such commands, however, are very much the exception to the rule. You can use redirection with the vast majority of UNIX commands, most of which don't care whether standard input, output, and error are defined as the terminal or as files.

Pipes

UNIX was designed to provide users with many small tools (commands), each of which is capable of performing one simple task, and to assemble these tools in various combinations to perform more complex tasks. Often, no single UNIX command can carry out an entire task by itself, but you probably can get the job done by processing data in several stages. Many UNIX commands were written not because they are useful by themselves, but because what they do is often useful in conjunction with other tools.

To combine tools, you use *pipes*. Most commands accept data from standard input and produce results on standard output. Redirection sends input or output to a file; a pipe sends input or output to another command.

The UNIX pipe symbol is a vertical bar, ¦, which you type between two commands. The shell simultaneously executes both commands and redirects standard output from the first command directly into standard input of the second command. The output produced by the first command thus becomes the input supplied to the second. The effect is not unlike a "bucket brigade" for data, in which each bit of data is passed from one program to another for some type of processing.

Note that the vertical bar often appears on-screen or on the keyboard as a solid bar (|). If your keyboard has the solid vertical bar, you can use it as the pipe symbol. Some keyboards have both the broken and solid vertical bar, and you can use either.

As an example of using the pipe symbol, suppose that you want a sorted list of everyone on the system. No single command can produce this list, but two commands working together can:

```
who ¦ sort
```

The who command produces a list of everyone on the system, which is piped directly into the sort command, which in turn arranges the list in alphabetical order and displays it.

Complex operations can be performed by connecting many commands with several pipe symbols. For example, to print (to the printer) a list of all files most recently modified in January, you would use the following command:

```
ls -l ¦ grep Jan ¦ lp
```

The ls -l command produces a list of all files in the current directory; grep sifts through this list and selects the lines containing the phrase Jan. (Note that this solution is not perfect, because grep also selects lines in which Jan is part of the file name.) This list in turn is passed on to the lp command, which spools its input to the printer.

You can achieve the full potential of many commands only with pipes. Consider the pg command (or the more command in Berkeley versions of UNIX), which displays a file one screen at a time. You also can use pg or more at the end of a pipe to display, one screen at a time, the output of another command. For example, consider the following command line:

```
who ¦ pg
```

The who command produces a list of everyone on the system and sends it, by way of a pipe, to pg, which displays the data one screen at a time.

When many commands are working together to process data through a pipe, one command may work faster than another. UNIX handles this problem automatically. If the command on the left of the pipe symbol produces output faster than the command on the right can accept it, UNIX temporarily suspends the command on the left until the command on the right catches up. If the command on the right accepts data faster than the command on the left produces it, UNIX temporarily suspends the command on the right until the command on the left produces enough data to be processed.

UNIX Pipes v. MS-DOS Pipes

MS-DOS also uses a pipe function, which it borrowed from UNIX. In fact, the syntax is almost identical, and it produces similar results. For example, consider this MS-DOS command:

```
DIR | SORT
```

In this command, DIR produces a list of files, and SORT sorts the list in alphabetical order. DOS, however, handles pipes much differently than UNIX.

In UNIX, all commands in a multipipe command line are started simultaneously; output produced by the first command is immediately fed into the second for processing, so pieces of data flow continuously through the pipe. This continuous transfer is an example of UNIX's multitasking capabilities, which enable several processes to execute simultaneously.

MS-DOS, however, is not a multitasking environment (Microsoft Windows notwithstanding); the operating system cannot run two programs at the same time. Instead, it runs the first program to completion, placing its output in a temporary file. When the first program completes its job, the second program is started and takes its input from the temporary file. When the command is complete, MS-DOS deletes the temporary file. This method makes much less efficient use of the computer's resources, and it requires disk space to hold the intermediate data.

UNIX Multitasking

One of the most powerful features of UNIX is its capability to provide *multitasking*—that is, to attend to many different tasks at the same time. Multitasking enables each user to run any number of programs simultaneously. In a nonmultitasking environment, you cannot start a new task until the previous one finishes; UNIX can carry out many separate activities together.

Background Execution

UNIX enables you to execute commands in one of two modes. The more common mode is *foreground execution*. When you type a command, the terminal is "tied up" with that command until it is complete. If the command requires input and no redirection was specified, you provide it from the keyboard. In most cases only one command at a time, per terminal, can run in the foreground (many windowing terminals, however, enable you to run many foreground programs simultaneously; see the discussion of X Windows in "Graphical User Interfaces," further in this chapter).

Background execution, on the other hand, enables you to submit a command that does not tie up the terminal. The command must not require interaction with you (a text editor would be a bad candidate), and it should be a program that requires a long time to finish. For example, a complex sort or spell command that requires several minutes to complete might be a good choice for background execution.

You can place a command in the background (to invoke it for background execution) simply by placing an ampersand (&) at the end of the command. For example, if you want to issue a background command that checks the spelling in a file called report and sends the misspellings to a file called badwords, you would use

```
$ spell report >badwords& <Return>
21893
$
```

The shell prints a special ID number for the task (in this case, 21893). This number is called the *process identification number (PID)*. The shell immediately displays the command prompt ($), enabling you to enter the next command while the computer continues to work on the background command. You may, for example, begin editing another file or issue any command that does not depend on the completion of the background spell command.

Commands running in the background differ from foreground commands in several important ways:

- Pressing <Break> or <Delete> stops only the foreground program; background programs continue to run uninterrupted.

- Unless you use input redirection, no standard input is available for background commands.

- As with foreground commands, standard output of background commands, by default, is the screen; however, sending the output of background programs to the screen is almost never desirable. If the background command produces output, its output spews across your screen, right in the middle of whatever else you are doing, unless the output is redirected.

You can place several commands in the background at a time, and the computer will work on all of them simultaneously; however, the following caveats apply:

- On some systems the number of programs that you can run simultaneously is limited.

- All UNIX systems have a limit on the total number of processes that can run on the computer system at one time. Although this limit usually is quite generous, it can be reached if many users issue a lot of background commands at the same time.

- Long before either of these limits is reached, system performance can suffer. The computer has only so much time to spend on programs, and the more programs running, the thinner that time must be spread. Especially on small computers, starting many background programs can slow all programs to a crawl. (The `nice` command may help; see the discussion of `nice` in the following section.)

Controlling Background Execution

Several UNIX commands enable you to perform various operations on background processes; these commands include `ps`, which displays the status of running programs; `kill`, which stops a program; and others, such as `nice` and `nohup`, which set various options.

The `ps` Command

The `ps` (*process status*) command displays a list of running programs. It is particularly useful for monitoring background commands. Various options are available, including options for listing other users' programs and for obtaining more than basic information about the programs. Consider the following sample `ps` command and its output:

```
$ ps -f <Return>
  UID    PID  PPID  C   STIME  TTY  TIME COMMAND
 mark 26201 26180 77 12:47:42    ?  0:11 sort list -o list
 mark 26205 26180 56 12:48:00  025  0:01 ps -f
 mark 26180     1  9 12:15:24  025  0:03 -sh
$
```

The -f option tells ps to list *full* information (without this option, only the fields PID, TTY, TIME, and COMMAND are shown). The exact output of this command varies somewhat from one UNIX system to another. This example shows that a sort command is running, probably in the background. Always shown is the ps command itself (after all, it must be running to produce this output) and sh, the shell. Shown for each command is the following information:

Field	Description
UID	The user ID of the person running the command
PID	The command's process identification number
PPID	The parent process identification number (the identification number of the program that started this process)
C	Processor utilization. This number normally is not of interest to users. It indicates how much of the computer's time this process has used lately; UNIX uses it to decide whom to work with next.
STIME	The time the program started
TTY	The terminal on which the program is running. On some UNIX systems, ps displays a question mark in place of the terminal ID to identify background processes started by UNIX at boot time and not associated with any particular terminal.
COMMAND	The approximate command line that started the program. Redirection characters and most special characters are missing from the command.

The `kill` Command

When you issue a foreground command, you can stop the command immediately by pressing <Break> (on some terminals, you press <Delete>); however, <Break> has no effect on background programs. UNIX provides a special command, `kill`, for stopping background programs.

To kill a background program, you must know its process ID number, which the shell displays every time you issue a background command. If the program's process ID number is no longer on-screen, the `ps` command displays the numbers associated with all your processes.

To issue a `kill` command, type **kill**, followed by the process ID number of the program you want to kill. For example, to kill the program associated with process ID 20261, type

    kill 20261

The basic `kill` command actually is a "suggestion" to the program, as though you were saying, "Excuse me, I'd like you to stop, if that's okay." Most programs are "well-behaved" and accept your request; however, a program occasionally refuses to stop, requiring stronger measures. The –9 option of the `kill` command is sometimes called the *sure kill* because the program you want to kill cannot refuse. Consider this example:

    kill -9 20261

Using this command kills the process. You should attempt a basic kill before using a sure kill because a basic kill gives the command a chance to shut itself down in an orderly fashion. A sure kill, on the other hand, is the UNIX equivalent of pulling the plug on the program.

The Origin of the –9 Option

The –9 option of the `kill` command is one of the more obscure options in UNIX. The name `kill` itself is a misnomer. The command does not kill anything; it actually sends a type of message, called a *signal*, to another program. The basic `kill` command sends the *software termination signal*. A sure kill sends another signal, which happens to be the ninth signal, hence –9. Depending on the version of UNIX, as many as 15 or more additional signals may be available; most of the others are of interest primarily to programmers.

The nohup and nice Commands

Two commands, nohup and nice, are useful for more precisely controlling background execution of commands.

Under normal circumstances, logging off terminates all background jobs you started. You can use nohup (*no hang up*) at the beginning of a command to indicate that the command should continue, even if you log off. (The nohup command gets its name from "no hang up," because if you are using a modem, you are logged off when you hang up the telephone.)

The following command, for example, starts the UNIX formatter troff in the background and specifies that it should not be terminated if you log off:

```
nohup troff -mm report >troff.out&
```

If you do not redirect the output from a command that begins with nohup, it is sent to a file called nohup.out.

Background programs normally compete on an equal basis with foreground programs for the computer's attention. If many users start a lot of background programs, however, a severe drop in system performance can occur. But users often start programs in the background precisely because they are in no hurry for those commands to finish. You can tell UNIX that a particular command is less urgent by placing the word nice at the beginning of the command:

```
nice sort bigfile -o bigfile&
```

This command receives much less than its normal share of the computer's attention and requires much more time to complete. If you are getting ready to go to lunch or leaving for the day, you might use nice with the last command you enter. The command will finish its job by the end of lunch or the next morning. The command is named nice because giving your own task a lower priority is a "nice" thing to do.

You can apply both nice and nohup to a command, in either order:

```
nice nohup spell problem.list >badwords&
```

```
nohup nice spell problem.list >badwords&
```

Both of these examples start the spell command as a background program (due to &). The program runs at a low priority (nice) and continues to run if you log off (nohup).

Other Types of Multitasking

In addition to running programs in the background, you can take advantage of multitasking in several ways:

- Using pipes involves multitasking. UNIX starts up all programs in the pipe at the same time, and output from one program is passed as input to the next.

- You simultaneously can work on several unrelated tasks by logging in at several different terminals at the same time. UNIX enables you to log in any number of times; some other multiuser operating systems don't.

- Some terminals, such as PC consoles and X Windows terminals, enable you to start up and run several programs on the same screen—multitasking at its best. You can type data for any program, which cannot be done with background programs.

Other Shell Command Features

In addition to the symbols for pipes and redirection, the shell provides many other special symbols that serve as typing savers or to increase the flexibility of the shell.

File Wild Card Characters

When choosing file names, you usually pick similar names for related files. The chapters in a book, for instance, might be named chap1, chap2, and so on. Annual sales reports might have names such as sales1989 and sales1990. The characters .c usually appear at the end of the name of a C language source file. This tendency to repeat character combinations in file names is nearly universal, whether it stems from a desire to be organized or just reflects a lack of creativity.

Wild cards—more properly known as *file generation characters*—enable you to create patterns that correspond to several file names. You thus can perform an operation on a group of files with similar names without typing each individual name. For example, by using wild cards you easily can remove all files with names beginning with temp or copy all files with names ending in .c.

You can use three types of special characters as wild cards to specify a file name pattern: the asterisk (*), question mark (?), and brackets ([and]). When the shell spots any of these wild card characters in a file name, it searches the current directory (or another directory, if a path is specified) for files that match the pattern. Internally the shell alters the command you typed, replacing the wild card with the actual names of all the files that match the wild card.

The Asterisk

The asterisk wild card (*) matches any number of characters that occur at that position in the pattern. For example, the pattern chap* represents all files with names that begin with chap. Thus, to remove all files that begin with chap, you would type:

```
rm chap*
```

The shell sees the wild card and searches the current directory for files that match its pattern. If it finds four files that match, such as chap1, chap2, chap3, and chap4, the shell then transforms the command into the following command:

```
rm chap1 chap2 chap3 chap4
```

This transformed command is the command that UNIX actually executes, and the rm command itself "thinks" you typed the four file names rather than the wild card.

The pattern *.c would match any file name ending in .c; the pattern sales*91 would match any name starting with sales and ending with 91, with anything in between.

You can use several asterisks in the same pattern. To find every file name containing 9, you can use the pattern *9*, which means "anything, a 9, and then anything."

The asterisk also matches the absence of characters. The pattern list* not only matches any file name beginning with list and followed by anything else; it also matches any file named simply list.

The Question Mark

The question mark wild card (?) matches any single character. Thus the command

```
lp memo?
```

prints all file names that begin the memo and are followed by a single character. The file name memo97 would not match because two characters follow memo. The pattern ??? would match any file name consisting of any three characters.

The Dot (Period)

Users of MS-DOS and of many other operating systems often forget that in UNIX the *dot* (or period) is just another character as far as wild cards are concerned. Thus the pattern a?c matches both abc and a.c. A similar pattern in MS-DOS would match only abc.

The shell treats the period specially only in file names that begin with a period. Because files with names beginning with a period are often special system files, wild cards never match them unless the wild card itself explicitly begins with a period. Thus, the command rm *file removes all files ending with file, except that it does not remove a file such as .profile—the file (.profile) begins with a dot, but the wild card (*file) does not. The command rm .*file, however, would remove .profile, because the wild card itself includes the beginning dot.

Brackets

A set of brackets ([and]) represents a single character, which can be any of the selections enclosed in the brackets. For example:

```
sort list[1589]
```

The wild card list[1589] represents any file whose name is list followed by one more characters, which can be 1, 5, 8, or 9. This command prints the sorted combination of the files list1, list5, list8, and list9 (assuming that they all exist). You also can specify a range: **letter[0-9]x** represents all files with names that start with letter, followed by a digit 0 through 9 and then the letter x.

You can use several sets of brackets in a wild card, enabling you to specify more complex patterns:

```
rm file[0-9a-z][3-58]
```

This command removes all files with file names that begin with `file`, followed by a digit 0 through 9 or a letter a through z, followed by the digit 3, 4, 5, or 8. (Note that [3-58] does not mean "3 through 58;" it means "3 through 5, or 8.")

Sometimes you may find that specifying what you don't want is easier than specifying what you do want. If the first character within a set of brackets is !, the shell looks for a character that is *not* one of the characters that follows it within in the brackets. Consider this example:

```
lp memo[!4-6]
```

This command prints any file whose name begins with `memo`, followed by a single character that is not 4, 5, or 6.

You also can construct patterns from combinations of wild cards, such as the following example:

```
cp [crs]* /usr/jim
```

This command finds all files beginning with c, r, or s and copies them to the directory /usr/jim.

Consider the following command:

```
cat x[0-9][A-Z]?6* >combo
```

Although perhaps a bit absurd, this command looks for any file name that begins with x, followed by a digit, followed by an uppercase letter, followed by any character, followed by a 6, followed by anything else; it concatenates all files whose names match this pattern into a single file named combo.

Especially if you are just beginning to experiment with wild cards, you may find this example complicated, and perhaps you simply would rather type the names of the files you want. With experience, however, even complex wild cards begin to seem natural.

> ## Maximum Command Line Length
>
> The maximum length of any UNIX command is 5,120 (5K) characters. Although this limit may seem impossibly large—who would ever type a command that long?—running up against a command of such length actually is possible.
>
> Consider the command to remove all files in a directory:
>
> ```
> rm *
> ```
>
> This seems to be a short command. If you use it in a large directory with thousands of files, however, the command may fail. Remember that the shell actually replaces wild cards with the matching file names. When the asterisk is replaced with thousands of file names, the resulting command could be longer than 5K.

Command Substitution

You often will use a command to produce information, such as a list of file names, and then use that information as part of another command. For example, suppose that you want to print to the printer all files that contain a reference to Chicago. You might first determine the files that contain the phrase *Chicago* with the grep command:

```
$ grep -l Chicago * <Return>
sales.1990
office.list
sites.illinois
$
```

This command searches all files in the current directory for the phrase *Chicago* and prints the names of the files. To print those files to the printer, you can then issue the lp command, specifying the files that grep found:

```
lp sales.1990 office.list sites.illinois
```

The shell, however, provides a simpler method for accomplishing such tasks, a method in which the output from one command forms part of another command. This capability is known as *command substitution*.

When you use command substitution, you type a command that contains another command, which you place within *backquotes*. A backquote (`` ` ``) is a single quotation mark that slants toward the right. Do not confuse backquotes with apostrophes ('). The shell executes the command inside the backquotes and uses the output to form part of the larger command. Using command substitution, you can print all files containing the phrase *Chicago* with the command

```
lp `grep -l Chicago *`
```

The shell executes the command inside the backquotes first, which yields a list of file names. Internally, the shell then replaces the inner command with the list of file names.

Consider, as another example, a file called garbage that contains a list of files that you want to remove. Using command substitution, you can type the following command to accomplish the task:

```
rm `cat garbage`
```

Normally, the command cat garbage displays the contents of the file, but because it is inside backquotes, the output from the cat command is substituted into the rm command instead, and rm removes the files.

Combining Commands

The shell provides several ways of typing more than one command on a single line. You can separate commands with semicolons, double ampersands, and double vertical bars. Each symbol has a slightly different meaning. Also, you can use parentheses to group commands.

The Semicolon

You can use a semicolon (;) to separate commands. The commands are executed in turn, just as if they had been typed on separate lines. Consider the following example:

```
cp file1 file2; rm file3
```

The cp command is executed, and then the rm command is executed.

The Double Ampersand

You also can use double ampersands (&&) to separate commands. Each command is executed only if the previous command was successfully executed. For example, in the command

```
grep Austin cities && vi cities
```

the grep command searches for the phrase Austin in the file cities. If it finds the phrase, the shell then executes the vi text editor, which enables you to edit the file cities.

The Double Vertical Bar

Double vertical bars (¦¦) also can separate commands. This command separator is the functional opposite of &&; each command is executed only if the preceding command fails. For example, consider the command

```
grep Florida states ¦¦ grep Mississippi states
```

which searches for Florida in the file states. If grep fails to find it, the shell executes the second command, which looks for Mississippi.

Parentheses

When several commands are on the same line, you can use parentheses to group them. This grouping starts up a new copy of the shell to execute the commands. Grouping has several practical uses:

- You can redirect commands as a group. For example, to execute two commands and have the output from both redirected to a file, type the following command:

```
(date; who) >output
```

- If one of the commands inside the parentheses is a cd command, cd applies only to the group of commands within the parentheses. Using parentheses, you can change directories and execute one or more commands, after which the shell returns to the original directory. For instance, if you want to rename (mv) and print a file in your old subdirectory, you can type

```
(cd old; mv sales.90 sales.1990; lp sales.1990)
```

This command changes to the old subdirectory, renames sales.90 as sales.1990, and then prints sales.1990. When the command completes, if you use the pwd command, you find that your current directory is the same as it was before you issued the preceding group of commands.

- You can place a series of commands in the background. Consider the following command, for example:

```
(spell doc >words; sort list -o list)&
```

This command creates a single background process that checks the spelling in doc and then sorts list. Without the parentheses, only the sort command would be executed in the background.

Variables

The shell enables you to create in the computer's memory small data storage locations called *variables*. Each variable has a name associated with it, and into the variable you place a *value*, which is the information you want to store there. Superficially, a variable is much like a file, which also is assigned a name and which also stores data. Variables, however, are stored in main memory and therefore are lost when you log off. Also, variables tend to hold individual nuggets of data, such as a single name, whereas files hold larger amounts of data.

Variables are of greatest interest to programmers who want to write shell programs, because shell variables serve the same purpose as variables in other programming languages. But even casual users can benefit from understanding variables, because many shell options are controlled by setting special shell variables.

To place a value in a variable—that is, to set a variable to a value—you use the following syntax:

```
variable=value
```

You do not place spaces on either side of the equal sign, and the value can contain spaces only if enclosed in quotation marks. Consider the following examples:

```
name=Belinda
```

```
city="Winter Park"
```

The first statement sets the variable name to the value Belinda; the second sets city to Winter Park. In the second statement, quotation marks are required because a space is present in the value (see "Quotation Marks," further in this chapter, for a detailed discussion of quotation marks).

After you set a variable, you can insert its value into any command typed thereafter. Whenever you type a dollar sign, which must be followed by the name of a variable, the shell replaces the combination of the dollar sign and variable name with the value in the variable. For example, if you type

```
grep $name phonelist
```

the shell replaces $name with the value of the name variable, Belinda. The command then becomes

```
grep Belinda phonelist
```

and the grep command searches the file phonelist for the name Belinda.

You can use this technique to avoid retyping frequently used phrases, especially path names. On an AT&T 3B1, for example, accessing a path that includes the lengthy name Filecabinet is quite common. You could create the following variable:

```
fc=/usr/douglass/Filecabinet
```

From then on, you could use $fc in any command in place of the entire path name /usr/douglass/Filecabinet.

Likewise, if you type

```
rm $fc/oldfile
```

the shell would change it into

```
rm /usr/douglass/Filecabinet/oldfile
```

The Special Variables

Several variables have a special meaning to the shell. By changing the values of these special variables, you can control various facets of the shell's behavior. This section describes the most important special variables; your system's reference manual describes many other useful special variables.

HOME

The HOME variable contains the name of your home directory. Although you primarily use it within shell programs, you also can use it as a typing shortcut. For example, you can delete a file called junk in your home directory by typing

```
rm $HOME/junk
```

The value of this variable is set automatically by the login program; you should have no reason to change the value of HOME.

PATH

Although a few commands are built into the shell, such as cd, most commands require the shell to execute a program. The standard UNIX commands can be located in any of several directories, and other directories may contain application programs that you want to invoke. When you type a command, the shell locates the associated program by searching a series of directories until it locates the program with the correct name. The special shell variable PATH contains a list of directories that you want the shell to search when you enter a command. A colon (:) separates the name of each directory. For example, a typical command to set the PATH is:

```
PATH=/bin:/usr/bin:/usr/lbin:/usr/mark/bin:.
```

With the PATH set to this value, entering a command causes the shell to look for the associated program, first in /bin, then in /usr/bin, then in /usr/lbin, then in /usr/mark/bin, and then in the current directory (.).

The login shell gives PATH a default value, but your .profile may change this value. If your system contains applications, you or your system administrator may have included a command to add additional directories to your PATH. Also, if you are a programmer, you eventually may write useful programs you want to invoke as commands. You might store these programs in a subdirectory (many users use the name bin for the subdirectory), and add this subdirectory to your PATH.

When you issue a command to change the value of PATH, you often specify the new value in relation to its old value. For example, to add a new directory to the existing PATH, type the following command:

```
PATH=$PATH:/usr/mark/bin
```

Actually, this command carries out two independent steps. The shell first spots $PATH and replaces it with the current value of the PATH variable. Then the resulting command sets PATH to its old value plus the new directory, /usr/mark/bin. For example, if the old value of PATH is /bin: /usr/bin:., this command sets its new value to /bin:/usr/bin:.:/usr /mark/bin.

CDPATH

The CDPATH variable is similar to PATH in that it contains a list of directories, separated by colons, which the shell uses to perform searches. When you type a cd command that does not begin with a slash or one of the special directory names . or . ., the shell searches the directories listed in CDPATH for a subdirectory that matches the cd command. For example, suppose that your .profile contains a command that sets CDPATH as follows:

CDPATH=/usr/mark:/usr/mark/letters:/usr/mark/reports

If you type **cd jim**, the shell checks first for /usr/mark/jim, then for /usr/mark/letters/jim, and finally for /usr/mark/reports/jim. As soon as it finds a matching path name, the shell changes to that directory and the cd command is terminated. (Note that the CDPATH variable is not available in all versions of the shell.)

MAIL

The MAIL variable contains the path name of your mailbox. The shell occasionally checks the mailbox for incoming mail and displays a message if new mail arrives. The shell does not set this value; you must set it, usually in the .profile. For example, consider the following command:

MAIL=/usr/mail/bobby

This command tells the shell that your mailbox is the file /usr/mail/bobby.

PS1

The PS1 variable is the primary shell prompt. Normally this prompt is a dollar sign, but you can be creative and set it to more exotic phrases. For example, if you set PS1 by typing

PS1="Yes, Master? "

the shell henceforth prompts with

Yes, Master?

rather than the usual dollar sign.

Most systems also have other special shell variables.

TERM

The TERM variable contains a code that indicates the make and model of the terminal you are using. On many systems, the login shell assigns a default value to this variable. On other systems, you can place a command in your

.profile to set this variable, or if you work on several different types of terminals, you can use several shell programming commands that ask you for the correct terminal type each time you log in. Consider the following sample command to set your terminal type:

TERM=vt100

On most systems, this command informs the shell that you are using a DEC VT-100 terminal.

Although the shell itself does not need to know your terminal type, many of the programs you often use under UNIX, such as vi, must know your terminal type to function properly. Programs such as vi use the terminal code to locate information about your terminal in a database of terminal capabilities.

Thousands of different types of terminals exist, and occasionally you may have trouble determining the proper code to use for your terminal. Your system administrator may be able to help you find a workable code. Especially for less popular terminals, several slightly different codes may work for the same terminal, increasing the likelihood that you will be able to guess a correct code. For example, if you use an AT&T 630 terminal on a 3B2 computer, you can set the TERM variable to 630, att630, ATT630, 630DMD, or 630MTG.

The Environment

The shell creates two separate areas of memory in which to store variables and their values. The first area—the one used by the shell unless you specify otherwise—contains variables used only by the shell, but not by any command or program. CDPATH, for example, is used only by the shell when you type a cd command. Commands used only by the shell are called *local variables*.

The shell uses the second memory area, called the *environment*, for storing variables, such as TERM, which are used by the shell and application programs. Every time you execute a command or program, the shell makes a copy of the information stored in the environment at that instant and makes this copy available to the program or command.

When you first specify the value of a variable, the newly created variable is automatically placed in the memory area associated with local variables and is therefore not available to programs and commands. For example, consider the following sequence of commands:

```
$ TERM=vt100 <Return>
$ vi junkfile <Return>
$
```

Even though the first statement defines the terminal type, the shell does not provide this crucial information to vi. Consequently vi responds with this strange message:

```
Visual needs addressable cursor or upline capability
```

vi is trying to tell you that it can work correctly only if it knows how to perform certain operations, but without knowing the terminal type, it cannot determine how to perform those operations. However, you can cause the shell to move TERM into the environment with this statement:

```
export TERM
```

After this step is done, vi will work correctly.

The shell automatically places some shell variables, such as HOME and PATH, in the environment; however, if one of the values associated with these variables is changed, you must enter a new export command for the new value to be placed in the environment.

Quotation Marks

Most symbols and punctuation marks have a special meaning to the shell. The question mark, for example, is used in wild cards, and the vertical bar indicates a pipe. Sometimes, however, you want these characters to be treated as normal characters in a command. Quotation marks tell the shell to ignore the special functions of these characters.

For example, suppose that you want to find the phrase huh? in all files in the current directory. At first, you might type

```
grep huh? *
```

The shell, however, not realizing that huh? is not a file name, spots the question mark and searches for files in the current directory that have names that begin with huh and are followed by one more character. To find huh?, you should type:

```
grep "huh?" *
```

The quotation marks (" and ", known as *double quotes*) tell the shell that everything enclosed within them is to be taken literally and treated as a single unit.

If you want to search a file for a phrase that contains more than one word, you would need to use quotation marks in your `grep` command. For example, consider the following command:

```
grep "Mary Sue" letter7
```

The space between `Mary` and `Sue` has a special meaning to the shell; it separates words on the command line. In the preceding command, the quotation marks tell the shell that even though a space exists between the two words, both words should be passed to `grep` as a single phrase, `Mary Sue`.

Double quotes do not hide all special characters from the shell; for example, the shell still looks for dollar signs within the quoted phrase, which indicates that you want to replace a variable with its value. For example, consider this command:

```
grep "Secretary $LOGNAME" employees
```

The shell will spot the dollar sign within the quotation marks and replace `$LOGNAME` with the value associated with the `LOGNAME` variable. If `LOGNAME` has the value `terry`, the `grep` command searches the file `employees` for the phrase `Secretary terry`.

Like quotation marks, you can use *single quotes* (' and ', or apostrophes) to enclose special characters to hide their special meaning from the shell. In most situations, you can use either double or single quotes; however, the shell does not look within single quotes for dollar signs. Thus, if you enter the command

```
grep 'Secretary $LOGNAME' employees
```

`grep` will search for the phrase `Secretary $LOGNAME`, exactly as entered within the single quotes.

Note that the purpose of single quotes, which hide the meaning of special characters from the shell, is quite different from the purpose of backquotes (`), which invoke command substitution, as discussed previously in this chapter.

The backslash (\) is also considered a kind of quotation mark because it also tells the shell to treat as a regular character the single, special character that follows it. Consider the following examples:

```
grep huh\? *

rm data?\?
```

The backslash in front of the question mark keeps the shell from attributing any special meaning to the question mark. The grep command in the preceding command is equivalent to grep "huh?" *. In the rm command, the first question mark (without the backslash) has the special meaning of "any character," but the second question mark (with the backslash) is a literal question mark. This rm command removes all files with names that begin with data, followed by any single character, followed by a literal question mark.

An Introduction to Shell Programming

UNIX users often think of the shell as providing two distinct services: a user interface and a programming language. Actually, these are two different aspects of the same function.

By default, the shell gets its input from the keyboard; however, you can use *shell programs* (also known as *shell scripts* or *shell procedures*) to perform complex or repetitious tasks automatically. When executing shell procedures, the shell does nothing more than get its commands from a file instead of from the keyboard.

You create a shell program simply by creating a file with a text editor and placing commands into the file. The commands you use within shell programs are exactly the same commands you can type from the keyboard. After you create the shell program, typing the name of the shell program causes the shell to read the commands in the shell program file and execute them. In effect, you can create new commands by combining existing commands in a shell program.

Creating a Simple Shell Program

To create a shell program, you first must create a text file containing the commands you want to execute. You can use any text editor for this task. For example, if part of your job requires you to monitor the number of customers logged in at the beginning of each hour, and if each customer's login name begins with the letters cust, you might place the following commands in a file called custinfo to print the current date and time and the names of the customers logged in:

```
date
who ¦ grep cust ¦ sort
```

After you create the file, you must add execute permission to the file, using the chmod command:

chmod +x custinfo

You need to perform this operation only once, even if you modify the file later. (For more information on the chmod command, see "Changing File Permissions" in Chapter 3.)

After you add execute permission to the file, if you type the name of the file, custinfo, each command executes in turn:

```
$ custinfo <Return>
Sat Jun 16 14:04:10 EDT 1990
cust719      ttya        Jun 16 11:05
$
```

UNIX Shell Programs v. MS-DOS Batch Files

Superficially, UNIX shell programs and MS-DOS batch files have many similarities. Both enable you to create a file that contains commands and to execute those commands simply by typing the name of the file.

Shell programs and batch files, however, differ greatly in many details. For example, by default, when you run an MS-DOS batch file, the commands are displayed on-screen as they are executed. Conversely, when you execute a UNIX shell program, the commands are not displayed unless you precede the command with sh -x, such as

sh -x myprog

More fundamentally, the MS-DOS batch feature was designed simply to enable you to execute a series of commands; it was never intended to be a full programming language. On the other hand, the shell provides a structured programming language and enables you to write complex programs that can perform almost any task.

Special Shell Program Commands and Features

In addition to the large number of regular UNIX commands, the shell includes a variety of commands and features designed specifically to make shell programs more useful. An exhaustive list would fill a book, but these commands and features can be grouped into several general categories:

- Commands that display information on-screen, such as echo

- Commands that read information from the keyboard, such as line and read

- Commands that evaluate various conditions and make decisions, such as test and if

- Looping commands that perform actions repeatedly, such as for and while

- Commands that perform arithmetic operations, such as expr

- Variables (discussed in the preceding section of this chapter), which serve the same function as variables in other programming languages

- Special variables that make important information available within a shell program, such as $*, which contains the words you typed on the command line to execute the shell program

Many UNIX commands, although useful in their own right, reach their full power only within shell programs. Many of these commands were included in UNIX not because of what they can do by themselves, but because of what they can do within a shell program in conjunction with other commands.

Shell commands are unique in that they must serve both as part of a user interface and as a programming language—that is, they must be meaningful both to human beings and to machines. Because they play this dual role, more complex shell programs sometimes have command syntax that is strange when compared with command syntax in other programming languages. Perhaps the oddest syntax is found in the command to add two numbers together and assign the sum to a variable:

```
total=`expr 5 + 9`
```

This command executes a program, expr, which computes the sum of 5 and 9 and, normally, would send this sum to the screen. Because the expr command is enclosed in backquotes, however, its output becomes the value assigned to the variable `total`. This rather obscure command is completely consistent with existing UNIX syntax and uses features with which an experienced shell user is already familiar.

Non-Bourne Shells

Although some kind of user interface is crucial to the operation of UNIX, the shell is not an integral, built-in part of the operating system. It is simply a program that accepts commands from the keyboard, interprets them, and causes an action to take place. Usually this command processing involves communicating with the kernel through system calls or by running a program.

The original shell—the Bourne Shell—is included on all UNIX systems, but on most systems it is not the only shell available. An experienced programmer can replace the shell with another program that accomplishes the same task. Although the Bourne Shell is an excellent user interface, many users have come to realize that working with the shell could be made easier. Although writing a shell is not a trivial task, many programmers have created their own versions of the shell. Most of these newer shells now include capabilities that were missing in the Bourne Shell. Two shells in particular— the C Shell and the Korn Shell—have gained widespread acceptance. Other shells, such as the Visual Shell and DOS Shell, were created by programmers attempting to meet a specific need and are discussed further in this section.

The C Shell

The University of California at Berkeley proved to be fertile ground for the development of new UNIX tools, one of which was the first major replacement shell to gain wide acceptance. Written by a student, Bill Joy, it was dubbed the *C Shell* because its built-in programming language strongly resembled the C programming language. Because most of the students and faculty using UNIX at Berkeley also were C programmers, modeling a shell on the C language was a natural course for Joy to take.

The C Shell includes a large number of features absent in the Bourne Shell. The bulk of these features falls into one (and sometimes more than one) of the following categories:

- Speed enhancements that enable the C Shell to perform some tasks faster than the Bourne Shell

- Typing shortcuts that make the C Shell easier to use because you use fewer keystrokes

- A complete overhaul of the built-in programming language

- Job control features that make better use of UNIX's multitasking capabilities

- Safety features that protect you from making common mistakes

The C Shell is included today with most UNIX versions that trace their lineage back to Berkeley, which include DEC's Ultrix and IBM's AIX. The actual program name of C Shell is csh, and you usually find it in the directory /bin or /usr/bin. Knowing when a C Shell is running is usually easy because the C Shell prompts with a percent sign (%) instead of the usual dollar sign ($).

The C Shell Command History

Probably the most important single contribution made by the C Shell is the addition of a *command history*. The C Shell maintains a list of the commands you have typed most recently, enabling you to repeat a command without retyping it or to repeat a command after making modifications.

When you log in, the shell begins recording commands. You determine (by setting a C Shell variable) the number of commands the shell can remember; 80 is typical. Using the history command, you can view a list of the most recently issued commands. Consider, for example, the following command and its output:

```
% history <Return>
    1       ls -l
    2       rm oldfile
    3       cd subdir
    4       find . -name 'test*' -print
    5       history
%
```

You can re-execute any command, which you can specify in any of several ways. For example, type !! to repeat the last command; type !2 to repeat command number 2; and type !r to repeat the last command that started with r.

When you type commands, C Shell provides new symbol combinations to save keystrokes. You often find that you need to use the same file name in several commands in a row. For example, suppose that you examine a file with the `cat` command and then decide to edit the file with the `vi` command. In the Bourne Shell, you would type such commands as follows:

```
$ cat /usr/spool/news/rec/humor/715 <Return>
$ vi /usr/spool/news/rec/humor/715 <Return>
$
```

In the C Shell, however, you would type the following commands:

```
% cat /usr/spool/news/rec/humor/715 <Return>
% vi !$ <Return>
%
```

In the `vi` command, notice that `!$` represents the last word in the preceding command. Many other command sequences are possible, such as `!18:3`, which represents the third word in command number 18.

The C Shell also provides a simple mechanism for reissuing previous commands in a slightly modified form. For example, suppose that you type the following sequence, accidentally misspelling `name`:

```
% find /usr/spool/uucppublic -naem 'temp*' -print <Return>
find: bad option -naem
%
```

Having to retype the entire command just to correct one typographical error is frustrating. In the C Shell, you simply type the following sequence to correct the mistake:

```
% ^em^me <Return>
find /usr/spool/uucppublic -name 'temp*' -print
%
```

Notice that you precede the incorrect characters and the corrected characters with carets (`^`). The sequence `^em^me` tells C Shell to re-execute the last command and change `em` to `me`. The C Shell then displays the corrected command and executes it.

You can specify the number of commands that you want kept in the command history by setting the `history` variable. For example, typing

```
set history=80
```

causes C Shell to keep the 80 most recent commands.

Aliases in the C Shell

The C Shell also introduced the concept of *aliases*. Essentially, an alias enables you to introduce abbreviations for commands that you use often. You type the abbreviation, and C Shell replaces it with the lengthier command.

For example, perhaps you often want to display a list of all your directory names. You can use the `find` command to produce such a list:

```
find /usr/yourname -type d -print
```

Typing such a command, however, becomes a chore when you use it frequently. A better alternative would be to assign an alias, as follows:

```
alias dirlist find /usr/yourname -type d -print
```

After you assign the alias, you simply type **dirlist** to execute the much longer `find` command. Normally you place `alias` commands in the `.cshrc` file, so that they are executed automatically every time you log in or start a new shell.

In the Bourne Shell you could use a small shell program to accomplish essentially the same task. Called `dirlist`, the shell program would simply contain the `find` command. The C Shell approach is superior to using shell programs, however, for two reasons:

- *Speed*. C Shell keeps the list of aliases in memory and can immediately convert commands, such as converting `dirlist` to the desired `find` command. A Bourne Shell program requires disk access and requires you to start a new copy of the shell to interpret the shell program, a much slower procedure.

- *Disk space*. Although a lesser consideration, each small shell program requires its own file, which is wasteful of disk space.

In recent years, the Bourne Shell has overcome these weaknesses by adding *functions*, which are actually more powerful than aliases. For simple tasks, however, such as this example using the `find` command, using functions is significantly less convenient.

The `alias` command also enables you to list all aliases currently in use.

Hashing in the C Shell

In the Bourne Shell, each time you issue a command that runs a program, such as `vi`, the shell must search through the directories listed in the PATH variable to locate the program. If you have many directories listed in the PATH, the shell may have to access the disk a great number of times just to find the program.

When you log in to the C Shell, one of its first actions is to scan through all the directories listed in the path and to construct a table, called a *hash table*, of the programs available in those directories. When you issue a command, the C Shell looks up the command in the hash table and therefore can access the program instantly—no disk searching is necessary. (The term *hash table* refers to the internal mechanism used by the programmer who wrote C Shell.)

C Shell must handle one part of the path—the current directory—as a special case. Although a name such as /usr/bin always refers to a specific directory, . represents your current directory, which changes each time you enter a cd command. Consequently, C Shell cannot prescan this directory when you log in, because the actual directory represented can change often. C Shell must search for files in the current directory in much the same way Bourne Shell does.

One problem with file hashing, often of special interest to programmers, occurs when programmers create new programs. If a programmer places a new program in /usr/bin, for example, a user already logged in cannot use it immediately. Typing the name of the command does not cause the C Shell to search the directories for the command, but simply to consult its hash table and display an error message after failing to find the program in the hash table.

The C Shell solves this problem by providing the rehash command, which tells the C Shell to abandon its current hash table and construct a new one by re-scanning the directories in the path.

Except when the occasional need to rehash arises, the hashing feature is completely automatic; you don't have to do anything except enjoy the faster performance.

Wild Card Enhancements in the C Shell

C Shell includes the Bourne Shell's wild card capabilities, which enable you to specify patterns of file names. For example, in either Bourne Shell or C Shell, you can delete all files with the characters temp in their name by typing

```
rm *temp*
```

C Shell, however, provides you with additional capabilities when you use wild cards.

You can use braces ({ and }) to surround a list of choices, each of which is separated by a comma. For example, to list the directories /usr/spool/lp, /usr/spool/uucp, and /usr/spool/news, you could type:

```
ls -l /usr/spool/{lp,uucp,news}
```

Similarly, consider this command line:

```
cp memo.{jim,pete,fred}.nr subdir
```

This command copies the files memo.jim.nr, memo.pete.nr, and memo.fred.nr to the directory subdir.

You also can use *tilde operators* in your path names. A single tilde (~) represents your home directory; thus, the path ~/things.to.do refers to the file things.to.do in your home directory. For example, when a user named Keith uses this notation, it might represent /usr/keith/things.to.do. Similarly, ~/memos/jim.1 refers to a file jim.1 in the subdirectory memos in the user's home directory; for Maria, it might represent /wpfiles/maria/memos/jim.1.

You can access files in other users' directories by following the tilde with a user's login name. For example, you could type ~diedre/choc.chip to access the file choc.chip in Diedre's home directory.

Programming in the C Shell

The C Shell's built-in programming language is very different than the language of the Bourne Shell, and the two languages are almost completely incompatible with each other. In many ways the C Shell's language resembles the C programming language, an association that is responsible for the C Shell's name. Many C programmers find it easy to program in the C Shell; however, other C programmers find the similarities more confusing than helpful, claiming that programming in two completely dissimilar languages is easier than programming in two languages that are similar but not identical.

Almost all C Shell programming statements are different than Bourne Shell statements and, in most cases, are improvements. To illustrate a simple difference, with C Shell you use the set command to assign a value to a variable. To assign such a value, a Bourne Shell programmer would type

```
name=betty
```

whereas a C Shell programmer would type

```
set name=betty
```

The C Shell also improved on the Bourne Shell by providing *arrays*—essentially lists of values, a concept common to most programming languages but missing from the Bourne Shell. The C Shell puts this feature to excellent use in setting the PATH variable. Recall that the PATH variable contains a list of directories to be searched when the shell looks for a command. In the Bourne Shell you cannot assign a list of values to a variable. You set PATH to a single value by typing a statement such as

```
PATH=/bin:/usr/bin:/usr/lbin:.
```

When the Bourne Shell searches for a command, it interprets this single string of characters as a list of separate directories. The C Shell has a much more natural way of expressing the same concept:

```
set path=( /bin /usr/bin /usr/lbin . )
```

A perplexing problem came up as Bill Joy was designing C Shell: How could it be made to coexist peacefully in a system that was already so heavily oriented toward the Bourne Shell? Getting rid of the Bourne Shell was unthinkable—too many programs had already been written for it; in fact, some of the important UNIX system commands are actually Bourne Shell programs. People would not want to use C Shell if it meant that they could not use existing Bourne Shell programs.

As a solution to this problem, the C Shell, when commanded to execute a program, looks at the very first line in the program. If the line begins with a pound sign (#), indicating a C Shell comment that C Shell otherwise ignores, the program is executed as a C Shell program. If the line is not a comment (does not begin with a pound sign), the C Shell invokes the Bourne Shell to execute the program.

Although this solution is not perfect (occasionally a Bourne Shell program starts with a comment, confusing the C Shell), it generally has worked over the years.

Job Control in the C Shell

Early in its history, UNIX acquired the capability to perform multitasking. Like the Bourne Shell, the C Shell enables you to place a program in the background by typing an ampersand (&) at the end of the command.

In versions of UNIX that are not derived from Berkeley UNIX, such as AT&T's UNIX System V, programs that you start in the background must remain in the background; similarly, you cannot switch programs that you start in the foreground to the background. When Berkeley began enhancing

UNIX in the late 1970s, however, the programmers added the *job control* feature, which enables you to switch programs between the foreground and background and to temporarily interrupt programs and continue them later. The result is a more flexible multitasking environment.

Note, however, that the C Shell alone does not guarantee that you can use job control; the operating system itself must support job control. On UNIX systems that are not from Berkeley, job control does not work, even if the C Shell is present.

Commands the C Shell introduced to support job control include:

Command	Action
<Ctrl-Z>	Pauses the program currently running in the foreground
bg (background)	Resumes in the background a program stopped in the foreground
fg (foreground)	Brings to the foreground a program run ning in the background
jobs	Produces a list of currently active programs
kill	Stops execution of a program

C Shell also includes minor conveniences. When you submit a background program in Bourne Shell, the shell does not notify you when the program has terminated. C Shell, however, displays a message for you whenever a background program terminates.

When you press <Ctrl-Z>, C Shell displays a prompt, enabling you to enter other commands. The stopped command, however, is still loaded in memory, suspended. You can resume the command at any time, using the bg or fg commands.

Consider the following example, which shows typical output of the jobs command:

```
% jobs <Return>
[1]  - Running          sort phonelist -o sorted.list
[2]    Running          troff -mm memo
[3]  + Stopped (signal) make
%
```

This output shows that three jobs are in the background; two are currently running, and one is temporarily stopped.

Although the `kill` command normally requires the process ID number of the program you want to kill, you instead can type the program's position number, shown in the `jobs` command list. You simply precede the position number with a percent sign. Using the preceding list of current jobs as an example, you could type the following command to kill the `troff` program:

```
kill %2
```

C Shell Safety Features

The C Shell includes several useful features to save you from certain careless mistakes you may make. Occasionally you may accidentally destroy the contents of a file by redirecting the output of a command into that file. For example, suppose that you type the following command:

```
who > list
```

The `who` command is executed and its output is written to the file named `list`. If `list` already exists and contains data, the contents of `list` are destroyed.

If, however, you beforehand set a special C Shell variable, amusingly called `noclobber`, the C Shell refuses to destroy existing files with redirection. To set the `noclobber` variable, type the following command:

```
set noclobber
```

If you want this file protection feature, you usually include the `set noclobber` command in your `.cshrc` file so that you don't have to set `noclobber` manually at each invocation of the C Shell. After you set `noclobber`, redirecting output to an existing file produces the following error message:

```
list: File exists
```

Placing an exclamation point after the redirection symbol, as shown in the following example, enables the C Shell to override the `noclobber` command and redirect output to files that already exist:

```
who >! list
```

Another safety feature prevents you from accidentally logging off when you press <Ctrl-D>, as can sometimes happen when you are running commands that accept input from the keyboard. For example, suppose that Doug wants to use the `mail` command to send a short message to Belinda, and he wants to enter the message from the keyboard. He types

```
% mail belinda
Hey, B: wanna go out for pizza? -- Doug
^D
```

Pressing <Ctrl-D> signals the end of Doug's message. If Doug accidentally presses <Ctrl-D> twice, the first instance ends the mail message, and the second causes him to log off the system. The resulting `login:` message tells Doug of his error.

Setting the special variable `ignoreeof` prevents you from accidentally logging off. (In UNIX, <^D> is an end-of-file marker; it signals the end of input. The variable name `ignoreeof` stands for "ignore end of file.") You usually set the variable `ignoreeof` in the `.cshrc` file by typing the following command:

set ignoreeof

After you set `ignoreeof`, the C Shell refuses to log off if you press <Ctrl-D>. Rather, you must type **exit** or **logout** to log off.

Other Differences

Many other minor differences exist between the C Shell and the Bourne Shell, some of which enable the C Shell and the Bourne Shell to coexist on the same machine without getting in each other's way. For example, the difference between the Bourne Shell default prompt ($) and the C Shell default prompt (%) enables you to tell at a glance which shell is currently active. Similarly, during the login process, the Bourne Shell executes a shell program, which you provide, called `.profile`. The C Shell instead executes a file called `.login`. In addition, whenever you start a new copy of the C Shell (for example, if you temporarily leave the `vi` editor with the `:sh` or `:!` commands), the file `.cshrc` is executed. A third file, `.logout`, is executed when you log off. The Bourne Shell has no equivalent to `.cshrc` or `.logout`.

The Korn Shell

The Korn Shell, or K Shell, was written by David Korn at AT&T Bell Labs in 1982; it is an attempt to integrate the best features of the Bourne Shell and the C Shell. Although it is the largest and most complex of the shells (except for the graphical user interfaces discussed in the following section of this chapter), it provides superior performance, running faster than any other shell and providing more conveniences.

The standard shell included with all UNIX systems traditionally has been the Bourne Shell, but the Korn Shell may be overtaking it. Although it originally began as an AT&T tool, the Korn Shell is now available from other sources. It is being included with AT&T's latest version of UNIX, System V Release 4, and it can be found on many UNIX versions compatible with AT&T's UNIX System V. The Korn Shell is provided with versions of UNIX from Hewlett-Packard and Apple. Aspen Technologies sells a version of the Korn Shell that you can use on many different machines. Even an MS-DOS version is available, included with MKS Toolkit, a collection of UNIX-like utilities for MS-DOS from Mortice Kern Systems. Other manufacturers sell the Korn Shell as an add-on or as part of a larger package of tools. AT&T, for example, sells the Korn Shell as part of the 386 UNIX VAR/ISV Software Developers Toolkit.

Unlike the C Shell, the Korn Shell is compatible with the Bourne Shell. If you are familiar with the Bourne Shell, you can begin using the Korn Shell immediately and will notice no differences. Bourne Shell programs can be run by the Korn Shell; however, the Korn Shell includes many features, some modeled after C Shell features, that are not available in the Bourne Shell.

The actual program name of the Korn Shell is `ksh`, which you may find in any of several different directories; `/bin`, `/usr/bin`, and `/usr/lbin` are common locations.

The Korn Shell Command History

Like the C Shell, the Korn Shell includes a command history. It remembers commands and can repeat them later. In most cases the syntax that you use for Korn Shell command history is slightly different from the syntax you use in the C Shell, as shown in the following comparison of commands used by Korn Shell and C Shell:

Action	C Shell Command	Korn Shell Command
List recent commands	`history`	`history`
Rerun command number 176	`!176`	`r 176`
Rerun last command starting with a v	`!v`	`r v`
Access last word of the preceding command	`!$`	`$_`

Despite the similarities, major differences exist between the C Shell and Korn Shell history mechanisms. For example, the C Shell keeps commands only while you are logged in; all commands are lost when you log off. The Korn Shell, on the other hand, keeps the commands in a file, so that you later can reuse the commands you used during a previous login session.

The Korn Shell provides sophisticated support for editing commands. When you press <Esc>, the Korn Shell enters edit mode, simulating a one-line vi editor (the Emacs editor is also available). Most vi commands are available for moving text, deleting text, and inserting new text. Keys that cause vi to move the cursor upward instead cause Korn Shell to display successively older commands, as recorded in Korn Shell's history file. For example, if command number 142 is currently displayed, pressing k ("cursor up" in vi) causes Korn Shell to display command number 141. You can modify the command displayed on the command line, and when you press <Return>, that command is executed.

You can use any UNIX text editor for editing complex commands—especially multiline commands. You can specify which text editor you want to use for complex tasks; vi is the common choice. The fc (*fix command*) command starts up the text editor and loads into the editing buffer the command you specify. For example, typing **fc 344** starts vi (or some other editor) with command 344 loaded. You then can edit this command and exit the text editor in the usual way. The edited command is then executed.

You can set several special shell variables to control the history mechanism:

- FCEDIT

  If you set FCEDIT, Korn Shell uses the value of FCEDIT as the name of the editor to use with the fc command. If you do not set FCEDIT, EDITOR specifies the name instead. If you do not set FCEDIT or EDITOR, Korn Shell invokes the ed editor when you issue the fc command.

- VISUAL

  If you set VISUAL, Korn Shell uses the value of VISUAL as the name of editor to be used when you press <Esc>. If you do not set VISUAL, EDITOR specifies the name instead. If you do not set VISUAL or EDITOR, you cannot use the command line editing feature.

- HISTFILE

  The HISTFILE variable specifies the name of the file in which the Korn Shell keeps the command history. If you do not set HISTFILE, Korn Shell uses a file named .sh_history in your home directory.

- HISTSIZE

  HISTSIZE specifies the maximum number of commands you can keep in the command history. The default is 128. Assigning an extremely large value to this variable can cause the Korn Shell to start up slowly.

Aliases in the Korn Shell

The Korn Shell contains a mechanism for assigning aliases that is essentially identical to the C Shell's, although the syntax is slightly different. If you want the alias to replace text that consists of more than one word, you must use quotation marks. For example, in the C Shell you would set an alias such as the following by typing

```
alias dirlist find /usr/jim -type d -print
```

The equivalent Korn Shell command is

```
alias dirlist="find /usr/jim -type d -print"
```

Tracked Aliases in the Korn Shell

The Korn Shell's *tracked alias* feature is similar to the C Shell's hash table in that it prevents the Korn Shell from searching for the same commands repeatedly. The C Shell, however, builds a table of every available command when you log in, whereas the Korn Shell builds the table more slowly.

The Korn Shell is constructed on the very appropriate assumption that most people run a few programs repeatedly. A technical writer, for example, might spend the whole day using almost nothing but the vi and troff commands. A programmer might use a dozen commands, such as vi, make, sdb, cc, and others.

The first time you use any specific command, the Korn Shell uses PATH to search for it, just as the Bourne Shell does. From then on, the Korn Shell remembers where it found that command, and the next time you use it, no searching is necessary. Thus you will notice no improvement in speed when you first use a command—only when you subsequently reuse it.

File Wild Cards in the Korn Shell

To specify file names, the Korn Shell supports the use of wild cards, including the C Shell's tilde operators: ~ represents your home directory, and ~*name* represents the home directory of the person whose login name is *name*. In addition, ~- represents the directory that was your current directory before your most recent cd command, and ~+ represents the current directory. The C Shell's braces ({ and }) are not supported in Korn Shell.

Job Control in the Korn Shell

The Korn Shell duplicates the C Shell job control commands. As with the C Shell, you can use these commands only if the underlying version of UNIX supports job control.

Programming in the Korn Shell

The most important point about Korn Shell programming is that it is compatible with the Bourne Shell. Although you cannot reasonably run a UNIX system under only the C Shell, you can run the system under the Korn Shell alone, because all existing Bourne Shell programs run under the Korn Shell.

The Korn Shell includes many important programming features not found in the Bourne Shell; many of these duplicate features in the C Shell. For example:

- *Numeric Variables.* The Bourne Shell uses only string variables; the Korn Shell uses true numeric variables as well. The statement NUMBER=17 assigns the string of characters 17 to the variable NUMBER in both the Bourne Shell and the Korn Shell; the Korn Shell statement let NUMBER=17 assigns the number 17 to NUMBER. The difference is subtle, and Korn Shell produces the same results in either case; however, the computer can work much more efficiently with numbers than with strings of characters. On some computers, numbers can be processed up to 30 times as fast as character strings.

- *Numbers.* The Korn Shell introduces simpler, more expressive ways of working with numbers. In the Bourne Shell, adding 1 to the variable X requires that you type the following cryptic statement:

```
X=`expr $X + 1`
```

In the Korn Shell, you can achieve the same result much more naturally by typing

```
let X=X+1
```

- *Built-in Commands.* The Korn Shell has a large number of built-in commands. When you use these commands, the Korn Shell does the work without calling an external program. Over the years, as many of these commands have been incorporated into the Bourne Shell, the Korn Shell has lost much of this advantage over the Bourne Shell.

- *Arrays.* The Korn Shell enables you to use arrays, much like the C Shell.

Because of the Korn Shell's additional features, programming in the Korn Shell is often easier than programming in the Bourne Shell. Even if you don't use these additional features, Korn Shell programs still run faster than Bourne Shell programs, largely because of the great number of built-in commands and tracked aliases.

Special Korn Shell Features

A large number of special shell variables are introduced in the Korn Shell. Perhaps the most useful is PWD, which contains your current working directory. You can use this variable to set your shell prompt so that the prompt includes the current path, a la MS-DOS:

```
PS1='$PWD> '
```

This command changes your prompt to the current path, followed by >. For example, the new prompt might be

```
/usr/fred/letters>
```

Korn Shell also provides features that you can use to simplify your use of the cd command:

- The command cd – causes the Korn Shell to return to your last working directory. This command is handy for switching back and forth between two directories.

- If cd is followed by two words, the Korn Shell repeats the cd command last executed, but substitutes the second word for the first. For example, if the last cd command switched you to the /usr/lib/uucp directory, typing **cd lib spool** switches you to the /usr/spool/uucp directory.

Read-Only Shell Programs in the Korn Shell

Sometimes a shell program contains sensitive procedures. The author of such a program may want to allow others to execute the program without allowing them to see how it was written. The Bourne Shell and the C Shell can execute shell programs only if the program has both execute and read permission; therefore, allowing users to execute a shell program that they cannot also read is impossible. The same is not true of the Korn Shell. If installed properly by the system administrator, the Korn Shell can run a program that has only execute permission; read permission is not necessary.

DOS Shells

As PCs running UNIX become more widespread and powerful, the number of people who come in contact with both UNIX and DOS is increasing. Many manufacturers provide some type of DOS interface for UNIX. In its simplest form, this interface may consist of tools for copying files between the UNIX file system and DOS diskettes. XENIX comes with such tools, and Emmet Gray's mtools is a collection of public domain DOS utilities that is widely available for most UNIX machines.

Other manufacturers go a step further and actually simulate the DOS environment with a *DOS shell*. For example, some machines from Sun Microsystems (running some versions of SunOS) and IBM (running AIX) provide shells that closely simulate DOS, including common commands such as DIR, TYPE, and COPY. In addition to providing an easy way to transfer files between DOS and UNIX, such DOS shells can serve to ease the transition to UNIX for people who are familiar with DOS.

On UNIX machines that are based on Intel processors (80286, 80386, or 80486), you often can run DOS programs as well, enabling you to take advantage of your favorite DOS programs. One such system from SCO, called VP/ix, essentially enables a machine to run UNIX and DOS at the same time. If you are comfortable with DOS, you will appreciate the familiar C> prompt and having all the DOS commands available to you. You also can run both DOS and UNIX application software.

Visual Shells

A *visual shell* is a menu-driven program. The most common visual shell is XENIX's vsh.

When you invoke vsh, a list of files in the current directory appears on-screen, along with a menu listing various tasks. To run a program or perform an operation on a file, you merely select the file or program you want, and you select an operation—such as Run, Copy, Delete, Edit, or Make Directory—from the menu. For some operations, vsh asks you for additional information; for example, if you ask to rename a file, vsh prompts you for the new name. For other selections, vsh displays a submenu. For example, if you select File System from the main menu, vsh displays a submenu listing operations such as Create, FilesCheck, SpaceFree, Mount, and Unmount.

Although experienced users often find vsh attractive, it is of greatest benefit to novices, who may have difficulty working with commands such as sort, which has dozens of options. Because it prompts for the information it needs, vsh makes formulating complex commands easier for the beginner. Experienced users, on the other hand, know the options required to accomplish a particular task and often would rather just type the command.

Finding Non-Bourne Shells

All UNIX systems include the Bourne Shell and restricted shell (see "Using Special Shells" in Chapter 9 for more information about the restricted shell). Many also include either the Korn Shell or the C Shell (only a few include both). You can type **ksh** or **csh**, respectively, to test for the presence of these shells. If an error results, either the shell is not present or it is located in a directory that is not in your search path. If no error results, UNIX runs the specified shell.

Graphical User Interfaces

The earliest computer applications were text-based; they used hardware that could print and display written text, and not much else. Early computers lacked the power to manipulate graphics, such as lines, squares, circles, and pictures. Their terminals could not display such objects anyway, so the lack of processing power hardly mattered. UNIX at first was such a system; it used printer terminals that were limited to text only.

As processors became more sophisticated and terminal displays became capable of displaying detailed graphical figures, many manufacturers devised systems that manipulated graphics as well as text. Although some systems were successful, none gained wide acceptance among computer manufacturers.

With the advent of PCs and workstations—powerful desktop computers serving a single user—graphics became more common. Many experts believe that the trend in computing today is away from text-oriented interfaces, such as the shells described in this chapter, and toward intuitive, easy-to-use *graphical user interfaces*, or *GUIs*. Instead of requiring complex commands, GUIs enable you to point at objects on-screen, using a pointing device such as a mouse, and select operations from menus. Many users find GUIs much faster to learn and much more efficient to use than shells. Companies find that their employees can be trained to use GUIs in much less time.

Windowing Systems

GUIs are also known as *windowing systems*. In most such systems, each running program creates one or more *windows*—rectangular areas on-screen in which programs display information and accept user input. On multitasking systems such as UNIX, windows are especially powerful. You can run many programs simultaneously, and information from each is displayed in a separate window. By pointing at the appropriate window with the mouse, you can switch from window to window and provide input wherever necessary.

Each window in which a program is running occupies a portion of the screen (charmingly known as *real estate*), or a single window may occupy the entire screen. When several windows are displayed on-screen simultaneously, they often overlap, causing one window to obscure part of another or hide it completely.

Using a windowing system is quite similar to working with sheets of paper at your desk. You can arrange papers in several piles, and as you move from task to task, you move the papers here and there on the desk.

Windows are normally arranged across the screen. When you want to work with a window that is partially covered up by another, you point to an exposed portion of the desired window with the mouse and bring it to the front, just as you would fish out a sheet of paper from the middle of a stack and place it on top. If the window you want is completely obscured by other windows, you can select the desired window from a list of windows.

You also can move windows to any position on-screen. Viewing two or more programs at the same time is easy; you need only to move the windows so that they do not overlap. You also can resize windows; that is, you can shrink or expand the window so that the desired information is showing. Windows are usually moved or resized by pointing to one of several symbols, called *icons*, that surround the border of the window.

You also can *iconify* or *minimize* windows, which replaces the entire window with a tiny icon. Minimizing a window is useful when you will not be working with that program for a while and want to clear some of the clutter from the screen. The program continues to run—it simply has no place to display results. You can restore the program to its normal window at any time.

The Growth of Graphical User Interfaces

As processing power increased and terminals capable of displaying graphics became available, GUIs steadily increased in popularity. Today a number of GUIs are available for different environments (see table 4.1). Note that OSF/1, AIX, Ultrix, and HP-UX are UNIX-type operating systems.

Table 4.1
Common Graphical User Interfaces

GUI	Operating System	Manufacturer
Windows	MS-DOS	Microsoft
Presentation Manager	OS/2	IBM
Open Look	UNIX	AT&T, Sun
Motif	OSF/1, AIX	Open Software Foundation, IBM
DEC Windows	Ultrix	Digital Equipment Corporation
PM/X	HP-UX	Hewlett-Packard
NeXTStep	Mach	NeXT

In the world of UNIX, virtually every GUI is built upon a graphical system developed at the Massachusetts Institute of Technology, a system known as the *X Windows* system, which began much like UNIX did.

The X Windows System

The X Windows system, developed for UNIX and widely used in it, has spread to other environments as well. X Windows offers these important features:

- X Windows runs applications either on your own machine or on another machine that you access across a network. Programs on other machines are indistinguishable from local programs.

- X Windows displays two-dimensional graphics, in monochrome or color, and multifont text (text in many different sizes and type styles).

- X Windows is independent of any particular operating system, language, or type of hardware. You can use any combination.

In the course of its development, X Windows has proved to be more powerful and flexible than similar systems for the Apple Macintosh, OS/2, or Microsoft Windows.

The History of X Windows

The X Windows system began in much the same way as the UNIX system itself did—it was designed to meet the specific needs of a small number of developers. In 1984, Robert Scheifler, at the Massachusetts Institute of Technology's (MIT) Laboratory for Computer Science, was working on a distributed system—a networking system that runs across several computers—called Argus. He found himself in need of a debugger (a program that helps programmers locate errors) that would enable him to watch activities on different computers at the same time. At the same time, Jim Gettys, an engineer with Digital Equipment Corporation (DEC), was assigned to Project Athena, an MIT project for undergraduate education. Both saw a need for a graphical system.

Paul Asente and Brian Reid, then at Stanford University, had previously developed a windowing system called W, which ran under Stanford's V operating system. In 1983, Asente and Chris Kent, as summer students at DEC's Western Research Laboratory, moved W to a DEC UNIX system and provided MIT with a copy. Scheifler and Gettys used this MIT copy as the basis for their windowing system.

W turned out to be slow and inefficient in a UNIX environment. Scheifler reworked parts of it to more closely match the way UNIX operates. He felt that these changes sufficiently distinguished his version from the original W (which was in use elsewhere at MIT) to warrant a new name. For lack of anything better, he chose the next letter of the alphabet, *X*, and by the time he gave the name more thought, users were already accustomed to using the name *X Windows*.

X Windows went through several revisions, and for a while, it was licensed by MIT to a small number of users. In September 1985, however, a decision was made at MIT that turned out to be of major importance: X Windows would no longer be licensed by MIT for a fee, but would be available to anyone simply for the cost of production. Pay for the postage and the tapes, they said, and you can have it.

This offer was more than hardware manufacturers could resist. DEC released the first commercial X Windows workstation, the DEC VAXstation-II/GPX, in January 1986. Other manufacturers, including IBM, Hewlett-Packard, Apollo, and Sun, adopted X Windows and contributed to it. By the fall of 1986, DEC had decided to use X Windows as a major element in its workstations operating under Ultrix (DEC's version of UNIX), MS-DOS, and VMS (DEC's proprietary operating system).

In January 1987, MIT announced the first X Windows technical conference. At the conference, 11 major hardware and software vendors announced their support for the current version of X Windows, X11.

The X Consortium

In January 1988, MIT formed the X Consortium, an open organization funded by its members, charged with supporting and continuing the development of X Windows. X Consortium members are listed in table 4.2.

Table 4.2.
X Consortium Members

Apple	Prime
AT&T	Rich
Bull	Sequent
CalComp	Siemens
Control Data Corporation	Silicon Graphics
Data General	Sony
DEC	Sun
Eastman Kodak	Tektronix
Fujitsu	Texas Instruments
Hewlett-Packard	UNiSYS
IBM	Wang
NCR	Xerox
NEC	

How X Windows Works

X Windows is an extremely complex system. It is designed to be used with a wide spectrum of hardware, operating systems, and programming languages. It is also designed to be as complete as possible, so that programmers can build any type of windowing interface.

X Windows is designed around what is known as *client/server architecture*, a term used to describe any computer design in which one component (the *server*) provides services for other components (the *clients*). The following list explains the components of the X Windows system:

- The *display server* is a program that handles the tasks of controlling a particular keyboard, mouse (or other pointing device), and a screen. The keyboard, mouse, and screen are collectively known as the *display*. (Actually, a server can control several screens that work together. You might have, for example, monochrome and color screens on the same terminal. Such configurations do not affect this discussion.)

- *Clients* are application programs that need access to the display. That is, each client needs to get input from the keyboard and mouse and to send output to one or more windows on-screen.

Clients cannot perform operations directly on the display; rather, they must access the display indirectly by using the display server as an intermediary. To communicate with each other, the clients and display server exchange messages. The clients, for example, send messages to the display server describing the type of text and graphics to be displayed on-screen; the server sends messages to the clients when the user takes some action, such as entering information at the keyboard or clicking the mouse within an area of the screen used by the client.

The client and display server most often communicate by using any of several possible interprocess communication facilities, which enable two programs to exchange data rapidly. Shared memory, message queues, or sockets are often used. (See Chapter 8, "Programming Languages and UNIX Software Development," for more information on interprocess communication.)

Because the clients and display server communicate exclusively by exchanging messages, they don't have to run on the same machine. Some or all of the clients can run on machines different from the machine running the display server, with messages passed across a network. This concept is powerful; on large networks, from a single display you can use programs that simultaneously are running on a variety of machines halfway across the continent.

As the popularity of X Windows grew, manufacturers adapted it for operating systems other than UNIX, such as DEC's VMS. Conceivably, you can simultaneously run one program using X Windows on a DEC VAX using VMS, another program on a UNIX computer, and still other programs on other computers running other operating systems, and you can have the output from each displayed in windows, side by side, on a single X Windows display. You can even use output display in one window as input for another program in another window.

X Windows does not require any particular type of network. It can run on any network that provides reliable, *in-order delivery*—messages must arrive in the same order in which they were sent. Making sure that messages arrive without errors of any kind is up to the network. Such a system is called a *reliable duplex byte stream*. TCP and DECnet are two examples of such mechanisms.

An important component of any X Windows system is the *window manager*. This special client, acting in conjunction with the display server, enables you to perform various operations on windows, such as moving, resizing, minimizing, and so on. The window manager also provides the *decorations* for all windows, which include title bars and various icons that border most windows.

Programming for X Windows

Writing programs, or clients, for X Windows would be inordinately tedious if the programmer had to worry about passing messages. Happily, this task is not necessary. Programmers writing programs for X Windows use an interface library, which enables them to specify the task they want to perform (drawing a circle, displaying some text); the interface library handles the details of getting the proper message to the display server. Different libraries are used for different programming languages. The most common library, used with the C programming language, is Xlib.

Note that the designers of X Windows did not intend to dictate what the screen should look like, what a particular mouse button should do, or any other aspect of a graphical user interface. Rather, Xlib provides programmers a means by which they can modify a GUI to suit their needs.

If, however, all programmers were to make up their own individual rules about how the screen should be laid out, running X Windows programs indeed would be confusing. So manufacturers and software organizations have developed *toolkits*—programming aids that not only enable programmers to accomplish tasks easily, but more importantly, standardize the look of their programs. Because all programs written with a toolkit are similar in appearance, you feel comfortable using them, and by learning a few basic rules, you can easily use most programs written in that toolkit.

Some common toolkits are Motif from Open Software Foundation, XUI from DEC, CXI from Hewlett-Packard, and XT Plus from AT&T.

Writing client programs for X Windows requires a slightly different way of looking at programming. X Windows uses what is called the *event model*. The client program sends messages that say, in effect, "Here are the possible events that I am interested in: The user might click the mouse on this icon, or type data into this area of the screen, or..." and so on. The client then goes to sleep (that is, becomes idle) and waits for the display server to notify it that one of the events has occurred. The client then wakes up and takes action.

X Windows and GUIs

X Windows is not itself a graphical user interface; rather, it is a foundation upon which most graphical user interfaces are built. Two of the most popular GUIs, both built on the X Windows system, are Open Look (available from AT&T and Sun) and Motif (available from Open Software Foundation, IBM, Hewlett-Packard, and others). Each has its own unique features, but both are based on the same powerful capability—running multiple processes simultaneously in individual windows.

Throughout its history, X Windows has typically required an expensive graphics terminal connected to a computer that runs the display server software. As the number of GUIs built on X Windows has increased, however, a new piece of equipment has appeared on the scene: the X Windows terminal. Available from a variety of manufacturers at prices starting around $1,000, this terminal has built-in display server software, and it connects to a computer by some type of network.

Chapter Summary

In this chapter you explored the various user interfaces available under UNIX. The standard UNIX shell—the Bourne Shell—provides sophisticated multitasking features and a powerful built-in programming language, both of which have strongly influenced the development of other user interfaces in other operating systems, most notably MS-DOS and OS/2.

Shells such as C Shell and Korn Shell provide a different collection of features. C Shell's features are radically different from Bourne Shell's features. Korn Shell's features build on Bourne Shell's; they add new capabilities, but they include all of Bourne Shell's features, thus maintaining compatibility between Bourne Shell and Korn Shell.

Other shells, such as the DOS Shell and Visual Shell, make UNIX easier to use for former DOS users and novices, respectively.

Finally, you learned about the X Windows system and a few of the graphical user interfaces available on many UNIX systems. These interfaces, many industry analysts believe, are the tickets to carry UNIX into the 21st century.

5

UNIX Tools

As more and more programmers began using UNIX—first within Bell Labs and later elsewhere—the urge to write nifty little programs for simple but helpful tasks was irresistible to many. These small programs have become known as *tools* because they simplify the work of programmers and users, just as do the tools of any other trade.

Many UNIX users use the words *tool*, *command*, and *program* interchangeably. Tools are simply small, general-purpose programs that you use as an aid to your work. You invoke tools by typing commands. Thus, when you type the command **cp**, for example, you are invoking the cp program, which you also can call the cp tool.

UNIX contains a large collection of tools, partly because writing these small but useful programs is so easy in UNIX. UNIX tools address tasks related to just about every aspect of working with a computer.

Many UNIX tools are discussed elsewhere in this book. File manipulation tools, such as cp and mv, are discussed in Chapter 3, text processing tools in Chapter 6, and software development tools in Chapter 8. Chapter 9, "UNIX System Administration," discusses tools used primarily by the system administrator. This chapter discusses useful tools that enable you to use and control the UNIX print spooling system and to run programs unattended using the UNIX batch execution tools.

UNIX Batch Facilities

In the early days of computing, most work with computers was oriented toward *batch processing*, which means that you gave the computer a list of one or more tasks (often on punched cards), and the computer processed

159

the tasks without intervention or interaction with the user. Results were usually printed on paper; if something went wrong, the computer printed information regarding what had happened, and the process was repeated until the job was performed satisfactorily.

UNIX, however, is strongly oriented toward interactive use. In this mode, you type commands and examine results, interactively supplying additional information with commands such as mail or vi. Batch processing orientation is nonetheless still useful. Some operations don't require interaction with you and don't produce results on-screen. Sorting a large file, for example, may require many minutes, or longer, during which the program does not need input from the terminal. When performing such tasks, you can indicate to UNIX that no terminal is required.

Chapter 4, "Understanding the UNIX Shell," explains that the simplest way to execute a command that does not require interactive input from a terminal is to place the command in the background by typing an ampersand (&) at the end of the command. To sort a large file called hugefile, for example, you can type

```
sort hugefile -o hugefile&
```

(The -o option specifies the name of the file to receive the sorted data—in this case, the same file that contains the original unsorted data.) The ampersand at the end of the command causes UNIX to execute the command in the background without access to user input. As soon as the command begins to execute, the command prompt returns, indicating that you can enter the next command. The sort command continues to execute in the background. Unless an error occurs, the command produces no output to the screen.

In addition to this simple background mechanism, UNIX contains several tools that enable you to execute background commands more precisely.

Executing Commands with batch

The batch command enables you to execute one or more commands in a *batch*—that is, in the background—with a number of useful characteristics. The batch command reads a series of commands from the terminal and executes those commands in sequence in the background. For example, to sort a file called big.list, check its spelling, and then print it to the printer, you type

```
$ batch <Return>
sort big.list -o big.list <Return>
spell big.list <Return>
lp big.list <Return><Ctrl-D>
<^D>
$
```

batch does not execute commands as you type them; it merely stores them for later use. As with most commands that accept input from the terminal, you press <Ctrl-D> to indicate that your input is complete. After you type <Ctrl-D>, the shell gives you your next prompt, indicating that batch no longer has use of the keyboard and that you can continue with more commands for the shell. Meanwhile, as you continue with other tasks, batch begins its work in the background without further interaction with you. One by one, batch executes the commands that you provided as input. This collection of commands is called a *job*, a term held over from the batch-oriented days of computing.

If the commands executed through the batch command produce any standard output (output that normally goes to the screen), you receive the output by UNIX mail.

Because no keyboard is available to commands executed by batch, no data is available to them on their standard input unless you specify redirection. For example, consider this command:

```
mail bob
```

This command attempts to read a message from the keyboard and send the message to Bob as mail. You would not expect to find this command in a batch job because no keyboard is available from which to read the message; however, you may find the command

```
mail bob <msg
```

in a batch job, because the redirection causes the command to get its input from the file msg (Chapter 4 discusses redirection in more detail).

Commands executed through batch are handled slightly differently than commands placed in the background with the ampersand (&) (see Chapter 4 for more information about background processing with &). These differences are as follows:

- The batch command handles any number of commands easily; the ampersand requires a more complex syntax to execute multiple commands.

- The system gives lower priority to a job you execute with `batch`, enabling other programs, most of which are interactive, to run more quickly. If you don't need the results of a task immediately, using the `batch` command provides a better environment for other users—it's the neighborly thing to do.

- Logging off the system kills commands executed with the ampersand, but batch jobs continue to execute.

- If you do not redirect output from a command executed with an ampersand, any output produced appears on-screen, usually rudely interrupting your current work. However, if any commands within a `batch` job produce output, `batch` sends you, through UNIX `mail`, the output as a mail message.

Delaying Command Execution with `at`

More powerful than `batch` is the `at` command, which enables you to specify the commands to be executed and exactly when they should be executed.

The `at` command requires you to specify when the commands should begin execution. You can specify a simple time and date:

```
at 8:15 am Feb 6 1991
```

As with the `batch` command, after you enter the `at` command, you type one or more commands. As you type commands, `at` stores them for later execution. After you type all the commands you want `at` to execute, press <Ctrl-D>. The shell displays the command prompt, and you can continue with other work. At the time and date you specify with the `at` command, UNIX will execute the commands you entered for `at`.

You may want to execute commands at a particular time for a number of reasons. For example, because a program that performs intensive calculations slows down the system, a considerate user issues an `at` command to run the program in the wee hours of the morning. A backup program also can be run during off-hours. The best time to run a communications program to send information to the home office is generally late at night when long distance charges are lowest. Conversely, a test program designed to measure a computer's performance during heavy load can be run at 3:00 P.M., when computer usage is high.

`at` enables you to specify the date and time in many different formats. You can specify times with or without a colon (`6:00` or `0600`), or as only the hour (`6`). You also can use `noon` or `midnight`, and you can place am or pm after the time. If you do not specify am or pm, the time is assumed to be on a 24-hour clock. Following the time with zulu indicates Greenwich Mean Time (Coordinated Universal Time). If you omit the date, it is assumed to be the present day or, if the time already has passed, the next day. In place of the date, you can specify today, tomorrow, or a day of the week (such as Monday). Finally, you can add a number of days, weeks, months, years, hours, or minutes, such as noon + 15 minutes to represent 12:15 P.M.

Consider the following examples of the at command:

Command	*Action*
at 9pm	Sets the job for 9:00 P.M. of the present day or, if issued after 9:00 P.M., 9:00 P.M. the next day
at noon tomorrow	Sets the job for 12:00 noon the next day
at 1100 Friday	Sets the job for 11:00 A.M. Friday (assumes a 24-hour clock if you do not specify am or pm)
at noon Friday + 2 weeks	Sets the job for two weeks from Friday noon
at 645pm next Tue	Sets the job for 6:45 P.M. one week from Tuesday
at 1430 zulu	Sets the job for 2:30 P.M. Greenwich Mean Time (Coordinated Universal Time)

When you use at to enter a job, UNIX displays a message that gives the time the command will run and a special identification code you can use later to identify the job.

Consider this example:

```
$ at noon Thursday <Return>
who <Return><Ctrl-D>
<^D>
job 679852800.a at Thu Jul 18 12:00:00 1991
$
```

The message displayed indicates that the job's identification (ID) code is 679852800.a, and that the job will execute at 12:00 on Thursday, July 18.

You can use the at command at any time to produce a list of all the jobs you have waiting to execute, including the time and date they are scheduled to run. To produce this list, specify the -1 (*list*) option, as shown in the following example:

```
$ at -l <Return>
679734000.a    Wed Jul 17 03:45:00 1991
679852800.a    Thu Jul 18 12:00:00 1991
$
```

This listing shows two jobs, their ID codes, and the times they will begin.

If you change your mind about a job, the command at -r followed by the job's ID code cancels the job. Consider this example:

at -r 679734000.a

This command cancels the at job with the ID code 679734000.a. Many system administrators prefer that only experienced people use at because the command enables you to schedule programs to run automatically, perhaps when no one is around to keep an eye on them. Two files enable the system administrator to control which users are authorized to use the at command: at.allow and at.deny.

If the file at.allow exists in the /usr/lib/cron directory, the file contains a list of all users who may use at. Users not listed may not use at. If at.allow does not exist, but the file at.deny does, at.deny contains a list of all users who are not authorized to use at. Users not listed are authorized to use at. If at.deny exists but is empty, all users may use at. If neither file exists, only the system administrator (root) may use at.

Executing Commands Repeatedly with cron

More powerful yet than at is cron (from the Greek word for *time*). cron executes commands automatically according to a schedule you define. You can execute commands daily, weekly, yearly, semimonthly, hourly, every few minutes, or in almost any imaginable pattern.

In many situations, executing the same command repeatedly is desirable. Typical situations include the following:

- *Backups*. On well-run systems, backups are performed on a regular basis.

- *Reminders*. You can use cron to send yourself mail every Tuesday to remind you of your staff meeting, every month to remind you to pay your rent, or even every year to remind you of your anniversary.

- *Data transmissions*. An example of a data transmission is a chain store transmitting its daily sales figures to the home office at a specific time each night.

- *Any repetitive task*. Almost anything you do repeatedly is a candidate for automatic execution with cron.

The Original cron System

The original cron system consists of two parts: a data file called crontab (cron *table*) and a program called cron. These elements are described in the following sections.

The crontab File

The crontab file (located in the /usr/lib directory) contains a list of the commands to be executed repeatedly and specifications regarding when each command is to be executed. Each line in the crontab file consists of six parts, separated by spaces or tabs. The first five parts specify the time when the command executes (the minute, hour, day of month, month, and day of week, respectively). The sixth element is the command to be executed.

The crontab file is a text file you can build with any text editor; however, the "old" scheme (still used in Berkeley versions of UNIX) enables only the system administrator to edit the crontab file. (The "new" scheme is discussed in the following section.) The examples throughout this section represent lines you might find in the crontab file.

In the first five parts, you can specify a number or an asterisk (*). An asterisk means *every possible value*. For example, an asterisk in the second field (hour) means *every hour*. In some contexts you may prefer to think of the asterisk as meaning *regardless of*; for example, when an asterisk is in the fifth field (day of week), you may understand the meaning more clearly as *regardless of the day of the week*. Consider the following example:

```
30 11 * * * who ¦ mail jim
```

This command mails a list of everyone on the system to the user Jim at 11:30 A.M. every day; literally, the command indicates that the command is to be executed at 30 minutes past 11:00 (on a 24-hour scale), every day of the month, every month, every day of the week.

For a second example, consider the following command that runs an accounting report early in the morning of the first day of each month:

```
5 3 1 * * monthly.report
```

This line specifies that the program `monthly.report` runs five minutes after 3:00 A.M. on the 1st day of the month, regardless of the month or day of the week.

Similarly, to print paychecks every Friday at 3:45 P.M., you may include the following line in `crontab`:

```
45 15 * * 5 paychecks¦lp
```

This command runs at 45 minutes after 3:00 P.M. (15:00 on a 24-hour clock), every Friday of every month (0 represents Sunday, 1 represents Monday, and so on).

Instead of a number or an asterisk, each of the first five parts can contain a list of numbers separated by commas (such as 3,8,12), a range of numbers separated by a dash (such as 6-12), or a combination (such as 3,5-10,14). For example, to run a program or command every 15 minutes during normal business hours, but not during lunch, the first five fields need the following information:

```
0,15,30,45 8-11,13-17 * * 1-5
```

This command executes at 0, 15, 30, and 45 minutes after the hour during the hours 8:00 A.M. through 11:00 A.M. and 1:00 P.M. through 5:00 P.M., on the days Monday through Friday.

To schedule new programs—and "unschedule" old programs—you simply edit the `crontab` file and add and delete appropriate lines.

The cron Program

The second part of the `cron` system is the `cron` program itself. This program starts automatically when the system boots, and it runs continuously, comparing the entries in the `crontab` file against the current time and date. When the time comes for a command to execute, the `cron` program gets the command started.

The following listing shows a sample `crontab` file from a small UNIX system:

```
0 4 * * * /bin/su uucpadm % /usr/lib/uucp/uudemon.admin > /dev/null
30 5 * * 1 /bin/su uucpadm % /usr/lib/uucp/uudemon.cleanu >/dev/null
30 5 * * 1 /bin/su root % /etc/cleanup.wk > /dev/null
3 3 * * 0 /bin/su root % /etc/clockupd.wk > /dev/null
03 * * * * /bin/su uucpadm -c "/usr/lib/uucp/uudemon.hour > /dev/null"
```

```
01 * * * * /bin/su uucpadm -c "/usr/lib/uucp/uudemon.poll > /dev/null"
14 18 * * * /usr/mark/Filecabinet/Reminders/daily
14 6 * * 0 /usr/mark/Filecabinet/Reminders/sunday.morning
31 3 * * 5 /bin/su root % /usr/mark/security/security ¦ mail mark
```

You really do not need to understand what purpose the individual commands in this example serve—you do not need to know, for example, what the uudemon.hour command does—but, by looking at the first five fields of each line, you should be able to determine when each command will execute. For example, cron executes the first command at 4:00 A.M. every morning (0 minutes after the 4th hour, every day of every month, regardless of the day of the week). The second command is performed at 5:30 A.M. on Mondays; the fourth command at 3:03 A.M. on Sundays.

The cron Command in System V

cron proved to be a tremendously useful facility, but in early versions of UNIX (prior to UNIX System V), most users were restricted from taking advantage of this facility because of two problems:

- Many programs run by cron performed important system functions, and system administrators couldn't risk users interfering with these programs by deleting or changing the associated lines in the crontab file.

- Programs run by cron were given root privileges, privileges normally restricted to the system administrator. If users were allowed to add any command to the crontab file, they could schedule commands to perform tasks not normally authorized.

These security problems could be managed only by restricting cron to the system administrator.

System V has eliminated these restrictions by replacing the single crontab file with many files—one for each user on the system. These individual files are no longer called crontab, but many users still think of them as "my crontab file," because collectively they serve exactly the same function as the older crontab file.

The simple change from a single crontab file to many crontab files solved the security problems in the following ways:

- Users can edit only their own crontab files, so the danger of these files interfering with each other or with the system administrator's crontab file no longer exists.

- Rather than executing all commands with root privileges, `cron` executes each user's commands with the same privileges normally afforded that user. Thus, users can use `cron` to perform only the same commands they are authorized to perform manually.

Under System V, each user has a personal crontab file. Each user's crontab file has the same name as his or her login name and is stored in the `/usr/lib/crontab` directory. For example, the path name of Jeff's crontab file is `/usr/lib/crontab/jeff`.

You cannot create your crontab file directly in the `/usr/lib/crontab` directory. Instead, you create your crontab file under any name you chose, in any directory, and use a command called `crontab` to install your file in the `/usr/lib/crontab` directory. (You may find it confusing to use a command called `crontab` to install your crontab file in the `crontab` directory.)

Suppose, for example, that Hillary uses a text editor to create a file called `auto.commands`, just as she does for any file. The file has the same format as the pre-System V `crontab` file, consisting of any number of lines, each made up of the six parts describing the command to be executed and the times to execute it. After creating the file, Hillary can install it as her `crontab` with the following command:

```
crontab auto.commands
```

In this example, the `crontab` command copies `auto.commands` to the `/usr/lib/crontab` directory and names the copy `hillary`. Later, if Hillary needs to change the contents of her `crontab`, she must edit her copy of the file (`auto.commands`) and then reexecute the `crontab` command, causing the new version of the file to replace the old in `/usr/lib/crontab`.

In fact, you can have several different files containing different combinations of commands, and you can install any of them as your official `crontab` by executing the `crontab` command with different file names. For example, Hillary may have one set of commands she wants executed when she is traveling on company business—perhaps in a file called `out.of.town`—and another set when she is spending time at the office in town—in a file called `in.town`. When she prepares to leave for a trip, Hillary uses the following command:

```
crontab out.of.town
```

This command copies the contents of the file `out.of.town` to `/usr/lib/crontab/hillary`. When Hillary returns, she use the following command to switch to the other set of commands:

```
crontab in.town
```

If Hillary decides to suspend her use of cron, she can type **crontab -r** to remove the file /usr/lib/crontab/hillary. She later can resume her use of cron by executing crontab with a file name.

Like at, cron has a set of files that the system administrator can configure to determine who is authorized to use cron:

- If the file cron.allow exists in the /usr/lib/cron directory, it contains a list of all users authorized to use cron. Users not listed may not use cron.

- If cron.allow does not exist, but the file cron.deny does, cron.deny contains a list of all users who are not authorized to use cron. Users not listed may use cron. If the file exists but is empty, all users may use cron.

- If neither file exists, only the system administrator (root) may use cron.

UNIX Print Spooling System

On a small UNIX system—with a single user, for example—you can access the printer directly to print documents. The special file /dev/lp represents the UNIX system printer, and you can send output to the printer simply by copying a file to /dev/lp, as follows:

```
cp memo /dev/lp
```

In this example, the cp command copies the file memo to the printer (/dev/lp).

Alternatively, you can redirect to the printer the output from a command, as shown in the following example:

```
who >/dev/lp
```

This command seems to be redirecting output to a file, but because the file /dev/lp is a special file representing the printer, UNIX actually sends the output to the printer.

Although this technique is adequate for small systems, it fails on larger systems for two reasons:

- If several users try to access the printer at the same time, their output may be intermixed on the printer—a few lines of one user's output may be followed by a few lines of another's.

- Accessing /dev/lp directly causes the terminal to be tied up until printing is complete. Because most programs that produce printed output don't need to interact with the user, tying up a terminal during printing is usually a needless waste of time.

Because of these problems, most UNIX versions do not provide direct access to /dev/lp for most users. Instead, users access the printer through a *print spooling system*, which manages the printer and supervises the details of printing documents for you.

System V Print Spooler

Under UNIX System V, the *print spooler* consists of two main parts. The first—the part you see—is the lp command. You can print a file by invoking the lp command, followed by the file or files to be printed:

```
lp sales.memo
```

This command causes the contents of the file sales.memo to print to the printer. You also can use the lp command at the end of a pipe to print the data produced by the pipe. To print a list of everyone on the system, for example, you can issue the following command:

```
who ¦ lp
```

The who command produces the list of users, which is sent to lp for printing.

The lp command does not actually print data; instead, it makes note of the file to be printed, or in the case of the pipeline command, copies the data to a temporary file and makes a note to print the file. The command prompt returns immediately, even though nothing has yet printed. Thus, the lp command does not actually print anything, but it enables you to request that a file be printed. Each use of lp is known as a *print request*.

The lp Command Name

lp is an abbreviation for *line printer*. During the early days of the development of UNIX, many computer centers owned line printers: machines the size of a small jukebox that print an entire line at a time, with 132 hammers striking a rotating drum or chain. Line printers are less common today, but the command name lp lingers on.

The second, hidden part of the print spooler is a program called lpsched (*line printer scheduler*). The lpsched program runs in the background at all times, never interacting directly with the user. lpsched is the program that accesses /dev/lp directly and attends to the details of printing a file.

This two-part scheme leads to two benefits:

- Because the actual printing is performed by the background program lpsched, not lp, the command prompt returns immediately, without waiting for printing to complete.

- Because a single program—lpsched—is responsible for printing the requested files, the program can ensure that one user's printout is complete before the next begins. Print requests are handled in an orderly, "first come, first served" fashion.

Daemons

Because lpsched executes apart from any terminal and seems to work by itself, it is sometimes known as the *print daemon*. Apparently the program reminded UNIX designers of a little gremlin inside the computer that attended to its own business by itself. Other programs that work in the background, such as cron, are also known as *daemons*.

The word *daemon* is a variant spelling of *demon* and is pronounced identically: DEE-muhn. Some users may say DAY-muhn, but they need to be kindly and gently shown a dictionary.

Large systems may have several printers available. Each printer is assigned a name by the system administrator. The name may indicate the printer's type (laser or dotmatrx), location (closet or mailroom), or may be a silly or famous name (mickey, minnie, goofy, and donald).

You can specify the name of the desired printer by using the -d option of the lp command:

```
lp -d goofy monthly.report
```

This command prints the file monthly.report on the printer named goofy. Other commands are available, mostly for use by the system administrator, to control the operation of the print spooler (see table 5.1 for a list of common print spooler commands available with UNIX System V).

Table 5.1
Print Spooler Control Commands

Command	Description
disable	Tells lpsched to stop printing on a particular printer. This command is useful when changing paper in a printer or performing maintenance. Users can continue to send requests to the printer, but nothing prints.
enable	Tells lpsched to resume printing on a particular printer
reject	Causes all new print requests for a printer to be rejected. All existing print requests, however, are honored. This command is useful when a printer is to be removed from the system, because it permits the printer to finish the work already requested.
accept	Enables new requests for a printer to be accepted
cancel	Interrupts a printout that is printing, or deletes an existing print request
lpstat	Lists information on existing print requests and the status of printers
lpadmin	Adds new printers, deletes printers, and changes the printer characteristics
lpshut	Shuts down the printer daemon lpsched
lpsched	Restarts the printer daemon

Other Print Spoolers

Many non-System V systems, most notably XENIX and UNIX variants based on Berkeley UNIX, use an alternate print spooler, lpr. Its use is almost identical to System V's lp command. For example, to print a directory listing on a XENIX system, you issue the following command:

```
ls ¦ lpr
```

The ls command produces a list of all the files in the current directory and sends that list to lpr for printing. Many of the options for lpr, however, are different from the options available with lp, and lp has a different set of tools. For example, on a version of UNIX based on AT&T's System V, you can request a list of all pending print requests with the lpstat command:

```
$ lpstat <Return>
laser-34013          mark          3482    Nov  6 21:39 on
laser
$
```

This output shows that the print spooler is currently managing a single print request. The print spooler has assigned the request an ID code of laser-34013. The print request was submitted by Mark on November 6, at 9:39 P.M., and consists of 3,482 bytes to be printed. The request is currently being printed on the printer called laser.

You can tell the print spooler to abandon this request with the cancel command:

```
cancel laser-34013
```

This command tells the print spooler to cancel the print request whose ID code is laser-34013.

On a Berkeley-based version of UNIX, you can display a list of pending print requests with the lpq (*line printer queue*) command:

```
$ lpq <Return>
Time        Rank  Owner  Job  Files        Total Size
21:57:03    1st   mark   867  /etc/passwd  14244 bytes
$
```

This output shows the same information as the lpstat command, except that if you are printing a file, lpq also shows the name of the file.

To cancel a print request on a Berkeley system, you use the lprm (*line printer remove*) command:

```
lprm 867
```

As with cancel, you must provide the print request's ID code, which is the job number in the fourth column.

Other UNIX Tools

UNIX includes a wide variety of useful tools. Almost every task you perform frequently has already caught the interest of a UNIX programmer, and the resulting tool resides today in UNIX's tool chest.

In many cases, a great deal of overlap exists in the various tools. Many simple operations, such as searching, pattern-matching, counting lines in a file, and so on, can be accomplished with different tools. Many times, a programmer realized that a tool existed to accomplish a particular task, but wanted to develop an easier or more powerful tool appropriate for a specific situation. Thus, different users may approach the same problem with different tools. Given a specific task, one user may use awk, another user may use sed, and yet another user may believe that a shell program best accomplishes the job. Although each of these tools—awk, sed, and the shell—has unique capabilities, these tools have many features and capabilities in common.

Few UNIX users ever learn to use all the tools available. Most users learn a useful subset and employ these tools to solve problems, even though in some cases another tool may be better. Learning a few tools well is more productive than learning a little about many tools.

The following list is a collection of tools useful in a variety of situations. For more information on these tools, consult a reference manual for your particular computer system or a book with a comprehensive command reference, such as Que's *Using UNIX*.

- cmp, comm, diff, and diff3

    These tools compare files and indicate where the files differ. They are useful for determining whether two files match or how one file differs from another. cmp, comm, and diff compare two files and display the differences in various formats. diff3 compares three files.

- compress and pack

    compress and pack are tools that greatly reduce the size of a file by analyzing the data within the files and determining a way to represent the data in less space. The packed or compressed file is much smaller than the original (reductions of 25 percent for pack and 45 percent for compress are typical).

    A file is unusable in its compressed or packed state, and you must issue the uncompress or unpack commands to return the file to its previous size and contents. These tools are useful whenever the size of a file is more important than ease of use. For example, files often are compressed before being transmitted over phone lines to cut long distance charges, and then uncompressed at the destination.

- cut and paste

  The cut command extracts parts of each line of a file. If each line of a file contains a customer's name, address, phone number, and yearly sales amount, for example, you can use cut to print only the name and sales amount, or name and phone number, or any other combination.

  The paste command performs the opposite function—it combines two files, pasting corresponding lines together. Thus, if one file contains 100 lines with customer names and another file contains 100 lines with the corresponding customer phone numbers, paste can combine them into a single file.

- grep, fgrep, and egrep

  This family of commands searches a set of files for one or more phrases or patterns. These commands can locate all files in which the phrase or pattern occurs, or can print all lines that contain a phrase or pattern. The name grep comes from a command available within the ed and vi editors that has the form: g/re/p. When you are editing a file, this command tells the editor to search the file globally (g) for a *regular expression* (re), or a pattern, and to print (p) each occurrence that it finds. grep performs a similar function.

  fgrep (*fast grep*) is the fastest but the least powerful: it can search only for specific words or phrases, not patterns. grep is slightly slower, but it can search for regular expressions (it can find, for example, all files with lines starting with an uppercase letter and ending in a period). egrep (*extended grep*) is the slowest, but it can search for more complex patterns and combinations of patterns.

- nl

  The nl (*number line*) command displays the contents of a file with line numbers on each line. It may be handy to use with technical papers.

- od

  The od (*octal dump*) command enables a file to be viewed as a series of octal or hex bytes or groups of bytes. Programmers find this technique especially handy when exploring the contents of a binary data file, which cannot be listed on-screen with a simple cat command.

- pg (AT&T UNIX) and more (Berkeley UNIX)

  These tools enable you to view a file one screen at a time. After displaying 23 lines from the file, these programs wait for you to press <Return> and then display the next 23 lines.

- split

  This tool splits a large file into smaller pieces and is especially useful for editing a large file. Most editors, such as vi, limit the size of files that can be edited. split enables you to break the program into editable pieces, which you later can recombine using cat.

- stty

  The stty (*set terminal*) command enables you to control various parameters of your terminal. This command is used most often by the system administrator, but you can use some of the features of stty to customize the way your terminal works. For example, perhaps you just acquired a new terminal on which you normally would press <Delete> to interrupt a command; however, you are used to working on a different terminal on which you press <Ctrl-C> to interrupt a command. Being a creature of habit, you can tell UNIX that you want to use <Ctrl-C> as your interrupt key by typing:

  stty intr "^c"

  (When entering the stty command, you actually type a caret (^) and then type c. But later, to interrupt a command, you press and hold <Ctrl> while you press c.)

- tr

  The tr (*translate*) command copies one file to another, translating one type of character to another. For example, tr can translate the contents of a file from uppercase to lowercase.

- units

  The units command serves as an on-line conversion table for all kinds of measurements. It converts feet to meters, days to seconds, light-years to furlongs, and dollars to pesos. Almost any imaginable conversion is possible.

- wc

  The wc (*word count*) command counts the number of characters, words, and lines in one or more files. If you specify multiple files, wc provides an individual count for each file and totals for the group.

- sort

  The sort command arranges a file in alphabetical or numerical order. It has many options that describe how the data in the file should be interpreted for the purposes of rearranging it in order.

- bc

  This tool performs calculations and is intended to take the place of a desk calculator.

- cal

  You can use the cal command to print a calendar for any month or year.

- calendar

  The calendar command provides a simple reminder service to help you remember upcoming appointments, birthdays, and such.

Chapter Summary

UNIX includes a variety of commands for accomplishing common tasks. You learned about many important commands that manipulate files and directories in Chapter 3, and you learned about the shell—one of the most important tools—in Chapter 4. In this chapter you learned about the tools for delayed and repeated execution: batch, at, and cron. You also learned about the UNIX print spooler, the commands to submit a print request (lp for System V and lpr for Berkeley), and commands to display and remove print requests (lpstat and cancel for System V and lpq and lprm for Berkeley).

Finally, you learned to recognize many of the tools commonly used by UNIX users, such as grep, compress, diff, and others.

You can obtain more information on these and other tools from your computer's user reference guide, or from a UNIX book with a command reference, such as Que's *Using UNIX*.

6

Text Processing in the UNIX Environment

U NIX is a general purpose operating system, not specifically designed for any one task, but excelling in the area of *text processing*, also called *word processing*. Text processing includes operations such as entering and editing text and formatting documents.

This facility with text processing is understandable because the young operating system was first applied to preparing patents in the Bell Labs Patent Department in the early 1970s. As the patent office staff's text handling requirements grew, researchers at Bell Labs developed new tools to meet the needs of the staff. By the time UNIX was released outside Bell Labs, it contained the most sophisticated facilities available for producing documents on small computers.

Although many popular PC word processing programs (such as WordStar and WordPerfect) are available through UNIX, UNIX was doing sophisticated text processing long before these programs were developed. The tools developed for the patent office were so powerful that they are still used today.

Producing a written document involves two distinct tasks: entering the text of the document and formatting the text. Many popular word processing programs now combine the two tasks into a single integrated operation, but earlier systems generally kept the two tasks discrete. UNIX uses separate programs to perform each task: a *text editor* to enter and edit text and a *formatter* to format a document for printing.

179

In this chapter, you learn about the tools that UNIX provides to accomplish these tasks. Text editors, such as `ed`, `vi`, and Emacs, enable you to create and edit documents. You learn about the function of a text formatter and explore the UNIX text formatters, such as `nroff`, `troff`, `tbl`, `pic`, and `eqn`. You also learn about other tools that enable you to manipulate text in various ways.

Text Editing

Almost all computer users create and edit files that contain text. Whether preparing letters, memos, and reports or writing programs, you need to work with text files.

Many programs or groups of programs are available to assist you in this task. These programs can be divided into three types of systems, from the most complex to the simplest:

- *Desktop publishing systems.* Magazine publishers and advertising companies use these sophisticated systems to design, lay out, and produce printed material that includes text, graphics, and photographs. In most cases, you can see the layout of the document on-screen as you construct it. The files created contain information on page layout, graphics, and text. These systems often require powerful computers.

- *Word processing programs.* These programs enable you to enter and edit text, specifying many attributes of the text and its arrangement on the page, including fonts, point sizes, and margins. Many are nearly as sophisticated as desktop publishing systems. Many popular PC word processing programs, such as WordPerfect and WordStar, are also available for UNIX.

- *Text editors.* These programs, usually much smaller and simpler than desktop publishing systems or word processing programs, create and modify pure text files—that is, files that contain only text, with no additional information concerning fonts or page layout. These programs are most commonly used with UNIX and are the focus of this chapter. Traditionally, UNIX has used text editors rather than word processing programs because text editors do not require powerful terminals and computers. (See table 6.1 for a list of some UNIX text editors that can perform various editing functions.)

Table 6.1
UNIX Text Editors

Text Editor	Description
ed	The original UNIX text editor; supplied with all UNIX systems
sed	The UNIX stream editor; used for special-purpose editing tasks
ex	A souped-up version of ed; written at Berkeley
vi	A screen-oriented editor; written at Berkeley
Emacs	A public domain full-screen editor; not supplied with the normal distribution of UNIX. You must purchase an editor such as Emacs separately.

The ed Text Editor

The ed editor is the original UNIX editor, written at Bell Labs. It was developed when CRTs (screens) were not as universal as they are today and when many users worked on printer terminals. Many of the terminals were made by Teletype Corporation and looked like a large typewriter with a roll of paper towels attached to the back. The output produced by the computer, as well as the input that you typed on the keyboard, was printed on the roll of paper. To be useful in the early days of UNIX, ed had to work on any kind of terminal, including the printer terminals.

ed works quite differently from the screen-oriented editors developed later. To enter and edit text with ed, you enter a series of commands that tell ed what to do and with which lines to work. Today's screen-oriented text editors always display some portion of the file. In screen-oriented editors, as you edit the file, the screen reflects the changes to the file, and the text is in an editing buffer in the system's memory. With ed, however, you must print some portion of the file to see the file's current condition.

Although ed seems cumbersome by today's standards, it remains a useful UNIX tool in some situations. It works on any terminal, even printer terminals. This capability can be important to a system administrator trying to configure a terminal that doesn't work correctly with other editors. ed is small, so it fits easily on any system or floppy diskette. Most importantly, the ed commands form a substructure for most of the other UNIX editors, including the most widely used UNIX editor, vi.

Introducing Basic ed Commands

You can invoke ed by simply typing ed, followed by the name of the file you want to edit; for example:

ed memo

If the file (memo in this case) exists, ed enables you to edit, or modify, the file; if the file does not exist, ed enables you to create it.

After you invoke ed, you carry on a conversation with ed, in a manner quite similar to the way in which you interact with the shell. You type commands, some of which are discussed in the following sections, and in response, ed adds, deletes, or modifies text in accordance with your commands. Certain commands cause ed to respond in some way; for example, ed might respond to certain commands by displaying the changes it made to your text in accordance with your commands.

ed has its own set of commands, which are not the same commands you learned to use within the UNIX shell. ed commands usually consist of just one letter, and most may be preceded by one or two line numbers that indicate the lines of the current text file to be changed. To display lines 20 through 35, for example, you use the p command:

20,35p

(p stands for *print*, a throwback to the old terminals on which *displaying* meant *printing*.) To delete these same lines, use the d (*delete*) command:

20,35d

ed automatically renumbers the remaining lines—the lines before line 20 and after line 35—so that the line that was line 36 becomes line 20.

If you want to affect only a single line, you enter just one line number. To delete line 14, for example, you type

14d

You can use several special characters in place of line numbers. A dollar sign ($), for example, represents the last line of the file. Thus, to delete from the 66th line to the end of the file, you type

66,$d

The Current Line

The ed editor uses a concept called the *current line* to simplify editing. Whenever you perform an operation on a line, ed makes note of the line number associated with that line and considers that line to be the current line. If the next command you type references the same line, you can omit the line number, and ed performs the command on the current line.

For example, suppose that you want to look at line 29; you type

29p

ed displays line 29 and now considers line 29 to be the current line. If you type

d

ed deletes the current line, line 29.

You use the a (*append*) command to add new text to the file. After you issue the a command, all lines you type thereafter are entered into the document as text until you type a period on a line by itself. Thus, to add three lines to the file after line 17, follow this format:

```
17a <Return>
January sales: 23000 <Return>
February sales: 67000 <Return>
March sales: 1000 <Return>
. <Return>
```

Searching and Substituting with ed

ed includes powerful searching and substitution commands. You perform a search by typing a slash (/) followed by the phrase for which you want to search. To search for the next occurrence of cats and dogs in your text file, for example, you type the following command:

/cats and dogs

A question mark (?) in place of the slash causes a backward search:

?cats and dogs

The s command performs substitutions. You use the following format:

lines **s**/*old phrase*/*new phrase*/

To change cat to dog on lines 40 through 99, for example, you can issue the following command:

`40,99s/cat/dog/`

The substitute command normally changes only the first occurrence of the search phrase on each line. Thus, the preceding substitute command changes the line

`He found cats here and cats there`

to

`He found dogs here and cats there`

If, however, you want to change the phrase every time it occurs on a line, you add a g (*global*) to the end of the command, as shown in the following example:

`40,99s/cat/dog/g`

Searching for Regular Expressions with ed

Besides searching for simple words or phrases, ed can perform much more complex searches, including searches for *regular expressions*—patterns that specify a complex search phrase. You also can use regular expressions with other UNIX commands that perform searching, such as sed, grep, and awk.

Suppose, for example, that you want to invoke a complex search such as for 3 at the end of a line or for a word beginning with th and ending in x. Regular expressions enable you to search for such phrases by using punctuation characters to specify the characteristics of the phrase you want to find. Some common regular expression characters follow:

- *Caret* (^). The caret represents the beginning of a line. When ^ is the first character in your search phrase, ed finds the phrase only if the phrase is at the beginning of the line. Thus, the command /^6 finds the next line that begins with 6.

  You also can use regular expressions in the search portion of a substitution command. If you type **20,50s/^cat/dog/**, for example, ed searches lines 20 through 50 for lines that begin with cat and changes cat to dog.

Note that ed is case-sensitive—that is, uppercase letters are distinct from lowercase letters. If you enter a substitute command that tells ed to change cat to dog, it does not change Cat to Dog.

- *Dollar sign* ($). The dollar sign represents the end of a line. You enter it as the last character of a search phrase when you want to find the phrase at the end of a line. The command /Que$, for example, finds a line that ends in Que.

  You can combine the caret and dollar sign in the same search phrase. The command /^open$, for example, finds a line that contains only the word open. It does not find a line that starts with open and ends in open.

  If a caret or dollar sign is out of place in the phrase, ed searches for it as a literal caret or dollar sign. Thus, the command /$100 searches for the phrase $100. The dollar sign represents the end of a line only when it is the last character of the search phrase.

- *Period* (.). The period represents any character. Searching for c.t finds the next instance of c and t separated by exactly one character. You can use any number of periods in an expression; th..4.8 searches for th followed by any two characters, followed by 4, any character, and then 8.

- *Brackets* ([ ]). A selection of characters surrounded by brackets represents a single character that must be one of the characters in the brackets. Searching for the pattern c[aou]t, for example, locates any word in which c and t are separated by a, o, or u. (In this case, the words cat, cot, cut, caterpillar, cutter, and cutlass qualify.) You also can specify ranges, so that 19[89][0-9] finds 19, followed by 8 or 9, followed by any digit 0 through 9.

- *Asterisk* (*). Always used with another character, the asterisk indicates that any number of the character that precedes it may occur at that position. In the search phrase lo*se, for example, the combination o* means "any number of o's." Thus, ed finds any occurrence of l and se separated by any number of o's. Zero o's is also considered acceptable, so lo*se also finds lse.

- *Backslash* (\). The backslash negates the special meaning of any regular expression character. This character is useful when the desired phrase actually contains a period, dollar sign, asterisk, or other special character. Searching for the pattern 6.2, for example, finds any occurrence of 6 and 2 separated by any one character. Searching for 6\.2, however, finds only the phrase 6.2.

Exiting ed

After you finish editing a document, you must write the new version of the document from the buffer to the file using the w (*write*) command. You then can exit ed with the q (*quit*) command.

If you attempt to exit ed without writing the buffer to the file (that is, without saving your changes), ed signals an error. This feature is designed to protect you against exiting ed if you have forgotten to save your changes. Occasionally, however, you actually may want to exit ed without saving—perhaps you were experimenting with a different arrangement of text within a report, but after seeing the new arrangement, you decide to leave the document as it was. The Q command enables you to exit ed, even though the changes you made during the editing session will be lost.

Table 6.2 summarizes the most commonly used ed commands.

Table 6.2
Common ed Commands

Command	Action
a (append)	Adds text after the specified line. 201a adds text after line 201. If no line number is specified, adds text after current line. Append command terminates when you type a period on a line by itself.
d (delete)	Deletes lines
i (insert)	Like a, except that text is inserted before the line specified (or, if no line number is specified, before the current line). 1i inserts text before the first line.
p (print)	Prints one or more lines to the screen
q (quit)	Exits ed
Q (quit without saving)	Exits ed even if the current changes have not been saved
s (substitute)	Enables a phrase or pattern on one or more lines to be changed to a different phrase
t (transfer)	Copies lines from one place in a document to another
w (write)	Writes the buffer's contents to the disk file

ed has many more features and capabilities than are listed here, but this chapter is intended to present an overview rather than a complete reference. If you want more information, consult your UNIX documentation or a book that covers ed in greater detail, such as Que's *Using UNIX*.

The vi Text Editor

The most common editor used today is the vi (*visual*) editor, developed at the University of California at Berkeley. Originally, vi was part of only Berkeley versions of UNIX, but it has become so popular that AT&T has adopted it for UNIX System V. Unlike the line-oriented ed, vi is a screen-oriented editor.

To many users, especially people experienced with editors in other environments, the vi editor is unconventional. A vi manual lists hundreds of commands, many of which may seem unusual to users experienced in other environments. vi was designed with specific goals in mind, however, and it is actually quite well suited to its purpose, providing power and portability for the UNIX user.

A good editor is simple enough for the novice, yet provides power and efficiency for the experienced user. To some extent, these goals diametrically oppose each other—user-friendly menus seem cumbersome to the experienced user, and terse, efficient commands seem obtuse to the beginner. Vendors therefore frequently provide two ways to perform an operation: a simple method for beginners and a fast one for advanced users.

vi takes a strong position in this battle: it was designed not for the occasional user but for the power user who needs an editor for daily use. Thus vi offers dozens of commands, many of which duplicate the functionality of other commands. For example, vi provides many different ways to delete text. You certainly could get by if you learn only a few of these commands, but each of these commands is faster—that is, requires fewer keystrokes—in certain situations. The more commands you learn, the faster you can perform editing tasks. Experienced users, who learn a large number of vi commands, can perform editing tasks more rapidly with vi than with almost any other text editor.

vi's portability is another important feature. Different terminals incorporate many different combinations of features, including different screen sizes and keyboard layouts. The designers of vi wanted to design vi so that it could be used from almost any of the hundreds of different terminals available. They succeeded, but many facets of vi can be understood only in light of the designers' desire to adapt vi for almost any terminal.

Understanding vi Basics

In the past, screen-oriented text editors were most often written for specific terminals and operating systems. The designers of those operating systems assumed that a standard screen and keyboard for that type of system was present. For example, all text editors (and word processing programs, for that matter) written for the IBM PC and its clones could assume the existence of arrow keys, at least ten function keys, and special keys such as Home, End, Delete, and so on. The situation for a DEC VT-100 on a VAX or an IBM 3270 on a mainframe is similar.

The designers of vi, however, faced a serious problem: because they wanted vi to work with virtually any terminal and because the terminals then available were so diverse, they could make few assumptions about the layout of the keyboard or the kinds of keys the terminal would have. The designers attempted to write a text editor that would work with any keyboard containing keys for the letters, digits, and ASCII punctuation.

They succeeded. You can indeed use vi from any terminal, regardless of the terminal's capabilities or keyboard configuration. vi consults a database of terminal capabilities and determines the capabilities and keyboard arrangement of your terminal (see Chapter 8, "Programming Languages and UNIX Software Development," for information about the termcap and terminfo databases). This information enables vi to use your terminal in the most efficient manner possible.

Most text editors and word processing programs in other environments rely on function keys to perform editing operations. To delete a paragraph in a particular text editor, for example, you might use the arrow keys to move the cursor to that paragraph, and you press F4. Some terminals, however, do not have an F4 key, and a few (mostly older) terminals don't even have arrow keys. Some users argued that vi could be forgiven for not working with such terminals, but the designers of vi were adamant: vi had to work with *all* terminals.

To solve these problems, vi's designers introduced the concept of *modes*. vi is always in one of two modes:

- *Text-entry mode*. In text-entry mode, the keys on the keyboard are used to enter text. Typing **x** enters x into the file.

- *Command mode*. In command mode, each key on the keyboard takes on an alternate meaning; in effect, every key becomes a function key. Thus, typing **x** in command mode does not enter x into the file; instead, it executes the x command, which deletes a character.

Knowing which mode is active is vitally important because the result of pressing a key always differs in the two modes. vi can help; it displays the current mode in the lower right corner on-screen if you configure it to do so, as described in "Setting vi Options," further in this chapter.

To create or edit a file, use the vi command with the name of the file. Consider this example:

vi dec.ind

If the file dec.ind exists, vi assumes you want to edit it and displays the first 23 lines of the file (see fig. 6.1).

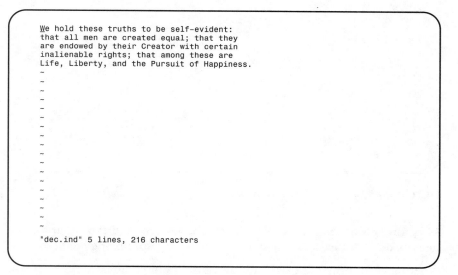

Fig. 6.1. *The first 23 lines of* dec.ind.

If the file does not contain enough lines to fill the screen, vi displays a tilde (~) to denote each unused line. The 24th line on-screen is reserved for editor communications and dialog. In this example, the last line shows the name of the file, dec.ind (Declaration of Independence) and the number of lines (5) and characters (216) in the file.

Note that these examples show a cursor that looks like an underline. The cursor on your terminal may be quite different, depending on your terminal. Many terminals use cursors that look like boxes. Some terminals use a blinking cursor; others use a solid (nonblinking) cursor. Many terminals enable you to select the appearance of the cursor through some type of terminal setup procedure (see the owner's manual associated with your terminal).

If the file you specify does not already exist, vi assumes that you want to create it and displays a (mostly) blank screen. For example, if you type **vi report**, but report does not exist, vi displays the screen shown in figure 6.2.

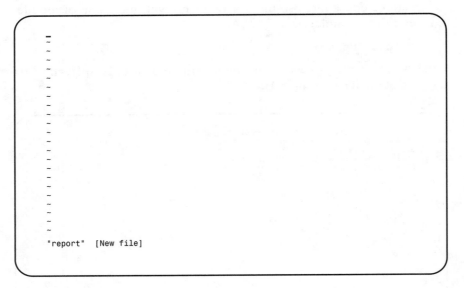

Fig. 6.2. *A blank screen for creating a new file.*

As before, tildes indicate unused lines. The last line indicates that the file report does not exist and that a new file is therefore being created.

Whether or not the file exists, vi always starts in command mode. If you want to enter text, your first command needs to switch to text-entry mode. Commands that switch vi from one mode to the other are discussed further in this chapter (see "Entering Text with vi").

Like ed, vi does not directly modify the file as it is being edited. Instead, vi makes a temporary copy of the file; this temporary copy is called the *edit buffer*. When you exit vi, it copies the contents of the buffer back to the file.

This approach has two important advantages:

- The text in the editing buffer is arranged in a form more convenient for vi. The difference is completely hidden from the user, but the buffer enables vi to work more efficiently.

- After making some changes, you may decide to keep the original file and discard the changes. When leaving vi, you can tell vi not to copy the contents of the editing buffer to the file, thus leaving the file in its original condition.

Introducing the Basic vi Commands

When vi is in command mode, every key on the keyboard represents a function to be performed. To advance the cursor one word, for example, you use the w command. You can precede most commands with a number to indicate how many elements (words, characters, lines, and so on, depending on the command) you want to affect. 16w, for example, advances the cursor 16 words.

In command mode, vi does not display commands on-screen as you type them; rather, you see the effect of the command. The x command, for example, deletes the character at the cursor's location without displaying x on-screen.

If you type a number before the command, you do not see the effect until you press the command letter. If you want to delete 40 characters, you enter the command 40x. As you type **4** and **0**, nothing seems to happen, but when you press the **x**, vi deletes 40 characters.

A few commands require more than one keystroke. The command z., for example, causes the line on which the cursor is currently located to become the middle line on-screen.

The edit buffer is just one instance of a buffer. You can think of a buffer as a temporary storage area where vi keeps text. Within the edit buffer, vi keeps a copy of the text from the file you are editing; however, vi has other buffers, used for storing other pieces of text. Throughout this chapter, you learn how to use other buffers to accomplish various editing tasks.

Moving within the Buffer

vi offers many ways to move the cursor within the buffer and view different portions of the buffer. A common operation is to move the cursor a few characters up, down, left, or right. This operation seemingly needs no explanation—you use the arrow keys, right? Wrong! vi instead uses h, j, k, and l.

At first glance (and maybe second), this scheme seems to be crazy, but two very good reasons exist for moving the cursor with these keys rather than the arrow keys:

- Although rare, some terminals still do not have arrow keys.

- More importantly, these keys are on the keyboard's home row, accessible by the three most powerful fingers of your right hand— an excellent example of vi's orientation toward the power user. Users accustomed to these keys can zip quickly around a buffer because they do not have to lift their hands from the keyboard to move the cursor. On most keyboards, the arrow keys are on the side, sometimes in inconvenient locations and often in strange configurations.

Most terminals do have arrow keys, and in fact, if the system has been configured correctly, the arrow keys move the cursor. (If the system has not been configured correctly, the arrow keys probably won't do anything.) Beginners generally appreciate the arrow keys, but if you expect to use vi regularly, do yourself a service and learn to use h, j, k, and l.

A plethora of other commands are available for moving within the buffer (see table 6.3 for a representative selection).

As with almost all vi commands, you can precede most of these commands with a number. In some cases, however, the number does not change the command. After all, what's the difference between going to the beginning of the line once or four times?

Table 6.3
Selected vi Cursor Movement Commands

Command	Cursor Action
h	Moves left one space
j	Moves down one line
k	Moves up one line
l	Moves right one space
\<Space\>	Moves right one space (same as l)
\<Backspace\>	Moves left one space (same as h)
w	Goes to beginning of following word
e	Goes to end of following word
b	Goes to beginning of preceding word
\<Ctrl-D\>	Scrolls down one-half screen
\<Ctrl-U\>	Scrolls up one-half screen
\<Ctrl-F\>	Scrolls forward one full screen
\<Ctrl-B\>	Scrolls backward one full screen
0	Goes to beginning of line
$	Goes to end of line
\<Return\>	Goes to beginning of following line

Command	Cursor Action
–	Goes to beginning of preceding line
H	Goes to top of screen
M	Goes to middle of screen
L	Goes to bottom (last line) of screen

In addition to the commands shown here, vi includes commands to go to the following or preceding sentence, paragraph, or section. (You configure what constitutes a section, although this technique is beyond the scope of this book. See your computer reference manual for details.)

vi also has a command that enables you to move the cursor directly to a specific line number: G. This command is unusual, however, because instead of preceding it with the number of elements you want to affect, you precede the command with the line number to which you want to move the cursor. For example, the command 145G moves the cursor directly to line 145.

As illustrated in table 6.3, a great deal of duplication exists in vi commands. For example, using only the four basic cursor-movement commands, h, j, k, and l, you can move the cursor to any location in the buffer; however, vi provides dozens of commands for moving the cursor in different ways. When moving the cursor across small distances, you may find h, j, k, and l convenient; when editing the wording within a sentence, w and b may be more convenient; when reviewing large sections of a document, <Ctrl-F> and <Ctrl-B> may seem to be the most flexible method. vi provides many different commands, with hopes that a knowledgeable user can perform almost any task with a minimum of keystrokes.

While the large number of commands can be intimidating, remember that you can use vi effectively with only a fraction of the available commands. Many beginning users select a handful of useful commands and master them before learning new commands. Most vi users never learn all vi commands.

Entering Text with vi

To add text to a document, you have to switch vi to text-entry mode. Upon switching from command mode to text-entry mode, the keys no longer execute vi commands; they simply become keys for entering text. Several commands enable you to switch vi to text-entry mode.

Consider the i (*insert*) command, for example. When you press i while in command mode, vi switches from command mode to text-entry mode. As you type text, the text is inserted into the document. When you finish typing, you press <Esc> to switch vi back to command mode.

Consider the following line from a buffer being edited in vi:

```
The quick fox jumps over the lazy dog.
```

The cursor is currently positioned on the f in fox. If you press i, nothing seems to happen, but vi has switched from command mode to text-entry mode. If you then type **brown** and press <Space>, vi inserts this text—character by character—before the f. When you are done, press <Esc>.

```
The quick brown_fox jumps over the lazy dog.
```

Notice that when you press <Esc>, the cursor backs up one character, to the space.

In this example, you insert only one word, but you can type any amount of text. Each time you press <Return>, vi inserts a new, blank line on which you can type, continually making room for additional text.

Remembering which mode—command or text-entry—vi is in is important because the keys function differently according to the mode. You have the option to display the current mode, which can be helpful to beginners (see "Setting vi Options," discussed further in this chapter). Experienced users find that the notion of modes becomes so familiar that they rarely lose track of which mode is in effect.

Note that when you are not sure which mode you are in, pressing <Esc> always returns vi to a known point. In text-entry mode, <Esc> switches vi to command mode. In command mode, <Esc> does nothing. Thus, after you press <Esc>, vi is always in command mode.

Many commands switch vi from command mode to text-entry mode (see table 6.4). These commands differ only in terms of where vi inserts the text you type.

Table 6.4
Commands for Switching to Text-Entry Mode

Key	Where vi Inserts Text
i (insert)	Before the cursor
a (append)	After the cursor

Key	Where vi *Inserts Text*
o (open)	At the beginning of a new line opened (inserted) below the current line
O (open)	At the beginning of a new line opened (inserted) above the current line
A (append line)	At the end of the current line
I (insert line)	At the beginning of the current line

Regardless of the key you use to switch to text-entry mode, the following rules apply:

- You can type as much text as necessary. Pressing <Return> always opens another blank line to make room for more text.

- vi switches back to command mode when you press <Esc>.

Again, notice the redundancy in vi commands. You can duplicate the A command, for example, with two other commands: $ (*go to end of line*) and a (*append text*). The $a combination requires two keystrokes, whereas A requires just one (albeit a shifted key). The designers of vi seem to have taken the attitude that whenever a common operation requires two or more keystrokes, a new command that requires just one keystroke should be added, if possible. Again, beginning users can easily get by with a small subset of the available commands, learning new commands later as their proficiency increases.

Using Markers

You can set as many as 26 *markers* within a buffer. Markers serve much like bookmarks, keeping your place in a document and enabling you to return to that same place later. You can use them much as you might use Post-it notes to mark pages of interest in a book.

As an example, suppose that you are editing a document, and something you read in the middle of the document reminds you of a change you need to make at the end of the document. You might set a marker at your current position and then move to the end of the buffer to make your changes. After you make your changes, you can return to your original position in the middle of the document by commanding vi to return to the marker you set.

You can set as many as 26 markers, named a through z, and tell vi to return to any marker at any time.

To set a marker at the current cursor position, press m and then press a marker letter (any letter). To return to the marker later, press the apostrophe (') and then the marker letter.

Markers are stored in one of vi's temporary internal bookkeeping areas and are not stored with the file on-disk. You therefore lose all markers when you exit vi.

Although markers are useful simply as a means to mark a location and return to it later, they are even more powerful when coupled with other commands, such as the delete commands described next.

Deleting Text in vi

The most basic commands for deleting text are x (*delete a character*) and dd (*delete a line*). You can precede either command with a number to indicate how many characters or lines you want to delete.

Even more powerful is the d command, which provides a versatile means for deleting pieces of text. After pressing d, you enter a single command to move the cursor. vi deletes everything from the previous cursor position to the new cursor position. The w command, for example, moves the cursor ahead one word; therefore, dw deletes the next word. You can include a number, of course, so that 12dw deletes the next 12 words.

Similarly, the command 20G tells vi to go to line 20, and d20G deletes all text from the current line through line 20. Thus, if you issue this command when the cursor is on line 50, vi deletes all text from line 50 back to line 20.

Markers are extremely useful with the delete command. You can move the cursor to the first (or last) line you want to delete, set a marker, move the cursor to the other end of the text you want to delete, and then type **d'a**, where a is the marker letter you have set. vi deletes from the current cursor position to the marker.

See table 6.5 for a list of some of the possible vi deletion combinations.

Table 6.5
Selected Deletion Commands

Command	Effect
x	Deletes a character
dd	Deletes a line
dw	Deletes a word
d0	Deletes to the beginning of the line
d$	Deletes to the end of the line
D	Shortcut for d$
dnG	Deletes to line n
d'x	Deletes to marker letter x
d/$word$<Return>	Finds the next occurrence of a word you specify, and deletes to that point
dL	Deletes to the bottom (last line) of the screen
dH	Deletes to the top of the screen
dM	Deletes to the middle of the screen

Modifying Text in `vi`

Many `vi` commands enable you to replace existing text with new text. In most cases, when you invoke one of these commands, two distinct operations take place: `vi` deletes the old text; then it switches to text-entry mode to enable you to enter new text in its place.

Consider the S (*substitute line*) command, for example. When you press **S**, `vi` deletes all characters on the current line, leaving a blank line. `vi` then switches to text-entry mode, enabling you to type a new line of text. As always, <Esc> exits text-entry mode. Thus, S enables you to substitute a new line for an existing line.

Note that you are not restricted to replacing the line with a single line. After you are in text-entry mode, you can type as many lines as you want. Each time you press <Return>, a new blank line opens. Thus, you can replace one line with any number of lines.

You can precede the S command with a number, in which case vi replaces the specified number of lines. 7S, for example, causes the next seven lines to be replaced by a single blank line. You then can enter as many lines as you want; you need not enter exactly seven lines.

The s (*substitute character*) command works similarly for characters and is commonly combined with numbers. Suppose, for example, that a line in vi contains the following text:

```
As we skipped merrily along
```

Typing **15s** tells vi to delete 15 characters and switch to text-entry mode. The text vi displays on-screen is somewhat unusual, however:

```
As we skipped merril$ along
```

Rather than deleting the text, vi places a dollar sign on the last character you want to delete, enabling you to see the old text as you enter new text. (The real reason is rarely a consideration today. The designers of vi didn't want to force slow terminals to perform the terminal I/O necessary to redisplay the line with the text removed.) As always, you can enter as much text as required; you need not enter exactly 15 characters. If you enter fewer than 15 characters, pressing <Esc> causes vi to remove from the screen the characters not overtyped. If you enter more than 15 characters, vi makes room for each additional character as usual in text-entry mode.

The c (*change*) command is often easier to use. Like s, it enables you to change one piece of text to another, but its format is similar to the d command. You always follow c with a single command for moving the cursor. Everything between the cursor and the specified location is deleted, and vi switches to text-entry mode. For example, w moves ahead one word, so cw changes one word. Again, you can precede the command with a number; for example, 5cw changes the next 5 words. As with the substitute command, any amount of text, from one character (or no characters) to many pages, can replace the text being changed.

Table 6.6 shows just a few of the combinations possible with the c command.

Table 6.6
Selected Change Commands

Command	Text Changed
cw	Word
c0	From current position to the beginning of the line
c$	From current position to the end of the line
cnG	From current position to line *n*
c'x	From current position to marker *x*
c/word<Return>	Finds the next occurrence of the word you specify, and changes to that point
cL	Current line to the bottom (last line) of the screen
cH	Current line to the top of the screen
cM	Current line to the middle of the screen

You can use two other commands to change text:

- The r (*replace character*) command replaces a single character. When you press **r**, vi displays a dollar sign on top of the current character and waits for you to press another key, which replaces the existing character. Because you can enter only a single character, you do not have to press <Esc> to exit text-entry mode.

- The R (*replace text*) command overtypes any amount of text. When you press **R**, nothing seems to happen, but vi enters a unique version of text-entry mode in which each character typed replaces the existing character. As usual, you press <Esc> to switch back to command mode. This mode is similar to the overtype mode available in many word processing programs.

Moving and Copying Text in vi

To move text from place to place in a document, vi uses the traditional *cut-and-paste* (in vi, *delete-and-put*) strategy. You first *cut*, or delete, the text you want to move and then specify another location in the buffer where you want to *paste*, or *put*, the text.

To cut text, you use any of the regular delete commands. When you delete text, vi moves the text from the document to an internal storage area called the *unnamed buffer*, where it is kept available in case you want to put it elsewhere in the document. (Do not confuse the unnamed buffer, which stores cut text, with the editing buffer, which stores the current contents of the file. vi has many buffers.)

The paste operation simply involves positioning the cursor elsewhere in the edit buffer and pressing **p** (*put*). vi copies the text from the unnamed buffer into the edit buffer at that position. vi also leaves the text in the unnamed buffer, enabling you to execute several put operations, using the same text in different places in the edit buffer. Simply move the cursor elsewhere and press **p** again.

Figure 6.3 illustrates a delete-and-put operation. To move three lines, you position the cursor on the first line to be moved, and type **3dd**. This command deletes three lines from the edit buffer, but places those three lines in the unnamed buffer. To insert those lines in a different location, move the cursor to a different location in the document and press **p**. vi copies the 3 lines of text from the unnamed buffer to the edit buffer at the cursor's current location.

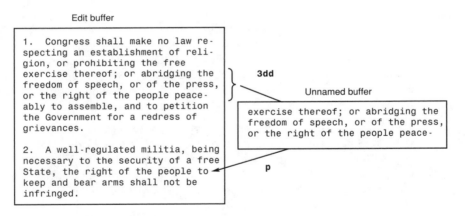

Fig. 6.3. *A delete-and-put operation in* vi.

Copying text from one place to another is a similar operation, except you do not remove the text from its current location. You use a series of commands called *yank* to copy text from the edit buffer into the unnamed buffer without deleting it. For every command that starts with d or D, an equivalent command exists that starts with y or Y.

To copy three lines, for example, you position the cursor on the first of the three lines and type **3yy**. This command is analogous to the delete command 3dd, which deletes three lines. Like the delete command, 3yy copies three lines to the unnamed buffer, but it also leaves them in the file. You then can move the cursor elsewhere in the document and press **p**, which copies the contents of the unnamed buffer into the edit buffer at the cursor location.

Note that each yank or delete operation overwrites the contents of the unnamed buffer. Thus, make sure you use a single command to yank or delete all the text you want to copy or move. To move three lines, for example, you must delete them with 3dd. Trying to delete the first two with 2dd and then the third with dd leaves only the last line in the unnamed buffer. Fortunately, the yank and delete commands are so comprehensive that you can almost always find one command to yank or delete the desired portion.

In addition to the unnamed buffer, 26 named buffers exist that you can use for moving and copying text, although you must press additional keys to use these buffers. Thus, you can simultaneously use up to 27 chunks of text (26 named buffers plus 1 unnamed buffer) for delete/yank and put operations. For information about the named buffers, consult your computer's reference manual or any of several books devoted exclusively to vi.

Searching with vi

vi inherited the searching capabilities of ed. To search forward for a phrase, you use the slash (/). The cursor jumps to the bottom of the screen and blanks a line on which you type a search phrase, using any of the regular expression characters (see "Searching for Regular Expressions with ed," a previous section in this chapter, for more information on regular expression characters). Pressing <Return> causes the cursor to jump to the next occurrence of that phrase.

If vi searches to the bottom of the buffer without finding the search phrase, it jumps to the top of the document to continue the search. A vi option enables you to change this approach (see "Setting vi Options," further in this chapter).

Pressing **n** repeats the search for the phrase for which you last searched.

As with ed, you can use a question mark (?) in place of the slash to perform a backward search.

The **ex** Editor

In addition to vi, the UNIX developers at the University of California at Berkeley created a line-oriented editor called ex, which started out as a souped-up version of ed. vi is built on ex and provides a visual (screen-oriented) interface. When you use vi, however, the ex editor is always available, and you can access ex commands directly within vi.

In vi, typing a colon (:) in command mode causes vi to accept an ex command. Most of these commands enable you to set options, make global changes to the buffer, or access files.

Few users ever invoke the ex editor as a distinct editor (although you can, with the ex command). Instead, most users interact with ex only as a part of vi. Thus many users commonly think of the commands in this section as vi commands, even though they actually are ex commands. Throughout this section you learn about commands described as ex commands, but you should understand that these commands also are available in vi.

When you type a colon, the cursor jumps to the bottom line of the screen, giving you a blank line on which to type an ex command. Unlike vi commands, ex displays commands on-screen as you type them, and the commands do not take effect until you press <Return>.

Almost all the commands available through the ed editor are also available through ex (although they must be prefixed by a colon to indicate that they are ex commands). Typing **:6,54d** and pressing <Return>, for example, deletes lines 6 though 54, just as this command does in ed. If you are familiar with ed, you may find some of the ex commands useful.

More importantly, all of ed's substitution commands, including regular expression patterns, are available. For example, suppose that you have a text file containing the stock numbers and descriptions of products you purchase in your business. You have been buying your widgets from Royalty Technologies' Chicago office; however, that office is now closing, and those widgets are no longer available. All stock numbers from that office start with RT, followed by two more digits, and ending in 3. To change all these stock numbers to old, you type the following command:

    :1,s/^RT..3/old/

Between line 1 and the end of the buffer, this command finds every line that begins with RT, followed by two more characters (represented by ..), followed by 3. The command then changes these five characters to old.

ex also enables you to use file commands, most of which are identical to similar commands found in ed. The :w command, which you can follow with a file name, writes the contents of the editing buffer to the specified file. If you omit the file name, the buffer is written to the file being edited. If you want to write only a portion of the editing buffer contents to a specified file, you can specify the line numbers you want to write. For example, if you type

```
:30,54w piece
```

ex writes lines 30 through 54 to the file piece.

Using the r command, you also can read the contents of another file into the current buffer. Consider the following example:

```
:r other.part
```

This command reads the contents of the file other.part into the current edit buffer. The new text is inserted after the line where the cursor is located.

ex can execute a command and read the output from that command into the buffer. It uses the r command and an exclamation mark. To produce a listing of the current directory and read it into the edit buffer, you type the following command:

```
:r !ls
```

You also can execute a command without placing its output in the edit buffer, but results display on-screen as usual. For example, to interrupt a vi session to read electronic mail, you type the following command:

```
:!mail
```

Setting vi Options

In the UNIX tradition, vi is easy to configure. You can control many options, each of which determines a particular facet of vi's behavior. You can set any option temporarily for a single vi session, or make any option effective every time you enter vi.

You set options in vi by typing the ex command **:set** followed by the names of options you want to turn on. Many option names are long and can be abbreviated to two or three characters (see table 6.7 for a list of some interesting vi options). Suppose, for example, that you want to see the line number of each line. The number option causes vi to precede each line with its line number. You turn on this option by typing

```
:set number
```

You turn off an option by typing **no** in front of the option name or abbreviation. You turn off the number option, for example, by typing

```
:set nonumber
```

Table 6.7
Selected vi Options

Option	Abbreviation	Default Setting	Description
number	nu	Off	Turns on the display of line numbers
wrapscan	ws	On	When vi searches for a phrase and reaches the end of the edit buffer, it "wraps around" to the top and continues. Turning off this option causes vi to stop at the end of the buffer.
showmode	smd	Off	Causes vi to display a message at the bottom of the screen when you enter text-entry mode
ignorecase	ic	Off	Causes vi to ignore case when searching for a phrase; for example, a and A are considered equivalent
magic	(none)	On	When turned off, all the regular expression characters lose their special meaning

Typing **:set** displays all the options you have changed from their default. Typing **:set all** displays the current setting of all commands, as shown in the following example:

```
noautoindent      nonumber                   noslowopen
autoprint         nonovice                   tabstop=8
noautowrite       optimize                   taglength=0
nobeautify        paragraphs=IPLPPPQPP LI    tags=tags /usr/lib/tags
directory=/tmp    prompt                     term=unknown
noedcompatible    noreadonly                 noterse
noerrorbells      noredraw                   timeout
flash             remap                      ttytype=unknown
hardtabs=8        report=5                   warn
noignorecase      scroll=11                  window=23
nolisp            sections=NHSHH HUuhsh+c    wrapscan
nolist            shell=/usr/bin/ksh         wrapmargin=5
magic             shiftwidth=8               nowriteany
mesg              noshowmatch
nomodelines       noshowmode
```

Some options have values associated with them and are not simply flags indicating whether an option is on or off. The window option, for example, is normally set to 23 to indicate that 23 lines are available for displaying the editing buffer. IBM PCs, however, have one extra line, so IBM PC users modify this option by typing

    :set window=24

You can configure vi to turn specific options on or off each time you invoke vi by placing set commands in a special file, .exrc, in your home directory. Each time you start vi, it looks for .exrc and reads any set commands located there.

Exiting vi

You normally exit vi by issuing the ZZ command. This command causes vi to write the contents of the edit buffer back to the file (if changes have been made) and exit.

Other commands for exiting vi are actually ex commands. The :q command asks to exit vi without saving anything. If you have made changes to the buffer, however, vi refuses to exit, warning you that all changes will be lost. Required instead is the following sequence:

    :q!

The exclamation mark confirms that vi should discard any changes to the buffer.

Other vi Capabilities

vi's capabilities are too numerous to list in full, but other features of interest include the following:

- vi can "take back" the last command that modified the buffer—modifications such as insertions, deletions, changes, or substitutions. Thus, you can experiment with commands without fear of permanently destroying an edit buffer.

- vi can repeat commands with a single keystroke.

- vi has extensive facilities for programmers. Various options enable programmers to enter programs with less typing or to find problems in programs. Programmers often find, for example, that their parentheses (or in C, braces) don't match. Placing the cursor on any brace, bracket, or parenthesis and pressing the percent sign (%) causes vi to jump to the matching brace, bracket, or parenthesis.

- vi can easily move text between files.

- vi enables you to switch from one file to another during editing without requiring you to exit vi and start again with a different file.

- vi has capabilities to change uppercase to lowercase and vice versa on any selection of text.

- vi includes automatic crash recovery. If your terminal is disconnected from the computer or if the computer crashes, vi can retrieve the edit buffer as it existed when the problem occurred. vi even sends you electronic mail, notifying you that an edit buffer has been saved and that you can retrieve it with the -r option to the vi command. The text in the mail explains how to use the command.

The capabilities described in the preceding list, as well as many other useful features, are described in much greater detail in your computer's reference manual and in many how-to books, such as Que's *Using UNIX*.

Using vi is a never-ending adventure; you continuously uncover new commands and new capabilities from books about vi or from computer reference manuals. Each new command enables you to perform your editing tasks slightly more efficiently, with less keystrokes. As your proficiency increases and vi's unusual aspects—such as the concept of modes—become second nature to you, perhaps you will begin to understand why accomplished vi users are so fiercely loyal to vi.

The Emacs Text Editor

Emacs, a popular alternative to the vi editor, was written by Richard Stallman of the Free Software Foundation (see Chapter 11, "Introducing the UNIX Community," for more information about this foundation). Although not a standard part of UNIX, Emacs is widely available in the public domain, and enhanced versions are commercially available from several sources.

Originally, Emacs—an acronym for Editor Macros—was a collection of macros (preprogrammed descriptions for certain tasks) for an editor called TECO (Tape Editor and Corrector) for the DEC PDP-10.

Many users prefer Emacs because it does not require vi's dual-mode operation (text-entry and command). Emacs depends much more heavily on Ctrl-key combinations, which can be cumbersome for touch typists, but you can customize it, enabling you to redefine keys and commands. A built-in programming language enables you to perform complex operations with a single command. In fact, you can customize Emacs so completely that it can even act like almost any other editor.

Another Emacs strength is its capability to edit multiple files simultaneously. Emacs can split the screen into multiple windows, enabling you to edit a different file in each window.

Emacs also provides on-line help.

The UNIX Stream Editor sed

The sed editor is the UNIX stream editor. The term *stream editor* implies that sed edits files as streams of data. Although ed and vi are capable of editing any part of a file at any time, sed works on the file like a worker does on an assembly line: sed reads each line from the file being edited, makes any changes you specify to that line, and then goes on to the next line. Just as an assembly line worker cannot go back to a piece that has already moved to the next work position, sed cannot back up to a line after going on to the next line.

Unlike ed and vi, sed is not an interactive editor; that is, you do not give sed one command, wait for sed to perform the command, and then give sed the next command. Instead sed is a batch editor: you provide it with all the changes you want to make to all the lines in the file, and sed performs these changes without further intervention. sed is most useful when you need to perform the same editing operations on a regular basis. For example, suppose that a branch office regularly sends you diskettes containing data files produced by a software package they use. You, in turn, have a software package of your own that uses the data file, but you must rearrange certain fields on each line and remove the parentheses from the area codes within the phone numbers. You can write a shell program containing sed commands to perform these operations automatically whenever you receive a new diskette.

You can use most ed commands in sed. A typical job for sed is to perform simple substitutions on a file, using a command such as the following:

```
sed "s/cat/dog/g" <catfile >dogfile
```

This command causes sed to copy catfile to dogfile, substituting dog for cat on each line. The quotation marks enclose a command that is identical to the ed substitute command. sed reads each line from the input file, makes the specified substitutions, and writes the resulting line to dogfile.

A single sed command can contain many commands that together perform complex operations. Consider this example:

```
sed "/John/d <Return>
s/Fred/Jim/g" <oldreport >newreport
```

This two-line command copies oldreport to newreport, deleting all lines that contain John and replacing occurrences of Fred with Jim.

sed is popular among shell programmers as a means for modifying data within a shell program.

Text Formatting

Early methods for formatting documents in UNIX arose in the same environment as the early text editors. As with the editors, the *text formatters* had to run on printer terminals or, at best, cheap ASCII display terminals. A text formatter is a program that accepts text along with formatting commands and rearranges the text according to the formatting commands. The commands tell the formatter how to arrange the text into paragraphs and which typefaces to use, such as italic and bold.

As is true with other aspects of UNIX, text processing with UNIX has always been oriented toward the power user rather than the novice. The tools described in this chapter, such as the `nroff` and `troff` formatters, were designed to enable experienced users to accomplish great things. To a beginner, the power and complexity of these tools can be both impressive and overpowering at the same time.

The UNIX Formatter `nroff`

The original UNIX text formatter is `nroff`, a descendant of `runoff`, a popular formatter that inspired many later formatters. In fact, `nroff` is a condensation of *new runoff*.

An `nroff` *document* is a text file—which you create with a text editor, as you do any text file—that contains not only the text you want to print, but also includes `nroff` commands that tell `nroff` how to format the text. You need not be concerned about making the text look nice within the file. Many lines in your files become uneven as you insert, delete, and move text within the file. When you complete the document, you invoke the `nroff` formatter to produce a neatly formatted document. `nroff` fills and adjusts uneven lines, inserts underlining and bold codes where requested, adds page numbers, places text inside margins, and so on. The output from `nroff` usually goes to a printer.

As a simple example, consider a file that contains the following text from the Declaration of Independence. This example shows uneven lines of text, just as they may have appeared on Thomas Jefferson's text editor after he finished inserting, deleting, and rearranging text.

```
When in the course of human events
it becomes
necessary for one people to dissolve the political
bands
which have
connected them to another
and to assume among the powers of the
Earth the separate and equal station....
```

Figure 6.4 shows part of a page of printed output resulting from using `nroff` to format the preceding text.

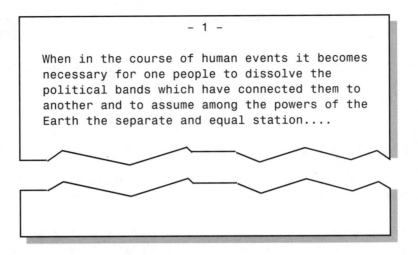

Fig. 6.4. *A sample printout from* nroff.

As you create nroff documents, you write not only the text you want printed, but also nroff commands that inform nroff about margins, page size, indentation, underlining, and other aspects of printing your document. nroff commands begin with a period, followed by a one- or two-letter command name. The name of the command often is followed by additional information, depending on the command. For example, if you use the .in command, which causes nroff to begin indenting text, you also must tell nroff how far to indent.

Suppose, for example, that an nroff document begins with the following lines:

```
.po .5i
.ll 7.5i
```

The .po (*page offset*) command tells nroff to insert a 1/2-inch space between the edge of the page and the beginning of each line. In effect, this command sets the left margin to 1/2 inch. The .ll (*line length*) command tells nroff that it has 7 1/2 inches for printing text on each line. Thus, the first 1/2 inch of each line makes up the left margin, and the next 7 1/2 inches make up the printable area. If the sheet of paper is 8 1/2 inches wide, 1/2 inch remains as the right margin. Without these commands, nroff uses 1-inch margins.

nroff uses inches as the unit of measurement in this example because the numbers in the nroff commands end with i. Many other units are available; 6c, for example represents 6 centimeters. If you do not follow the number with a letter, nroff reads the numbers as characters for commands that deal with horizontal distances and as lines for commands that deal with vertical distances.

In addition to specifying absolute values, you can use + or – to specify relative values. .po +1i, for example, tells nroff to increase the page offset (that is, increase the left margin) by 1 inch. Similarly, .ll –1i tells nroff to shorten the line length by 1 inch.

Even though your nroff document may contain lines of different lengths (again see fig. 6.4), nroff attempts to make all printed lines approximately the same length, a process called *filling*. nroff places as many words as possible on each printed line, breaking or combining lines as necessary to make each line the same length.

Although filling is usually desirable, you may want to print some parts of a document exactly as written. Suppose, for example, that a letter contains an inside address such as the following:

```
Acey Deucy Deucy Hardware Company
175 E. Missouri Avenue
Houston, TX  77048
```

If not instructed otherwise, nroff fills the text, possibly generating the following output:

```
Acey Deucy Deucy Hardware Company 175 E. Missouri
Avenue Houston, TX  77048
```

The .nf (*no fill*) command tells nroff to suspend filling, printing the lines exactly as you typed them in the file. The .fi (*fill*) command tells nroff to resume filling. Thus, you surround the inside address of a letter with these commands as follows:

```
.nf
Acey Deucy Deucy Hardware Company
175 E. Missouri Avenue
Houston, TX  77048
.fi
```

The .br (*break*) command interrupts filling. When nroff encounters a .br, it prints the partial line that it has accumulated since it last printed a full line.

In a related process, the .ad (*adjust*) command tells nroff to adjust the text—often called *right justification*—inserting spaces between words so that each line is exactly the same length, evenly aligning the text at the right margin. If you begin the sample document shown in figure 6.4 with .ad, nroff adjusts the text by inserting extra spaces between the words (see fig. 6.5). Note that nroff does not adjust the last line in a paragraph.

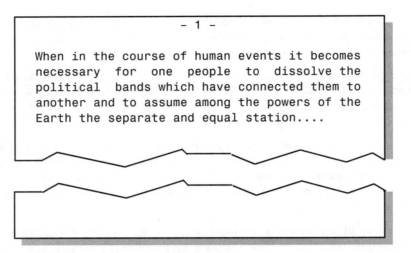

Fig. 6.5. *Sample text adjusted with* `.ad`*.*

Table 6.8 contains a list of common `nroff` commands.

Table 6.8
Selected `nroff` Commands

Command	*Description*
`.ad` (adjust)	Turns on adjusting. Follow with `l` to adjust only the left margin, `r` to adjust only the right margin, `b` to adjust both margins, or `c` to center each line.
`.bp` (break page)	Causes `nroff` to jump to the following page
`.br` (break)	Causes `nroff` to print the lines it is accumulating and begin a new line
`.ce` (center)	Centers the following line of text. No adjusting or filling is performed. After `.ce`, you can specify the number of lines you want to center.
`.fi` (fill)	Activates filling
`.ft` (font)	Changes the letter style. `.ft I` switches to italic (producing underlining), and `.ft B` switches to bold. `.ft` alone switches back to the previous font, as does `.ft P`.

Command	Description
.hy (hyphenate)	Turns automatic hyphenation on or off. The number you specify for the .hy command tells nroff whether to turn hyphenation on or off and, when turned on, specifies the details of how nroff is to perform hyphenation.
.in (indent)	Sets indentation. For example, .in +10 indents all successive lines by ten characters.
.ll (line length)	Sets the amount of printable space on each line
.ls (line spacing)	Sets text to be single-spaced (.ls 1), double-spaced (.ls 2), and so on
.na (no adjust)	Turns off adjusting
.nf (no fill)	Turns off filling
.pl (page length)	Sets the length of the paper, including top and bottom margins
.po (page offset)	Determines the amount of space between the left edge of the paper and the left margin
.sp (space)	Causes nroff to insert a blank line. If you specify a number with the command, such as .sp 5, nroff inserts that many blank lines.
.tl (title)	Defines the title you want to print at the top of each page
.ul (underline)	Turns underlining on

The troff Formatter

nroff works best with character-oriented devices such as terminals and daisywheel printers. As sophisticated printers, such as laser printers, and typesetters became more common, a version of nroff called troff (*typesetting nroff*) was developed to make full use of these printers' capabilities. troff included commands for selecting various fonts and point sizes, performing more sophisticated adjusting, and handling simple graphics.

The .ft (*font*) command enables you to select different fonts, identified by a one- or two-letter abbreviation (*font name*). .ft I, for example, switches to italic; .ft HB changes the font to Helvetica bold; and .ft RI switches to Roman italic. The special command .ft P switches to the previous font.

Thus, if you type

```
He was a
.ft I
very
.ft P
good boy when he wanted to be.
```

`troff` produces this output:

He was a *very* good boy when he wanted to be.

Which fonts you have available, and what letters you use as their one- or two-letter abbreviation, varies slightly from one manufacturer's version of `troff` to another. Some abbreviations are standard, such as R for Roman, and HB for Helvetica bold. Others are less consistent; for example, the constant-width font Courier is abbreviated CW (constant width) on one version of `troff` and TT (teletype font) on another.

To save typing time, you can embed the \f command, a special version of the .ft command, in your text. You follow the sequence \f with a single-letter font name, and `troff` changes fonts at that point. To use \f with the preceding example, you type

```
He was a \fIvery\fP good boy when he wanted to be.
```

The character sequence \fI tells `troff` to switch to italic, and \fP tells `troff` to switch back to the previous font. If you want to use a two-letter font name, you use the sequence \f(, followed by the font name. (Note that you do not type a closing parenthesis.) In this example, to print the word *very* in Helvetica italic, you type

```
He was a \f(HIvery\fP good boy when he wanted to be.
```

The sequence \f(HI tells `troff` to switch to Helvetica italic. The parenthesis is crucial to the meaning; it tells `troff` to consider the next *two* characters as the font abbreviation, not just the next single character. Without the parenthesis—if you type **\fHI**—`troff` thinks you want to switch to regular Helvetica (font abbreviation H) and that the I is the first character to be printed in Helvetica.

The .ps command adjusts point sizes. For example, .ps +2 causes the following text to print two points larger:

```
Jupiter is a
.ps +2
big
.ps -2
planet.
```

This sequence produces the following output:

Jupiter is a big planet.

As with fonts, you can save typing time by embedding a special point-size command, \s, in your text, rather than using .ps. To generate the preceding output, you also can type

```
Jupiter is a \s+2big\s-2 planet.
```

In this example the characters \s+2 tell troff to increase the point size by 2; similarly, \s-2 tells troff to decrease the point size by 2.

nroff and troff are completely compatible, and many users produce drafts of documents in nroff and print the final document with troff. nroff simply ignores commands that make no sense to a character-oriented formatter. It ignores, for example, requests for changing point sizes with .ps or the \s sequence.

Other commands may produce slightly different results. For example, the command .sp .6i causes troff to space down 0.6 inches. nroff, however, cannot skip exactly 0.6 inches (the equivalent of about 3.6 lines), so it simply comes as close as it can.

Macro Packages

Although nroff and troff provide the necessary commands for formatting most types of documents, you sometimes have to repeat long command sequences several times at different places in the same document. A macro facility enables you to define new commands in terms of existing nroff and troff commands.

Macros are simply new commands that you define as abbreviations for long sequences of nroff or troff commands. If you discover that you repeatedly use the same sequence of commands within a document, you can define a macro that represents this long sequence of commands.

Most examples in this book, for instance, are indented and printed in constant-width font. To create such an example, you type the following troff commands at the beginning the example:

```
.ft CW
.in +.5i
```

This sequence switches to a constant-width font (usually Courier, depending on your version of troff) and indents text 1/2 inch. You must type a similar sequence at the end of the example:

```
.ft P
.in -.5i
```

This sequence tells troff to switch back to the previous font and reduce the indentation by 1/2 inch. You can use a macro to eliminate the repetition of these commands. Near the top of the document, you can enter the following commands:

```
.de SE
.ft CW
.in +.5i
..
```

The .de (*define macro*) command tells troff you are defining a macro you want to call SE, a name that you selected, perhaps as an abbreviation for *start example*. All commands up to .. are part of the macro definition. Now that you have defined the .SE macro, placing .SE in the document causes troff to execute the commands you specified in the definition. You can define a similar macro, calling it EE for *end example*, which executes the commands you need at the end of each example.

Over the years, many users of nroff and troff developed collections of macros, called *macro packages*, which other users found generally useful for accomplishing everyday tasks. Many of the macros packages were developed by writers at Bell Labs and included sophisticated and powerful macros for technical writing tasks. Using these macro packages, writers at Bell Labs could—with only a few troff commands—print a beautifully formatted cover page for a technical paper or produce a properly formatted memo, complete with the Bell System logo in the corner.

Eventually most of these macro packages were distributed by various manufacturers as a standard part of their nroff and troff software. Table 6.9 lists some of the macro packages in widespread use.

Table 6.9
Common Macro Packages

Macro Package	Description
ms	Original macro package developed at Bell Labs but no longer supported by AT&T. Still widely used, it is shipped with many Berkeley versions of UNIX.
mm	Large, general-purpose macro package. Many features to aid in producing letters, memos, proposals, reports, and technical papers.

Macro Package	Description
man	Macro package useful for formatting manuals
mptx	Special-purpose macro package for printing a permuted index, a type of cross-reference index used to format UNIX manuals
me	General-purpose macro package available on some Berkeley systems

mm (*memorandum macros*) is an especially popular macro package. Originally intended for memo and letter writing, it is helpful for almost any kind of document. mm provides macros that take care of the details of formatting many different types of documents so that you can concentrate on the text of the document rather than the formatting.

Among its many capabilities, mm contains easy-to-use macros for specifying headings, footnotes, and lists of items. The .AL (*automatic list*) macro, for example, starts an automatically numbered list. You precede each item in the list with the .LI (*list*) macro, and you use the .LE (*list end*) macro to terminate the list.

Consider the following portion of text containing an automatic list:

```
Bob and I discussed the problems you are
having with installing new software updates
and recommend
the following changes:
.AL
.LI
Each office should install a modem that
enables us to dial in and verify that
the installation was performed correctly.
.LI
Your personnel should maintain a written
log of the times and dates that updates
are installed.
.LI
Updates will now be distributed on tape
cartridges to simplify installation.
.LE
```

Figure 6.6 shows part of a page of output resulting from formatting this document with nroff and specifying that the mm package is to be used.

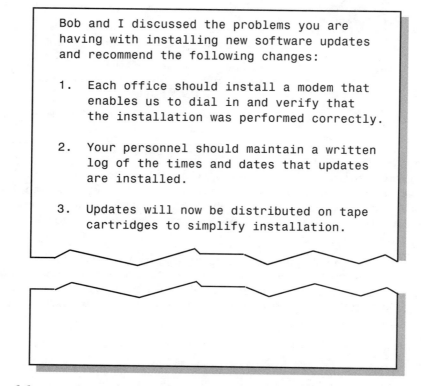

Fig. 6.6. *A sample printout from* nroff *using the macro package* mm.

Notice that the names of all nroff and troff commands are lowercase. The authors of the mm macros chose uppercase macro names so that you can easily distinguish built-in commands from macros.

UNIX Preprocessors

Several programs, called *preprocessors*, are usually included as part of the nroff and troff software. The three most common preprocessors enable you to describe tables (tbl), pictures (pic), and mathematical equations (eqn) within your document. Given these descriptions, the preprocessors produce commands that tell troff how to draw the table, picture, or equation.

Formatting Tables

Many documents include tables of various configurations. A special program, tbl, is available for formatting tables.

tbl accepts as input any document with nroff or troff commands, text, and table specifications. As output, it produces an identical document with the table specifications converted to the necessary troff commands—which are often quite complex—for printing the table. It then provides this output as input to troff, which processes the commands tbl has produced, along with the rest of the document. tbl is called a *preprocessor* because it alters the document before the main processing program (troff) works with it.

Consider the following sample table:

```
.TS
center,box;
c s s
c c c
l n n.
Ball Bearing Sales
.sp
City    Zone    Sales
.sp
Chicago 17      238,920
Cincinnati      22      15,900
Orlando 8       563,100
Seattle 14      1,320,700
.TE
```

The .TS (*table start*) command tells tbl that what follows is a table to be formatted. All tables consist of three parts:

- *Options.* Options specify the attributes of the table as a whole. In this example, the options center and box specify that the table is to be centered horizontally and surrounded by a box. A semicolon terminates the list of options.

- *Formatting specifications.* These lines indicate the table layout: the number of columns in the table, the width of each column, and the arrangement of the data in each column. The format specifications are the three lines following the options, beginning with c s s. Each line in the formatting area corresponds to a line of data that will be printed in the table. If fewer formatting lines than lines of table data exist (the usual case), the last formatting line applies to all remaining lines of table data.

Thus, `c s s` tells `tbl` that the first line of the table is to be centered across all three columns (literally, that the first column is to be centered and slide across the other two columns). The next line, `c c c`, indicates that the second line of the table consists of three columns, each of which is to be centered. Finally, the third format line, `l n n`, applies to the remainder of the table. The first column is to be left-justified, and the second and third columns contain numbers that are to be centered.

- *Table data.* The remainder of the table contains the table data. You can intersperse `troff` commands as needed to set fonts, control line spacing, and so on. Tabs separate each column, but you can change the tabs to any character you want to use.

The final print table displays as follows:

```
      Ball Bearing Sales

     City       Zone    Sales

   Chicago       17    238,920
   Cincinnati    22     15,900
   Orlando        8    563,100
   Seattle       14  1,320,700
```

Formatting Equations

UNIX began in a research environment in which researchers often wrote technical papers requiring complex mathematical equations. Although `troff` has the capability of handling these equations, the commands necessary can be lengthy and complex. Another preprocessor, `eqn`, was developed to make such formatting easy.

Like `tbl`, `eqn` accepts a document as input and produces a document as its output. `eqn` watches for special codes that surround the description of an equation and converts that description to the equivalent `troff` commands. `eqn` output is then passed to `troff`, which formats the document.

Words and symbols describe the equations, often reading very much in the way a mathematician would say the equation. The description is surrounded by a set of codes (typically `.EQ` and `.EN`, but you can define others) that identify the equation to `eqn`.

Simple equations read almost like English. For example, the commands

```
.EQ
a over b
.EN
```

produce the following formula:

a

––

b

Other, more complex functions are possible, however. Consider the following equation:

```
.EQ
lim from {i -> inf} sum from j=0 to i x sup i
.EN
```

This description produces the equation shown in figure 6.7.

Fig. 6.7. A sample equation formatted with eqn.

Although this description may seem obtuse to nonmathematicians, people who work with such equations find the description relatively straightforward and much simpler than the equivalent troff commands.

Drawing Pictures

The third program in the preprocessor trilogy is pic, which enables you to describe a simple picture in English-like terms. Like tbl and eqn, pic reads a document looking for special commands that identify a picture and changes the picture description into the much more complex troff commands.

Picture descriptions are surrounded by the .PS (*picture start*) and .PE (*picture end*) commands. Everything in between is taken by pic to be a description of a picture. A sample of a picture description follows:

```
.PS
move right 1.6i
ellipse "char" "a"
move right
ellipse "double" "b"
more right
ellipse "short" "c"
move to 2nd ellipse
move down; move down
box "typical" "function"
arrow from .b of 1st ellipse to 1/2 of the way between \
    last box.nw and last box.n
arrow from .b of 2nd ellipse to last box.n
arrow from .b of 3rd ellipse to 1/2 of the way between \
    last box.ne and last box.n
move to .b of last box
arrow down
ellipse "int"
.PE
```

The description reads very much like English (.b represents *bottom* and last box.nw represents *the northwest corner of the last box*). The result is the diagram shown in figure 6.8.

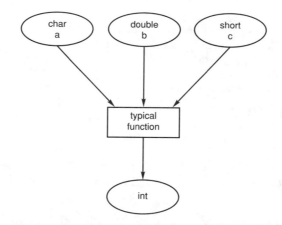

Fig. 6.8. *A sample picture formatted with* pic.

The UNIX Spelling Checker

The UNIX spelling checker, `spell`, produces a list of misspelled words found within a document. Although not overly remarkable by today's standards (spelling checkers are commonplace today), `spell` does understand `nroff`, `troff`, and the preprocessors well enough that it does not try to check the spelling of commands such as `.pl`. It also recognizes font constructions and, therefore, understands that `\fIextremely\fP` prints *extremely* in italic; it does not include `fIextremely` or `fP` in its list of misspelled words.

The Workbenches

Perhaps the most fascinating aspect of text processing with UNIX is a product never designed to be commercially available. Developed at Bell Labs, the Writers Workbench (WWB) is an amazing attempt to get computers to analyze and proofread documents. Although parts of it are available on many UNIX systems, WWB is not universally available and is not considered a standard UNIX product.

The `style` program analyzes a document and determines the percentage of passive versus active sentences, types of verbs, types of sentences, and other aspects of grammar. Most interesting are the first few lines of its analysis, which attempt to determine, using several different algorithms, the grade level of the writing. The following output is the first few lines of a sample `style` report:

```
readability grades:
        (Kincaid) 10.4   (auto) 10.9   (Coleman-Liau) 10.3
        (Flesch) 10.8
```

According to this report, the writer is writing at a tenth- or eleventh-grade level. Although the algorithms produce slightly different results, the report provides a general idea of the level of writing. Surprisingly, `style` most often indicates that the writer's level of writing is too high rather than too low.

Table 6.10 is a list of some other interesting WWB programs.

Table 6.10
Selected WWB Programs

Program	Description
abst	Attempts to determine the level of abstractness of a document
acro	Searches for the first occurrence of an acronym; helps ensure that each acronym is defined when first used
diction	Searches for overworked, wordy, or misused words and expressions and offers suggestions for improvement. For example, suggests replacing *at this point in time* with *now*, or changing *personal opinion* to *opinion* (all opinions, by definition, are personal).
double	Looks for a word that occurs twice in a row
punct	Checks punctuation
sexist	Looks for sexist words and expressions and suggests improvements; for example, suggests that *chairman* be changed to *chair*

Chapter Summary

In this chapter you learned about the UNIX tools for editing text (ed, ex, vi, and sed) and formatting text (nroff, troff, tbl, eqn, and pic). All of these tools are designed for the power user who needs text processing tools that can accomplish any task.

This chapter has only scratched the surface of UNIX's powerful text processing capabilities and is designed to present the concepts of UNIX text processing, rather than to teach you how to use the tools described. As with any good text processing system, you can find books devoted entirely to UNIX text processing. In addition, as with any good text processing system, the thrill of discovering new tricks and techniques is always present. Few users indeed know everything there is to know about nroff and troff.

7

Understanding Communications and Networking

I n Chapter 1, "Introducing the UNIX Operating System," you learned that UNIX was developed in an environment that encouraged sharing, cooperation, and the exchange of ideas and information. As the UNIX market expanded, this same philosophy of sharing was one of the many features that attracted new users to UNIX. This chapter looks at some of the features of UNIX that are specifically designed to enable users to exchange information.

UNIX provides a number of ways for you to communicate with other users. In this chapter, you learn about electronic mail, with which you can send messages, data, programs, and other types of information to friends and colleagues, whether they work on your computer or almost any other computer anywhere in the world. Alternatively, through the write command, you can carry on an electronic conversation with other users on your computer.

In this chapter, you also learn about the techniques your system administrator can use to keep the users on your computer informed.

Finally, you learn about networking and about a few of the systems available to enable you to transfer information between computers, whether they're in neighboring buildings or neighboring countries. You learn about the UUCP networking system and commercial products such as RFS and NFS.

Electronic Mail

Electronic mail—sending and receiving messages by computer—is changing the way the world thinks about exchanging information. It has invaded every type of computing—not just the UNIX world—and revolutionized the way we look at communicating. Electronic mail is not restricted to simple text messages; it can include almost any kind of data, such as programs, spreadsheets, databases, and even voice and pictures. You can exchange mail either with other users on your computer or with users on other computers that use a compatible mail system.

Billions of electronic mail messages every year are delivered cheaply and quickly, in most cases virtually instantaneously. These messages are sent not only on UNIX systems but also through local area networks, mainframe networks, and commercial services such as MCI Mail. The U.S. Postal Service is watching the industry warily as electronic mail handles a growing number of messages formerly sent by first class mail. Almost every major company has discovered the benefits of electronic mail, which include the following:

- *Low cost.* Electronic mail is an extremely cost-effective way to move information around, especially when it must be moved quickly. A three-page letter costs $10 to $15 to ship overnight or $4.50 to send by telex. That same letter can be sent by electronic mail for a few cents locally or for about $1 long distance.

- *Speed.* Electronic mail can be delivered almost as fast as the wire can carry it.

- *Flexibility.* Because electronic mail is sent between computers, you have much greater flexibility in how you use the mail. If a co-worker in another city sends you a copy of a spreadsheet by fax and you want to experiment with the data, you first must enter the data into your computer. If, however, the co-worker sends you the same spreadsheet by electronic mail, it arrives directly on your computer, often ready to use. You have complete control over what to do with the information—print it, edit it, incorporate it into a report you are preparing, or use it as input data for some other program.

- *Waste reduction.* Electronic mail goes a long way toward reducing the clutter of paper in the modern office, not to mention saving a lot of trees.

The UNIX mail system was developed in the early days of UNIX, and it provides a powerful facility for moving information between users, both on the same machine and to other machines throughout the world. On the computer, you can prepare letters, memos, and data and distribute them with a few simple commands.

Using the UNIX `mail` Program

The original UNIX mail program is called `mail`. Although it is not the most sophisticated mail package available under UNIX today (see "Using Other UNIX Mail Programs," further in this chapter), it is available on all UNIX computers and performs most functions that users need. You use the `mail` command for both sending and receiving mail.

UNIX Mailboxes

Each user on a UNIX computer has a "mailbox," where incoming mail is stored until it is read. Mailboxes are kept in the `/usr/mail` directory, and each mailbox is named after the user whose mail is stored in it. Thus, Jane's mailbox would be called `/usr/mail/jane`. Permissions on the mailboxes are set such that you can read and modify your own mailbox but not those of other users—except, of course, when you send mail to them.

Sending Mail

You can send mail by issuing the `mail` command with the name of the receiver on the command line, such as

```
mail martha
```

The `mail` program reads information from the standard input (the keyboard, by default). When you issue a command to send mail, the `mail` command waits for you to type your mail message. Your message can be any length and in any format. You press <Ctrl-D> when you are finished, and `mail` then places your message in the receiver's mailbox (Martha's, in this example). Consider the following example:

```
$ mail martha
Martha --
Don't forget to mail me those reports from
yesterday's sales meeting. Cathy is breathing
down my neck to give her my sales figures for
this month. Thanks!
                        -- Rob
^D
```

Terminating Mail Messages with a Period

Whenever you supply keyboard input to a command, you terminate
the input by pressing <Ctrl-D>. Thus, you can terminate your mail
message by pressing <Ctrl-D> at the end of the message. However,
with mail (unlike every other UNIX command), you also can terminate input by typing a period (.) on a line by itself. Perhaps the designers of mail thought that typing a period was easier than pressing
<Ctrl-D> and so, foreseeing the heavy use to which mail might
someday be put, decided to add this shortcut as a convenience.

You can send the same message to any number of people by listing on the
command line the login names of all receivers. Consider this example:

```
$ mail dale mark terryl terrys tom
Gang --
Today is Jim's birthday, in honor of
which we will be meeting at Bob's Chili
for lunch. Bring the Rolaids.
     -- Joyce
^D
```

The mail command provides an excellent opportunity to use command
substitution, which enables you to use the output from one command as
part of another command (see Chapter 4, "Understanding the UNIX Shell,"
for a discussion of command substitution). If you often send mail to a
particular collection of people, such as the folks mentioned in the preceding
birthday example, you can create a file with a list of their login IDs. For
example, suppose that you call this file gang and that it contains the
following IDs:

```
dale
mark
terryl
```

```
terrys
tom
```

To send a message to these folks, you type the following:

mail `cat gang`

The backquotes tell the shell to invoke command substitution. The shell first executes the command inside the backquotes.

The cat gang command produces the list of names as its output; that output in turn becomes part of the mail command, and mail is sent to the folks in the list.

Typing messages from the keyboard is fine for short messages such as those shown here, but for longer messages, this technique is inadequate. While composing your message, you may want to review, proofread, correct, and rearrange your message. Simply use a text editor (such as vi) to create a file containing the message you want to send. Using input redirection, you can send the contents of that file as your mail message (see Chapter 4 for details about redirection).

For example, if you prepare a message to Karen in a file called my.message, you can send that message to her by typing the following command:

mail karen <my.message

This technique has the added advantage of leaving you with a file that contains the message you sent to Karen. You can use this file as a "carbon copy" for later reference, if you need to remember the contents of the message you sent to her.

Similarly, you can send any file as a mail message. If Ken calls and says he needs a copy of an expense report program (named expense.c) you wrote in C, you can mail it to him by typing the following command:

mail ken <expense.c

The source program expense.c is sent as the text of the message. When Ken reads his mail, the program will appear as a message, which he can save to a file.

Reading Mail

UNIX uses several means to notify you that you have received mail that is waiting for you:

- Each time you log in, UNIX checks for mail and prints the message `You have mail` if any mail is in your mailbox.

- Most versions of the shell can be set to check for mail periodically. When new mail arrives, the shell displays a message such as

  ```
  You have mail in /usr/mail/jenny
  ```

- Many UNIX systems have programs that check for incoming mail at some set interval and display some kind of indicator on your terminal when new mail arrives. For example, on the AT&T 3B1, a program called smgr (*status manager*) watches for incoming mail and displays an envelope symbol on the top line of the console when mail arrives.

- You can check for mail at any time by typing **mail** with no arguments. If your mailbox is empty, the `mail` program displays the message `No mail`; otherwise, `mail` shows you the first mail message in your mailbox.

Each message in your mailbox appears exactly as the sender typed it, except that the `mail` program inserts one or more *headers* at the beginning of the message. Headers tell you who sent the message and when it was sent. For example, a message from Jon might look like this:

```
From jon Tue Dec 31 10:11 EST 1991
Hi there - is it lunchtime yet?
I'm starving!!!
```

The first line is the header, which has been added by the `mail` program. The remaining two lines are Jon's message, exactly as he typed it.

The `mail` program displays each message one at a time. After each message, `mail` prompts with a question mark, which is its way of asking what you want to do with the message. By entering the appropriate command, you can keep the message in your mail box (press <Return>), delete the message (type **d**), save the message to a file (type **s**, followed by the name of the file), or forward it to one or more users (type **m**, followed by the names of the users). After you tell `mail` what to do to each message, `mail` displays the next message.

A typical mail session might look like this:

```
$ mail
From diedre Tue Dec 17 13:06 PST 1990
```

```
Bob --
The report for Mr. Jenkins has been faxed to
his office. If you want to look it over, it's stored
in /usr/diedre/reports/jenkins. Read it and
call me.    -- D
? s from.diedre  <Saves the message to a file named from.diedre>

From mike Tue Dec 17 11:05 PST 1990
Dear Bob,
Your wife called. Something about your basement
and 3 feet of water.
? d  <Deletes the message>
$
```

After you tell `mail` what to do with your last message, the `mail` program terminates.

Although most messages have a single header, some messages have multiple headers. A message often has a multiple header when it is forwarded from one user to another. Each time the message moves from one mailbox to another, a new header is added to the beginning of the message. For example, if Al sends Betty a message, who in turn forwards it to Charles, who then sends it on to you, the message would look like this:

```
From charles Thu Aug 1 16:01 CDT 1991
>From betty Thu Aug 1 14:42 CDT 1991 forwarded by charles
>From al Thu Aug 1 14:03 CDT 1991 forwarded by betty
The new project status forms are available in the copy
room. Grab all you need. -- Al
```

The headers, read from the bottom up, show the progress of the message as it was passed from user to user. For example, the last header shows that the message originated with Al. The phrase `forwarded by betty` tells you that Betty was the initial recipient of the letter and that she forwarded it to someone else. By reading upward through the headers, you can determine who received the message and what those recipients did with it.

Exchanging Mail with Users on Other UNIX Computers

Much of the real power of electronic mail lies in the ability it gives users to exchange information with other users on different computers, saving you the trouble of printing and faxing material to friends and co-workers, or of relying on the postal service or an express delivery company.

Sending mail to users on other computers is usually no more complex than sending mail to users on your own computer. All UNIX computers have names. To send mail to users on other computers, you must give the name of the computer on which the user works and the user's name, separated by an exclamation point. Suppose that you type the following command:

```
mail comet!barney
```

This command waits for you to type a message and then sends the message to Barney, who works on a computer called `comet`. When you finish typing the message, your prompt returns immediately, and, while you continue with other tasks, the computer attends to the job of contacting `comet` and transferring the mail. In most cases, your computer places a phone call through a modem, although networks are commonly used today as well. The transfer may take only a minute or so; however, delays sometimes occur—for example, if the receiving computer's modem is busy—so your computer may have to try repeatedly until it can make contact. The entire process of transferring the mail, and retrying if necessary, happens automatically.

UNIX and the Exclamation Point

Using an exclamation point to separate the computer name and the user name is sometimes known as *bang notation*. UNIX users (and for that matter, specialists in any field) shun long words and phrases, so UNIX users usually refer to an exclamation point as a *bang*, feeling that the five syllables in "exclamation point" are simply too many for a lowly piece of punctuation. Thus `comet!barney` is commonly pronounced "comet-bang-barney." You may also hear the exclamation point called a *ball bat*, which the exclamation point resembles to those with visually active imaginations.

Before your computer can contact other computers, someone has to tell it how, which is an important task of the system administrator. He or she first must identify the computers with which you and your co-workers want to exchange mail and then configure your computer with the information necessary to contact these computers. This information often includes the other computers' phone numbers, network addresses, or other information. Similarly, the system administrators for the other computers must provide their computers with the same information about your computer. If your system administrator tells you that your computer "knows about" another computer, it means that your computer has been properly configured to contact that computer.

Occasionally you may want to send mail to a user who works on a computer that your computer doesn't know about. For example, suppose that you are working on a computer called hypatia, and you want to send mail to Alex on a computer called wizard. Your computer can't know about every other computer in the world; perhaps your computer doesn't know about wizard, and vice versa. You can still send mail to Alex, however, if you can find a *pass-through* computer.

The uuname command produces a list of all the computers your computer knows about. In comparing lists, you and Alex might notice that although your computers don't know about each other, they both know about a computer called dagwood. Thus, you can send mail to dagwood and have the mail *passed through* to wizard by typing this command:

```
mail dagwood!wizard!alex
```

This command tells your computer to send mail to dagwood, with instructions for dagwood to forward the mail to wizard, where it is delivered to Alex, as shown in figure 7.1.

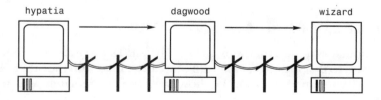

Fig. 7.1. *An example of a pass-through computer,* dagwood.

Even longer, more complex paths are possible. Consider this example:

```
mail oyster!auxnj!icepit!leslie
```

This `mail` message is sent to a computer named `oyster`, which forwards it to a computer called `auxnj`, which forwards it to a computer called `icepit`, where it is delivered to Leslie.

When the mail arrives, it includes a complete record of where it has been:

```
From uucp Sat Apr 27 15:35 EST
>From uucp Sat Apr 27 15:22 EST remote from auxnj
>From uucp Sat Apr 27 15:12 EST remote from oyster
>From gwen Sat Apr 27 12:10 PST remote from cbis2

Leslie --

The sales figures you wanted are being sent via
overnight delivery. Call if you have questions.
                    -- Gwen
```

The last mail header tells you that the message originated from gwen on cbis2. Reading upward, you can see that the mail was passed to oyster, then to auxnj, and then to Leslie's computer, where it was delivered to Leslie. Each header shows the time at which the message was transferred to the next computer. Gwen sent the message at 12:10 P.M. Pacific time, and it was delivered to Leslie 25 minutes later, at 3:35 P.M. Eastern time.

Using Other UNIX Mail Programs

Although the UNIX `mail` program has proved to be a powerful workhorse over the years, programmers have been tempted to write better mail programs. Many programmers have tried; some have succeeded. A few of these other mail programs are discussed in the following sections.

The `mailx` Mailer

One popular `mail` alternative is `mailx`. The `mailx` program is compatible with `mail`, so that messages sent with one can be read with the other. When you read your mail with `mailx`, however, you immediately will notice differences.

The following example shows what you might see when `mailx` starts:

```
mailx version 3.1  Type ? for help.
"/usr/mail/jerry": 1 message 1 new
>N  1 mark           Thu Aug  8 17:43    8/349
 N  2 jim            Thu Aug  8 16:18    2/112
 N  3 sarah          Wed Aug  7 08:54   19/1208
?
```

Rather than displaying the first message, `mailx` immediately shows you how many mail messages you have, who sent them, and when they were sent. The pair of numbers at the end of each line shows the size of each message, in lines and characters. You can read the messages in order, as with `mail`, or begin with any message you want.

The `mailx` program has other helpful capabilities:

- With `mailx`, you can send "carbon copies" to users other than the addressee.

- You can use `mailx` to create groups of users, a technique that enables you to send messages to many users at once by specifying the name of their group. For example, if you define a group of your co-workers under the name `staff`, you can type the command **mailx staff** to send a mail message to everyone in your work group.

- The `mailx` program enables you to invoke an editor, such as `vi`, so that you can edit the message you are sending.

- With `mailx`, you can automatically include several canned lines of text at the end of your message. Typically this text might include your name, telephone number, and other information, serving much the same purpose as letterhead.

- You can include the contents of a file or the output from a program as part of your message in `mailx`.

Although `mail` is available on all UNIX systems, many manufacturers provide `mailx` as an alternate mail program.

The `elm` Mailer

Many popular mail programs were originally written for fun by imaginative programmers, who later contributed the programs to the UNIX community at no charge. Many computers around the United States, called *archive sites*, make a point of collecting such public domain software and making it available to anyone who wants it.

Perhaps the most sophisticated of these public domain mail programs is `elm`, written by Dave Taylor at Hewlett-Packard Laboratories in Palo Alto, California, with contributions from dozens of other UNIX users. The `elm` program is a screen-oriented mail processing system that enables you to send and receive mail much more easily than you can with other mailers.

The `elm` program has great flexibility and power. The author of `elm` was familiar with many other popular UNIX mail programs and carefully picked the features he liked best from each. It has all the capabilities of other UNIX mailers, such as `mailx`, but it also displays information in an especially simple and clear way.

One very useful feature of the program is its header system. Like many other mail programs, `elm` automatically attaches more information to the beginning of each message than just the sender's login name and the date the mail was sent. A typical `elm` message looks like this example:

```
From joe Thu Aug  8 22:50 EDT 1991
Subject: Weekly pizza party
To: barbara (Barbara King)
Date: Thu, 8 Aug 91 22:50:13 EDT
From: Joe Harris <crescent!joe>
X-Mailer: ELM [version 2.2 PL0]

Barbara --

The weekly pizza party will be held at Pizza City on
north US 321. Be there at 11:30 Friday.
                                        -- Izzy
```

In this example, the lines at the beginning of the message tell you the subject of the message, the complete names of the sender and receiver, the version of `elm` used to send the message, and the complete login name and computer name of the sender (`joe` on the computer named `crescent`).

The `elm` mailer is extremely user-friendly and simple to use, even for most beginners. Moderately complex steps are easy because the program guides you through each procedure step by step. In fact, you may find that you can use most of `elm`'s basic functions without reading any of the manuals. If you do need documentation, however, `elm` includes an extensive, thorough set of well-written manuals stored in text files on-disk. (If you want printed copies, you must print them yourself.) The program also is highly configurable; that is, you can define every facet of its behavior. A configuration file, which you create, tells `elm` what to do in a variety of situations.

In the past, an office worker needing information from an employee mailed a form—such as an IRS Form W-4, a travel authorization, or a problem report—to the employee, requesting that it be filled out and returned. With `elm`, you can perform the same function electronically, by sending a special kind of mail message called a *form*. Like a paper form, an `elm` form is a message with blanks for filling in information. When you send a form, you specify where the blanks in your message are. When you receive a form, `elm` prompts you to insert information into the blanks, and then `elm` returns the completed form to the sender.

Another practical feature of `elm` is its *mail filter*. As electronic mail becomes more popular, you may find that your mailbox begins to accumulate messages that don't really interest you—the electronic equivalent of junk mail. Within `elm` is a program that enables you to specify an action to be taken automatically with certain types of mail. For example, you might tell `elm` to delete mail automatically from certain users. Similarly, if a member of your group always sends out a joke of the day, which doesn't particularly interest you, you can tell `elm` to delete any message with the word *joke* in its subject description. Or, if you like the jokes, you might instruct `elm` to save the daily jokes in a file automatically. If you have an assistant, you can instruct `elm` to forward certain types of mail automatically to your assistant for processing. If you receive a heavy volume of mail, the `elm` filter can dramatically reduce the amount you have to read.

Other UNIX Mail Programs

Many other mail programs have been written and distributed by ambitious programmers or are available with various versions of UNIX (see table 7.1 for a list of other mail programs).

Table 7.1
Other UNIX Mail Programs

Program	Description
Berkeley	This powerful but often overly complex mailer is delivered with the Berkeley version of UNIX.
MH	Like Berkeley, this program is a powerful, complex mailer.
NMail	This mail program is delivered with the AI Workstation Software Environment from Hewlett-Packard.
PMX/TERM	Part of the AT&T Mail software, PMX/TERM is sold separately by AT&T. Its forms are much like those in `elm`.
fmail	Supplied with the AT&T Toolchest, this program provides a screen-oriented interface but uses the regular `mail` program to do the work of sending and receiving mail.

Carrying On Electronic Conversations with `write`

Although electronic mail is undoubtedly the most useful way of communicating with other users, UNIX provides another way that is even more fun. The `write` command enables you to carry on a "conversation" with another user. Lines you type on your terminal are displayed on the other user's terminal, and lines typed by the other user appear on yours. In effect, `write` provides a type of on-line CB radio.

When using `write`, both users must be logged in, and both must use the same computers. Because communication is instantaneous, `write` does not save messages for later retrieval, as `mail` does, nor can it pass information between computers.

Although `mail` enables you to send the same message to many users simultaneously, `write` allows you to communicate with only one user at a time.

Suppose that Bob wants to "talk" with Liz. Bob invokes the `write` command, listing Liz as the receiving user, as in the following example:

```
write liz
```

A message immediately appears on Liz's terminal:

```
Message from bob (tty42) [ Fri Aug 9 11:52:32 ] ...
```

By typing this command, Bob has set up a one-way conversation. Each time he types a line and presses <Return>, the line appears on Liz's terminal. If Liz wants to, she can ignore the messages and continue her current task, or she can engage in a conversation by typing a `write` command directed at Bob, such as:

```
write bob
```

Another one-way conversation is set up, this one from Liz to Bob. Each line that Liz types is now displayed on Bob's terminal. Thus, to be accurate, `write` actually sets up two simultaneous one-way conversations, rather than a single two-way conversation.

To terminate a `write` command, press <Ctrl-D>. Note, however, that when you press <Ctrl-D>, you disconnect the communication line only from yourself to the other user. Your friend can still send messages to you until she or he also presses <Ctrl-D>.

Why use `write` instead of picking up the telephone?

- You may be logged in at a terminal that does not have a telephone nearby.

- Some companies with offices in several cities pay a flat charge for leased data lines, but must pay long distance charges when a telephone call is placed. Thus, using a `write` conversation to communicate may be cheaper for your company than placing a telephone call.

- Using `write` is fun.

In some cases, you may not want to allow other users to interrupt you with `write` messages. For example, you may not appreciate receiving a friendly invitation to lunch right in the middle of an important sales demonstration with potential customers. You can prevent other users from interrupting you by turning messages off with the `mesg n` command. Users attempting to `write` to your terminal receive an error message. Later, you can be sociable again by turning messages on with the command `mesg y`.

The `mesg` command affects only `write` messages. You still can receive mail to your mailbox.

Getting System Information Electronically

Some of the most vital communication takes place between the system administrator and the users. The system administrator is usually the one person who knows the most about new equipment, broken equipment, and important upcoming events that concern the computer, such as backups and maintenance. The system administrator can communicate information to the users in any of several ways, depending on the urgency of the information.

The Message of the Day

Each time you log in on a UNIX system, the system automatically displays a welcoming message called the *message of the day*. By changing the message of the day, the system administrator can make all users aware of important subjects, from the company picnic to upcoming maintenance schedules.

The message of the day is stored in the file /etc/motd. This file is a regular UNIX text file that the system administrator can edit using any text editor, such as vi. Often asterisks or other punctuation marks surround the message to make it stand out, ensuring that all users see the message when they log in (see fig. 7.2 for an example of a typical message of the day).

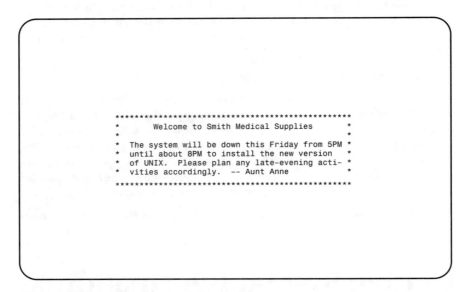

```
****************************************************
*           Welcome to Smith Medical Supplies      *
*                                                  *
*   The system will be down this Friday from 5PM   *
*   until about 8PM to install the new version     *
*   of UNIX.  Please plan any late-evening acti-   *
*   vities accordingly.  -- Aunt Anne              *
****************************************************
```

Fig. 7.2. *A sample message of the day.*

The message of the day is especially appropriate for messages such as this example, which are not urgent but which all users need to see.

The wall Command

For extremely urgent messages, the system administrator can use a command called wall (*write all*). The wall command functions similarly to write in that the message is immediately displayed on users' terminals; however, it differs from write in the following ways:

- wall sends the message to all users currently logged in.
- Only the system administrator can use the wall command.

- Conversation is strictly one-way, from the system administrators to the users. Users cannot respond to a `wall` message.

- Users cannot turn these messages off with the `mesg` command.

A `wall` message is also known as a *broadcast message* and almost always involves some imminent event, such as a system crash, fire, or other catastrophe. The following example is a typical broadcast message:

```
Broadcast message from danc (console) Jul 29 16:41:32
...

The data center reports that the sprinkler system was
triggered accidentally by the weenie roast being held
by the assistants outside. The data center will have to
shut the system down in 60 seconds. Log off now!!!!

P.S. -- Free weenies in the parking lot.
```

You should not ignore broadcast messages; they almost always contain critical information. In this case, the message also contains a notice of free food.

The UNIX News System

Information of limited importance can be distributed by the UNIX news system, available on systems running UNIX System V. (Do not confuse this system with the Usenet NetNews system, described in Chapter 11.) In effect, the news system provides the system administrator with a simple electronic bulletin board on which to post short articles of interest to some users. Articles may include information about new services or equipment, notices of new employees, or almost anything else of interest to the users of the machine. As the user, you can read the articles that interest you and skip those that don't.

The system administrator posts a new article by adding a file to the `/usr/news` directory. The name of the file is the name of the article, and it therefore should give a hint of what the article is about, such as `new.employee` for information about a new staff member or `wordperf.hints` for useful tips about WordPerfect.

You can use the `news -s` command to determine if any new news articles have been posted by the system administrator since the last time you read the news. This command prints a message if new articles are available. Many users place this command in their .profile so that the existence of new news articles is brought to their attention each time they log in.

You can read all new articles with the news command. From the shell prompt, type **news**:

```
$ news <Return>

new.employee (danc) Jul 17, 1991

Folks -- Please join me in welcoming Henry Smith to
our ranks. Henry comes to us with 6 years of UNIX
experience and will be a big help to us on the
upcoming project.
$
```

New articles usually begin with a *header*, which is a line that identifies the name of the article (new.employee in this case), the person who wrote the article (danc in this example), and the date the article was made available.

You can read any individual article by typing **news** followed by the name of the article:

```
$ news petey.is.dead <Return>

petey.is.dead (anne) Aug 2 1991

Well, the ol' PDP-11 finally died yesterday. The guy
from DEC said the power supply would have to be
replaced, and Cindy decided it wasn't worth the cost.
No one's decided what to do with it yet, but all the
user files have been moved over to the VAX, and
petey has been taken off the network for good. So
long, old buddy!
$
```

You can obtain a listing of all available articles simply by listing the files in the /usr/news directory, using the ls command.

Networking on UNIX Systems

One of the reasons for the explosive growth of UNIX is its capability to exchange data with other computers, especially other UNIX computers. This capability, known as *networking*, makes it possible to distribute new programs very quickly and to manage many computers from a central site. These factors were all important in the early days of UNIX at Bell Labs, and they are just as important today.

The UUCP Networking System

The oldest, and perhaps most important, UNIX networking system is *UUCP*, which stands for *UNIX-to-UNIX copy*. UUCP is available on almost all UNIX computers that are in any way connected to other computers or have access to a telephone line. As the name implies, one of the major functions of UUCP is copying files from one computer to another, and in fact its most often used command is called uucp.

However, UUCP has other capabilities. In addition to transferring files from computer to computer, UUCP enables users to execute commands and perform administrative and maintenance tasks on distant computers.

Although UUCP has been made to run under other operating systems, such as MS-DOS and VMS, it was designed to run on UNIX computers. UUCP uses other UNIX tools to do much of its work—such as the shell, the mail program, and cron—and therefore is less complex than it might be were these tools not available.

UUCP can operate using just about any kind of connection between computers, including:

- Dial-up telephone lines (the public telephone network)

- PBX systems

- Direct connection (a cable that physically connects two computers located close together)

- Networks, such as Internet (discussed further in this chapter)

Figure 7.3 illustrates these possibilities.

Because UUCP can use the public telephone network, many people look upon all UNIX computers (at least, computers that have modems—most computers do) as a *loosely linked network*. That is, not all UNIX computers are connected to each other at all times, but any two computers have the capability of being connected, by virtue of the telephone lines to which they have access.

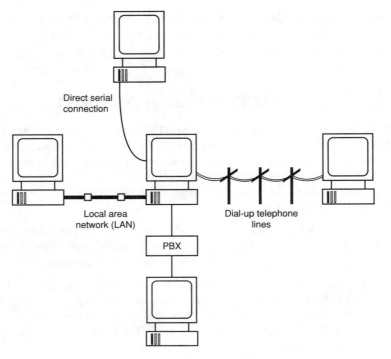

Fig. 7.3. *Types of UUCP connections.*

The History of UUCP

UUCP was originally written by Mike Lesk at AT&T Bell Labs in late 1976. At the time, UNIX computers had become widely distributed throughout Bell Labs, and Lesk was looking for a way to administer these computers remotely. A second, more powerful version was written in 1978 by Lesk and Dave Nowitz, a version that Bell Labs used through 1983, when problems with security and performance forced Bell Labs to commission work on another version.

After much discussion among UNIX experts, Peter Honeyman, Dan Nowitz, and Brian E. Redman began work on the new UUCP. Officially AT&T refers to it as *Basic Networking Utility*, or *BNU,* but in typical UNIX fashion, it is almost universally called *HoneyDanBer UUCP,* from the login names of the three key designers (respectively honey, dan, and ber—Redman's initials). Most versions of UNIX use HoneyDanBer UUCP.

The Operation of UUCP

The commands that make up the UUCP system are easy to identify: they all start with uu.

The uucp command, the namesake of the UUCP system, copies files from one UNIX computer to another. When you issue a uucp command, the uucp program itself performs only the initial stages of the process for copying a file between computers. The program verifies that your request is valid— for example, that the files you want to copy exist and that the computer name or names you specify are valid—and it creates control files in the /usr/spool/uucp directory that contain the details of what you want to do. At this point, uucp's work is done; it invokes another program to continue the work, but you get the shell prompt back and can continue with other tasks.

The program invoked by uucp is called uucico. (uucico stands for *UNIX-to-UNIX Copy-In Copy-Out*; it is pronounced by sounding each letter: "yoo-yoo-see-eye-see-oh" or "You, you see? I see. Oh!") After consulting configuration files stored in the /usr/lib/uucp directory, uucico contacts the destination computer, usually by telephone (see the following section, "UUCP Configuration Files," for more information about these files). When the other computer answers, uucico on your computer logs in using a special login name and password provided to your system administrator by the system administrator of the other computer. Because of the special login used, the other computer does not invoke a shell, as it would for a regular user, but invokes its own copy of uucico.

The uucico on your machine and the uucico on the other computer exchange identification information. Your computer takes the controlling role, telling the other computer which files are to be transferred. In the parlance of UUCP, your computer becomes the *master*, and the other becomes the *slave*. For each transfer, the slave makes sure that the request does not violate its security configuration and tells the master that it will or will not allow the transfer.

When your computer has no more work to do—that is, when it has transferred all the files listed in its control files—it asks the slave whether the slave has any work to do involving your computer. The slave checks for control files of its own that request file transfers to your computer. If the slave has work, the two computers switch roles—yours becomes the slave, and the other computer becomes the master. When the other computer has completed its work, the computers again switch roles, in case your computer now has new work that was created by users executing more uucp commands after your computer became the slave. The computers continue exchanging roles until neither has any more work to do; at that point both computers hang up.

Sometimes uucico may not be able to connect with the other computer immediately. Your computer's modem, or the other computer's modem, may be busy. Or the system administrator may have told UUCP that transfers on certain computers are to take place only at certain times of the day (usually late at night), and UUCP contacts those computers only at those times.

If UUCP is unable to transfer your files immediately, it tries again periodically. By using cron, the system administrator can configure uucico to start automatically at certain times to look for unfinished work.

UUCP uses one or more *protocols*, which specify the format that the data will take as the computers exchange files. Common to all UUCP systems is the g protocol, designed by Greg Chesson at Bell Labs. UUCP uses telephone lines. Using this protocol, the sending computer transmits, along with the data, additional information the receiving computer can use to verify that no data was corrupted during transmission. Telephone lines are notorious for introducing errors in transmitted data. If errors do appear in the data, the receiving computer can request that the sending computer transmit the data again.

Another popular protocol, found in many UUCP systems, is the e (*error-free*) protocol. UUCP can use this protocol over networks, such as Internet, that themselves ensure the arrival of data without errors. These networks relieve UUCP of the burden of checking for errors and of transmitting extra error-checking information.

Other protocols include d (*Datakit*), x (*X.25*), f (*Telnet*), and t (*TCP*), all used on various kinds of networks.

UUCP Configuration Files

The /usr/lib/uucp directory contains numerous control files that the system administrator uses to tell UUCP how to contact other computers. The control files in this directory include the following files:

Control file	Contents
Systems	A list of all the computers that UUCP can contact and information such as telephone number, baud rate, and login password. Because this file contains passwords for other systems, ordinary users cannot look at it.
Dialers	A description of how different kinds of modems can be controlled. The modems used by UUCP must be listed here. If one of your computer's modems is not listed in the dialers file, your system administrator must add an entry explaining how UUCP can control the new modem.
Devices	A list of how many of each type of modem your system has and to which ports (connectors) the modems are connected
Permissions	A list of the commands and directories that other systems can use, along with other information pertaining to UUCP security

Restricted and Unrestricted Uses of UUCP

When discussing UUCP, differentiating between what UUCP can do and what it is allowed to do is important. Especially in today's computing environment, in which computer worms, viruses, and other bugs are running rampant (see "The Internet Worm," further in this chapter), almost every system administrator places restrictions on what UUCP is allowed to do. For example, on almost every computer, UUCP is restricted to copying files into a single directory, /usr/spool/uucppublic. You can think of this file as a loading dock where UUCP is allowed to pick up and deliver files. Allowing other computers access to other directories of your computer can create serious security problems.

Many of the commands described here, therefore, may not work on your system if your system administrator has restricted them.

Copying Files with uucp

The form of the uucp command is very similar to that of the UNIX cp command; it differs in that the file is copied to a different computer.

For example, to copy the file /usr/janet/accounts from your computer to /usr/sheryl/accounts on a computer named bronco, you use the following command:

uucp /usr/janet/accounts bronco!/usr/sheryl/accounts

This command looks like a cp command, except that the destination file name is written in bang notation, which specifies a machine name. This notation tells UUCP to copy the file to that machine.

When you issue a uucp command, your prompt returns within a second or two, but do not be fooled into thinking that the file has been copied to the other computer. The uucp command simply completes the first step in getting the file copied. The bulk of the work is handled in the background by UUCP, which must contact the other system and complete the file transfer. Most likely, the UUCP system on your machine has to place a telephone call to bronco to copy the file, which may take some time. In addition, if the file is large and the modems on the computers are slow, it may take a significant amount of time to transfer the file across the telephone lines.

The -m option to uucp enables you to request that UUCP send you mail when the copy has been completed successfully. Or you can use the uustat command to check on the status of the copy periodically (see "Other Useful UUCP Commands," further in this chapter).

On most machines, however, the uucp command used in the example does not actually work, because the system administrator on bronco probably has restricted UUCP so that it is not allowed to copy files to /usr/sheryl.

Instead, you might have to send the file to UUCP's public directory with the following command:

uucp /usr/janet/accounts bronco!/usr/spool/uucppublic/accounts

Because so many UUCP commands reference this directory—and because the name of the directory is so long—you can use the shorthand symbol ~ (*tilde*) in place of /usr/spool/uucppublic:

uucp /usr/janet/accounts bronco!~/accounts

You also can ask UUCP to send mail to Sheryl when the copy is complete. Specify the –n (*notify*) option, followed by the name of the user on bronco whom you want to notify:

```
uucp -nsheryl /usr/janet/accounts bronco!~/accounts
```

You can notify yourself and Sheryl with the following command:

```
uucp -m -nsheryl /usr/janet/accounts bronco!~/accounts
```

Executing Commands on Other Computers with uux

The uux command enables you to execute a command on another machine or to execute a command on your machine that involves files on other machines. After the word uux, you type a valid UNIX command, enclosing it in quotation marks; however, you must write the name of the command and all files you use in bang notation, indicating the system on which the command or files reside. An exclamation point with no system name in front of it indicates your computer.

For example, to obtain a list of users logged in on the computer named peanut, type:

```
uux "peanut!who > !~/whos.on.peanut"
```

This command executes the who command on peanut and places its output in a file called whos.on.peanut on your machine—at least, that's the illusion perpetrated. In reality, uux places the output of the who command in a file on peanut, and that file is then automatically copied to whos.on.peanut on your system. As with uucp, the tilde (~) represents the directory /usr/spool/uucppublic.

Similarly, to execute the sort command on your machine, using the namelist file from the computer named pebbles, and to send the output to a file sorted.names on the computer named bambam, you type the following:

```
uux "!sort pebbles!/usr/jeff/namelist >bambam!/usr
/mary!sorted.names"
```

Again, UUCP automatically performs several intermediate steps:

1. UUCP copies /usr/jeff/namelist from pebbles to a temporary file on your computer.

2. UUCP sorts the file and places the output in another temporary file on your computer.

3. UUCP copies the output file from your computer to /usr/mary /sorted.names on bambam.

Although the capabilities of uux are very powerful, they also are very dangerous; in fact, probably none of the uux commands shown here will work on your computer. You can imagine the problems involved in letting anyone and everyone call your computer and execute commands that can modify or delete important data files. On most computers, uux is heavily restricted.

Other Useful UUCP Commands

The following UUCP commands also are useful.

Command	Description
uulog	Produces a report of files copied and commands recently executed by UUCP
uuname	Lists all the computers with which you can communicate
uustat	Lists pending UUCP operations, including files waiting to be copied to or from another computer and commands waiting to execute on another computer
uucheck	Used by the system administrator; verifies that all configuration files used by UUCP are present and produces a report on UUCP security
uuto	Provides a simpler means of using uucp. You simply name the files you want to copy and who is to receive the files (computer name and user name). uuto then issues the appropriate uucp command with appropriate options to send mail to you and the recipient. For example, to copy a file status.report to Greg on the computer midget, type **uuto status.report midget!greg**.
uupick	A timesaving shell program that enables you to "pick up" files sent to your computer from another computer. It lists the files that have arrived and the computer that sent them, and it enables you to copy them easily to other directories.

UUCP and the Future

Even though UUCP is the oldest and least sophisticated of the UNIX networking methods, it probably is here to stay. You will find UUCP on almost all UNIX systems, it is extremely flexible and powerful, it meets the needs of a wide variety of applications, and—perhaps most importantly— it's cheap. UUCP requires nothing more than a modem and a telephone line, and yet it can take advantage of many powerful types of networks when they are available.

Networking with RFS and NFS

Two common products for linking UNIX computers—RFS and NFS—were developed independently by AT&T and Sun Microsystems, respectively.

RFS (*Remote File Sharing*) was developed by AT&T and was introduced with UNIX System V Release 3. Originally it could be used only in conjunction with AT&T's STARLAN network, but it was later modified to work with other networks as well.

NFS (*Network File System*) was developed by Sun Microsystems in 1984 for Sun's version of UNIX, SunOS. NFS has since been implemented on more than 100 different types of computers; it now runs under many different versions of UNIX, including Berkeley 4.2 and 4.3, XENIX, AT&T UNIX System V Release 2 and Release 3, DEC's Ultrix, Cray's UNICOS, Amdahl's UTS, and IBM's AIX. It also runs under several non-UNIX operating systems, including IBM's VM for mainframes, DEC's VMS for the VAX line of computers, and MS-DOS for PCs.

Although they are quite different in their underlying structure, RFS and NFS are similar in the way in which you use them:

- The system administrators of one or more of the computers on the network *advertise resources*; that is, they make directories on their systems available for sharing. They not only must tell their computers which directories they will share, but they also must let other system administrators know.

- Administrators on other computers *mount* the remote resources; that is, they use the `mount` command to tell their computers to connect to the directories from other systems.

After the resources are mounted, you can access the directories on the other systems as though they were directories on your system. Thus a simple `cp` (*copy*) command specifying a directory on another system copies files from that system to your system or vice versa.

Computers that provide directories for other systems to use are called *servers*; computers that use these directories are called *clients*. Note that the same computer can be both a client and a server if it uses other computers' directories at the same time that it makes some of its own directories available for other computers to use. (See fig. 7.4 for an illustration of this arrangement. In this example, Computer A is a server, and Computer B is a client.)

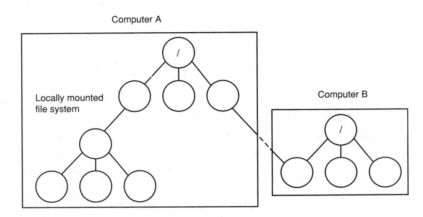

Fig. 7.4. *A remotely mounted file system.*

TCP/IP and the Internet

In 1969, the Defense Advanced Research Projects Agency (DARPA) of the Department of Defense (DOD) sponsored an experiment involving major DOD computing centers and centers at academic and commercial sites working on defense contracts. The centers were connected through what eventually became ARPANET, a network spanning the globe. In most cases, the computers at these centers already were organized into networks; ARPANET did not so much connect computer to computer as connect network to network. Such a network of networks is called an *internetwork*, and ARPANET became one of the best-known and largest internetworks.

Throughout the 1980s, DARPA funded the development of a set of protocols that smoothly integrated different kinds of networks. TCP/IP (Transmission Control Protocol/Internet Protocol) is a set of these networking protocols developed by DARPA. They describe how networks can be interconnected and communicate with each other.

TCP/IP was included in Berkeley's version of UNIX, and by 1983, all computers on ARPANET were using TCP/IP. By 1990 ARPANET included hundreds of networks around the world, many of which included dozens of computers. Not all computers on ARPANET use UNIX, but all use TCP/IP to communicate.

Throughout the 1980s, ARPANET became the beginning of an even larger internetwork. Computing centers and organizations involved in defense work connected to ARPANET, and other organizations—often not involved in defense work—in turn connected to those networks. Eventually, enormous numbers of computers were part of ARPANET, or were connected to computers that were part of ARPANET, or were connected to computers connected to computers that were part of ARPANET, and so on. Before long, every major computer center in the country, and many throughout the world, could exchange files, mail, and other information.

DARPA, however, controlled only the networks that linked computers that were part of ARPANET. The other computers, networks, and the equipment that connected them to each other were controlled by somebody, but no single organization or agency controlled everything. This conglomeration of interconnected computers and networks, with no central control, became known as the *Internet*.

By the close of the 1980s, ARPANET was beginning to show its age. Most of its internetwork lines communicated at 56,000 bits per second, an impressive speed in the early days of ARPANET, but no longer state-of-the-art. Furthermore, DARPA was a research agency that did not relish its position as a provider of services, and ARPANET had become a service.

In 1984, the National Science Foundation (NSF) began forming an internet of its own, which was not restricted to researchers involved in government work, as was ARPANET. Called NSFnet, it was designed to include several very high-speed connections between major computing centers—in the language of networking, these connections were the *backbone*. Data was transmitted over the backbone at speeds up to 1.5 million bits per second initially, reaching speeds of 45 million bits per second by 1990. In turn, smaller networks connected to the major computing centers through regional networks. NSF donated some $14 million over a period of five years, and in 1987, the first portions of the backbone began to operate. At about the same time, DARPA began phasing out ARPANET.

NSFnet had certain advantages. Anyone could hook in—it was not restricted to defense-related work. And it had a much greater data-carrying capacity. ARPANET was funded by the government, however, and was available essentially free of charge to its users. Users of NSFnet were expected to pay their way.

NSFnet continues to grow as a major component of the Internet. NSF expects to upgrade all lines to 45 million bits per second eventually, although technical problems exist that must be solved first.

The Internet Worm

In late 1988, a graduate student at Cornell University disabled an estimated 3,000 UNIX computers for several days with a kind of program known as a *worm*, a program—usually written with malicious intent—that duplicates itself from computer to computer. The computers were all connected to Internet, but only certain kinds of computers were affected: DEC VAXes and Sun workstations, all running versions of Berkeley UNIX. Although this worm did not destroy or damage any data, an estimated 8,000 hours were required to clear it, costing $10 million in lost time.

The story began at about 8 P.M. on Wednesday, November 2, 1988. Cornell graduate student Robert Morris released onto the Internet a worm that he had written. He intended it as an experiment, in which the worm would benignly spread itself from computer to computer. However, like a creature in a science fiction thriller brought to life, the worm went awry. By guessing passwords and exploiting known flaws in some electronic mail systems, the worm spread across the country. Within two hours it had infected a major network access point at the University of California at Berkeley, and within four hours it had reached every computer on the Internet that was susceptible to its attack.

Many of the affected computers were owned by universities, such as Cornell University, the University of California at Berkeley, and Carnegie-Mellon University. The National Cancer Institute was infected. Perhaps more chilling, other infected computers were owned by government research agencies involved in classified work, such as Lawrence Livermore National Laboratories and the Army's Aberdeen Proving Ground.

The worm proved incredibly difficult to stop. A VAX 8600 at the University of Utah was infected at 9:46 P.M. (MST). By 10:06 P.M., the worm had made so many copies of itself on the computer that the computer was rendered useless. At 10:20 P.M., a system administrator killed the worm, but by 10:41 P.M., the computer was infected again and unusable. Shutting down the system and killing the worms didn't stop the problem; the computer kept getting reinfected.

In a desperate attempt to avoid reinfection, many sites disconnected their computers from the Internet, crippling the Internet and its ability to carry electronic mail. Ironically, the collapse of the Internet's mail capability prevented the delivery of several mass mailings that contained information on fighting the worm.

Within days the frantic efforts of system administrators cleared the so-called *Internet Worm*. Manufacturers made changes to many of the programs that enabled the worm to spread; however, the Internet Worm remains the most notorious example of the damage that can occur when networking security is too permissive.

(Most of this information about the Internet Worm is based on an excellent summary by Frank Hayes in the June 1990 issue of *UnixWorld*.)

Chapter Summary

UNIX has a long tradition of sharing information, a tradition that dates back to the earliest days of UNIX at Bell Labs. UNIX provides many ways for you to share information with other users—on your system and on other computers. You can send and receive electronic mail with any of several electronic mailers, such as `mail`, `mailx`, and `elm`. Alternatively, for more immediate interaction, you can carry on a conversation with `write`.

UNIX also provides many ways for the system administrator to provide information to the computer's users. By editing the message of the day, your administrator can distribute important information in a timely fashion. For more urgent information, the `wall` command sends a message to all users currently logged in. For lengthy items or items of specialized interest, the news system enables the system administrator to post news articles on an electronic bulletin board.

UNIX enables you to exchange data with users on other systems with the UUCP system, available on almost all UNIX systems. Depending on security, you also may be able to execute commands on other machines. Most powerful of all, computers can be connected into networks using RFS and NFS, and can exchange information at very high speeds.

As you have seen in this chapter, electronic communications provide our society with one of the greatest benefits of the computer age, but also with one of its greatest problems. Safe-guarding information in an era when all computers are interconnected presents today's computer experts with a very challenging situation.

8

Programming Languages and UNIX Software Development

U NIX began as an operating system written by programmers for programmers. Thompson, Ritchie, and the other creators of UNIX did not set out to design a commercial product, but rather an environment in which to do their own work. Consequently, today UNIX is one of the richest program development environments available.

Many of the major software development companies today are *UNIX shops*, computer slang for "a place where UNIX is used." In fact, some companies that market software for other operating systems—mainframes, PCs, and minis—use UNIX to develop software and then *port*, or transfer, the software to the desired environment.

UNIX provides an ideal environment for writing software. Throughout the history of UNIX, dozens of programmers have developed specialized tools to ease the task of developing software, tools that have contributed to the UNIX community.

In this chapter, you explore many of the software tools—such as debuggers, cross-reference programs, code analyzers, and databases—and programming languages that UNIX programmers commonly use. This chapter is intended primarily for people involved in program development, such as programmers, analysts, and software development managers; however,

257

even if you are new to software development, you will find interesting information in this chapter about the tools and languages with which UNIX programmers work.

UNIX Programming Languages

UNIX provides an attractive environment to programmers, regardless of the language in which they program. As UNIX's popularity increased, so did the incentive for companies and individuals to make new languages available under UNIX. Colleges and universities encouraged students to write compilers and interpreters for the schools' UNIX computers. Vendors saw increasing markets for various language products as more and more software developers began using UNIX. Researchers at AT&T Bell Labs, where UNIX grew up, continued their tradition of creating new programming languages, and researchers increasingly developed these languages under UNIX. Many of the languages that began under UNIX are now major players in the computer industry in both the UNIX environment and elsewhere.

Today all major programming languages, as well as a vast number of not-so-major languages, are available on one or more UNIX computers (see table 8.1 for a comparison of some of the major UNIX programming languages). These languages—and many others available with UNIX—are discussed in the following sections.

The C Programming Language

Of all the languages born under UNIX, the C programming language has made the greatest impact on the computer industry. Designed by Brian Kernighan and Dennis Ritchie—original participants in the development of UNIX—C is one of the most popular and widely used programming languages.

UNIX and C share a special relationship; they share not only designers, but design philosophies. The designers of C wanted a language that would enable them to do their work and produce fast, efficient code. They wanted the "Ferrari" of high-level languages, which is what C has proved to be.

Table 8.1
Common UNIX Programming Languages

Language	Type	Common Uses	Advantages	Disadvantages
APL	Interpreted	Matrix manipulation; mathematical modeling	Very powerful built-in math operators	Difficult to read; poorly structured; requires special keyboard and display for Greek math symbols
awk	Interpreted	Report writing; file manipulation; data retrieval; data verification	Powerful C-like language has a built-in understanding of files and records	Slow compared to C
BASIC	Interpreted	Small applications, especially by inexperienced programmers	Easy to use; applications can be developed rapidly	Somewhat slow compared to other languages; different dialects are incompatible
C and C++	Compiled	System utilities; text processing; databases; numerical analysis	Very fast; efficient; portable	Difficult for beginners
FORTRAN	Compiled	Numerical analysis	Fast; well-suited for scientific and engineering work; wide base of existing software.	Poorly structured; poor text manipulation capabilities
COBOL	Compiled	Business applications	Extremely well-suited to business applications and file processing; highly standardized	Wordy; slower than C or FORTRAN
Shell	Interpreted	System utilities and batch files	Programs can be written quickly using existing UNIX commands	Relatively slow; programs are sometimes obtuse

Understanding the Characteristics of C

The distant ancestor of C is a language called BCPL, written by Martin Richards in 1967. Ken Thompson, one of the creators of UNIX, was attracted by many of the features of BCPL, but found that the small computers under which UNIX then operated could not support BCPL. He created a more modest version of BCPL for UNIX, called B, in 1970. Both BCPL and B were low-level languages that dealt with only one type of object—the machine word. By 1971, Kernighan and Ritchie saw a need for a more powerful, flexible language, and they designed and implemented a new language, briefly called NB, but later known as C. The major advance of C over B was its typing structure. Rather than dealing with a single type of object, C provided a wide variety of different data types and representations.

C has several notable features, which are outlined in the following sections.

Size

C is often described as a "small" language because, compared to many other programming languages, C has a small number of different statement types, and the entire language can be described completely in a small book. Programmers familiar with other languages can learn the basic syntax of C quickly, and C compilers are comparatively cheap and easy for software developers to write.

Closeness to the Hardware

C is a relatively low-level computer language. The designers of C wanted to create a language that enabled programmers to stay close to the machine; as a result, C deals with the same types of objects that computers do. Computers are adept at shifting, "bit-fiddling," and manipulating binary numbers, and C is oriented toward these types of operations. Because of this orientation toward operations that machines do well, C programs tend to produce extremely fast, efficient code. This low-level view makes C an ideal candidate for writing system utilities and even operating systems. In fact, all UNIX tools and commands, and almost the entire UNIX operating system, are written in C.

Kernighan and Ritchie knew that in some languages, notably PL/I, program statements that seemed simple to the programmer caused the computer to perform very complex operations. Programmers were sometimes amazed at how inefficient their programs were, not realizing that a single language statement represented a large amount of work for the computer.

C's designers avoided this trap; in a 1978 edition of *The Bell Labs Technical Journal*, Ritchie wrote, "Programmers like to feel that the cost of a statement is comparable to the difficulty in writing it." That is, if a statement is easy to write, it should be easy for the computer to perform. Consequently each type of C statement represents an operation that is basic to a computer and that can be executed efficiently.

Portability

One of C's most important attributes is its portability. Although originally designed for the DEC PDP-11 under UNIX, C is independent of any particular machine or operating system. Programmers can write carefully crafted C programs that run on many machines and under many different operating systems. To a great degree, the portability of C is responsible for the proliferation of UNIX on so many different machines.

C goes to great lengths to handle input and output in a consistent manner across many different types of environments. Thus, the same program can read and write data on a UNIX system and on a mainframe, even though each environment stores data quite differently.

Operators

C has an unusually rich set of operators, including the conventional operators, such as addition and subtraction, and more unconventional operators, such as *bit shifting*. (Bit shifting is the process of moving bits around within a binary number. Such operations turn out to be useful in some situations.)

Subroutine Library

The C compiler includes an extensive library of subroutines that programmers can call from within a C program. Included are routines for manipulating strings, performing I/O, sorting data, manipulating blocks of memory, and many other functions. C programmers rely heavily on this library to perform much of the processing in a C program.

Pointers

Pointers are one of C's most powerful features (but also the most vexing to new C programmers). Essentially machine addresses, *pointers* enable programmers to deal with where data is located, as well as the data itself. Through pointers, C provides an especially elegant way of expressing algorithms, which are very efficient for the machine.

Introducing a Sample C Program

This section presents a sample C program that copies its standard input to its standard output one character at a time, converting all lowercase letters to uppercase.

```
1    #include <stdio.h>
2    #include <ctype.h>
3
4    main ()
5    {
6    int c;
7
8        while ((c = getchar ()) != EOF)
9            putchar (toupper );
10       exit (0);
11   }
```

Lines 1 and 2 locate system files that contain definitions required by this program and most other programs, and then they include these files in the program. Both files are located in the /usr/include directory; the compiler knows to look for them there. stdio.h contains definitions for the standard I/O routines; ctype.h contains definitions for the character classification and conversion routines. Lines 4 and 5 begin the main program. Line 6 declares an integer variable, c. Line 8 begins the main loop of the program. This portion of the program, using the getchar function, reads a character from the standard input, assigns the character to the variable c, and performs the body of the loop if the end of file is not reached. The body of the loop, line 9, consists of converting the character to uppercase and printing it. When the end of file is reached, the loop falls through to line 10 and exits the program with a return code of 0, which indicates to the operating system that the program worked successfully. The blank lines, lines 3 and 7, help make the program easier for people to read.

Compiling a C Program

You use the cc command to compile C programs. Many options are available; a simple cc command follows:

```
cc testprog.c -o testprog
```

This command compiles the source file `testprog.c` and, if no errors occur, produces an executable program called `testprog`.

Although you type a single cc command to compile a program, at least four programs are executed to do the work. The programmer may not be aware (and, in fact, need not be aware) that the following programs are invoked:

- *Preprocessor.* The preprocessor (`/lib/cpp`) reads the user's C source program, looking for *preprocessor directives*, which are special commands that begin with # and provide a number of programming facilities, such as macros. The preprocessor produces a temporary output file that is also C source code, but with the macros expanded and various other changes.

- *Compiler.* The compiler (`/bin/comp` in UNIX System V) translates the C source code from the preprocessor into assembly language.

- *Assembler.* The assembler (`/bin/as`) converts the assembly code into machine code.

- *Linker.* The linker (`/bin/ld`) combines the pieces of a program into an executable file. Large programs are written as several source files, and the linker combines these files into a single executable program. The linker also searches the appropriate libraries for library functions used within the program and links them into the program.

A few of the options for the cc command vary from one version of UNIX to another. Under most versions, the cc command provides an option that causes cc to display the four (or more) commands normally executed with the announcement that it is being executed behind the programmer's back.

Standardizing C

The original book describing C was *The C Programming Language*, written by C's designers, Kernighan and Ritchie. For many years the computer industry considered this book to be an indispensable guide for all C programmers, and most compilers boasted that they were "K&R compatible;" that is, that they adhered to the description of C described in Kernighan and Ritchie's book. Compiler designers, however, added new features to their C that were not part of the original description.

As C spread beyond UNIX, the computer industry saw an increasing need to standardize the language across all computers and environments. In the mid-1980s, the American National Standards Institute (ANSI) formed a committee, known as X3J11, to prepare a standard description of C. The final standard was released in 1990 in the book *Programming Language C*. Ironically, many of the C compilers on the PC, such as those from Borland International and Microsoft Corporation, were among the first to adhere to the ANSI standard. Because so many existing UNIX compilers were firmly entrenched, UNIX was relatively slow to switch to the version of C mandated by ANSI.

Object-Oriented Programming and the Rise of C++

Various software developers designed and implemented a number of new and improved versions of C. In particular, some tried to include features for a new method of programming known as *object-oriented programming*, or *OOP*. OOP invites the programmer to look at a problem in a different way than the programmer traditionally does. The programmer using the traditional approach concentrates on the procedure and the data the procedure uses to get a job done. By contrast, the programmer using an object-oriented approach focuses on the things the program must manipulate, called *objects*, and how these objects interact. Objects are constructed so that they contain both the procedure and the data. Object-oriented programming is based upon these three cornerstones:

- *Encapsulation.* Traditional (non-object-oriented) programs usually describe in one part of the program the data to be manipulated and describe elsewhere the procedures to manipulate the data. Object-oriented programming combines the description of an object's data with the procedures that manipulate the data, forming a single, integrated unit.

- *Inheritance.* Objects can inherit features and attributes of other objects. When an object-oriented programmer determines that two types of objects share common features, these common features need be defined only once. A new object can be defined simply and quickly by specifying how it differs from an existing object. An example of typical object-oriented thinking is: "A newspaper is just like a magazine except...."

- *Polymorphism.* Different objects react to the same operation in different ways. Performing common types of operations on different objects may be possible, yet what actually happens may vary, depending on the characteristics of the object. For example, an installation operation can be defined for a computer, a washing machine, and a VCR, but the procedure differs for each object.

Many practical advantages flow from these features, including the following:

- Object-oriented programs tend to be resilient to change. Because objects are packaged as integrated units (data and procedures), you can make changes within the object with a minimum chance of affecting code outside the object.

- Maintenance time often is greatly reduced because changes to one part of the code tend not to break other parts.

- Object-oriented programs are usually smaller and can be written more quickly because inheritance can reuse code that is already written.

- Because of inheritance, code written on one project is more likely to be usable without modification on another.

Some object-oriented versions of C, such as *Objective C*, acquired moderate success, but one in particular, *C++*, has achieved widespread acceptance. C++ was developed in the early 1980s by Bjarne Stroustrup of AT&T Bell Labs. The name C++, suggested by Rich Mascitti, is a pun on the C operator ++, which means "add one." Stroustrup wrote the first book on the subject, *C++ Programming Language*, in 1986.

Like its parent, C, C++ has taken hold and spread throughout the UNIX environment and beyond. C++ is the first language that combines object-oriented theory with the practicalities of commercial programming. Today C++ has more than 150,000 users, a number that increases daily. This language promises to become a major player in the development of MS-DOS software with the release of C++ compilers from Borland International and Zortech, Incorporated.

In the UNIX environment, most implementations of C++ are based on a translator called `cfront`, written by Stroustrup. `cfront` accepts C++ source code as its input and translates this code into C source code, which is then compiled using the standard UNIX C compiler.

C++ has had an effect on its parent, C, as well. Many of the features that originated in C++ were adopted by the ANSI C committee as part of their standard. ANSI is working on a C++ standard, which is scheduled to be completed in 1994.

The FORTRAN Language

FORTRAN was the first major high-level computer language. Developed between 1954 and 1957 by an IBM team headed by John W. Bacus, FORTRAN predates UNIX by a considerable margin. FORTRAN's forte is *number-crunching*—the processing of large amounts of numerical data—and this language is still used today by many scientists and engineers. FORTRAN is not a modern, state-of-the-art program, but it remains appealing because of the vast body of scientific and engineering software written over the years using FORTRAN. In the early days of UNIX, FORTRAN was even more popular than it is today. As UNIX developed and spread beyond Bell Labs, the FORTRAN compiler of choice was `f77`, a compiler that adhered to the 1977 ANSI version of FORTRAN.

Other FORTRAN compilers that attempted to solve some of FORTRAN's shortcomings eventually evolved. Two such compilers, `ratfor` (Rational FORTRAN) and `efl` (Extended FORTRAN Language), provide FORTRAN dialects that include structured programming constructs, which standard FORTRAN lacks. The new statements in both dialects are based on structured control statements from C. `ratfor` and `efl` are translators that convert Ratfor or EFL source code into standard FORTRAN code, which is then compiled by the standard FORTRAN compiler.

The COBOL Language

COBOL (Common Business Oriented Language) is the most widely implemented computer language in the world. Originally developed for the large computers of the early 1960s (by the standards of those days), COBOL is largely based on the work of Dr. Grace Murray Hopper of the U.S. Navy. COBOL is intended to be very English-like, with language keywords composed entirely of English words, assembled using a syntax very similar to English. Even though COBOL programs tend to be long and verbose, they are usually easy to read and understand.

COBOL is unique, both for the features it includes and the features it omits. With COBOL's strong orientation toward business applications, it addresses the needs of business applications and omits features frequently found in languages of little use in the business world. Business applications tend to do large amounts of input and output, and COBOL provides efficient methods for processing massive amounts of file data. Decimal arithmetic, ideal for processing money, is another of COBOL's strong suits. On the other hand, COBOL is weak in computational power and utterly lacks scientific and engineering functions such as logs, trigonometric functions, and the like, because such functions rarely are needed for business applications.

Short COBOL programs are nonexistent; some are just less long than others. Even the following simple program to print the phrase *Hello World* is lengthy:

```
IDENTIFICATION DIVISION.
PROGRAM-ID.      HELLO.
AUTHOR.              SCHULMAN.
DATE-WRITTEN.    MAY 25, 1991.
DATE-COMPILED.

ENVIRONMENT DIVISION.
CONFIGURATION SECTION.
SOURCE-COMPUTER.    ATT-3B2-600.
OBJECT-COMPUTER.    ATT-3B2-600.
INPUT-OUTPUT SECTION.
FILE-CONTROL.
    SELECT PRINTER ASSIGN TO UT-S-PRINTER.

DATA DIVISION.
FILE SECTION.

FD  PRINTER
    LABEL RECORDS ARE OMITTED
    DATA RECORD IS PRINT-LINE.
01  PRINT-LINE.
    05  FILLER      PIC X(80).

PROCEDURE DIVISION.
HERE-WE-GO.
    OPEN OUTPUT PRINTER.
    MOVE "HELLO WORLD" TO PRINT-LINE.
    WRITE PRINT-LINE.
    CLOSE PRINTER.
    STOP RUN.
```

COBOL programs always are divided into four major parts, called *divisions*. The IDENTIFICATION DIVISION identifies the program and its author; the ENVIRONMENT DIVISION defines the program's interaction with the computer and the outside world; the DATA DIVISION declares the records, fields, and variables that the program manipulates; and the PROCEDURE DIVISION contains the code that the program executes. In COBOL programs that are more useful than this example, the DATA and PROCEDURE divisions are usually quite long—a listing of the entire program may be dozens, or even hundreds, of pages in length.

Although COBOL always has been popular on mainframes, its path to UNIX has been slow. Several COBOL compilers are available for UNIX (see table 8.2).

Table 8.2
Selected COBOL Vendors for UNIX

COBOL Product	Vendor
AcuCOBOL-85	AcuCOBOL, Inc.
Micro Focus COBOL/2	Micro Focus, Ltd.
RM/COBOL	Ryan McFarland Corp.
Sun COBOL	Sun Microsystems, Inc.
VIS/COBOL	VISystems, Inc.

Assembly Language

Assembly language, notable because of its almost complete absence from UNIX, is essentially the language that the computer directly understands. In the early days of computing, at least until the mid-1950s, all programs were written in assembly language; some programs were entered via toggle switches on the control panel of computers. Other high-level languages, such as those described in this chapter, were developed somewhat later (late 1950s). Programs written in assembly language always were more efficient than the equivalent program in a high-level language written by an equally skilled programmer. Although assembly language programs were more tedious to write than programs in other languages, programmers continued to turn to assembly language because of its efficiency. The first version of UNIX was written in assembly language, as were all operating systems of the time.

Today, C has replaced assembly language in UNIX. C is easier to use than assembly and yet is almost as efficient. By their nature, assembly language programs are intimately tied to a single machine, but most UNIX programmers want to write programs that can run on many machines. C offers much of assembler's efficiency, but provides the portability that assembler does not.

In 1973, UNIX was completely rewritten in C, and by 1978 Dennis Ritchie could write that C was "sufficiently expressive and efficient to have completely displaced assembly language programming on UNIX."

Programming Languages Available in UNIX

The programming languages described previously in this chapter can be found in many environments other than UNIX. If you have studied computer languages, you probably are familiar with these languages, even if you never before have heard of UNIX. UNIX programmers, however, also have access to several useful languages found mostly or exclusively on UNIX computers. These languages are described in this section.

awk

Although often considered a tool, awk also can make a serious claim to being a programming language. awk was developed by three Bell Labs researchers—Alfred Aho, Peter Weinberger, and Brian Kernighan—and its name is formed simply from the last initials of its authors.

awk's designers were all C programmers, and many awk statements have formats borrowed directly from C. Consequently, C programmers find awk especially easy to use. But awk is designed specifically for processing and examining files in various ways and goes far beyond C in these areas. awk has a built-in understanding of files, records, and fields and can perform a large number of file manipulation tasks with very short programs.

awk programs consist of one or more pairs of *patterns* and *actions*. Patterns describe which records awk should select from the file, and actions specify what awk should do with those records.

Some common uses of awk, with examples, include the following:

- *File Manipulation.* awk can be used to rearrange, combine, or edit files in many different ways, such as rearranging fields, removing obsolete fields, and adding new data. For example, an awk program to keep records only in which the eighth field is Delaware follows:

```
$8 == "Delaware" { print }
```

This program tells awk to select all records in which the eighth field is Delaware and to print them. You can redirect this information to another file, creating a file of only Delaware records.

- *Reporting.* awk programs can collect data from files and produce reports, requiring little effort from you. For example, suppose that a file contains records in which the fifth field is a sales office location and the seventh is the amount of a sale. An awk program to print all records for the Cincinnati office and produce a total follows:

```
$5 == "Cincinnati" { print; total = total + $7 }
END { print total }
```

The first line tells awk to locate records for which the fifth field is Cincinnati. awk prints all such records, and keeps a running total of the seventh field. When all records have been printed (at the END), awk prints the total.

- *Data Validation.* awk programs can check files for proper content, such as checking field sizes and values. Suppose that a file consists of records, each of which should contain twelve fields and in which the third field is supposed to be a seven-digit part number. A simple awk program to verify these aspects of the file follows:

```
NF != 12 { print "Record", NR,
                    "does not contain 12 fields." }
length($3) != 7 { print "Part number for record",
                    NR, "wrong size." }
```

This program first says that if the number of fields (NF) is not 12, print a message that includes the record number (NR). Then, if the length of the third field is not 7, print a message.

awk can accomplish a large number of complex tasks with programs only a few lines long. Longer awk programs can accomplish correspondingly more complex tasks. awk is one of the most valuable tools you can learn, because it combines the capabilities of many other tools, such as sed, cut, paste, and others, with capabilities not found elsewhere, except in other programming languages (see Chapter 3 for a detailed discussion of cut and paste, and Chapter 6 for a discussion of sed).

The Shell

The primary purpose of the shell is to serve as an interface between the operating system kernel and the user; however, the shell also provides a programming language through which you can write batch files, utilities, and even applications. Several shells are available under UNIX. (In this section, the term *shell* refers to the Bourne Shell.)

Most of the statements—sometimes all of them—within a shell program are the same UNIX commands you issue from the keyboard: mv, cut, sed, and others. Flow control statements, such as tests and loops, are special, built-in statements. Together, the combination leads to flexible, but often unusual, shell programs.

For example, consider a shell program to send a one-line message to another user. If the user is logged in, the program immediately sends him or her a message via the write command; otherwise, the UNIX mail command is used. A sample program follows:

```
echo "User to send a message to: \c"
read user
echo "Your message (1 line only): \c"
read msg
if echo "$msg" ¦ write $user
then
    echo "Message sent via the write command."
elif echo "$msg" ¦ mail $user
then
    echo "Message sent via the mail command."
else
    echo "Message could not be sent."
fi
```

The first four lines prompt you to enter the name of the user to whom you want to send the message, and then prompts for the one-line message. if attempts to send the message through the write command. If the attempt is successful, the programs displays a confirmation message; otherwise, it attempts to send the message through mail. If that attempt succeeds, the program displays a confirmation message; otherwise, the program displays a failure message.

You can use the looping features in the shell to execute commands repeatedly. For example, suppose that you are about to make changes to files in the current directory, but first want to make a copy of each file, adding the extension .old to the name of each copy. You can accomplish this task with the following simple shell program:

```
for i in *
do
    cp $i $i.old
done
```

The for loop determines the name of every file in the current directory and then performs the statement between do and done, once for each name found. The variable i takes on a different file name each time. The cp command makes a copy of each file. The name of the copy is the name of the old file, with the extension .old appended.

Complex applications with the shell are possible; in fact, Ray Swartz, who writes a monthly column for the magazine *UNIXWorld*, advertises a complete general ledger package written entirely in the shell.

Shell programs are not compiled in any way; the files containing the shell program source are directly interpreted by the shell. By turning on execute permission for the source file using the chmod command, the programmer indicates to the shell that the file is an executable shell program. (Refer to Chapter 3, "Understanding Files and Directories," for more information about the chmod command.)

Because shell programs are interpreted rather than compiled and because many shell statements involve starting other programs, shell programs usually run slower than equivalent programs in other languages. This slowness, however, usually is offset by the speed with which shell programs can be designed, coded, and tested. Many tasks that cannot be economically solved with C, COBOL, or FORTRAN programs can be solved quickly and cheaply with the shell. For this reason, programmers often use the shell to *prototype* a program; that is, to create a throwaway version of the program in the shell to get a feel for what the program will look like. From the shell prototype, programmers can gain valuable insight about how the program should work, before they code the final program in C or other compiled language.

Other Languages Available in UNIX

A wide variety of other languages are available under UNIX. Many of these languages are common computer languages developed in other environments and brought to UNIX.

APL

Though not a big player in the UNIX world, APL occasionally has made its way to UNIX systems. APL was first described in 1962 by Kenneth Iverson in a book called *A Programming Language*. The name of the language is simply an abbreviation of the title of the book. APL is known as an excellent language for mathematical and matrix operations. The spread of APL has been severely limited by its unusual character set; APL requires a special terminal with numerous special characters, including the Greek alphabet.

Following is a sample of an APL program:

```
∇ RES←PRIMES N;T
RES←2, T  3
→0 X ι N < ρ RES
T←T + 2
→3 X ι ∨/0 = RES | T
RES←RES, T
→2
∇
```

BASIC

Long a popular language on small computers, Beginner's All-Purpose Symbolic Instruction Code (BASIC) was designed in 1965 at Dartmouth College by John Kemeny and Thomas Kutz. As the name implies, Kemeny and Kutz developed BASIC as a teaching tool and a programming language for people who did not want to bother with an in-depth knowledge of computers and programming. BASIC began as a simple language, easily implemented on any computer and mostly suited for mathematical work. Over the years, however, many vendors added features, turning BASIC into a viable development language, at least for small- and medium-sized applications.

Versions of BASIC from different vendors make use of widely varying dialects; no standard exists that is analogous to the ANSI standards for C, FORTRAN, and COBOL. Versions of BASIC from different manufacturers usually are incompatible with each other.

bs

bs is a curious combination of BASIC and SNOBOL (a text-process language from Bell Labs), with some influences from C. Like BASIC, bs programs can be thrown together and debugged quickly. bs was developed at Bell Labs.

Forth

Forth is a general purpose language developed by Charles Moore in the late 1960s. The language is especially popular on microcomputers and used in robotic control applications.

lex

lex is a lexical analyzer designed by M.E. Lesk and E. Schmidt at Bell Labs. A lex program is made up of text patterns and actions, intermixed with C code. The output of lex is a C program that finds those patterns in input data and takes the specified actions. lex is especially powerful when combined with yacc.

yacc

yacc (*yet another compiler compiler*) is a tool that enables you to provide a specification for a programming language or structured input data and to produce a compiler for that language. In effect, yacc is a tool for defining the structure of input data and for specifying actions that should be taken when the various constructs are recognized. This tool is an extremely powerful aid if you are writing compilers or processing extremely complex input data.

LISP

LISP is a list processing language developed in 1960 by John McCarthy at the Massachusetts Institute of Technology. One of the oldest computer languages still in use today, LISP is especially popular in artificial intelligence applications.

Pascal

Pascal is a popular general-purpose structured programming language developed by Niklaus Wirth of the Eidgenossische Technische Hochschule (Federal Institute of Technology) in Zurich, Switzerland. Wirth originally designed Pascal as a teaching language and based it on ALGOL, a structured language developed in 1960 that was popular in Europe but found little use in the United States. Since its inception, Pascal has been popular as a teaching language and as a general-purpose programming language.

Modula-2

Modula-2 is a general-purpose structured programming language, very similar to Pascal. This similarity is not surprising because Modula-2 was implemented in 1979 by Pascal's designer. Wirth intended Modula-2 to be a successor to Pascal. Like its structured brethren, C and Pascal, Modula-2 can be used for scientific, engineering, and business applications.

SNOBOL

SNOBOL was popular in the earlier days of UNIX. SNOBOL was developed in the 1960s at Bell Labs and is especially adept at text and string processing. It contains extensive facilities for defining new data types and data structures.

Debugging UNIX Programs

Experienced programmers know that programs never work the first time, at least almost never. Large programs are simply too complex for most programmers to get every detail right the first time. Initially, most programs contain mistakes, called *bugs*.

Most programmers spend a large portion of their time finding and fixing bugs, a process known as *debugging*. Like most environments, UNIX has a variety of sophisticated tools to help programmers find and fix bugs in their programs. Most of these tools were developed at Bell Labs. UNIX provides a wealth of tools for debugging programs, especially C programs. The following sections describe some of the debugging utilities available on most UNIX systems.

lint

The designers of C viewed a compiler as performing two important functions:

- Analyzing a C source code program for errors
- Generating machine code (translating the C program into executable machine code)

When the first C compiler was implemented in 1971, it was developed on a minicomputer that was underpowered even by the standards of the time. The DEC PDP-11 restricted the maximum size of any program to 64K, about one-tenth the memory available on even a bare-bones PC today. On such a small machine, designers found that producing a compiler that did an adequate job of finding errors and generating code was impossible.

Designers circumvented the machine's limitations by creating two versions of the compiler. One version, the cc command described earlier in this chapter, performed only simple syntactical error checking, which enabled this version to concentrate on its primary goal of generating executable programs. A second version generated no code. Known as lint (because it cleaned the "fluff" out of programs), it was relieved of the responsibility of translating the program into machine code and could do an exhaustive job of checking the program for errors.

In theory, programmers were supposed to first use lint to check programs for errors. After lint gave the green light, the programmer could use the cc command to generate the machine code. In practice, programmers usually went straight to cc, turning to lint only when their programs didn't work correctly.

UNIX machines today are far more powerful than the original PDP-11, and the compiler invoked by cc does a better job of error checking than its predecessor. lint, however, is still the premier program analyzer for locating possible sources of problems. lint analyzes programs not only for syntactic errors, but also for many common, logical bugs; commonly misused constructs; statements that may cause portability problems if the program is moved to a different type of machine; and wasteful constructs, such as program code that cannot be reached.

lint has a reputation for being extremely verbose, because it complains about anything it finds suspicious. Programs that pass lint's scrutiny are as free of errors as any machine can possibly determine. In some ways, lint complains too much; programmers must often work to "shut lint up." Because it prints warning messages about any construct it finds questionable, lint sometimes complains about lines with which nothing is wrong. You can imbed several special sequences, which look like C comments, within a program to tell lint to keep quiet about some specific aspect of the program.

Shown below is a small portion of the output from lint when run against a public domain utility:

```
(263)   warning: main() returns random value to invocation environment
(296)   warning: pid unused in function DumpTempFile


===============
value type used inconsistently
    malloc      llib-lc(339) :: cpr.c(628)
value type declared inconsistently
    strcpy      llib-lc(422) :: cpr.c(629)
```

```
    strcat      llib-lc(418) :: cpr.c(652)
function argument ( number ) used inconsistently
    malloc( arg 1 )        llib-lc(339) :: cpr.c(628)
function returns value which is always ignored
    strcpy         strcat          printf
```

Each of these messages warns you about something that lint finds suspicious. The second message, for example, tells you that one of your variables was never used and probably can be removed from your program. Most of the rest of the messages tell you about a misuse of a C library function. Your computer's reference manual can provide more information on reading lint messages.

UNIX Debuggers

Two major debugging tools, or *debuggers*, have been supplied with UNIX throughout its evolution, and one or the other is found on almost all UNIX systems on which program development occurs. Both enable the programmer to gather information about a program that has failed (a kind of postmortem examination), or to dynamically monitor the operation of a program as it executes under the control of the debugger.

The oldest debugger, adb (*absolute debugger*), was oriented toward machine-language programs. This debugger dealt with machine instructions and machine storage locations. adb was helpful with C programs too, but not easy to use because the programmer had to deal with machine-language-oriented concepts rather than C-oriented concepts.

On most systems, adb has been replaced by sdb (*symbolic debugger*). Rather than working with machine instructions and storage locations, sdb deals with C source statements and C variables, and most programmers find it much easier to use.

Both adb and sdb have the following features:

- *Examination of a* core *dump.* When a UNIX program *crashes* (encounters an unrecoverable problem), the operating system takes a snapshot of what its memory and CPU looks like and, with this information, creates a file called core. The debuggers enable a programmer to determine what the program was doing when it terminated and what the values of its variables were at that time.

- *Variable access.* During controlled execution of a program, the debugger enables the programmer to inspect the values of variables and, if desired, to modify them. sdb displays the variable's value in a way that is meaningful for the variable's type: numeric data is displayed numerically, strings are displayed as alphanumeric characters, and so on. adb cannot generate this display.

- *Setting breakpoints.* You can instruct the debugger to insert special markers, or *breakpoints*, into a program being tested. During controlled execution, the program stops when it encounters a breakpoint. The programmer can then examine variables or perform other debugging functions and then, if desired, tell the debugger to resume execution of the program where the debugger stopped.

- *Single-step execution.* The programmer can tell the debugger to execute the program one machine instruction (adb) or C statement (sdb) at a time.

- *Function testing.* The debuggers enable you to test a single, individual function without running all parts of the program.

UNIX Profilers

Programmers sometimes find their programs running more slowly than expected and may have no idea what portion of the program is taking so long. The *profiler* enables you to collect statistics, while your program is running, on the functions within your program. After your program terminates, the profiler can print a report detailing which functions your program called and how much time it spent in each function.

To profile a program, you compile the program in the usual way, except that you must use the -p option of the C compiler. This option causes the compiler to include special profiling code in the executable program. When you run the program, this code collects statistics on the number of times each routine is called and amount of time spent within the routine. When the program terminates, the profiling code creates a file called mon.out, and dumps the statistics it has gathered during program execution to that file.

The mon.out file is illegible; you must use the prof command to produce a readable report. The prof command extracts the statistics from mon.out and creates a report with information about each of the program's functions. The following example shows the first few lines of a sample report.

```
%Time  Seconds  Cumsecs  #Calls  msec/call  Name
 37.5     3.02     3.02     815      3.70     expand
 33.1     2.67     5.68      82     32.5      write
```

10.4	0.83	6.52	166	5.02	substr
4.6	0.37	6.88	815	0.45	PutLine
2.7	0.22	7.10	1017	0.213	_doprnt
1.7	0.13	7.23	1025	0.130	fwrite
1.2	0.10	7.33	829	0.12	memccpy
1.2	0.10	7.43	2292	0.044	strlen
1.0	0.08	7.52	816	0.10	fgets
1.0	0.08	7.60	47	1.8	read
0.8	0.07	7.67	1051	0.063	memcpy
0.6	0.05	7.77	970	0.05	fprintf
0.4	0.03	7.80	1	33.	List
0.2	0.02	7.90	1	17.	ctime
0.2	0.02	7.92	3	6.	open
0.2	0.02	7.94	1	17.	unlink

This report presents a wealth of information. As an example, consider the information on the third routine, substr. This report provides the following information:

Report heading	Description
%Time	The program spent 10.4 percent of its time executing this routine.
Seconds	The program spent a total of 0.83 seconds executing substr.
Cumsecs	This routine and all the routines preceding it account for 6.52 seconds of execution time.
#Calls	This routine was called 166 times.
msec/call	The average time spent in each call was 5.02 milliseconds.

You should note two factors on profiling. First, the number of seconds reported for each routine is not exact because the profiling causes the program to run more slowly than it otherwise would; however, profiling is still useful for determining the relative amount of time the program spends in each routine. Secondly, to create the mon.out file, the program must exit normally. Programs that crash cannot be profiled.

UNIX Program Maintenance

Developing software involves many complex tasks beyond simply writing the programs. Especially in a team environment, in which many programmers are working with interrelated parts of a system, someone must keep track of which programmers are working on what pieces of software. Over the years, programmers have developed many tools to aid in the development of large software systems, and today UNIX includes numerous tools for maintaining and constructing these systems.

Libraries

Like most operating systems, UNIX enables you to collect often-used functions in a *library* or alternatively, an *archive* (see "Building Libraries," following, for a more detailed explanation of libraries and archives). Virtually all C and FORTRAN programs use functions stored in one of the standard UNIX libraries, and many programmers create their own libraries of commonly used functions to use with their programs. Traditionally names of libraries end in .a (archive).

The last stage of compiling a program is called *linking*. This process is performed by the UNIX linker, ld. If a program uses library functions, ld searches the libraries for the necessary functions and copies the functions into the executable program.

Standard Libraries

Each language has a set of standard functions that programmers can call from any program. These functions are stored in libraries. For C programs, the standard library is /lib/libc.a; for FORTRAN, the intrinsic functions are in /usr/lib/libF77.a and the I/O functions are in /usr/lib/libI77.a. When a programmer compiles a C or FORTRAN program, the linker searches the appropriate library automatically.

Additional libraries are available. You can search for them by including the library name on the command line. For example, you can search for the C math library, which includes the log and trig functions among others, by specifying -lm on the command line.

Building Libraries

Strictly speaking, libraries and archives are not necessarily the same thing. An *archive* is a collection of files grouped together and formed into a single file using the UNIX archiver, ar. A *library* is an archive that contains program functions. In practice, almost all archives are also libraries.

To create a library, you first must write functions that you expect to be useful when writing programs. These may include functions that you—or someone else—wrote for a previous software project. You must place each function, or possibly group of related functions, in its own source file and compile each source file into an object file. For example, you might call a function to remove trailing spaces from a string rmspace and place it in a file called rmspace.c. You would then compile the file with the command:

```
cc -c rmspace.c
```

This command generates an object file, called rmspace.o.

After you compile all the individual functions, you collect the object files into a library with the ar command, as in the following example:

```
ar r mylib.a parse.o rmspace.o expand.o shift.o
```

ar is the name of the command; r specifies that the library will be created if the library does not exist, or that functions will be replaced in the library if the library does exist. mylib.a is the name of the library to be created; the remaining files are compiled object files.

ar combines the object files into a single archive file, with a table of contents at the beginning to enable the linker to locate functions within the library quickly. After you create the library, you can use its functions in programs simply by listing the name of the library in the compiler command. For example, if a program called test.c used one or more functions in the library mylib.a, you would use the following compilation command:

```
cc test.c mylib.a
```

You can use the ar command not only to build libraries, but also to list the files within a library and to extract or delete files from a library.

The curses Library

You expect most sophisticated applications, on any computer, to perform basic screen operations, such as clearing the screen, moving the cursor, highlighting screen areas, and accepting input from various areas on-screen.

Although X Windows enables you to use these operations, and more, on graphics terminals, most UNIX systems still work primarily with "dumb" character terminals. Though these screen operations are simple in concept, they present major problems in the UNIX environment:

- Under proprietary operating systems, a vendor can mandate that you must use a particular make and model of terminal. Under VMS, for example, you must use DEC VT-100-series terminals, and IBM mainframes require IBM 3270-series terminals. Because all terminals are the same, you can create programs that issue the proper control codes to make the screen work in the desired way. Under UNIX, this approach is not possible. UNIX is designed to work with virtually any type of terminal from any manufacturer, and no set of control codes is universal.

- Because terminals often are connected to the computer with relatively slow serial cables, programs seem to run fastest if the programs can perform as little I/O as possible.

UNIX solves these problems with the curses library, developed by the University of California at Berkeley. When a program using curses begins execution, the curses library determines the type of terminal being used and then consults a database of terminal capabilities to determine exactly what the terminal can do and what control codes are necessary to make the terminal perform those actions. Throughout the program, the programmer can invoke functions to clear the screen, move the cursor, and so on, and curses sends the correct codes, as provided by the database. The programmer can concentrate on what actions are to be performed; curses takes care of the details of making the actions happen.

curses also analyzes your screen operations to reduce screen I/O, a process called *optimization* (in fact, the name curses is derived from *cursor optimization*). Using curses functions, you describe how the screen should look; then, you call a function called refresh. This routine compares what is on-screen with what you want on-screen and determines how to make the former into the latter with the least amount of I/O. For example, if some of the text on-screen matches what you want, curses is smart enough to leave that text as it is.

In earlier versions of UNIX, the entire database of terminal capabilities was kept in a single text file called /etc/termcap. A sample portion of the termcap file for a DEC VT-100 terminal follows:

```
d0¦vt100¦dec vt100:\
    :cr=^M:do=^J:nl=^J:bl=^G:co#80:li#24:cl=\E[;H\E[2J:\
    :le=^H:bs:am:cm=\E[%i%d;%dH:nd=\E[C:up=\E[A:\
    :ce=\E[K:cd=\E[J:so=\E[7m:se=\E[m:us=\E[4m:ue=\E[m:\
    :md=\E[1m:mr=\E[7m:mb=\E[5m:me=\E[m:is=\E[1;24r\E[24;1H:\
    :rs=\E>\E[?3l\E[?4l\E[?5l\E[?7h\E[?8h:ks=\E[?1h\E=:ke=\E[?1l\E>:\
    :rf=/usr/lib/tabsetvt100:ku=\EOA:kd=\EOB:kr=\EOC:kl=\EOD:kb=^H:\
    :ho=\E[H:k1=\EOP:k2=\EOQ:k3=\EOR:k4=\EOS:ta=^I:pt:sr=5\EM:vt#3:xn:\
    :sc=\E7:rc=\E8:cs=\E[%i%d;%dr:
```

Although this entry seems to be a meaningless jumble of nonsense, it is actually a concise description of the codes sent and received by a VT-100. The first line gives the name and description of the terminal; the remaining lines define various characteristics, each one denoted by a two-character code. For example, the sequences co#80 and li#24 on the second line tell curses that the VT-100 has 80 columns and 24 lines, respectively.

Similarly, at the beginning of the next-to-last line, the sequence ho=\E[H tells curses that to move the cursor to the home position (upper left-hand corner on-screen), curses must send to the terminal an <Esc> character, followed by [and H. These characters do not appear on-screen; the screen recognizes them as a code sequence and moves the cursor to the home position. A sequence in the middle of the third-to-last line, kd=\EOB, tells curses that if the user presses the down-arrow key, the terminal transmits to the computer an <Esc> character, followed by O and B. curses recognizes this sequence and tells the program that the user pressed the down-arrow key.

The termcap descriptions can be hard on your eyes, but they are relatively easy for the computer to process. Nonetheless, the termcap file on many computers is so long—often thousands of lines—that programs using curses often take several seconds to find the entry for the appropriate terminal.

With UNIX System V, AT&T introduced an improved database of capabilities, terminfo. Rather than storing all entries together in a single file, each terminal entry is stored as a separate file, which is named after the terminal described by the file. The /usr/lib/terminfo directory contains numerous subdirectories, each with a one-character name. Each subdirectory contains the files for the terminals whose names begin with that letter. Thus curses can find the data for a VT-100 in the /usr/lib/terminfo/v directory under the name vt100.

Under `terminfo`, `curses` almost instantly can locate the appropriate terminal entry simply by accessing the appropriate file. In addition, the entry is encoded in a format that makes the entry extremely easy for `curses` to read.

Most UNIX systems are delivered with hundreds of terminal definitions. An AT&T 3B2/600 running UNIX System V Release 3, for example, is delivered with 570 terminals defined. Programmers who find themselves working with a terminal for which no `terminfo` definition exists can write such a definition by combining a little patience and a lot of experimentation with the provided tools.

SCCS

In most cases, after software is written, it undergoes a series of modifications. You may discover bugs in the software (or worse, your customers may discover them) and have to make changes to fix the bugs. Alternatively, in response to a change in your customers' needs, you may add new features or change the way the software works. Various software packages, known as *change management systems*, are available to control, coordinate, and track changes made to software. The most common of these packages under UNIX is Source Code Control System (SCCS). On most UNIX systems, SCCS is provided with the standard UNIX software development tools.

The name Source Code Control System is slightly misleading. You can effectively use SCCS with any text file subject to a series of changes, such as documentation or data files.

SCCS provides two major classes of benefits:

- *Version Control.* SCCS keeps a complete history of each file, including who modified the file, the date and time of modification, and what modifications were made. Also, SCCS enables you to retrieve any previous version. This feature can help you locate the version in which a bug appeared and enables you to "throw away" recent changes to return to an older, more reliable version of the software.

- *Change Control.* SCCS prevents the unauthorized modification of software. A project administrator can specify exactly who is allowed to make changes to particular files. SCCS also prevents simultaneous changes. It tracks who is currently working with specific files and prevents two programmers from making changes to the same file. SCCS can even provide information on who is working on which files at any time.

The key to SCCS is the *s-file*, which serves as the central repository of information on files tracked by SCCS. For every file tracked, you must create a corresponding s-file whose name is the same as that of the tracked file, with s. prepended. For example, the file s.prog.c contains the SCCS information for the file prog.c.

S-files contain information on the changes that have taken place in a file, who made the changes, when the changes were made, and other information. You never edit s-files directly; they are acted upon by the dozen SCCS commands.

You can think of the collection of s-files for a software system as a public library. Initially, you must place each file under SCCS control, equivalent to placing a book in a library. When you want to make changes to a file, you must "check out" a copy of the file from SCCS. SCCS enables only one person at a time to make changes to the file, and it checks its security information to ensure that you are authorized to check out the file. After you make the changes you want, you "check in" the file, back to SCCS. This process is known as the *change cycle* (see fig. 8.1).

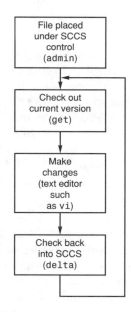

Fig. 8.1. The SCCS change cycle.

To create the initial SCCS file, you use the `admin` command. As with almost all SCCS commands, dozens of options are available. The following simple command, for example, places the file `prog.c` under SCCS control by creating its s-file:

```
admin -iprog.c s.prog.c
```

After you create the s-file, you use the `get` command to check out a copy of the file. As before, numerous options are available, some of them quite complex. The following command is an example:

```
get -e s.prog.c
```

After you make the changes you want, you use the `delta` command to check in the file:

```
$ delta s.prog.c <Return>
comments? Fixed a bug in the main loop
1.2
3 inserted
1 deleted
43 unchanged
$
```

The `delta` command prompts you for a comment that describes the kind of changes you made—in this example, **Fixed a bug in the main loop**. SCCS keeps the commentary in the s-file; the commentary serves as written documentation of the changes you and other programmers have applied to the file. `delta` then assigns the next version number to your new version—in this example, `1.2` (the first version of an SCCS file is 1.1). Finally, `delta` reports that, compared to the previous version, you inserted 3 new lines, deleted 1 line, and left 43 lines unchanged. SCCS then adds the new version to the s-file.

You can request from SCCS any past version of a file, but SCCS does not keep a copy of each version in the s-file; rather, it keeps the very first version and the *changes* from one version to another. Thus, in the preceding example, the information added to the s-file specifies which line was deleted and specifies the text and location of the three lines that were inserted. In a very real sense, SCCS causes each file you check out to "relive" its entire past. SCCS starts with the initial version of the file and rapidly applies, in order, all the changes that have been made to the file throughout its history.

Because the s-file contains only the changes you have made against a file and because the number of lines changed in each version is usually small compared to the size of the entire file, the s-file generally takes up far less space than would be required to store complete copies of each version.

Other SCCS commands control various attributes of a file (such as who is allowed to make changes to it) and produce reports about the changes made to files.

Another software package worth mentioning is RCS (Revision Control System), which serves much the same purpose as SCCS. RCS is public domain software, freely distributed from various sites. Although many people consider RCS to be more powerful, it is not nearly as widespread as SCCS. RCS, however, has an advantage that is important to some users: RCS is available under MS-DOS for PCs.

The make Utility

Complex programs often are made up of a number of source files individually compiled and then linked together into a single, executable program. Large software systems can consist of dozens of programs compiled from hundreds of intricately related files. The problem of building and maintaining such large systems is twofold:

- Compiling and linking a large system may involve a complex sequence of commands, which must be executed in the correct order. The designers of a software system must carefully define the steps for building the system.

- When programmers make changes to the system, rebuilding the system is often a problem. Programmers can recompile the entire system from scratch, but for simple changes this procedure is often far more work than is necessary. Keeping track of which parts of the system have changed and must be recompiled, and which have not changed, is difficult, time-consuming, and prone to human error.

UNIX provides a powerful yet simple utility called make that simplifies the maintenance of such systems. The key to make is a configuration file called a *makefile*—which is, in fact, usually called makefile—through which the programmer defines the way in which the parts of a program interrelate. When you create the makefile, you list each program within the system, along with the files from which the program is built and the commands required to build it from those files.

make solves the software maintenance problem. The makefile precisely documents the procedure for building the system. make can execute the procedure automatically, building the entire system from its components.

When you make changes to the system, a single, simple make command can accurately determine which files have changed and can execute exactly the commands necessary to rebuild just those programs that use the changed files.

The following is a sample makefile for a single program:

```
prog:     file1.o file2.o file3.o
          cc file1.o file2.o file3.o -o prog

file1.o:  file1.c
          cc -c file1.c

file2.o:  file2.c
          cc -c file2.c

file3.o:  file3.c
          cc -c file3.c
```

This makefile describes an executable program called prog, which is built from three C source files: file1.c, file2.c, and file3.c. The three source files are individually compiled into object files (ending in .o) and then linked together into an executable program.

The makefile contains two types of information: dependencies and commands. *Dependencies* define which files are components used to build other files. In the preceding sample makefile, the first line is a dependency. The file on the left (prog) is the target to be built, and the files on the right (file1.o, file2.o, and file3.o) are the components from which the target is built. *Commands* define the UNIX commands—usually involving the compiler or linker—that must be executed to build the target. The second line is a command explaining how prog is built from the three object files.

make forms a hierarchy of dependencies. From this file, make sees that prog is dependent on the three object files that, in turn, are dependent on individual C source files. make understands that the object files first must be built from the C source files; then the executable program prog can be built from the object files.

If the directory contains no files other than the C source files and the makefile, typing **make** causes make to print and execute the following commands:

```
$ make <Return>
      cc -c file1.c
      cc -c file2.c
      cc -c file3.c
      cc file1.o file2.o file3.o -o prog
$
```

make realizes that the entire system must be built from scratch. make first compiles the C source files into object files and then links the object files to create the executable program. If errors occur during the process, make stops at that point.

After the system is built, make can easily rebuild the system if changes are made. If file2.c were changed, issuing a make command would generate this output:

```
$ make <Return>
      cc -c file2.c
      cc file1.o file2.o file3.o -o prog
$
```

In this example, make realizes that recompiling file1.c and file3.c is unnecessary, so make recompiles only the changed file and then relinks the object files to produce the executable file.

If make is invoked but nothing has changed, make produces the following output:

```
$ make <Return>
'prog' is up to date.
$
```

The makefile shown here is much more verbose than necessary. make has a set of built-in rules that provide a knowledge of certain types of files; make understands, for example, that object files are dependent on their corresponding C source files, and it knows how to issue a compile command to build the former from the latter. Thus, you can write the preceding makefile simply as

```
prog:     file1.o file2.o file3.o
          cc file1.o file2.o file3.o -o prog
```

make can infer everything else it needs from its built-in rules.

Among the other useful features of make are the following:

- For complex software systems, you may need a makefile hundreds of lines long to define the dependencies of all the files. make provides many shortcuts to simplify this task (for details on these shortcuts, refer to your computer reference manual or a book devoted entirely to make).

- make is not restricted to building C language programs; you can use it with any language. For example, make includes built-in rules for FORTRAN and includes methods that enable programmers to define rules for any compiler for any language. make can even automate nonprogramming applications such as text formatting. Any situation in which files are built from other files by issuing commands is likely to find make useful.

- make has a built-in understanding of SCCS and works efficiently with SCCS s-files.

- make has proved to be such a useful utility that it has found its way into non-UNIX environments. Both Microsoft Corporation and Borland International include a version of make with their compilers for the IBM PC under MS-DOS.

Databases and Software Development

Most serious application programs require the services of a *database*—a file manager that enables computers to perform complex and sophisticated storage and retrieval of information. Because no single database system can meet the needs of all programmers, UNIX does not have a standard, built-in database. Rather, you can purchase any of dozens of database systems separately from third-party vendors (see table 8.3 for a list of some databases available today).

Most database packages provide numerous tools to aid in the design and construction of databases. They also provide libraries of functions that programmers can call from within a program to store, retrieve, and modify data. These functions are called much like the standard I/O functions in C or FORTRAN.

Table 8.3
UNIX Databases

Database	Vendor
Informix	Relational Database Systems
Oracle	Oracle Corporation
Unify	Unify Corporation
db_Vista III	Raima Corporation
dBase IV	Ashton-Tate
c-tree	Faircom

Other Program Development Tools

Many other program development tools are available under UNIX, including the following:

- cb

  cb (*C beautifier*) adjusts the way a C program is indented, improving its readability in the eyes of most programmers.

- cxref

  cxref produces a cross-reference listing of identifiers used in a C program.

- m4

  The m4 macro processor accepts input text and modifies it in numerous ways, as defined by the programmer. Included are macro definition and invocation.

- nm

  nm displays a symbol table of functions and variables defined in an object module or executable program.

- time

  The time command enables a programmer to time a program and produce figures on the amount of elapsed time and CPU time required by the program.

Chapter Summary

Because of its history as an operating system written by program developers for program developers, UNIX provides an environment rich in tools for creating and maintaining software.

Almost all popular programming languages are available under UNIX, and many languages that were originally developed under UNIX have since found widespread use under other operating systems. Two "homegrown" UNIX languages have become especially popular: today C is one of the most widely used programming languages in MS-DOS, OS/2, and VMS, and C++ is rapidly gaining a loyal following outside of UNIX. Other languages, long popular under UNIX, have also found their way into other environments; these include `awk`, `lex`, and `yacc`.

UNIX also provides strong software development support with powerful debuggers, a program maintenance tool (`make`), and function libraries. Databases, available from third-party vendors, round out UNIX's software development tool chest.

UNIX's rich collection of languages and tools and its strong orientation toward programmers have led many software development companies to see UNIX as the premier software development environment.

UNIX System Administration

When you buy a computer, you have certain tasks in mind that you hope to accomplish more efficiently by using the computer. Perhaps you want to write more professional letters, use spreadsheets to get a better handle on your sales accounts, or use accounting software to keep your company's books. Whatever the task for which the computer was purchased, you encounter tasks that you must perform to keep the computer running, tasks that have nothing to do with your original purpose. Maintenance, backups, and installation of software upgrades are all important, sometimes complex, tasks that have nothing to do with keeping books or writing memos. These computer-oriented, nonapplications tasks are collectively known as *system administration*. The person who performs these tasks is known as the *system administrator*.

On small computers, system administration may require only a few minutes a week; in fact, if you own a small system, such as a PC, you may be your own system administrator. On larger systems, administration may keep someone busy full time. On mainframes or groups of minis used for round-the-clock data processing, a crew of people, sometimes working in shifts, may be necessary to keep up with all the administrative chores.

In this chapter, you learn some of the important tasks that are the responsibility of the system administrator, and you learn some of the UNIX commands used by UNIX system administrators.

You may find, as you explore your UNIX system, that some details do not exactly match what is written here. Nowhere do versions of UNIX differ from one another more than in the area of system administration. Because system administration is concerned with the types of equipment connected to the computer and with the underlying functions of UNIX, you sometimes find manufacturers providing different tools to accomplish the same task.

The Responsibilities of the System Administrator

The system administrator is responsible for performing all administrative tasks, such as adding new users, diagnosing system problems, and performing backups. On large systems, the duties of the system administrator are usually quite well defined. On smaller systems, however, the users themselves may be responsible for many administrative tasks; for example, they may be responsible for backing up their own files. On the smallest systems—desktop PCs—the system administrator and the user usually are the same person, and the responsibilities merge.

UNIX is used most widely on medium-sized computers, typically costing a few hundred thousand dollars and supporting a few dozen users. This chapter focuses on the responsibilities you would assume as a UNIX system administrator responsible for such a system. The fundamental duties, however, are the same, regardless of the system. Typically you would perform many of these tasks only rarely on a stand-alone PC, tasks that you would carry out every day on larger systems.

As a system administrator, your primary tasks probably fall into the following categories, each of which is discussed in detail in this section:

- Maintaining the system
- Diagnosing and repairing (or arranging for the repair of) all kinds of computer problems
- Anticipating the needs of the computer and your users
- Installing new equipment and software as needed

In addition to fulfilling these duties, you as the system administrator are an important resource for users. They expect you to be knowledgeable about the computer, its version of UNIX, and the principal activities that take place on the computer. Because individual users usually are concerned only with their personal work, they often come to you for information on how their specific tasks will interact—or interfere—with the work of other users on the system. They expect you to know "the big picture."

Preparing a Site for a New Computer

As system administrator, you often are involved in the earliest stages of installing a new computer, including the preparation of the site before the computer is delivered. If you are installing a small computer—such as a Sun workstation or a MicroVAX—just about all you need is a sturdy table in a room with normal air conditioning. For larger systems, preparing the site may be more complex. Here is a checklist of factors to consider when you install a new computer:

❑ *Machine dimensions.* Know the dimensions of your new machine. This advice may sound obvious, but system administrators who "plan" for a machine only to find that it won't fit where they thought it would are legion.

❑ *Access.* Do not sandwich a machine into a corner in such a way that you cannot access its cables and connectors. You may want to add or move cables while the machine is running, especially if the machine is large. Leave yourself plenty of room, because you *never* should move a running computer.

❑ *Electrical power.* Be sure that you have the proper power outlets. Some computers require 220-volt outlets. Also, give special consideration to an *uninterruptable power supply* (UPS), which supplies power to your computer for a short period of time (up to an hour) if the electricity goes out. Surge protectors, often built in to UPSs, also provide an important safeguard, lest an errant spark in the power line should barbecue a circuit board inside your computer.

❑ *Ventilation and cooling.* Be sure the computer is located in a cool, well-ventilated room. The manufacturer specifies temperature guidelines. The larger the computer, the more important it is to take into account the heat generated by the computer. A room that is perfectly cool and comfortable under normal conditions can warm up considerably when your computer really starts humming. Even a small minicomputer can draw 2,000 watts of electricity, and it will have exactly the same effect on room temperature as a

2,000-watt heater. Remember that every watt of electricity the computer consumes will eventually wind up as heat in the room. Thus, in a room with optimum air conditioning, the heat generated by a 2,000-watt computer requires a bit more than one-half ton of additional cooling capacity.

❑ *Humidity.* The manufacturer specifies a humidity range, which you should follow carefully. Many computer rooms are equipped with hygrometers, devices for measuring relative humidity. Too little humidity can result in a buildup of static electricity, which can damage delicate circuit boards and possibly cause data loss. Too much humidity can cause condensation within the computer, possibly causing short circuits. If the humidity level is unacceptable, you may have to install a humidifier or dehumidifier.

❑ *Supplies.* You should have necessary supplies at your fingertips. Supplies include blank diskettes and tapes, printer paper, cleaners, printer ribbons or toner cartridges, spare cables, and a few essential tools, especially a screwdriver.

❑ *Documentation.* Have handy the documentation that came with the computer, a copy of your service contract, and the telephone number for technical service and support.

❑ *Console.* Prepare a convenient and comfortable site for the computer console; as system administrator, you may spend a lot of time at the console.

You also need to allow for growth. Very few computer sites shrink; most grow. Planning ahead never hurts, nor does deciding where you might want to put that expansion cabinet or extra tape drive when the time comes.

Arranging for Maintenance

After the computer is up and running, you may find these tips helpful:

- Regularly clean the equipment filters and disk drive heads. A small hand-held vacuum cleaner is great for cleaning out computer air filters. A head-cleaning diskette, used sparingly, keeps your disk drives working well.

- Check hardware connections, especially cables. Most cables have screws that enable you to fasten them tightly in place. Even though these screws make moving the cables more difficult, they prevent cables from falling out by themselves.

- Maintain a log book of everything you do on the system. Record all pertinent information about backups, service calls, the name of the technician who worked on your computer, problems, panics, and installation of new hardware and software. This log can be an invaluable aid when diagnosing problems.

- Keep magnets out of the computer room. Magnets are the great destroyer of data.

- Keep the system physically secure. In many companies, computer rooms are locked and require special keys or pass cards to gain entrance. On any computer, your data is only secure insofar as miscreants cannot get their hands on the equipment.

Using the root Login

As system administrator, you have a regular login name—such as dave or jenny—like everybody else, but you also have access to the special login name root. Also known as the *superuser*, root is different from other users in two ways:

1. All UNIX security is waived for root. No matter what the permissions setting, root can read, modify, create, or delete any file. (Only encrypted files are safe from being viewed by root, but root can still delete them.) Users occasionally will call upon you to help out with a chore that they cannot perform because they lack the proper permissions. For example, they might need access to a protected file that belongs to a former employee.

2. Some operations can be performed only by root. For example, only root can install a new device or shut down the system.

Logging in as root carries a great deal of responsibility. With a single command, root can destroy a disk or crash the system. You should give the root password only to users who absolutely need it—the fewer, the better. Furthermore, use root only when necessary; you can perform many—perhaps most—of your system administration tasks under your regular login name. Many system administrators log in as root in the morning and spend the whole day doing work as root. This practice has two disadvantages:

1. As root, if you mistype a command, you can perform operations with tragic consequences. As a regular user, the system is much more likely to refuse any command that leads to disaster.

2. Logged in as root, if you leave your terminal unattended, you are at the mercy of any troublemaker who comes along and types a command.

Spend as little time as possible logged in as root. Do your work carefully and make sure you log off (or switch back to your regular login name). On many UNIX systems, root can log in only at the system console. From any other terminal, you must login under your usual login name and then perform an su command to become root.

For most users, the shell uses the dollar sign ($) as the default prompt—that is, the prompt you see unless you change it. If you log in as root, however, the shell uses the pound sign (#) as the default prompt. This constant yet subtle reminder helps you remember that you are wielding the special powers of root and that you should exercise greater caution than you otherwise might.

Forgetting the root Password

For the average user, a forgotten password is not a tragedy. The system administrator can change anyone's password to a known value at any time. However, as system administrator, remembering the root password is imperative. On some systems, you have to go to great lengths to change the password to a known value.

The Radio Shack *TRS-XENIX Operations Guide* notes the following statement about a forgotten root password: "There is nothing to be done. The only remedy is prevention: *make sure you don't forget the root password* [italics theirs]...."

Today few systems lock you out forever if you forget the root password, but the procedure for resetting it is usually tedious, is different for every type of computer, and usually involves shutting down the computer, which does not make your users happy.

An old XENIX user's guide offers the best advice. The section entitled "Forgetting the root Password" simply states, "Don't."

Booting the Computer

Booting a UNIX computer is a complex process for the computer, but it is simple for the system administrator. In most cases, simply turning on the computer causes it to perform the boot process automatically, usually without any intervention on your part. Some systems may ask you to enter the current time and date.

The Boot Procedure

If you are accustomed to watching PCs boot, you will find that UNIX computers take much longer, perhaps as much as ten minutes on large systems. The procedure a large computer carries out in checking itself and setting up a multiuser environment is a complex task that involves the following stages:

1. The computer reads and executes the *bootstrap program*, a very short, simple program located on block 0 of the first hard disk.

2. The bootstrap program loads the UNIX kernel into the computer. The kernel typically is stored in a file in the root directory, under the name /unix, /xenix, or a similar name.

3. The kernel configures itself by setting up its memory and testing for the presence of various types of hardware.

4. The kernel starts the init process, which controls the creation of login processes as long as UNIX is running (see Chapter 10, "Understanding the Internal Structure of UNIX," for more information about init). The kernel has now finished its role in starting up the system; the remainder of the procedure is controlled by init.

5. The init process starts up various daemons (background processes) and starts a shell to execute the initialization script /etc/rc.

6. Finally, init switches to multiuser mode and begins starting gettys, which enable users to log in.

The /etc/rc File

As system administrator, you will be most interested in the initialization performed by init in step 5 of the preceding list. The init process runs a special shell program called /etc/rc (rc stands for *run commands*). As system administrator, you can place any command in rc that you want executed each time the system boots. Typically, rc performs the following tasks:

- Loads the system date and time. Depending on the system, rc may include a command to ask the user for the current time and date, or it may load the time and date from a battery-operated clock within the computer.

- Checks the file systems for problems, using fsck

- Mounts file systems on the appropriate directories

- Starts daemons, such as the print spooler and cron

- Initializes network services

- Runs the preserve program, which recovers any work in progress in vi when the system went down

- Deletes all files in the /tmp and /usr/tmp directories. These directories are intended for temporary files only, and most UNIX systems clean them out each time the system starts.

Many system administrators add their own commands to rc to perform security checks or other tasks that are useful as the system boots. On some systems, a separate file is used for commands added by this system administrator.

Shutting Down the Computer

Few UNIX computers are turned on each morning and off each night, as is common for PCs. Most UNIX computers are designed to be turned on and run continuously until they must be shut down for some reason, such as repair or maintenance.

To shut down a UNIX computer, you should not simply turn off the power. Even if no users are currently logged in, a UNIX computer may still be busy performing routine housekeeping chores. Rather than pulling the plug on the computer, you must ask the computer to finish up any important activity and prepare itself to be turned off.

In most versions of UNIX, you tell UNIX to shut itself down with the shutdown command. The exact format of the command varies from one version of UNIX to another, but a typical command, from System V, is

```
shutdown -i0 -g300
```

The -i0 option requests a full shutdown (other options enable some system services to be stopped without completely stopping UNIX). The -g300 option allows users a 300-second (5-minute) grace period to finish their work and log off.

On most systems, shutdown is a shell script that performs the following operations:

1. It disables logins so that no new users can log in.

2. If a grace period is specified, shutdown sends messages to all logged-in users at regular intervals, urging them to finish up and log off. As the grace period progresses, the messages become increasingly urgent.

3. When the grace period expires, it shuts down the system daemons, such as cron and the line printer spooler.

4. It issues a series of *sync* commands (short for *synchronize*), which tell the kernel to save its work and "get to a good stopping point."

5. It signals init to terminate.

6. On many systems, you now can safely turn off the power. On others, shutdown performs a final act, telling the CPU to halt, in effect killing the computer.

The time from the end of the grace period to the halting of the CPU is typically about one minute or less.

System Administration Files and Commands

The /etc directory contains most of the files that control the operation of UNIX. As system administrator, you will often need to modify these files. /etc also contains commands that are used almost exclusively by the system administrator.

Configuring Terminals for UNIX System V

On systems based on AT&T UNIX System V, two files control the configuration of terminals: inittab and gettydefs, both in the /etc directory.

The inittab File

The /etc/inittab file controls the operation of init, an important UNIX daemon with a variety of responsibilities. Chapter 4, "Understanding the UNIX Shell," discusses the crucial role of init in the login process, and Chapter 10, "Understanding the Internal Structure of UNIX," outlines its function in process management.

Each line in the inittab file tells init when certain key processes should be started automatically. For example, some processes need to be started when the system boots; others (on some systems) must be started when the power fails. Each line in inittab consists of four parts, separated by colons:

1. A two-letter process ID, used internally by init

2. One or more characters representing the *run state* under which the process is to be started (typically, 1 represents single-user mode, which is the initial mode of UNIX when it first starts up, and 2 represents multiuser mode, to which UNIX switches as part of the start-up process)

3. An instruction, describing how the process is to be started

4. The process (command) to be started

As system administrator, you are most concerned with the role of init in the login process and the use of the inittab file to control terminals. You need to modify inittab to add new terminals, remove terminals, or temporarily disable terminals.

Chapter 4 explains that getty is the starting point in the login process. For a user to log in at a particular terminal, a getty must be running to prompt for a login name. Without a getty, the process cannot begin and no one can log in. The inittab file must be configured to tell init to run getty on idle terminal lines.

A typical line in the inittab file controlling a terminal follows:

```
34:2:respawn:/etc/getty tty34 9600
```

This line tells init that when the system goes into multiuser mode (run state 2), the /etc/getty command is to be started. The respawn instruction tells init to restart getty again when the process dies (which in the case of getty means that the user has logged off). The next user can then log in. The getty command itself contains the terminal number 34 (tty34). Most system administrators think of 9600 as the baud rate, but it actually identifies a line in the gettydefs file.

You can disable a terminal line by changing the third field for a terminal entry in /etc/inittab from respawn to off. Essentially, off in the third field tells init to stop any getty currently running on that terminal and to disable any further logins.

The gettydefs File

The gettydefs file controls the actions of the getty command. Recall that getty is responsible for setting the terminal characteristics (such as the baud rate), prompting the user for a login name, and accepting the login name from the keyboard. The getty command then passes control to another program, login, which completes the login process.

Each line in the gettydefs file consists of five fields, separated by pound signs (#). Each time init executes a getty command, getty searches the gettydefs file for a line that begins with the command's second argument. Thus if init executes the command

```
getty ttyb3 9600
```

getty looks for a line that begins 9600, such as the following example:

```
9600 # B9600 CLOCAL BRKINT IGNPAR ISTRIP IXON IXOFF
ECHO OPOST ONLCR # HUPCL BRKINT ISTRIP ICRNL IXON OPOST
ONLCR B9600 CS8 CREAD ISIG ICANON ECHO ECHOE ECHOK TAB3
#Please login: # 4800
```

The first field—9600 in this example—is the line tag and serves simply to identify the line. The tag can be any word, but system administrators often find that using a baud rate is convenient.

The second field contains a series of strange-looking words—ten of them in this case—that tell getty how to configure the terminal line before the user logs in. Your UNIX System Administrator's Reference Manual lists all the possible words that may appear here and their functions; for example:

- B9600 sets the baud rate to 9600.

- CLOCAL indicates that this terminal line is "connected locally;" that is, it is directly connected to the terminal by a serial cable (as opposed to a connection through a modem, data switch, or network).

- IGNPAR tells getty that the terminal should ignore parity (error-checking) on the characters received from the keyboard.

The third field consists of similar words and tells getty how to configure the line after the user has entered a login name.

The fourth field is the login prompt issued by getty, in this case the simple phrase Please login:.

The final field is a tag that refers to another line in the gettydefs file—4800 in this case. This tag tells getty that if it is unable to establish a connection with this set of configuration parameters, it should try the set labeled 4800.

The next two lines in gettydefs might look like the following:

```
4800 # B4800 CLOCAL BRKINT IGNPAR ISTRIP IXON IXOFF
ECHO OPOST ONLCR # HUPCL BRKINT ISTRIP ICRNL IXON OPOST
ONLCR B4800 CS8 CREAD ISIG ICANON ECHO ECHOE ECHOK TAB3
#login: # 2400

2400 # B2400 CLOCAL BRKINT IGNPAR ISTRIP IXON IXOFF
ECHO OPOST ONLCR # HUPCL BRKINT ISTRIP ICRNL IXON OPOST
ONLCR B2400 CS8 CREAD ISIG ICANON ECHO ECHOE ECHOK TAB3
#login: # 9600
```

Notice that the line labeled 4800 ends with the label 2400, which tells getty to try that line next. The line labeled 2400, in turn, ends in 9600, sending getty back to the line labeled 9600. Thus, in this case, getty tries the line representing 9600 baud, then 4800, then 2400, and then 9600 again, repeating this cycle until it receives a login name.

Configuring Terminals for Berkeley UNIX

Systems based on the Berkeley version of UNIX use a slightly different set of files than System V for configuring terminals. Versions before 4.3BSD use three configuration files in the /etc directory—gettytab, ttys, and ttytype—to tell getty how to configure terminal lines. In Version 4.3BSD, ttys and ttytype are merged into a single file, ttys.

The Original ttys File

In versions of Berkeley UNIX prior to 4.3BSD, the ttys file contains lines— one for each terminal—that determine how each terminal will be configured. Each line consists of the following three parts:

- The first character is 1, indicating that the terminal currently is on (that is, a user may log in if the terminal is not being used), or 0, indicating that it is off (that is, users may not log in).

- The second character determines the speed (baud rate) of the line. Any character is valid, as long as it matches a line in the `gettytab` file that specifies the line speed.

- The remainder of the line is the name of the terminal.

Typical lines in a `ttys` file might look as follows:

```
12console
03tty004
```

The `ttytype` File

The `ttytype` file contains one line for each terminal on the computer and relates the name of each terminal to its type. For example, a typical line follows:

```
ttya    vt100
```

This line tells `getty` that terminal `ttya` is a DEC VT-100 terminal.

The New `ttys` File

Version 4.3BSD of Berkeley UNIX combines the functions of `ttys` and `ttytype` into a single file. For example, the following lines are typical:

```
console "/etc/getty console-9600" vt100   on  secure
tty000  "/etc/getty std.9600"      att5420 off
```

The first line specifies the `getty` command (in quotation marks) that is to be run on the console. It also specifies that the console is a DEC VT-100 terminal, is currently on (that is, logins are allowed), and that `root` may safely log in on this terminal (`secure`). The second line specifies the `getty` command for `tty000`, but it also specifies that the terminal is off (logins are not allowed) and that the terminal is an AT&T model 5420 terminal.

The `gettytab` File

The `gettytab` file contains a table listing the terminal speeds supported by the computer. A typical line is

```
2¦std.9600¦9600-baud:sp#9600:
```

The first set of words, separated from each other by vertical bars and from other fields by a colon, specifies the names by which this entry can be referenced—in this case, 2, std.9600, and 9600-baud. The code sp#9600 specifies that these names all refer to a 9600-baud setting. 2 can be used in an old-style ttys file, and the other names can be used as part of a getty command in a new-style ttys file.

Administering the passwd File

As its name implies, the passwd file contains the login passwords for all users, but it also includes other important information about each user. Each line in the passwd file describes a single user and contains these seven fields, separated by colons:

- The user's login name
- The user's encrypted password
- The user's numeric user ID
- The user's numeric group ID
- The full name of the user
- The user's home directory
- The program that is executed when the user logs in, usually one of the shells

A typical entry in the passwd file is

```
scott:1VPbSUWAA.8iA:205:300:Scott Sutherland:/usr/
scott:/bin/ksh
```

The most interesting field is the second field, which contains the user's encrypted password:

- Regardless of the length of the password it represents, the encrypted password is always 13 characters long.

- UNIX can encrypt a password in 4,096 different ways; therefore, even if two users have the same password, their encrypted passwords may—and almost certainly will—look completely different.

- If a user is no longer allowed access to the computer—for example, if an employee leaves the company or transfers to another department—the system administrator usually changes the encrypted password to NONE, VOID, NOLOGIN, or some similar word; for example:

```
scott:NOLOGIN:205:300:Scott Sutherland:/usr/scott:/bin/ksh
```

Because a valid encrypted password is always 13 characters in length and because none of these replacements is 13 characters long, no users may log in using this login name.

- If the password field has never been filled and therefore is empty, the user does not have to supply a password to log in.

The passwd file plays an important role in UNIX, especially because of its ability to correlate numeric user IDs with login names. Users like to think in terms of login names, yet internally the kernel works exclusively with numeric user IDs. Many commands, such as ls, use the passwd file to convert one to the other. When ls obtains information on a file, the numeric user ID is among the information; ls then finds the user ID in the passwd file and displays the associated login name.

Although only the system administrator can modify the passwd file, all users must be able to read it, because so many UNIX commands depend on its information. In some recent versions of UNIX, the encrypted password is no longer kept in the passwd file but in a separate file, called the *shadow password file*, which cannot be read by anyone but the system administrator.

While examining the passwd file, you probably will notice that the first few entries describe users you have never heard of, with strange names like daemon and sys. These names do not represent actual people, and nobody is allowed to log in under these names. Every UNIX file must have an owner, and most of these login names were created by the designers of UNIX simply for the purpose of assigning ownership to files that don't logically belong to any specific user. For example, the "user" lp owns all files associated with the print spooling system. Other pseudo-users include bin, adm, and uucp.

Still other user names allow people—or computers—to log in for special purposes. For example, most systems have a login name nuucp, which is often used by other computers logging in to your computer to transfer files.

Another special-purpose login name is uname. On some computers, anyone is allowed to log in as uname—no password is required. When you login as uname, however, the system simply identifies itself and then logs you off. This procedure can be handy if you're not sure which computer is connected to a specific modem or terminal; however, because uname helps hackers identify the system they have reached, many system administrators consider uname a security risk and therefore remove it.

Administering the group File

The group file lists the groups of users, including group name and numerical group ID, and lists the users who are included in the group. Similar to the passwd file, the group file allows commands such as ls to correlate numerical group IDs with group names. Each line contains 4 fields, such as the following typical line:

```
clerks:NONE:320:pat,mary,jim,jerry
```

The first field is the name of the group (clerks). The second is the encrypted password; anyone who knows the password can become a member of this group. The word NONE indicates that no valid password exists (encrypted group passwords, like login passwords, are always 13 characters long); therefore, only the users listed (Pat, Mary, Jim, and Jerry) are members of the group. The group's numerical ID is 320.

Maintaining the System for Users

If you administer a medium- to large-sized UNIX system, one of your most common—and most visible—tasks is adding new users to your system and removing departing users from your system.

Adding Users to the System

As system administrator, part of your job, especially in medium-sized companies, is that of computer ambassador. You welcome new users to their new computing environment, point out sources of help, and explain who is responsible for certain tasks.

The first step in preparing for a new user is to make sure that the user has a working terminal. The new user may be using a terminal that is already installed. If setting up the terminal is your job, you need a terminal, an empty port on your computer to which the terminal can be connected, and the correct cables and connectors.

The actual installation depends on how the terminal is connected to the computer. You may need to summon technicians to run cables, connect to a data switch, or tie a terminal into your network. Follow local custom or consult the manufacturer's instructions.

After the terminal is connected, you must create a home directory for the user and appropriately modify several files. As an example, suppose that Keri D. User has just joined your group as a programmer. To add her to your system, follow these steps:

1. *Pick a file system for her home directory.* Usually, several file systems are available on which to place her home directory. You may have a reason to place her on a specific file system. For example, you may pick the file system with the most space available, which you can determine with the df command. Or perhaps you assign all programmers to the /usr3 file system. In this case, suppose that you select /usr3.

2. *Make an entry in the* /etc/passwd *file.* Each user must have a line in the password file that contains information required by the system. For Keri, the line might be

   ```
   keri::2016:300:Keri D. User:/usr3/keri:/bin/ksh
   ```

   The number in the third field, 2016, is Keri's numeric user ID. You can select any number that is not already in use. The second number (in the fourth field) is the numerical group ID, which should be the number from the /etc/group file associated with the group to which Keri is assigned, probably corresponding to programmer or develop. The second field is the encrypted password, but because it is blank, no password is required for Keri to log in. You need to take care of this security hazard next.

3. *Assign a password.* Using the passwd command, assign a password to Keri. You can use a password that Keri has chosen, or you can assign a random combination of letters, which Keri can change later.

4. *Modify the* /etc/group *file.* Add Keri's name to the list of users for her group in the /etc/group file. If Keri is the first member of a new group, you must add a new line for the new group.

5. *Create a home directory.* Using mkdir, create Keri's home directory, /usr3/keri. Make Keri the owner of the directory using chown, assign the directory to Keri's group using chgrp, and set the permissions appropriately (probably 755) using chmod. The following commands create her home directory:

   ```
   # mkdir /usr3/keri

   # chown keri /usr3/keri

   # chgrp develop /usr3/keri

   # chmod 755 /usr3/keri
   ```

6. *Create a* .profile. If Keri is not an experienced UNIX user, you need to create a .profile for her in her home directory, probably by copying the .profile from another experienced user. If Keri is knowledgeable about UNIX, let her create her own .profile.

7. *Configure* /etc/inittab *or* /etc/ttys. If Keri is using a terminal that has just been installed, you must add an entry to /etc/inittab (UNIX System V) or /etc/ttys (Berkeley UNIX) so that her terminal prompts for a login.

On many systems, a tool is available to perform these tasks for you. For example, AT&T UNIX includes sysadm, which performs this task and other system administration tasks. Berkeley UNIX includes mkuser, which adds a new user for you.

Using Special Shells

In Chapter 4, you learned about the most common shells that are available; however, as system administrator you have different concerns than ordinary users. Additional considerations may influence the shell you allow users to use.

If some of your users carry out only certain specific tasks on your computer, you may want to consider having them use the *restricted shell* (rsh). This special version of the Bourne Shell enables you to control exactly what a user is allowed to do. If set up correctly, rsh does not let the user run any programs or modify any data files beyond those chosen by you.

If /bin/rsh is placed in the seventh field of the user's passwd entry, UNIX runs the restricted shell for a user during login. When that user logs in, rsh executes the user's .profile in the usual (unrestricted) way. After .profile is complete, however, the shell goes into restricted mode. The restricted shell does not permit the user to

- Change the current directory with the cd command

- Change the PATH variable

- Use a slash (/) in the name of a command

- Use output redirection (> or >>)

By restricting the user from these four operations, you can precisely control what the user is allowed to do. In most cases, you need to create a directory—often called /usr/rbin—to contain the programs that restricted users are allowed to use. Within that user's .profile, you can set the PATH variable to contain only the directory /usr/rbin, thus restricting the user to only those commands. The user cannot change the PATH to include other directories. Although a nonrestricted user can execute any program—even if it is not in the search path—by specifying the full path name of the program, restricted users cannot, because of the restriction against using slashes in the name of a command. Because redirection cannot be used, the user also cannot create new files, except through the available programs and commands.

If any shell programs (shell scripts) are available within the restricted user's search path, restricted mode is turned off while the user executes the shell programs. Thus, you can provide shell scripts to perform operations that are otherwise restricted.

Note that making a text editor, such as vi, available to a restricted user is dangerous because, in most cases, a text editor enables the user to defeat the purpose of the restricted shell. With a text editor, a user can modify his or her .profile to include other directories, and shell programs (which are unrestricted) can be created to perform any task.

Another common trick is used in high-security environments by hackers, saboteurs, and other undesirable types. If certain security holes already exist on a UNIX system, troublemakers sometimes substitute a program of their own for a system tool or application program. For example, an electronic intruder might try to wreak havoc by copying the rm command into a company boss's directory, but names the copy cat. Now, under some circumstances, if the boss types **cat report** to examine a file, the file is actually deleted.

If your version of UNIX supports *trusted programs*, you can protect your users from this tactic with a *trusted shell*. For example, IBM's AIX includes a trusted shell called tsh. When you, as the system administrator, install system tools and application programs, you tell the operating system, with a certain command, that the tool or application is *trusted*, in effect giving it your seal of approval. In a trusted shell, users are allowed to execute only these trusted programs. Programs from any other source, such as those installed or written by users or, using the preceding example, the copy of the rm command, are not trusted, and the trusted shell refuses to run them.

Deleting a User from the System

Just as new users arrive, existing users occasionally depart. They may leave the company, transfer to another department, obtain a computer of their own, or simply stop using the computer in their jobs.

When people depart, they usually leave their work behind. For example, assistants who leave the company may leave behind hundreds of important files that you do not want to erase. When they leave, you may do nothing more than disable their logins by placing a word, such as VOID, NOLOGIN, or GONE, in the password field of their lines in /etc/passwd, preventing them from logging in. (This precaution is especially important on computers that have modems attached, so that disgruntled ex-employees do not call and exact revenge after they have been terminated.)

Occasionally you may want to remove a user completely from your system. For example, Wil was just transferred to another department that has its own computer. Being a knowledgeable UNIX user, he used uucp to transfer all his files from your computer to his new department's computer and has now told you that he will not be using your computer any more. To remove him, you would follow these steps:

1. *Back up his home directory.* Being a cautious administrator, you know that making a backup of Wil's home directory won't hurt, just in case he discovers later that an important file is missing. Store the backup for a couple of months; if you haven't heard from him by then, reuse the tape or diskettes for something else.

2. *Remove his home directory.* You can remove his home directory and all of his files with a single rm command, such as:

   ```
   # rm -r /usr4/wil <Return>
   #
   ```

3. *Remove his entry from* /etc/passwd. Find Wil's entry in the /etc/passwd file, and delete it.

4. *Modify the* /etc/group *file.* Find all listings for Wil in the group file and delete them. If Wil was the only member of any groups and if you don't expect to have any new members for those groups, you can delete the entire group entries.

5. *Modify the* /etc/inittab *file.* If no one else will be using Wil's terminal, find the entry for the terminal in the /etc/inittab file, and delete it or turn it off (by changing respawn to off). If someone else will be inheriting the terminal, omit this step.

Performing Backups

One of the most crucial tasks you perform as system administrator is creating *backups*. No matter how careful you and your users are, an important file is occasionally destroyed. Backups are simply copies of files, stored on disks or tapes, that you make as a contingency against lost or damaged files. When a user discovers that a file is missing, you hope that you or one of your assistants have recorded a copy of the file on a backup.

The following events can cause you to lose files:

- Hardware failures, especially disk drives

- Bad disks or diskettes

- Program bugs

- Human error, such as deleting the wrong file

- Sabotage, such as computer "viruses," "worms," or theft

- Lightning strikes or power surges

On PCs, users are usually required to make their own backups. On large multiuser computers, backups are almost always the responsibility of the system administrator.

Determining Backup Procedures

As system administrator, you must make a number of decisions concerning how you will make backups. Two considerations are especially important: What medium should you use? How often should you make backups?

Selecting a Backup Medium

In the UNIX environment, you can make backups onto one of three different media: diskettes, tapes, and hard disks. Diskettes are the most economical—your computer probably has a diskette drive already, and diskettes are cheap. Making diskette backups, however, is slow and tedious. Several varieties of tapes are available, and backups to tape are much more convenient; however, tapes are more expensive, and tape drives are much more expensive than diskette drives. Streaming tape drives are less expensive, slower, and less convenient than nine-track tape drives. Most convenient of all is a hard disk drive, but this backup medium also is the most expensive.

You probably will choose the fastest backup medium that your budget, or your company's, allows.

Setting Up a Backup Schedule

Deciding on a backup schedule—that is, how often to make a backup—is always a compromise between conflicting interests. The more often you make backups, the more likely that, when information is lost, you will have a copy of the destroyed files on a recent backup. But backups cost time and money; the more often you make backups, the greater the cost. Determining a backup schedule requires a delicate balance of benefits and costs.

Typically, when deciding how often to perform backups, you should base your decision on the following considerations:

- *How much risk do you run of having a catastrophe?* Look at the risk factors mentioned in the previous section: Is your hardware reliable? Are your programs usually free of bugs? Are your users especially knowledgeable and reliable? Is your electrical power consistent? If your answer to each of these questions is "yes," you run less risk of catastrophe. Each "no" answer increases your need for frequent backups.

- *What is the cost of a catastrophe?* To some people, losing any amount of data is a tragedy. Consider an airline's reservation system. Airlines go to herculean efforts to ensure that not a bit of data is lost, because the consequences of lost reservations are too horrible to contemplate (see the following aside, "Fault-Tolerant Systems"). On the other hand, consider a clerk entering sales invoices into a general business system. If a catastrophe strikes and the work is lost, the clerk simply re-enters the invoices. Although this consequence is time-consuming and boring, it is not of the same magnitude as a crippled airline reservation system.

Note that the two decisions—backup media and backup schedule—interact. If backups are crucial and you need to perform them frequently, you are more likely to opt for one of the more expensive backup media.

Fault-Tolerant Systems

In situations in which users must be sure that no data is lost, ordinary backup procedures, such as those described in this chapter, are inadequate. Such users may need to turn to *fault-tolerant* systems. Though expensive, they provide the greatest protection against data loss.

A fault-tolerant system contains two or more of every system component, including memory, CPUs, and disk drives. Every component has at least one duplicate, and components are constantly monitoring each other for signs of failure. If any one component fails, its backup component is ready to take over at any time, without any loss of data.

Fault-tolerant systems duplicate not only hardware but data as well. For example, when the computer writes data to disk, it writes simultaneously to two disk drives. If one disk fails, the other takes over. In effect, such systems perform a continuous backup.

Most fault-tolerant systems are designed so that failed components can be replaced while the computer is running, in contrast to other computers, which must be turned off when parts are replaced. Thus a fault-tolerant computer can run indefinitely, in spite of occasional component failures.

Perhaps the most interesting example of fault-tolerance is the space shuttle orbiter. During all phases of a mission, five computers perform all calculations, constantly monitoring each other and comparing results. Three of the computers actively control the shuttle while the other two stand by, ready to take over at any time. As long as any one of the five computers continues to function, the shuttle can operate safely. (Note, however, that the mission rules require that all five computers must be working perfectly before a launch can take place. NASA intended the fault-tolerance to protect the shuttle in case of an in-flight failure, not to permit a launch when one computer had failed. Ironically, although this rule increases overall safety, it has worked to delay the shuttle on occasion, because the chance of having a bad computer is greater with five computers than with one.)

Performing a Backup

Several standard UNIX commands enable you to perform backups. In addition, many manufacturers of disk and tape drives supply special programs that work especially well with their drives.

Working with backups involves three types of operations:

- Making, or creating, the backup is the most common operation. You perform this operation on a regular basis, copying files from your file system to backup media.

- Listing the contents of a backup enables you to determine which files are stored on a backup and when the backup was made. You perform this operation on an as-needed basis.

- Restoring a backup—the operation you hope you never have to perform—copies files from the tape or diskette back to the file system. You perform this operation only after files are lost or erased.

The tar Command

The `tar` (*tape archive*) command originally was intended to copy a set of directories and subdirectories to tape, but it now works with diskettes too. If a catastrophe occurs and you need to fetch a file from disk or tape, `tar` also can retrieve files. The format of a `tar` command is as follows:

> `tar options directories`

For example, the command to make a backup on diskette of the `/usr2` and `/usr3` directories is

> `tar cvf /dev/diskette /usr2 /usr3` <Return>

The options `cvf` specify that you want to create a new backup, that you want `tar` to list what it is doing as it does it (`v`, for *verbose*), and that the file name of the device (`/dev/diskette`) follows next on the command line. Finally, the directories to be backed up are listed. Note that `tar` is unusual among UNIX commands: you do not precede the options by a dash (-). The designers of `tar` felt the dash was not necessary because the "options" (actually a misnomer) are not optional and must be present with every `tar` command.

Because you specified the `v` option, `tar` tells you about each file it saves to diskette. A few lines from the output follow:

```
a /usr2/charles/.profile 1 blocks
a /usr2/charles/environment 1 blocks
a /usr2/charles/.kshrc 1 blocks
a /usr2/charles/letters/b.sommers/bernie.doc 6 blocks
a /usr2/charles/letters/chris/chris1.ltr 8 blocks
a /usr2/charles/letters/chris/chris2.ltr 9 blocks
a /usr2/charles/letters/chris/chris3.ltr 9 blocks
a /usr2/charles/letters/financial/mutfunds.ltr 1 blocks
a /usr2/charles/letters/financial/fund.list 3 blocks
```

The a at the beginning of each line indicates that the file is being *added* to the tape or diskette. tar also shows the size of each file, in 512-byte blocks.

If you need to retrieve files from a backup disk, use the x (*extract*) option in place of the c option. To retrieve all files, use this command:

tar xvf /dev/diskette

If you want to retrieve only certain files, list the names of the files on the command line as follows:

tar xvf /dev/diskette /usr/michelle/memo/fred.1

This command retrieves /usr/michelle/memo/fred.1 from the backup.

Finally, you can list the files stored on a backup with the command

tar tvf /dev/diskette

The tar command is easy to use and sophisticated enough for most backup purposes; however, tar has limitations in choosing files for backup. For example, you cannot tell it to back up all files whose names begin with *a*, nor all files that have been modified in the last week. Programmers at AT&T saw the need for a better backup program, and they created cpio.

The cpio Command

With UNIX System V, AT&T provides a new backup command, more powerful than tar, called cpio. To produce a backup, type the cpio command as follows:

cpio -ocv >device

Most system administrators simply type the options o, c, and v as a single unit (ocv), never giving a thought to their individual meanings. o (*output*) tells cpio to create a backup; c (*character*) tells cpio to write header information in character format (see the following aside, "cpio Headers"); and v (*verbose*) tells cpio to list files as it backs them up.

By itself, the cpio command is not very useful; noticeably missing is the list of files or directories to be backed up. The AT&T programmers who designed cpio sought to design a flexible backup program that could not only backup entire directories, but also select files to be backed up based on almost any criteria, such as date of the last modification, size, permissions, name, or file type. In this endeavor, they took an extremely novel approach: they passed the buck.

The AT&T group noticed that the find command was already capable of selecting files based on almost any criteria. They wrote cpio to simply accept, on its standard input, a list of files to be backed up, relying upon find to produce that list. (For more information about the find command, see Chapter 3, "Understanding Files and Directories.") Thus, to back up the /usr directory, you type the command

```
find /usr -print ¦ cpio -ocv >/dev/mt0
```

In this example, the find command produces a list of all files and directories in the /usr directory and pipes this list to cpio, which backs up the listed files to /dev/mt0 (tape drive 0).

To select specific files, you can use various options for find to modify the list it feeds to cpio. For example, to back up only files that have been modified within the last seven days, use this command:

```
find /usr -mtime -7 -print ¦ cpio -ocv >/dev/mt0
```

The cpio command is the same, but the find command is different; it locates all files in the /usr directory that have been modified within the past seven days.

If you have a specific list of files that you want backed up, even if the list has no pattern, cpio can handle that task as well. If, for example, you have a file called backup.list that contains a list of files to be backed up, you can type:

```
cpio -ocv <backup.list >/dev/mt0
```

You don't need a find command in this case, because the list of files is supplied on cpio's standard input using redirection rather than a pipe.

cpio Headers

For each file that cpio backs up, cpio writes a *header* on the tape or diskette; the header contains the file name and information about the file. The header can be written in one of two formats: *binary* or *character*.

Binary headers (the default) store information in a format that is most convenient for a particular machine; they are therefore slightly more efficient and take up slightly less room on the tape or diskette. However, a backup tape or diskette written with binary headers on one machine may not be usable on a different make and model of computer. Thus, backup files written on a DEC VAX, for example, could not be restored on a 386-based XENIX computer.

Character headers, however, contain information written with ASCII characters instead of binary numbers. Character headers, specified with the c option, take up slightly more space, but they are compatible across all machines. This compatibility can be very handy if your VAX breaks and is in need of lengthy repairs. If you made your backups with character headers, you can retrieve important files on your friend's 3B2; if you used binary headers, you have to find another VAX. This capability is so valuable that most system administrators use the c at all times, without a second thought.

In retrieving files, cpio works much like tar. If file names are specified on its command line, cpio retrieves only those files; otherwise, it retrieves all files on the tape or disk. A typical command to retrieve all files is

```
cpio -icvdmu </dev/mt0
```

As with the options used to create a backup, most system administrators consider icvdmu a word, not a series of separate options. The following list describes what each options means:

Option	Action
i (input)	Restores a backup
c (character)	Uses character headers
v (verbose)	Lists the files as they are restored
d (directories)	Creates directories as needed

Option	Action
m (modify time)	Date-stamps the restored files with the dates they had when they were backed up, rather than with the current date
u (unconditional)	Restores files, even if they already exist on disk

As with tar, you can list all the files on a backup with the command

```
cpio -icvt </dev/diskette
```

Hard Disk Backup Programs

The fastest, most convenient way of making a backup is to copy files from one hard disk to another. The hard disk receiving the backup may be a non-removable hard disk, or it may be a removable disk pack that you can remove from the computer and store elsewhere, much like a floppy. Backups made from hard disk to hard disk are attractive because the computer can make them rapidly; the data transfer rate between two hard disks is faster than between a hard disk and any other storage medium.

Hard disk backups, however, have important disadvantages:

- Hard disk drives are expensive.

- Removable disk packs are expensive.

- If removable disk packs are not used, then the backup is not very safe; a fire that destroys the original disk is likely to destroy the backup as well.

For these reasons, hard disk backups almost never replace, but rather supplement, tapes or diskettes. For example, you may perform a tape backup every week and a hard disk backup every day. Thus, in the event of a typical problem—a user accidentally deletes a file—you have the hard disk backup available. In the event of a *real* catastrophe, however, such as a fire in the computer, you can fall back on the tapes.

You can use any of several programs for backups from hard disk to hard disk:

- dcopy

  The dcopy command, available on UNIX System V, copies all files from one hard disk to another, and reorganizes the files as they are copied. As you learn in Chapter 10, the data blocks that make up a file on a hard disk can, over time, become scattered, increasing the time UNIX requires to access the file. As dcopy copies files, it stores all the data blocks for a file together, which means that the copy is arranged more efficiently than the original. Many system administrators perform a dcopy at regular intervals, such as weekly; after the dcopy is complete, they consider the original to be the backup copy and use the new copy as the "real" copy that users can access.

- copy

  The copy command, available on Berkeley UNIX systems, performs the same operation as dcopy.

- volcopy

  The volcopy command rapidly copies every block from one disk to another disk. The resulting copy is an exact image of the original. The receiving disk must be the same size and type as the original. One disadvantage exists: volcopy copies every block on the disk—even unused space—and therefore takes longer than dcopy or copy when copying disks that are mostly empty.

Backup Tips

A number of techniques are available that you can use to minimize the inconvenience of performing backups. In most cases, some kind of trade-off is involved: in exchange for easier backups, you must pay additional costs or incur inconvenience at some other time.

You also must pay particular attention to ensuring the integrity of your backups. Because of their very nature, you hardly ever know that your backups are unusable until a catastrophe occurs and your backups remain as your only hope.

The following list provides some helpful hints for making, maintaining, and using backups:

- *Back up only data, not programs.* Most UNIX systems contain a large number of files and programs that never change or that are easily replaceable, which include almost all files in system directories, such as /bin and /usr/bin. Similarly, only some files in /etc need to be backed up, such as passwd. Backing up only user files can result in a huge savings in the time required for a backup.

- *Mix full backups with incremental backups.* An incremental backup makes copies of only those files that have changed since the last backup. The find command, which is used in conjunction with cpio, has the capability of selecting only files that have changed within a specified period. You might perform a full backup each Monday and then an incremental backup on Tuesday through Friday. Because relatively few files change between backups on most systems, incremental backups usually require less time and significantly fewer diskettes. However, because incremental backups contain only files that have changed, you may not be able to find a copy of a lost file on your most recent backup. You may have to search backward through the incremental backups to find the most recent retrievable copy of the file.

• *Rotate backups.* Too many system administrators conscientiously perform backups with the same set of diskettes or tapes. These media can become worn, and in a moment of crisis when users turn to their backups, they find that the backups have errors. Instead, have several sets of tapes or diskettes available, and use a different set each time in a repeating cycle.

• *Store some backup sets off-site.* What good are backups if your office burns down, taking both the computer and the backups with it? For maximum effectiveness, you should make an extra set of backups and store them away from the computer—at home, at a friend's house, or in a safe-deposit box.

• *Verify backups.* Don't assume your backup is usable; check it! You can do a simple test by commanding tar or cpio to list the contents of the backup. If this operation succeeds, you at least can access all the files on the backup.

• *Label everything.* Knowing that you made a backup is of little help if you can't find it. Every tape or diskette should have a stick-on label indicating when the backup was created, who made it, what it contains, and how it should be restored.

Monitoring System Performance

Another important task you must carry out as system administrator is to monitor the performance of your system. As part of your daily routine, you need to look at how efficiently your system is performing and, in some cases, take steps to help it run better.

Few computer systems have all the disk space they need, and as system administrator you should know how your disk space is being used. The df command tells you at any time how much space is available on each file system. You should use this command on a regular basis, watching for trends. If a file system has been growing at a consistent rate and is in danger of filling up, you need to take action—a good system administrator anticipates the problem before it becomes critical. Often you can solve disk space problems by asking your users to delete unnecessary files (most users tend to keep everything until told otherwise) or by removing inappropriate programs such as games. You may be able to move files to file systems with more free space. If you truly are out of space, however, you may need to purchase additional disk drives; the sooner you can anticipate this need, the less chance you have of running out of space before ordering and installing the new drive.

Monitoring other system resources may be just as important as monitoring disk space, but their shortages may be less obvious. For example, programmers on your system may use a kernel resource called *message queues*. When UNIX was originally configured for your machine, somebody (perhaps the manufacturer) specified a maximum number of message queues. If not enough are available, your users, especially programmers, will complain, and you may have to reconfigure the operating system. (This procedure varies from one system to another.) Your computer's system administrator's reference guide lists other such resources that you may have to manage (also see "Tunables" in Chapter 10).

Most versions of UNIX provide tools to monitor the performance of your computer, such as sar, included in UNIX System V. Interpreting the information provided by sar requires a good knowledge of the internal workings of UNIX (see Chapter 10 for an introduction to internals), but can be helpful in analyzing computers that perform slowly.

A List of Suggestions for System Administrators

As system administrator, you can adopt many habits that can help you perform your job better:

- *Automate.* If you are able, write shell programs and C programs to automate tasks and help decrease your workload. Not only will your job be less tedious, but you can test and verify automated procedures, thus reducing the number of mistakes. Learn and use cron so that you don't have to rely on your memory to ensure that important tasks get done.

- *Communicate.* Keep in touch with your users. They often can serve as a valuable source of information about your computer's performance. No matter how efficiently you think things are running, your users may have other impressions, and they may have suggestions for improvement.

- *Subscribe.* Read as much as possible about what's going on in the UNIX community. Chapter 11, "Introducing the UNIX Community," lists many excellent magazines that can both keep you informed about advances in UNIX and offer tips to simplify your job.

- *Join.* Join as many user groups and organizations as you can, such as UniForum, USENIX, and local groups. Members of these groups often have solutions to problems you encounter. If at all possible, connect to Usenet for a continuous barrage of tips, tricks, and insights into administering UNIX systems.

- *Learn.* Never pass up an opportunity to take a class in system administration or UNIX.

Chapter Summary

Many people find the job of system administration to be the best of all possible worlds. It provides the perfect mix of skills, requiring sharp technical skills on the one hand and providing constant opportunity for interacting with people on the other. Too many computer-related jobs are strictly machine oriented or people oriented; few offer such a blend of technical and social challenges as does system administration.

In most settings, the problems of the system administrator are unending; however, if you know your computer, UNIX, and your users, system administration can be a prestigious and rewarding job. You will find a great deal of satisfaction when another user exclaims, "How did you solve that one so fast?"

10

Understanding the Internal Structure of UNIX

I n Chapter 2, "Understanding UNIX Basics," you were introduced to the parts that make up the internal structure of UNIX. This chapter presents in greater detail some of the components underlying the features you have seen in previous chapters. This chapter, however, can present only some of the basics to you. Entire books have been devoted to the internal workings of UNIX, and many of them only scratch the surface.

Although UNIX is a complex software package—*any* operating system is complicated, for that matter—UNIX is not too complex for most users to understand, if they have the desire to explore it. You certainly can make the argument that a deep understanding of the internal workings of UNIX is not necessary for most users to use it effectively, yet in many situations you may be able to perform tasks more effectively if you know how UNIX works. If you write programs, such knowledge can help you choose between several possible ways of writing a portion of your program. Similarly, most system administrators find that they can make effective decisions about how to administer their system only by understanding how UNIX uses those decisions.

In this chapter, you learn about the components that make up a UNIX system. You explore how UNIX runs a program and how UNIX organizes a disk to make the disk seem to have directories and subdirectories. You come to understand the internal parts of the kernel. Finally, you will see how UNIX manages its memory and how UNIX perpetrates the illusion that it has more memory than is actually available.

325

Files and Processes

To a computer running under UNIX, the essence of the world can be expressed in two words: *files* and *processes*. This computer is like a tiny kitchen in which processes are the chefs following their recipes, and files are the ingredients for great feasts.

UNIX Processes

UNIX is a multiprocessing system, which means that it can attend to many tasks at one time. Each of these tasks is called a *process*; each represents a program running on the computer. In most cases, when you type a command, you are running a program and thus starting a process.

In a sense, processes in the computer are competing against one another. The computer has only a limited amount of memory, CPU time, and other resources, and each process on the computer is vying for these resources. The UNIX kernel must decide how much of these resources to allot to each process.

The term *program* and *process* are not exactly synonymous. A program is a set of instructions that causes the computer to do useful work if the computer follows them; it represents potential. A process is what the computer carries out when it actually follows those instructions.

Note that several processes can be running the same program simultaneously. For example, if several users happen to be checking the spelling of their documents at the same time, they all are using a single program—the spell program—but each instance represents a distinct process. Similarly, you might notice that many people are editing data files simultaneously. This editing involves one program—vi—but many processes.

The Organization of Processes

The folks at Bell Labs who designed UNIX thought of processes in very anthropomorphic terms. Because they thought of processes as though they were people, they used human terms to describe the relationships between processes.

A new process is created when an existing process asks the kernel to create it. The existing process makes this request through a system call named fork. When the process makes this call, the kernel creates two processes out of the one process that made the request. The original process is called the *parent*, and the new process is called the *child*. In most cases, when you type a command at the UNIX prompt, the shell reads your command and starts a new process to perform the task you have requested with your command; the shell is the parent, the new process is the child.

In many cases, the parent sits idle while the child does its work and then continues when the child is finished or, in the parlance of UNIX, when the child *dies*. When you run a command from the shell, the shell ordinarily waits idly while the child does the work; when the child completes its task, the shell resumes and asks you for your next command.

Sometimes the parent does not wait for the child to die. For example, when you run a shell command in the background (by placing & at the end of the command), the shell immediately displays the prompt and asks you for another command while the child continues its work in the background. In fact, the major difference between a foreground command and background command is that the former makes the shell wait for the child and the latter lets it continue immediately.

A parent process has certain responsibilities to its child processes, and UNIX must keep track of the relationship among the processes—for each process, UNIX must keep track of its parent and children, if any. The responsibilities of a parent are not important to a general discussion of processes, but programmers must take these responsibilities into account when they work with more than one process at a time.

All processes must have a parent; that parent process in turn must have a parent; and so on. If you follow the lineage back far enough, you eventually come to a special process—process 1—that runs a program called init.

The init (*initialize*) process is the ancestor of all processes: the parent, grandparent, great grandparent, or perhaps a more distant relationship. When a UNIX computer boots, init is the first process started, and it is the only process that does not have a true parent. The init process is always running while UNIX is running, and if init dies because of an error, UNIX cannot function correctly.

The init process performs many important functions. It starts a new process on each terminal (called getty) that allows a user to log in (See "Booting the Computer" and "The inittab File" in Chapter 9 for more information about init).

If a process dies while any of its children are still alive, the children become *orphans*. One of init's most interesting functions is that of an *orphanage*—it becomes the parent for all orphans and assumes the responsibilities of parent for these processes.

Zombies

When a process dies, UNIX cannot remove it completely from the system until the parent acknowledges that its child has died; the parent gives this acknowledgment through the `wait` system call. In what is perhaps the strangest example of the anthropomorphic twist to UNIX processes, a process that has died but whose parent has not performed a `wait` becomes a *zombie*. Like the zombies of horror classics, a UNIX zombie has died but cannot leave the system of the living until it is exorcised with a `wait`. Zombies usually are a symptom of improperly written programs, which create new processes but do not interact with them correctly.

Figure 10.1 illustrates the relationship of a sample of processes running on a UNIX computer.

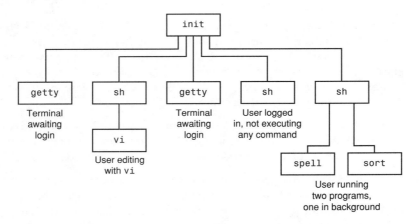

Fig. 10.1. Sample processes and their relationships.

You may be both amused by and skeptical of the terminology used in this chapter—parents and children and orphans and zombies—but the actual UNIX program source code gives instructions for manipulating these entities. Programmers often find it helpful to think of abstract programming concepts in terms of how they resemble more familiar everyday objects (zombies excluded).

The Process Table

In an area of memory reserved for the kernel's use, UNIX maintains a table of processes running on the computer, called the *process table*. Here the kernel stores important information about each process, to which the kernel must have immediate access. For example, the process table stores scheduling information, which the kernel uses when deciding which process to run next. Also included is the information required to locate the areas of memory containing the various parts of the process.

The Parts of a Process

Each process consists of several parts, each occupying an area of memory:

- *The user block.* The process table contains critical bookkeeping information about each process, to which the kernel must have access at all times. Other bookkeeping information is required by the kernel only when the process is actually running, and this information is stored in the user block. Information stored in the process table tells the kernel how to find each process's user block. Most importantly, the user block serves as an index for the rest of the process's memory; stored within the user block is the information for finding the other parts of the process.

- *The data area* and *the stack.* The data area and the stack are two separate areas that together contain the information being manipulated by the program. The difference between the two requires an understanding of programming and is not important here.

- *The text.* The text contains the program—the machine instructions—that tells the program what to do. This term may be somewhat confusing, because you often use the term *text files* to denote files that contain only ASCII characters. In the context of the kernel, however, *text* instead refers to the executable machine instructions that make up a program.

Figure 10.2 illustrates how the kernel locates the various parts of a process. The process table contains the information needed to find the user block, and the user block in turn contains the information needed to locate the other parts of the process.

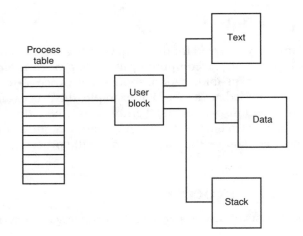

Fig. 10.2. *The parts of a UNIX process.*

If two or more processes on a computer are running the same program, they each must have their own data, because the data with which they work are not necessarily the same. The processes, however, can share the machine instructions, which are always the same for a specific program. For example, if two users simultaneously are using vi to edit files, each user is calling upon machine instructions contained in the vi program; however, the data involved—the files being edited, the location within the file, the contents of buffers, and other information—certainly is different for the two processes.

As an analogy, consider two cooks baking identical cakes. Although both cooks need their own eggs, flour, sugar, and frosting, they certainly can share the recipe from which they will prepare their cakes.

Figure 10.3 shows an illustration of how UNIX views shared text. When two processes run the same program, their user blocks both contain a reference to the same machine instructions. When either process is running, the computer is executing instructions from that text. The two processes, however, do not have to be doing the same thing at the same time. For example, you might be using the instructions within vi to copy a block of text while another user is executing the instructions to save a file.

The Effective User and Group IDs

On any machine running under a multiuser operating system such as UNIX, certain operations are forbidden to most users. For example, most users have only read permission on the password file (/etc/passwd); they can look at but not modify this file. The password file must have these permissions; otherwise, any user could change or remove anyone's password, and the concept of system security would become meaningless. Yet, under carefully controlled circumstances, UNIX sometimes must let you perform operations normally denied to you. For example, when you change your own password with the passwd command, the net effect must be that the password file is modified to reflect your new password. When you run the passwd command, how does UNIX allow you to perform an operation that it otherwise does not allow you to do?

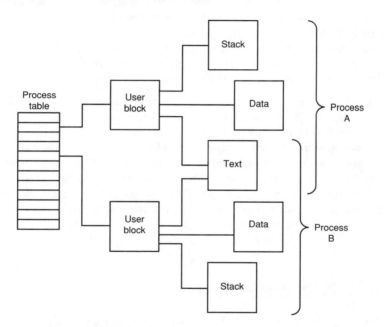

Fig. 10.3. *Two processes sharing text.*

UNIX solves this problem with the *set user ID bit*. The set user ID bit (or more commonly, *set UID bit*) is an attribute of a program that can be turned on by the owner of a program. When you run a program that has the set UID bit turned on, you temporarily gain the privileges afforded to the user who owns the program. For example, if Kathy creates a program and you run it, you usually are afforded your usual privileges while running the program. However, if she also turns on the set UID bit, you gain the rights to do anything Kathy can do when she runs the program. In UNIX terminology, kathy becomes your *effective user ID*.

In the case of the passwd command, the passwd program is owned by root (the system administrator) and has the set UID bit turned on. When you run the passwd command, you temporarily inherit some of root's privileges, and thus you can change the password file under passwd's control.

Because programs with the set UID bit turned on allow users to take on the rights of other users, they must be carefully written so that they allow you to perform only specific functions. For example, when you run passwd you become root, and therefore have the permissions—so far as UNIX is concerned—to change any password in the password file; however, the passwd command itself does not let you change any password other than your own. Programmers writing programs for which the set UID bit will be enabled must exercise caution. Their programs must carefully control which operations it allows users to perform, so that users do not abuse the new privileges granted by the set UID bit.

A related bit, the *set group ID bit*, allows you to assume the rights afforded to the group to which a program belongs. Programmers use the set group ID bit much less frequently than the UID bit, but set group ID is used in the UNIX mail system. All users' mailboxes belong to a group called mail, and the permissions on them are set so that members of the mail group can modify these files. The mail program itself is owned by the mail group and has its set group ID bit turned on. Thus, although you ordinarily cannot modify another user's mailbox, you gain the capability to do so—and therefore to send mail to other users—when you run the mail program, because you gain the privileges of the mail group.

The UNIX File System

In Chapter 3, "Understanding Files and Directories," you learned that the files within the UNIX file system are organized into *directories*. This structure, however, is actually an illusion perpetrated by the kernel, an illusion that is useful as a way to visualize the organization of the file system. In this section, you learn how a UNIX file system really is organized and how the kernel uses hierarchical directories to make it seem organized. This internal organization is normally invisible to a UNIX user.

In the early days of UNIX, the terms *disk* and *file system* were synonymous. As larger disks became available, however, system administrators began the practice of dividing disks into sections—called *partitions*—each of which contained a file system and, therefore, seemed to the user to be a separate disk. Today a single, large disk can contain a dozen or more partitions, each of which is a file system.

The Parts of a UNIX File System

Ken Thompson at Bell Labs, one of the original creators of UNIX, first described how the UNIX file system would be organized, and his design is still used today in UNIX System V, with only minor changes. The designers of other versions of UNIX, most notably the Berkeley UNIX, made modifications and improvements, but the basic design presented here also applies to other UNIX versions. The details in this chapter apply to UNIX System V.

All UNIX file systems are composed of these parts: the *boot block*, the *superblock*, the *i-node list*, and the *data blocks*. Figure 10.4 illustrates the arrangement of these parts.

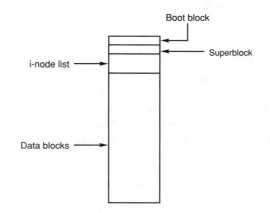

Fig. 10.4. The parts of a UNIX file system.

The Boot Block

The boot block occupies the first 512 bytes of the file system and contains a small program, called the *boot program*. When you first turn on the computer, the computer must fetch the UNIX kernel from disk and load the kernel into its memory. At this point, however, the computer doesn't know how to find the kernel, but it *is* smart enough to load the boot program from disk 0 and execute the boot program, which loads the UNIX kernel and begins executing it.

Every file system contains a boot block, but the computer uses only the boot block for the first file system (usually numbered 0).

The Superblock

The boot block is followed by the *superblock*, a small bookkeeping area that contains information that applies to the disk as a whole. This information includes the following:

- The size of the disk

- Information about the unused areas of the disk

- The name of the file system

MS-DOS users may be interested to know that the UNIX boot block corresponds to the DOS boot sector, and the superblock corresponds very roughly to the DOS File Allocation Table.

The I-Node List

The next area of disk space, after the superblock, is the list of *i-nodes* (information nodes). The total size of this area of disk varies, depending on how the system administrator configures the disk (see "Making a File System with `mkfs`," further in this chapter). Each i-node is 64 bytes long, and a typical UNIX file system contains a list of several thousand. UNIX uses one i-node for every file or directory on the file system, to store important information about that file or directory. Usually, many of the i-nodes are unused, available when you create new files. The i-nodes are numbered, starting with *1*, according to their position in the list. Internally UNIX identifies a file not by its name, but by the file's i-node number. When all i-nodes are being used, you cannot create anymore files on that disk.

UNIX attaches a special meaning to the first couple of i-nodes. The first i-node—i-node 1—is never used. The programmers who designed UNIX discovered that their task of writing the kernel was simplified if they avoided using i-node 1. I-node 2 is always the root directory.

Each i-node contains the following information about a file or directory:

- The *mode* of the file, which includes the file type, permissions, and (for programs) whether or not the set user ID or set group ID bits are enabled

- The number of links to the file (names by which the file is known)

- The user ID number of the owner

- The group ID number to which the file belongs

- The size of the file

- The time and date of the last file modification

- The time and date of the last file access

- The time and date of the last i-node change

- Location information for data associated with the file or directory

You may notice that the information stored in an i-node is the same information presented when you issue the `ls -l` command. Notably missing from the i-node information is the name of the file. File names are not stored in the i-node list. Instead, directories provide the missing information, as explained in the next sections.

The Data Blocks

Following the i-node list, the remainder of the disk is dedicated to *data blocks*. On early UNIX systems, the size of each data block was 512 bytes. Most UNIX systems today, however, use 1024-byte data blocks, and some (such as mainframes from Amdahl) use 4096-byte data blocks.

UNIX stores each file's data within the data blocks. UNIX allocates the appropriate number of data blocks to each file, one data block for every 1024 bytes of data or portion thereof (on most versions of UNIX). Thus, every file from 1 byte to 1024 bytes in length actually uses the same amount of disk space: one data block.

The data blocks that contain the data for a specific file may be scattered throughout the data block area of the disk. UNIX uses the i-node associated with a particular file as a table of contents for locating the data blocks that contain the data for that file. Figure 10.5 illustrates this relationship—the figure shows a file, the data for which is stored in four data blocks. The i-node associated with that file contains the information UNIX uses to access the proper data blocks. Although you cannot tell the exact size of the file from this figure, the file must contain between 3073 and 4096 bytes to use four data blocks.

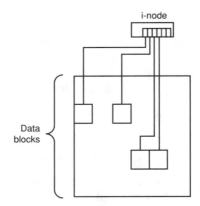

Fig. 10.5. A typical file's i-node and data blocks.

Disk Fragmentation

When the first few files are created on-disk, UNIX stores the data in contiguous data blocks—that is, the data blocks for each file are together and in order. However, the data blocks for a particular file do not have to be stored together, or even near each other. As files are created, removed, and changed, the data blocks associated with those files tend to become scattered throughout the data block area of the file system, a situation known as *fragmentation*. UNIX requires more time to access a badly fragmented disk, resulting in a slower system. The system administrator can defragment a disk with any of several tools, such as dcopy or copy. (See "Hard Disk Backup Programs" in Chapter 9 for more information on dcopy and copy.)

Directories

In Chapter 3, you learned that UNIX uses directories as tables of contents listing other files. In this section, you learn the details of how UNIX stores and uses a directory.

UNIX stores data within a directory just as it stores data in a file: each directory has an associated i-node, and the directory contents are stored in data blocks. The purpose of a directory, from the point of view of the file system, is the correlation of file names to i-node numbers. When you type commands, you reference files by name, but for UNIX to use them, it must know the i-node number. Directories provide the crucial link.

Each directory consists of a collection of 16-byte entries, one for each file listed in the directory. Within each 16-byte entry, UNIX uses 14 bytes to store the file name and 2 bytes to represent the number (in binary) of the i-node associated with that file. Note that a 2-byte binary number can contain values from 0 to 65,535. The numbers 0 and 1 do not represent i-node numbers (i-node 0 does not exist, and i-node 1 is never used), so a UNIX file system can hold at most 65,534 files and directories. Figure 10.6 illustrates the contents of a sample directory.

.	182
..	34
expenses	76
timesheets	2093
sales.rpt.91	0
memo.to.bill	479
jenny.memo	1377
class-list	755
shipping	0
bills.memo	479
sales.rpt.90	811

Fig. 10.6. *Contents of a sample directory.*

Figure 10.6 illustrates several important points:

- Like all directories, this sample directory begins with entries for . (*dot*, or current directory) and .. (*dot-dot*, or parent directory).

- The entries in the directory are not listed in any particular order. (When you list the directory with ls, you see the files and directories listed in alphabetical order only because ls sorts the list before displaying it.)

- When you delete a file, the kernel leaves the name in the directory but changes the file's i-node number to 0. Commands that search and display directories—such as ls and find—are programmed to skip these entries. The kernel reuses these slots as you create new files. In this example, two entries—sales.rpt.91 and shipping— show i-node numbers of 0 and therefore represent files that no longer exist.

- Two files in this example—`memo.to.bill` and `bills.memo`—have the same i-node number and therefore represent the same file.

Indirection

UNIX is designed to work most efficiently with small files, and on early UNIX systems, most files were small. Because of the way UNIX stores the roadmap to the data blocks within the i-node, modern UNIX systems can access the first 10K bytes (10,240 bytes) most efficiently. Beyond 10K, the kernel must employ a technique called *indirection* to fetch data blocks. The i-node contains enough space to hold the locations of only 10 data blocks. For blocks beyond the first 10, the i-node tells the kernel where to find a supplemental list with information that enables the kernel to access additional data blocks.

As an analogy, suppose that all books were required to have a table of contents no longer than one page, and that one page turned out to be just long enough to list ten chapters. Beyond the first ten chapters, the table of contents merely referred you to an auxiliary table of contents, located elsewhere in the book. In such a situation, you obviously could find information in the first 10 chapters more quickly than you could find information that occurred later in the book. Because all i-nodes are the same size, and have enough space to list only the first 10 data blocks, UNIX gives you an incentive to keep files at or below 10K.

Past 266K (272,384 bytes), the situation worsens. The kernel must use an even more complex method, *double indirection*, to access the data blocks. Thus, if you cannot keep a file below 10K, at least keep it below 266K. With files of much larger sizes, *triple indirection* is also possible.

Although few people worry about size limits for data files, you should respect these limits for directories. At 16 bytes per entry, a 10K directory can contain 640 file entries. UNIX always uses two entries for . and .., so you should limit the number of files and subdirectories in a single directory to 638.

File Location and Retrieval

When you access a file, what seems like a simple operation is actually a complex sequence of events. This section presents an example illustrating how UNIX locates a file from a path name. The numbers in the example are taken from a real UNIX system, although the numbers on your system probably are different.

Suppose that you issue the date command. For the sake of simplicity, assume that you use a full path name:

/bin/date

(Using a full path name simplifies the problem because the shell PATH variable does not come into play.) What does UNIX have to do to find the disk space in which the date program is stored? The following steps explain the procedure, which is illustrated in figure 10.7.

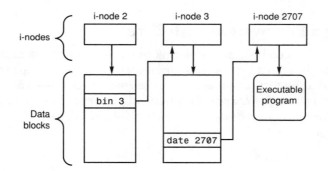

Fig. 10.7. *Locating the* date *program.*

1. The kernel must find the root directory. This task is easy, because the kernel knows that the i-node for the root directory is always i-node 2. The kernel reads i-node 2 and uses it to find the data blocks that contain the root directory.

2. The kernel searches the root directory, looking for an entry for bin. It finds this entry:

   bin   3

   This entry tells the kernel that i-node 3 contains the information for the bin directory. The kernel reads i-node 3 and uses the information within it to find the directory's data blocks.

3. The kernel searches the bin directory for date and finds this entry:

```
date      2707
```

This entry tells the kernel that i-node 2707 contains the information for the date program. The kernel reads i-node 2707 and fetches the executable program from the data blocks listed in that i-node.

File System Commands

Most UNIX systems have numerous commands that manipulate file systems in some way. Three of these commands—mkfs, fsck, and df—are discussed here. Note that only the system administrator can use mkfs and fsck for hard disks on most systems.

Making a File System with mkfs

You cannot use a completely blank disk or partition until you make it into a file system. You must write a valid superblock to the beginning of the disk, create a root directory, and mark the remaining i-nodes and data blocks as *free*. The mkfs (*make file system*) command performs these operations. It takes as its argument the device name of the disk or disk partition. Consider this example:

```
mkfs /dev/rfp020
```

(The device name for disks varies from one system to another.) This command sets up a file system on disk /dev/rfp020.

The mkfs command enables you to specify how many i-nodes you want to allocate on the disk; choosing this value can be tricky. For every 16 i-nodes you allocate, you must give up one data block. If you create too many i-nodes, you can run out of disk space on the disk because too much space is used by i-nodes. If you allocate too few i-nodes, you may find yourself unable to create a new file—even though plenty of disk space is still available—because all i-nodes are in use.

A good rule of thumb for general disk use is to allocate 1 i-node for every 4 data blocks. Thus, on a 10,000-block disk, you would allocate 2,500 i-nodes, which require 157 blocks of disk space. If, however, you know that the disk will contain only a few, very large files, you can allocate fewer i-nodes. Similarly, if you know the disk will contain lots of small files, more i-nodes may be required.

Figure 10.8 shows the output from a sample `mkfs` command, in which a file system is created on a floppy diskette.

```
# mkfs /dev/rfp021 <Return>
slice 1
bytes per logical block = 1024
total logical blocks = 395
total inodes = 96
gap (physical blocks) = 2
cylinder size (physical blocks) = 20

#
```

Fig. 10.8. *Sample output from the* `mkfs` *command.*

The output shows that each block has 1024 bytes, and that the disk contains a total of 395 blocks. The `mkfs` command allocates 96 i-nodes (roughly 395 divided by 4), which require 2 blocks (64 i-nodes per block).

Checking a File System with `fsck`

A healthy file system should have certain characteristics. Like a set of accounting books, various figures in a file system should balance. For example, every i-node that is used should be listed in at least one directory (otherwise the file represented by the i-node is inaccessible); similarly, every data block should either belong to an i-node or appear in the list of unused data blocks. The `fsck` command (*file system check*) provides you with a method for checking the integrity of a file system and repairing it if it is damaged.

How can a file system become damaged? Hardware errors, though rare, can occur and cause problems in a file system. More common, however, is damage—usually minor—caused by surges or interruptions in the electrical power supply.

Figure 10.9 shows a sample output from fsck.

```
# fsck <Return>
/dev/fp002
File System: filsys  Volume: usr

** Phase 1 - Check Blocks and Sizes
** Phase 2 - Check Pathnames
** Phase 3 - Check Connectivity
** Phase 4 - Check Reference Counts
** Phase 5 - Check Free List
5233 files 78130 blocks 40922 free

#
```

Fig. 10.9. Sample output from fsck.

The fsck command normally performs its work in five phases, each of which contains a series of checks. In this example, fsck produces no complaints; the file system is in good shape. The report shows that the disk contains 5,233 files and 78,130 blocks, of which 40,922 are unused.

Unfortunately, fsck sometimes reports bad news. See figure 10.10 for a sample of output generated after executing the fsck command on a corrupted disk.

In this example, fsck finds the following four problems and asks you for permission to fix them:

1. I-node 822 contains information for a file (1986 bytes long, owned by mark), but that file is not listed in any directory and therefore has no name. fsck flags it as an unreferenced file and asks whether you want to reconnect it to a directory. If you answer **y**, fsck lists it in a special directory called lost+found, under the name 000822 (its i-node number). The lost+found directory serves exclusively as an attachment point for unreferenced files found by fsck.

2. I-node number 1022 is also an unreferenced file; however, because the file contains no data (SIZE=0), fsck simply deletes it.

3. The superblock contains a count of the number of unused i-nodes. When fsck counted the number of i-nodes, however, the actual count didn't match the number in the superblock. fsck therefore offers to fix this problem.

4. fsck found one data block that was neither part of a file nor included in the list of unused data blocks; fsck asks whether you want to add this data block to the list of unused data blocks.

```
# fsck <Return>
/dev/fp002
File System:  Volume:

** Phase 1 - Check Blocks and Sizes
** Phase 2 - Check Pathnames
** Phase 3 - Check Connectivity
** Phase 4 - Check Reference Counts
UNREF FILE  I=822  OWNER=mark MODE=100644
SIZE=1986 MTIME=Aug 16 18:57 1991  (NOT EMPTY)
RECONNECT?

UNREF FILE I=1022  OWNER=mark MODE=10000
SIZE=0 MTIME=Aug 16 18:59 1991  -- CLEARED
FREE INODE COUNT WRONG IN SUPERBLK
FIX?
** Phase 5 - Check Free List
1 BLK(S) MISSING
BAD FREE LIST
SALVAGE?
** Phase 6 - Salvage Free List
5233 files 78130 blocks 40922 free
#
```

Fig. 10.10. *The results of running* fsck *on a corrupted disk.*

Whenever you use fsck, it checks the following conditions, all of which should be true for a healthy file system:

- Every data block should be claimed by a single i-node or should appear in the list of free data blocks.

- No i-node should refer to a data block number that does not actually exist on the disk. For example, no mention of data block 5000 should be on a floppy disk, because data block 5000 does not exist.

- The number of links recorded in the i-node should match the actual number of entries found for that file in directories.

- The number of data blocks used by a file should be consistent with the size of the file as recorded in the i-node.

- Because directories are composed of 16-byte entries, the size of a directory always should be evenly divisible by 16.

- A directory should not list any i-nodes that are not in use.

- Various numbers recorded in the superblock must be within certain values. For example, the number of i-nodes allocated on the disk should not exceed 65,535.

Listing File Systems with df

The df (*disk free*) command lists the file systems available and the number of unused data blocks and i-nodes. The output from df varies from one system to another; the following output is just one example:

```
# df -t <Return>
/           (/dev/dsk/c1t1d0s0):     3068 blocks     2215 i-nodes
                 total:    25830 blocks    3216 i-nodes
/usr        (/dev/dsk/c1t1d0s2):     8112 blocks    22254 i-nodes
                 total:   221444 blocks   27680 i-nodes
/usr2       (/dev/dsk/c1t3d0s8):    48364 blocks    61702 i-nodes
                 total:   276420 blocks   65488 i-nodes
/tmp        (/dev/dsk/c1t3d1s8):    19714 blocks     2484 i-nodes
                 total:    20060 blocks    2496 i-nodes
/usr3       (/dev/dsk/c1t3d1s9):    20320 blocks    31724 i-nodes
                 total:   256360 blocks   32032 i-nodes
#
```

(Note that the –t option tells df that it should list not only the free space on each file system, but also the total size of the file system.)

This listing shows five file systems. For each, df shows the device name, the number of blocks and i-nodes used, and the total number of blocks and i-nodes present on the disk.

Compare this df output with the following df output, which was produced by a computer running a different version of UNIX:

```
# df <Return>
Filesystem          kbytes      used    avail capacity  Mounted on
/dev/zd0a            16439     10620     4175    72%     /
/dev/zd4g           381919    243948    99779    71%     /u3
/dev/zd3g           254987    222148     7340    97%     /u5
/dev/zd3h           245458    179315    41597    81%     /u4
/dev/zd2g           381919    333342    10385    97%     /u6
/dev/zd2h           373443    237553    98545    71%     /usr
/dev/zd2a             8459       439     7174     6%     /tmp
/dev/zd1d           519894    448139    19765    96%     /acct
/dev/zd0d           433344    223248   166761    57%     /u2
felix:/share        532428    470256     8928    98%     /felix
#
```

This listing shows the device name, the total size of the disk (in kilobytes), the amount of disk space used and available (in blocks), and the percentage of disk space used. Note that the last entry represents a file system on another machine that has been mounted on this computer through a network using NFS (see Chapter 7, "Understanding Communications and Networking," for information on NFS).

The UNIX Kernel

The *kernel* is the resident portion of UNIX. The boot program loads the kernel into a portion of the computer's memory when you turn on the computer, and the kernel occupies that memory continuously until you shut down the computer.

The kernel is unquestionably the most complex part of UNIX, but two portions of it—*device drivers* and the *tables*—merit some attention here because they may have an effect on your work with UNIX.

Device Drivers

Device drivers are software components that directly control pieces of equipment, such as disk drives, tape drives, printers, and terminals. When any other portion of the UNIX kernel needs to access a device (that is, a piece of equipment), that portion of the kernel makes a request of the device driver to perform the necessary operation. The device driver then supervises the necessary details.

Within the parts of the kernel other than the device drivers, all devices are treated alike. The kernel recognizes a common set of operations that all devices can perform, such as reading or writing data. When one portion of the kernel needs to write data to disk, it calls upon the proper device driver, provides the device driver with information about the data to be written, and lets the device driver attend to the details of manipulating the disk drive (see fig. 10.11 for an illustration of this relationship).

As a real-world analogy, consider an air traffic controller. During the course of a day, the controller issues the same commands—take off, turn left, climb, descend, begin the final approach—to the pilots of many different types of aircraft. Although the controller issues the same command, the pilots of two different types of aircraft perform different tasks in complying with the command. The pilots are experts of their own type of aircraft and know what must be done when the controller tells them, for example, to "descend to 5,000 feet." In the same way, the kernel issues generic requests to the device drivers, which perform the particular operations necessary to complete those requests on specific types of equipment.

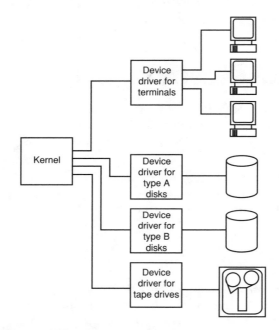

Fig. 10.11. *The relationship of the kernel to devices.*

When you attach a new type of equipment to your computer, you also must install a device driver for that type of equipment, which involves two steps:

1. You must obtain a device driver for the equipment. Often the vendor who sells you the equipment supplies you with its device driver; otherwise, you may have to enlist an experienced programmer to write a device driver. Several books have been written on the subject, and many manufacturers publish guides describing how to write device drivers for their machines. For example, AT&T publishes *Block and Character Interface (BCI) Driver Development Guide*, a massive tome that is anything but light reading, which tells you how to write a driver for almost any type of device that you may want to connect to an AT&T computer.

2. You must install the device driver in the kernel. This procedure varies dramatically from one system to another. On some

computers, you simply copy the device driver to a special directory. On others, you must perform a complex series of tasks. Your computer's reference guide is your best source of installation information.

Data Tables

Much of the internal workings of UNIX centers around a series of *data tables*. These tables are simply areas of memory in which the kernel stores information about various facets of the computer's activities. The kernel refers to the information in these tables frequently and modifies the information within the tables as various events occur. For example, whenever a new process starts, the kernel makes an entry in one of its tables about the new process. Tables are stored in memory reserved for the kernel's use and can be accessed exclusively by the kernel. Some of the important tables that UNIX must maintain are listed here:

- *The shared text table.* Earlier in this chapter, you learned that when two or more users run the same program, they share a single copy of the text (machine instructions). In the shared text table, UNIX keeps track of each text on the system and the number of users who are using it.

- *The i-node table.* A file's i-node contains important information about the file, and the i-node normally is stored on the same disk as the file. When the file is being used, however, the kernel copies the i-node into memory for faster access. These "in-use" i-nodes are stored in the i-node table.

- *The file table.* The file table contains information specific to the way in which a particular process is using a file. It contains information such as current location of the process within the file and whether the process is reading or writing, or both, to the file. Note that if several processes are accessing the same file at the same time, only one entry is in the i-node table, but multiple entries are in the file table, one for each process.

- *The mount table.* The mount table describes the mounted file systems and the directories onto which they are attached.

- *The callout table.* The callout table is the UNIX kernel's equivalent of Post-it notes. Occasionally the kernel undertakes a task that must be interrupted temporarily and completed at a future time. The callout table provides a place for the kernel to enter reminders to itself that it needs to perform an operation sometime in the future.

- *The process table.* The process table contains one entry for each running process. Much of the important information UNIX keeps on each process is stored in the process table: the current status of the process (that is, what it is doing or waiting for), the priority of the process, the ID of the user and group to which the process belongs, the process ID number (PID) of the process, the PID of the process's parent, and more.

Tunables

When a system administrator or technician installs UNIX on a computer, he or she can adjust a large set of parameters that affect system performance. These parameters are called *tunables* because they enable the system administrator to fine-tune the operating system. Choosing values for the tunables requires a thorough understanding of UNIX and a knowledge of how the computer will be used. In some cases, the value of a tunable is critical; in others, a poorly chosen value simply results in an operating system that doesn't run as fast as it could.

Many of the tunables specify how large certain tables, such as those listed in the previous section, should be. In no case do you want to make the tables any larger than necessary, because the unused portions of the table waste memory. On the other hand, if the tables are not large enough and they become full, users will not be able to perform certain operations. For example, if the process table is full, users cannot start new processes; if the file table is full, users cannot open new files. Worse, if the callout table is full and the kernel needs to place another entry in the table, a *panic* results.

Kernel Panics

If nothing else, the designers of UNIX chose colorful terminology. In their terms, the kernel doesn't encounter a fatal error; it panics. A *panic* occurs when the kernel encounters a situation—such as a hardware error or some type of internal inconsistency—that it cannot handle. The kernel prints an error message on the console, which includes a description of what happened and some internal information that programmers can use, and then the kernel stops dead. To continue, the system administrator must reboot the computer. On a properly functioning computer, panics are rare.

Swapping and Paging

On multiuser systems such as UNIX, the programs being run by the users on the system sometimes require more memory than is present in the computer. This situation occurred even more frequently years ago, when memory was more expensive than it is today and, consequently, computers had less memory. Like most multiuser systems, UNIX ensures that new processes can run, regardless of the amount of memory currently in use, by employing one of two techniques: *swapping* or *paging*.

Swapping

The original UNIX systems used a technique called *swapping*, which enabled the kernel to use disk space instead of memory when memory was in short supply. On a swapping system, when you start a new process, the kernel tries to find an unused area of memory large enough to hold the program and its data. If enough memory is available, the kernel loads your process into that memory area and begins execution. If not enough memory is available, however, the kernel looks for another process that is already running but not currently busy. The kernel moves that process's program and data from memory to a special area on-disk called the *swap space*. That process is said to be *swapped out*, and the memory previously occupied by that process is now available for your process.

Later, when the swapped-out process is ready to continue, the kernel must swap the process back in. The kernel searches for an unused area of memory and moves the process's program and data from the swap space back into main memory. If many processes are running, the kernel must swap out one process to swap in another.

Figure 10.12 illustrates a system in which some processes are in the computer's memory (swapped in) and others are on-disk (swapped out).

Although swapping enables many more processes to run than otherwise can be supported by the computer's memory, swapping is an enormous drain on system resources. Users often can tell when memory is full and the kernel is swapping, because the system slows down noticeably. If the processes running require far more memory than the computer has available, the system may spend most of its time swapping programs in and out and very little time actually doing useful work. Such a computer is said to be *thrashing*.

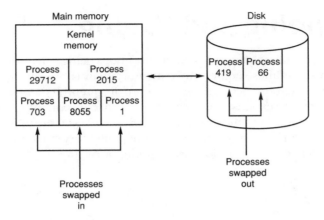

Fig. 10.12. *Processes 419 and 66 swapped out.*

Virtual Memory and Paging

The Berkeley version of UNIX introduced a technique called *paging*, also known as *virtual memory*. Paging has since become standard in almost all versions of UNIX. Like swapping, paging enables the kernel to use disk space in place of main memory, but much more efficiently than swapping. The area on-disk is called the *paging area*, rather than swap space, indicating a slightly different memory-management technique.

On a paging system, all main memory is divided into chunks of memory of equal size, called *pages*, which on most UNIX systems contain 4,096 bytes each. Similarly, programs are divided into portions of the same size, also called pages.

When you start a new process, the kernel does not have to find enough free memory to load your entire program and its data; it needs only a single page of memory, into which it loads the first page of your program. As your program executes, it eventually needs to use data or program instructions on a different page, at which point it finds that the desired data or instructions are not loaded into memory. This condition is called a *page fault*. Your program temporarily suspends its work while the kernel searches for an empty page of memory and loads into that page the data or instructions required by your program. The kernel maintains a table of the parts of each process loaded into memory pages.

If a page fault occurs and all memory is in use, the kernel makes room for the required data by *paging out* other data. The kernel searches for the page of memory least-recently used, moves that page to the paging area on-disk, and then moves your requested data into the now-vacant page.

Note that in computers that use paging (virtual memory), all pages belonging to a single process are not necessarily located together in the computer's memory. Figure 10.13 shows a computer's main memory, highlighting the pages in memory that belong to a single process.

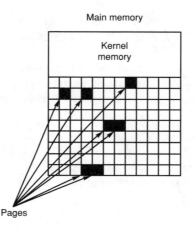

Fig. 10.13. Pages for a process.

Other pages, not shown in this example, are on-disk (paged out). Because of this scattering of data throughout the computer's memory, paging systems require assistance from the computer's hardware—the computer's CPU must include special circuits, called *virtual memory management* hardware—to keep track of where the parts of a process are located. Fortunately, most computers today are designed with the appropriate hardware.

Paging is much more efficient than swapping, for a variety of reasons:

- Only small pages (approximately 4K bytes) are transferred to and from disk at a time, rather than entire processes.

- At any given time, most processes use only a small portion of their data and instructions. Swapping requires that both the used and the unused portions of the program are loaded together; paging requires that only the portions currently in use be in memory. Thus, an amount of memory that is inadequate in a swapping environment may be fine for a paging environment.

Chapter Summary

In this chapter, you have learned a little about how UNIX works internally.

UNIX focuses on two main concepts: files and processes. Most of the work performed by the UNIX operating system involves manipulating these two types of entities.

UNIX groups files together into an organization called a *file system*. UNIX presents the illusion that file systems are organized into directories and subdirectories, but at a lower level, this illusion is simulated by the components of the file system. A file system is actually composed of a boot block, a superblock, a list of i-nodes, and an area of data blocks. Directories become nothing more than special files that associate the name of a file with its i-node number.

In this chapter, you also learned about the important information that UNIX stores in memory tables. These tables play an important part in the duties of the system administrator, who must configure these tables in a new computer and manage these tables from time to time in existing systems.

Finally, you learned about the UNIX memory management schemes—paging and swapping—which enable UNIX to provide more storage space for running programs than is actually available in main memory.

11

Introducing the UNIX Community

W henever large numbers of people become interested in a common topic, groups, magazines, and conferences develop to form a community through which people can exchange ideas, information, and fellowship (and in the case of computers, software). Because UNIX extends to so many different types of hardware and environments, UNIX users have become immersed in an especially rich user community. As UNIX has grown, so have the user organizations that support it. Some groups have been formed by the vendors to promote the sale of their products, and others by end users (that is, people who use UNIX in their jobs) to exchange ideas and information with other users. This chapter looks at the groups, and the resources available through them.

UNIX Vendor Organizations

Throughout the late 1980s, a major source of concern among UNIX users and vendors was the divergence of UNIX systems into two broad categories: those based on AT&T's UNIX System V, and those based on Berkeley's versions of UNIX. In 1988, AT&T (whose systems were based on UNIX System V) and Sun Microsystems (whose systems were based on Berkeley UNIX) sought to merge the features and capabilities of both by cooperating on the development of a combined version of UNIX. Other major UNIX vendors, such as DEC, IBM, and Hewlett-Packard, feared that such a collaboration would give Sun an unfair competitive advantage. These vendors asked to be allowed to participate in the effort. When AT&T refused,

353

IBM and its allies formed the Open Software Foundation (OSF), dedicated to developing its own UNIX-like operating system and promoting the development of open systems. Not to be outdone, AT&T and Sun gathered together their own corporate comrades and formed UNIX International (UI).

The UNIX version of the feud between the Hatfields and McCoys rages on today, with both OSF and UI claiming to have the operating system of the future. Both groups are engaged in ongoing research and development of new technologies for UNIX, including graphical user interfaces, increased security, support for multiprocessing and transaction processing, and networking.

OSF and UI have made several efforts to negotiate an end to the divisions that separate them. OSF members want AT&T to separate its UNIX operation into an independent corporation, the stock of which could be purchased by other UNIX vendors. AT&T, on the other hand, wants to retain ownership of this valuable asset and vows that it never will relinquish majority control over the future of UNIX System V.

Table 11.1 shows the largest members of UI and OSF. Some companies, listed in the middle column, belong to both organizations.

Table 11.1
Selected UI and OSF Members

UNIX International (UI)	Both	Open Software Foundation (OSF)
AT&T	Intel	Digital Equipment Corp.
Sun	Informix	Hewlett-Packard
UNiSYS	Stratus	IBM
Control Data	Ingres	Carnegie-Mellon
Fujitsu	Motorola	Boeing
SCO	Wang	Mitre
Citibank	Toshiba	Visix Software
Integrated Solutions	Data General	
	Oracle	

UNIX System Laboratories

As the 1980s came to a close, AT&T formed a separate organization to guide the future of UNIX System V. Originally called the UNIX Software Operation (USO), AT&T changed the name to UNIX System Laboratories (USL) in mid-1990. In early 1991, USL sold approximately one quarter of its stock to outside vendors and added outside personnel to its board of directors. As always, however, AT&T stands firm in retaining a major controlling interest in USL. USL, in turn, has become the guiding force behind UNIX International.

At the UniForum conference in January 1990, USL announced the System V Roadmap, which charts the course of System V development for the next five years. USL initially released UNIX System V Release 4 (SVR4), which combines features of the three best-selling UNIX versions: UNIX System V, Berkeley UNIX, and XENIX. Table 11.2 shows the major versions of SVR4 expected over the coming years.

Table 11.2
System V Release 4 Versions
(SVR4 Roadmap)

Version	Scheduled Release	Features
SVR4	1991	Open-look graphical user interface, network file system, internationalization, virtual file system
SVR4 MP	1991	Multiprocessing support
SVR4 ES	1992	Enhanced security
SVR4 MP Plus	1992	Additional multiprocessing capabilities
SVR4 NC Plus	1993 or 1994	Network computing support

The Open Software Foundation

OSF released OSF/1, its version of UNIX, in October 1990. This version strongly resembles UI's UNIX System V Release 4 and includes support for many of the same features, including enhanced security, a graphical user interface, and multiprocessing. OSF initially expected to adopt IBM's AIX version of UNIX, but later switched to Mach, a UNIX-like operating system developed at Carnegie-Mellon University. A key factor in OSF's decision was Mach's excellent support for multiprocessing. The command set was borrowed from IBM's AIX Version 3.1. To date only two OSF members—Digital Equipment Corporation and Groupe Bull—have announced their intentions to replace their own versions of UNIX with OSF/1.

OSF is seeking to solve many of the challenges facing UNIX today by issuing Requests for Technology (RFT), in which OSF invites vendors—both OSF members and nonmembers—to submit new solutions to problems facing open systems. OSF members develop these solutions into new technologies that are then made available to all OSF members. Table 11.3 shows the RFTs issued by OSF as of 1991.

Table 11.3
OSF Requests for Technology

RFT	Description
ANDF	Architectural Neutral Distribution Format. Requests a format in which software can be distributed across differing computer hardware.
DCE	Distributed Computing Environment. Requests technology for computing across multiple machines.
DME	Distributed Management Environment. Requests technology for managing different types of hardware across network environments.
GUI	Graphical User Interface. This RFT is the only one that has been completed; OSF adopted Hewlett-Packard's Motif graphical user interface.

While many observers in the UNIX community long for vendor consensus on a standard, industry-wide version of UNIX, not everyone considers the division of vendors into two groups harmful. Although a duplication of labor exists between OSF and UI, the competition spurs both groups on toward better features and greater sophistication.

UNIX User Associations

Although UNIX vendors are busy organizing themselves for commercial purposes, UNIX users have long been organized and continue to form common-interest groups. Especially in earlier days, when UNIX documentation was written poorly and user support was nonexistent, novice UNIX users gained from the experience of more knowledgeable users through user associations. In many cases groups like */usr/group* (now UniForum) and USENIX were the only sources of help when difficult problems arose. In addition, groups such as the Free Software Foundation provided software at little or no cost to solve many common problems that users often encountered.

UniForum

UniForum, the International Association of Open Systems Professionals, is the largest organization devoted to the promotion of UNIX and open systems. UniForum serves as a forum for the exchange of information about all aspects of UNIX, including hardware and software vendors, applications, and the development of new versions of UNIX. A nonprofit association, UniForum is independent of any individual vendor and works for the advancement of UNIX and open systems in general, rather than any specific vendor implementation. Although many of UniForum's members—more than 7,000 members worldwide—are employed by UNIX vendors, 40 percent are end users interested in developing their UNIX skills. Working with UniForum are 26 affiliate groups and 61 sponsor companies in the United States and around the world. UniForum is represented by affiliate groups in countries on every continent except Antarctica, including Japan, the United Kingdom, and the People's Republic of China.

UniForum was established in 1980 and incorporated the following year as */usr/group*, the name of which was a pun on UNIX's directory structure. The /usr/group Standards Committee produced perhaps the first UNIX standards document, the */usr/group Standard*, in 1984. That document became one of the foundation documents for the evolving POSIX standards, developed under the sponsorship of IEEE. (See Chapter 12, "UNIX and the Market," for more information on the POSIX standard.) In 1989 /usr/group officially changed its name to UniForum.

UniForum is best known for its annual conference of the same name. The first UniForum conference was held in Los Angeles in July, 1981, and attracted 300 attendees and 12 exhibitors. By January, 1990, the UniForum conference in Dallas attracted over 22,000 attendees and 275 exhibitors, including such major players as Sun, AT&T, IBM, Novell, Apple, Amdahl, and DEC. The conference focuses on the needs of UNIX users, especially end users. Each year at the conference, UniForum presents an award for outstanding individual contribution in the development of UNIX systems and a technical award for the best paper presented at the conference.

UniForum's Technical Committee provides an important part of UniForum's contribution to the UNIX community. Managed by the Technical Steering Committee, it is composed of working groups, which develop standards proposals, and special interest groups, which provide discussion forums for users and developers. Table 11.4 lists the five working groups and special interest groups.

Table 11.4
UniForum's Technical Subcommittees

Group	Area of Focus
C++ Special Interest Group	The C++ programming language
Internationalization Working Group	Adding features that make UNIX easier to use in European and Asian environments
Performance Measurements Special Interest Group	Standard methods for measuring and improving the performance of UNIX
Real Time Working Group	UNIX systems that must operate with time-critical applications
Security Special Interest Group	Enhancing UNIX security features

The Technical Committee also produces a number of publications on POSIX and other technical areas, such as networking, electronic mail, internationalization, and open system procurement.

The UniForum Publications Department produces four general publications, including its monthly magazine, *UniForum Monthly* (formerly *CommUNIXations*), and its biweekly newsletter, *UniNews*.

Virtually all major UNIX hardware and software vendors contribute to UniForum; its corporate sponsor list reads like the who's who of the computer industry. Included are Altos, AT&T UNIX Systems Laboratories, Amdahl, Apple, Cray, DG, DEC, Harris, HP, Hitachi, IBM, Intel, Motorola, NCR, OSF, Pyramid, SCO, Sequent, Sony Microsystems, Sun Microsystems, Tandem, Toshiba, UNiSYS, and WordPerfect Corporation.

A general membership in UniForum costs $100 annually and entitles the member to all association publications and services. General members may serve on UniForum's technical subcommittees and on its board of directors.

Associate members pay $50 annually, receive *UniForum Monthly*, and are entitled to discounts on other publications and services. Members of both classes receive discounts on registration for UniForum conferences and events.

Appendix F lists UniForum affiliate groups.

Free Software Foundation

With the exception of MS-DOS, probably no environment has more free software available than UNIX. The savvy UNIX shopper often can find needed software at little or no cost. One of the major sources of this free software is the Free Software Foundation.

The Free Software Foundation (FSF) was founded by Richard Stallman, a UNIX expert whose beard and long, dark hair epitomize the stereotypical image of a UNIX software guru and hacker. Stallman believes that all software should be free to individuals, and he has set out to provide one of the most comprehensive arrays of UNIX software, all free. Distributed under the name *GNU*, which stands for *GNU is Not UNIX*, the Free Software Foundation distributes everything from operating systems and compilers to applications and tools. Everything is distributed for the cost of only the disk or tape on which it is distributed. Programs are distributed in source form, allowing you to make changes to the software, if you have the desire and the technical ability. You are restricted only from reselling the software; you, of course, may distribute copies to others for free.

Although most software is distributed with a copyright prohibiting copying, GNU software is distributed with a notice that Stallman calls a *copyleft*, which encourages copying. In a document distributed with FSF's Emacs editor, Stallman writes about the legal meaning of the GNU copyleft:

> The legal meaning of the GNU copyleft is less important than the spirit, which is that Emacs is a free software project and that work pertaining to Emacs should also be free software. "Free" means that all users have the freedom to study, share, change and improve Emacs. To make sure everyone has this freedom, pass along source code when you distribute any version of Emacs or a related program, and give the recipients the same freedom that you enjoyed....If you still want to find out about the legal meaning of the copyleft, please ask yourself if this means you are not paying attention to the spirit.

Stallman's unique method of distributing software is motivated by a belief that hoarding information—including software—is against the best interests of society. Although other companies are selling software for profit, FSF is dedicated to contributing to the greater good. Among the major products available from FSF are a C compiler, a C++ compiler (called G++), a debugger, the Emacs editor, and a shell called BASH (Born Again Shell), which is similar to Korn Shell.

FSF has had a major effect on the industry. Many of its products are distributed or used by major hardware vendors, such as DEC, Hewlett-Packard, and the Open Software Foundation. Due to grants and other assistance from these vendors, FSF receives the support needed to continue its service.

FSF is not the only source of free software; the federal government is another. The National Technical Information Service makes available thousands of software packages for a minimal cost. Other government agencies, such as NASA, are major producers of free UNIX software.

USENIX

USENIX is the oldest UNIX user association, founded in 1975 and incorporated in 1980. USENIX is dedicated to the development and distribution of information about UNIX and UNIX-like systems and is most famous for founding the Usenet news network (discussed further in this chapter). As of 1991, USENIX boasts of having approximately 4,500 members, with 13 associated local groups throughout the country.

USENIX plays an important role in keeping its members informed of the latest events that affect the development of UNIX. Beyond reporting, USENIX plays an active role in the development of UNIX systems and standards, actively participating in various standards efforts by ANSI, IEEE, and ISO.

USENIX publishes *Computing Systems* quarterly in conjunction with the University of California Press. The magazine contains technical papers on advanced computing topics. USENIX also publishes a bimonthly newsletter, *;login:*, which keeps members apprised of USENIX activities and news in the UNIX community. This newsletter also contains calls for papers, book reviews, and information about various UNIX standards activities.

USENIX sponsors two large technical conferences each year, which include technical presentations and tutorials. Special BOF (Birds of a Feather) sessions bring together users with common interests in specialized fields.

The summer conference includes an exhibition of new technical products. USENIX also sponsors other mini-conferences and workshops throughout the year.

USENIX offers five classes of annual membership: student ($15), individual ($50), corporate ($300), educational ($150), and supporting ($100, for organizations that want to offer additional support to the association). Members receive subscriptions to *;login:* and *Computing Systems*, discounts on various UNIX publications, and discounts on technical conferences and workshops.

Usenet

One of the most fascinating developments of the UNIX explosion is the spread of Usenet, also known as NetNews. Although superficially resembling an enormous, worldwide bulletin board, Usenet is unlike any other bulletin board in the world. Run by USENIX and originally designed to enable UNIX users to exchange ideas, data, and software, Usenet has grown into a global forum for hundreds of topics, both technical and nontechnical, ranging from computers to social issues and hobbies of every kind. Users can exchange ideas about the latest computer hardware, find information about the latest shuttle mission, or toss out a question about the best restaurants in Paris. Amazingly, this massive source of information, conversation, and recreation is virtually free.

How Usenet Works

Electronic bulletin boards have become common throughout the world; many large cities have hundreds. Most bulletin boards are small, implemented by companies or individuals who attach modems to their computers (often PCs) and invite the world to call. Users call in by their own modems, and after they are on-line, browse through files or exchange mail messages. A few bulletin board services, such as CompuServe or Prodigy, are run by large companies for a profit, and charge users for access to their computers.

Usenet—often referred to as *The Net*—is fundamentally different. Most UNIX computers already have the capability to exchange files with each other by networks or the UNIX UUCP software system (see Chapter 7, "Understanding Communications and Networking"), of which Usenet takes advantage. Most other bulletin board services operate by enabling the user to call a central computer manually and perform operations on that computer. Usenet operates by automatically distributing files, programs, mail, and other data—individually known as *articles*—directly to the computers of all the sites that participate in Usenet. The user doesn't call the bulletin board; the bulletin board comes to the user. Usenet, therefore, is a conglomeration of the thousands of computers of all the people who use this network.

Usenet articles are not distributed directly from a central site, but instead make their way through an almost infinite variety of routes. Each article originates on one of the thousands of computers that participate in Usenet and is transferred automatically from the originating computer to one or more nearby computers that also participate in Usenet. These computers, in turn, contact other computers and pass the article along to them, like a chain letter. Known as a *flooding routing algorithm*, each article received on a particular computer may have travelled a different route as it weaved its way through the maze of computers. Articles from nearby computers may arrive within minutes; articles from around the world may take days. At any given instant, millions of bytes of Usenet data are being transferred world-wide in this manner.

USENIX, which administers Usenet, maintains a system called uunet—a system that enables the association to distribute news articles and archive the UNIX software distributed across Usenet. All articles eventually make their way to uunet, and computers connected directly to uunet are assured of getting every article. USENIX charges a small fee for connecting directly to uunet. Most computers, however, get articles indirectly through other computers, and the only cost for them, if any, is the cost of the phone call required to transfer the articles.

When articles arrive on a computer, the NetNews software automatically examines them and collects them into directories that represent the various newsgroups, which are explained in the following section. Users can read the articles at their convenience. After a predetermined period of time—anywhere from a week to a month—articles are erased to free disk space and make room for more articles.

Usenet Newsgroups

Each day computers participating in Usenet receive thousands of articles, far more than any user could possibly read. To organize this wealth of data, the writer of each article assigns the article to one or more categories, called *newsgroups*. When you read articles, you easily can request only the newsgroups in which you are interested.

Newsgroups—about 700 of them—are divided into a number of broad categories (see table 11.5).

Table 11.5
Usenet's Major Newsgroup Categories

Newsgroup Category	Includes
alt	Unusual newsgroups that don't seem to fit anywhere else
bionet	Newsgroups relating to biology and the environment
comp	Computer-related newsgroups
gnu	Software distributed by the Free Software Foundation
misc	Miscellaneous newsgroups on a wide variety of unrelated topics
news	Newsgroups relating to Usenet software or of general interest to all users
rec	Newsgroups relating to recreational activities
sci	Newsgroups relating to sciences other than computers
soc	Newsgroups for social interaction or social topics
talk	Newsgroups for extended discussions, such as politics or religion

Each of these categories is divided into topics, which may in turn be subdivided into subtopics. For example, the comp category is divided into numerous topics dealing with computers. One of them, lang, deals with computer languages. The topic lang is further divided into subtopics for different languages. The name of a newsgroup consists of its category, topic, and subtopic separated by periods, such as comp.lang.c++, which is devoted to the discussion of the programming language C++.

In addition to Usenet's major categories, listed in table 11.5, other categories may exist that address the interests in small geographic areas. The fl category, for example, contains newsgroups concerning jobs, organizations, and fun things to do in Florida.

Since 1986, the number of newsgroups has grown from approximately 200 to over 600 today, not including local groups. A complete listing of the hundreds of newsgroups is impossible in this text, but table 11.6 contains a tiny sample of some of the available newsgroups and their official descriptions (taken directly from the NetNews software configuration file). These groups illustrate the wide diversity of interests represented on Usenet.

Table 11.6
A Selection of Usenet Newsgroups

Newsgroup	Description
alt.atheism	People without religious holidays
alt.cyberpunk	High-tech low-life
alt.gourmand	Recipes and cooking information
alt.kids-talk	A place for the precollege on the network
alt.rock-n-roll.metal	For the headbangers on the network
alt.romance	Discussions about the romantic side of love
alt.sex	Postings of a prurient nature
bionet.jobs	Scientific job opportunities
comp.lang.c	Discussions about C
comp.music	Applications of computers in music research
comp.os.cpm	Discussions about the CP/M operating system
comp.sources.games	Postings of recreational software
comp.sys.att	Discussions about AT&T microcomputers
comp.unix.cray	Cray computers and their operating systems
misc.jobs.offered	Announcements of available positions
misc.legal	Legalities and the ethics of law
rec.aquaria	Keeping fish and aquaria as a hobby
rec.arts.startrek	Star Trek: the TV shows and the movies
rec.equestrian	Discussions about equestrian topics

Newsgroup	Description
rec.games.bridge	Hobbyists interested in bridge
rec.humor	Jokes (may be offensive)
rec.music.folk	Discussions about folk music
rec.skydiving	Hobbyists interested in skydiving
rec.sport.football	Discussions about American-style football
sci.med.aids	AIDS: treatment, pathology and biology of HIV, and prevention
sci.space.shuttle	The space shuttle and the STS program
soc.college	College, college activities, campus life, and so on
soc.culture.china	About China and Chinese culture
soc.singles	Newsgroup for single people, their activities, and so on
soc.women	Issues related to women, their problems, and their relationships
talk.bizarre	Discussions about the unusual, bizarre, curious, and often stupid
talk.politics.soviet	Domestic and foreign Soviet politics
talk.religion.misc	Religious, ethical, and moral implications

As new newsgroups are created, and obsolete newsgroups are discontinued, special control articles are distributed throughout Usenet. These articles are posted to a special newsgroup called control, which actually is not intended to be read by anyone. Instead, the NetNews software spots special messages in these articles that tell NetNews to add a newsgroup, delete a newsgroup, cancel an article, or perform some other administrative function. For example, the following sample shows what a control article might look like:

```
Control: cancel <1991Mar11.050950.16973@watdragon.waterloo.edu>
```

This message tells the NetNews software to cancel an article, perhaps because it was accidentally sent twice by its author. The obscure sequence of characters following cancel is the unique message identification that the NetNews software assigned to the message.

Using Usenet

Each incoming news article on Usenet is represented by a file on the computer. You can read news articles simply by listing the contents of these files, but most users invoke a special program called a *news reader*. Public domain (free) news readers—such as vnews and rn—are available from many sources. News readers keep track of the newsgroups that interest you and keep track of which articles in those groups you already have read. When you want to read new articles that have arrived, you invoke the news reader. Some news readers display summaries of available new articles, enabling you to select which groups and articles to read next.

A typical news article begins with a dozen or so lines, called the *header*, that describe the origin of the article. Figure 11.1 shows the contents of an article.

```
Path: icepit!peora!masscomp!know!sdd.hp.com!cs.utexas.edu!
hellgate.utah.edu!mmoore
From: mmoore%hellgate.utah.edu@cs.utah.edu (Michael Moore)
Newsgroups: comp.unix.questions
Subject: grep
Keywords: grep, recursive
Message-ID: <1991Apr14.214414.9815@hellgate.utah.edu>
Date: 15 Apr 91 03:44:14 GMT
Organization: University of Utah, CS Dept., Salt Lake City
Lines: 29

    Does anyone know if there is an easy way to recursively
search for a pattern down the entire file tree of a
directory?
    ...
```

Fig. 11.1. A Usenet news article.

In figure 11.1, the article's header contains the following information:

• Path

  Path shows the complete route the article took, in reverse order, from the originating computer to the user's computer. In this example, the message originated from a user with login name mmoore on computer `hellgate.utah.edu` and made its way from computer to computer, eventually arriving on `icepit`.

- `From`

  `From` identifies the sender and the sender's computer; in this example, `Michael Moore` is the sender, on a computer called `hellgate.utah.edu`.

- `Newsgroup`

  `Newsgroup` specifies the newsgroup to which the article has been posted. This part of the header may specify several groups if the same article has been posted to several related groups. In this example, the newsgroup is `comp.unix.questions`.

- `Subject and Keywords`

  The `Subject` and `Keywords` lines describe the article's subject matter. In this example, the subject is the `grep` command and whether it can be used recursively.

- `Message-ID`

  `Message-ID` is a unique code that identifies the article.

- `Date`

  `Date` identifies when the article was submitted—April 15, 1991 in this example.

- `Organization`

  `Organization` is the owner of the computer, a company or an individual—the University of Utah in this example.

- `Lines`

  `Lines` is the number of lines in the article—29 in this example.

News readers enable you to do more than read an article on-screen. If you find a particularly interesting or useful article, such as programs, you can print it or save it to a file in your directory for later use. Most readers also enable you to respond to the article by electronic mail or to submit material to the newsgroup.

When you want to contribute to Usenet—either by participating in a conversation, submitting software that you have written, or even telling a joke—you *post an article*. You can post an article from within the news reader software or from a separate program. The software prompts you for the material you want to submit, which you can enter into a text editor or pull in from an existing file. The software then automatically transfers the article to one or more nearby computers, and thus begins its travel through Usenet. Within days, the article distribution is complete.

Many articles are distributed worldwide, but this distribution is not always appropriate. Although new software may be of interest to users everywhere, a discussion of this month's events in a Boston computer club is probably of interest only to Bostonians. When you post an article, the software asks you how widely you want the article distributed. You can respond with any of dozens of codes, such as New England (ne), the United States (usa), North America (na), or worldwide (world). You even can restrict distribution to computers within a single company or organization, such as AT&T (att) or NASA (nasa).

Most newsgroups are *unmoderated*—you can post an article to the newsgroup at any time; however, a few groups, such as those concerned with the distribution of software, are *moderated*. You cannot post articles directly to these groups, but instead must send the article by electronic mail to a person serving as a *moderator*, who reviews the article and approves it for posting. In the case of software, the moderator usually makes a cursory inspection of the software, checking to ensure that the software compiles and loads correctly and inspecting it for viruses and copyrighted material.

Participating in Usenet

To join Usenet, you need only to find another site that already participates and is willing to provide your computer with a *feed*; that is, to pass along to you the articles that they receive. The system administrator at that site configures his or her computer to pass incoming batches of news to your computer. Most colleges and universities participate, and their networks often are used by individuals who want to connect to Usenet.

To receive a *full feed*, which includes every article in every newsgroup, you must have many megabytes of disk space. Many sites, especially individuals with home computers, cannot afford the space, nor can they afford to have their phone lines tied up by the huge quantity of data transferred in a full feed. These sites opt instead for a *partial feed* and inform their source that they want to receive only certain newsgroups.

Complex software is required to run and maintain a Usenet site, but fortunately this software is widely available at no cost. You usually can obtain the software from the computer site providing the feed or from one of several archive sites that allow you to call by modem and retrieve software.

Usenet Statistics

Because Usenet is decentralized and runs across public networks with no central control, estimating the total volume of information that moves across the network is tricky. Nonetheless, several groups attempt this feat. One such group is the Network Measurement Project at the DEC Western Research Laboratory in Palo Alto, California. Brian Reid and his group gather sample usage statistics from almost 800 Usenet computers and then, from that data, draw conclusions about all of Usenet in much the same way that companies such as Arbitron collect television statistics with which to produce ratings. Each month Reid and his group share the results with the Usenet community.

As of April 1991, Reid estimates that 38,000 sites participate in Usenet, with an average of 39 readers per site. The computers on the network process an average of 8,626 articles daily across the newsgroups, which represents almost 20 megabytes of information, programs, discussion, graphics, and lists shipped from computer to computer by networks and phone lines.

Most telling are Reid's Top 40 lists, which show the most-used newsgroups, rated by number of articles, number of users who read the group, and volume of data. The volume of data (megabytes of traffic) can be deceiving because newsgroups that ship graphics files easily top the list. In fact, `alt.sex.graphics` is number one by this ranking method.

Table 11.7 shows the top ten newsgroups, ranked by the number of users who read the group. This ranking doesn't always indicate the most active groups. One group, `news.announce.important`, had only one article that month, but it was widely read.

Table 11.7
Most Widely Read Usenet Newsgroups

Rank	Estimated Readers Worldwide	Articles per Month	Kilobytes per Month	Newsgroup
1	170,000	3,028	6,656.4	`alt.sex`
2	150,000	77	181.6	`rec.humor.funny`
3	140,000	461	898.7	`misc.jobs.offered`
4	130,000	1,071	1,269.5	`misc.forsale`
5	120,000	1	1.8	`news.announce.important`
6	120,000	51	345.5	`news.announce.conferences`

continued

Table 11.7 *(continued)*

Rank	Estimated Readers Worldwide	Articles per Month	Kilobytes per Month	Newsgroup
7	100,000	1,805	2,873.4	`rec.humor`
8	100,000	1,062	2,136.3	`news.groups`
9	100,000	11	302.8	`rec.arts.erotica`
10	100,000	931	1,671.5	`comp.lang.c`

Usenet's capability to convey information is different from any facility available in any other environment, making Usenet a truly unique development of the UNIX community.

UNIX Publications

As the popularity of UNIX has increased, a variety of publications have become available to keep users informed of market trends, provide information on new products, and explain UNIX features. A few of the better-known publications are discussed in this section.

UNIXWorld, published monthly, includes the latest industry news, reviews of new hardware and software products, tutorials on various UNIX facilities and tools, and columns by experts in the UNIX arena. Regular columns include "The Wizard's Grabbag" by Dr. Rebecca Thomas, in which readers submit short programs or shell scripts of general interest to UNIX users; "Answers to UNIX" by Ray Swartz, which provides a question-and-answer forum; and "New to UNIX" by Augie Hansen, which features a monthly tutorial on basic UNIX tools and techniques. A typical issue contains approximately 150 pages. Annual subscriptions are $18. Software presented in *UNIXWorld* is available through two bulletin boards by calling (408) 247-4810 or (604) 533-2312. The account name is `uworld`; the password is `code4me`.

UNIX Today!, a biweekly newspaper (albeit a very flashy one), carries the latest UNIX industry news and focuses on the marketing factors that affect UNIX software and hardware vendors. A typical issue contains 76 oversized pages. *UNIX Today!* is free to qualified industry professionals; $59 annually to others.

UniForum Monthly (formerly *CommUNIXations*) is UniForum's monthly publication. About 54 pages per issue, this magazine focuses on industry trends, UNIX-related events, technical and marketing issues, and UniForum activities. Regular features include a monthly column by the director of UniForum, book reviews, and tutorials for new UNIX users. *UniForum Monthly* is available, at no extra cost, only to UniForum members as part of their membership.

UniNews is a biweekly newsletter published by UniForum. Typically four pages long, this newsletter used to be called */usr/digest*. *UniNews* includes analyses of the latest UNIX news, and information on upcoming events. The newsletter is free to UniForum general members, $30 annually to associate members, and $60 annually to nonmembers.

UNIX Review, a general interest UNIX magazine, is published monthly. In addition to industry news, articles focus on software development and new products. Regular contributions include Stan Kelly-Bootle's "Devil's Advocate" column, an often hilarious look at the lighter side of UNIX, and Eric Allman's "The C Advisor." New hardware is reviewed in "Tested Mettle," and UNIX-related books are examined in "Off the Shelf." A typical issue contains approximately 110 pages. Annual subscriptions cost $55.

In addition to these publications, UNIX frequently appears in general computing magazines. Vendor-specific magazines—which focus on specific vendors and their systems, such as IBM and DEC—often publish articles on the versions of UNIX provided by those vendors, such as IBM's AIX and DEC's Ultrix. Even PC-oriented publications, such as *Byte*, *Dr. Dobb's Journal*, and *PC Magazine*, now routinely examine the impact UNIX has on the PC world.

Chapter Summary

This chapter touches on the resources available to you, both commercially and through an extensive user network, when you join the UNIX community.

For an exhaustive compendium of UNIX magazines, user groups, organizations, and product vendors, see *The UNIX Products Directory*, published annually by UniForum. The 1990 edition features more than 6,000 UNIX-related products and services from 1,540 vendors. The directory, which is available from UniForum, is free to general members, $35 annually to associate members (and for additional copies to general members), and $75 annually to nonmembers.

Also see Appendixes E and F in this book: Appendix E lists addresses for UNIX information and publications, and Appendix F lists UniForum affiliate groups.

## 12

UNIX and the Market

S ince its beginning as an experiment in AT&T's Bell Labs, UNIX has become a major part of the computer industry and is now available from most of the world's major computer vendors. In this last chapter, you learn how UNIX fits into this global market, what measures are being taken to promote its growth, whither it is going, and whence comes its competition.

Open Systems

From the earliest days of the computer industry through the 1970s, most systems sold were *proprietary*. A proprietary system is designed, owned, sold, and controlled exclusively by a single manufacturer. When vendors released new computer systems, the hardware, operating systems, and application software often were designed exclusively for that computer system and could not be used elsewhere. Although this self-contained approach encouraged innovation among manufacturers, proprietary systems forced consumers to rely on a single manufacturer for all their needs.

UNIX is the centerpiece of a growing movement in the computer world toward *open systems*—hardware and software not controlled by any single manufacturer and available from a wide variety of suppliers. Vendors tout open operating systems because their hardware and software are capable of functioning with systems from other vendors; UNIX is such a system. Vendors are adopting UNIX because it opens new markets to them, and consumers of computer systems increasingly are demanding open systems because they offer certain important benefits:

- *Greater freedom of choice.* Purchasers of open systems can choose from among a variety of suppliers of operating systems, application software, and equipment.

- *Easier integration.* Equipment and applications based on the same open systems are more likely to work together than disparate pieces designed to work with proprietary systems.

- *Lower training costs.* Users trained on open systems are equipped to work on computers from any vendor that supplies the same systems.

- *Lower software development costs.* As a company moves from one make and model of computer to another, it need not redevelop software.

- *A larger market for software vendors.* An independent software vendor (ISV) who develops software for one open system can market the same software for any computer using that system.

- *Longer product life.* As new computers are developed, the same open system will continue to work on the new computer. Software developed for an open system is therefore more likely to survive longer, because it does not have to be rewritten when old computers are discontinued and new computers introduced.

UNIX Standards

The key to UNIX and open systems is the development of *standards*. For many vendors to claim that they sell UNIX systems is fine, but if many of the features differ from one system to another, users gain little. The history of UNIX standards is discussed in this section, but the future development of standards also is crucial to UNIX and is the focus of intensive efforts by many dedicated people throughout the computer industry.

As UNIX spread throughout the 1980s, a number of organizations set about to produce standards, assuring users that versions of UNIX from different manufacturers would be functionally identical.

POSIX

In 1981, /usr/group (now UniForum) formed a committee to define a standard version of UNIX (see Chapter 11, "Introducing the UNIX Community," for more information about UniForum). Their report was published in 1983 and formally adopted by /usr/group in 1984. For many years, the /usr/group standard was the best available for UNIX and was commonly adopted by companies that needed a standard.

The /usr/group standard became the basis for the most important UNIX standard, developed by the Institute of Electrical and Electronic Engineers (IEEE). This standard, known as IEEE 1003, was published in April 1986 and entitled *Portable Operating System Standard for Computer Environments*; it became widely known as *POSIX*.

POSIX is not itself an operating system—you never see a vendor selling POSIX; rather, it is a description of how users or programs should interact with certain aspects of an operating system. In more technical terms, POSIX defines an *interface*.

As an analogy, consider an automobile. Car engines vary enormously from one make to another. Transmissions are different in different cars, yet you can sit down in most American cars and drive off without thinking twice about it. The reason is that in all American cars, the interface is the same—a steering wheel, gas and brake pedals, and an ignition key. When you drive, you deal only with the interface, not the internal workings of the engine. (Actually, the interface has two forms, if you consider manual and automatic transmissions.)

In the same way, programs and users deal only with the interface to the kernel, not the underlying workings. POSIX is not concerned with the inner details, only with the interface and the way in which it interacts with users and programs. POSIX is actually a series of standards, each describing how a particular facet of an operating system should work. For example, the first POSIX standard, P1003.1, describes the interface between an application program written in either the C or the C++ programming language and the operating system. The second standard, P1003.2, describes how the shell and various commands interact with the user. (See table 12.1 for a list of current POSIX standards.)

Table 12.1
POSIX Standards

IEEE Standard Number	Standard Title	Description
P1003.1	Operating system interface	Defines how C and C++ programs interact with the kernel

continued

Table 12.1 *(continued)*

IEEE Standard Number	Standard Title	Description
P1003.2	Command language and tools	Defines how the shell and tools work
P1003.3	Verification test procedures	Defines test procedures
P1003.4	Real-time extensions	Defines how real-time (time-sensitive) features work
P1003.5	Ada binding for POSIX	Defines how a POSIX system should interact with programs written in Ada (a programming language developed by the Department of Defense)
P1003.6	Security	Defines security features
P1003.7	System administration	Defines system administration features
P1003.8	Networking	Defines networking interfaces

Any operating system that interacts according to POSIX standards is *POSIX-compliant*. Thus, any program that runs on one POSIX-compliant computer (and does not make use of any extra features on that computer that are not part of POSIX) should run on any other computer that also is POSIX-compliant. Similarly, a user familiar with commands on one POSIX-compliant computer should be able to issue commands on any other POSIX-compliant computer.

Although POSIX is largely based on UNIX, an operating system does not necessarily have to be based on UNIX to comply with POSIX; it merely has to comply with all the standards that POSIX specifies. Other operating systems, such as DEC's VMS and Microsoft's OS/2, are working to be POSIX-compliant. Although much of the design of these operating systems draws on UNIX, they are certainly not versions of UNIX, yet they can be made POSIX-compliant.

Since the mid-1980s, the United States government—the largest purchaser of computers in the world—increasingly has begun to mandate the use of POSIX-compliant computers in bid requests. In doing so, it has raised the POSIX standard almost to the status of law, because no computer manufacturer wants to produce a computer system that cannot be sold to its largest potential customer. Through the rest of the decade, the standards produced by POSIX will continue to play an increasingly important role in the growth of UNIX.

ANSI C

Until the mid-1980s, the C programming language—like UNIX—was available from many sources in slightly different versions. The American National Standards Institute (ANSI) formed a committee known as X3J11, charged with the task of developing "a clear, consistent, and unambiguous Standard for the C programming language which codifies the common, existing definition of C and which promotes the portability of user programs..." (*Rationale for the Draft Proposed American National Standard for Information Systems, Programming Language C*). Although the ANSI committee paid close attention to the way in which C was used in the UNIX environment, the goal of the committee was the production of a C standard that applied equally to PCs running MS-DOS, mainframes running MVS, and computers running UNIX.

Although it would not be strictly a UNIX standard, a C language standard would have a far-reaching effect on UNIX, because the future of UNIX is intimately tied to C. Almost all of the UNIX kernel (in all versions of UNIX) and virtually all the UNIX utilities are written in C. Certainly the various parts of UNIX are only portable—that is, transferrable to other UNIX systems—insofar as they are written in a widely accepted dialect of C.

ANSI sought to preserve existing practice wherever a common existing practice could be found. So they turned to the original book on C, *The C Reference Manual*, written by one of the developers of C, Dennis Ritchie. A version of this document was published as an appendix in *The C Programming Language*, the first commercially published C book, by Brian Kernighan and Dennis Ritchie; however, the ANSI committee also sought to include extensions that had come into common use since *The C Reference Manual* was published. In considering some areas of the language, the committee found the work of other groups helpful, especially POSIX.

The ANSI standard for C, entitled *Programming Language C*, has been universally adopted by suppliers of C compilers. Many compilers already conform to the ANSI standard, and all suppliers plan to switch to ANSI-compatible compilers in the near future.

X/Open

X/Open is a nonprofit, international consortium of computer manufacturers. The goal of X/Open is to define a *Common Applications Environment* (CAE), a set of standards that defines how application programs interact with an operating system. X/Open produced a document, *X/Open Portability Guide*, that defines their CAE. In January 1987, X/Open announced that they would base all future versions of this guide on the POSIX standards.

Commercial Consortia

UNIX International (UI), a consortium composed of AT&T and other companies with an interest in AT&T's UNIX System V, has been both a provider and follower of standards. AT&T's early System V Interface Definition (SVID) influenced the development of POSIX, and AT&T's latest release of System V—Release 4—is in turn designed to be compliant with the latest POSIX standards.

Similarly, the Open Software Foundation (OSF), a consortium composed of IBM, DEC, Hewlett-Packard, and vendors interested in a UNIX-like operating system not controlled by AT&T, has based its standard operating system, OSF/1, on POSIX.

Figure 12.1 shows the relationship between the various standards discussed in this section.

UNIX Competitors: DOS and OS/2

Most computer industry analysts agree that during the 1990s, manufacturers of operating systems, including UNIX, will be competing fiercely for the desktop market—those users who buy computers that sit atop their desks, more commonly known as PCs and workstations. UNIX already commands most of the market in high-end computers. Its chief rivals in the desktop market include MS-DOS, OS/2, and the quasi-operating system Microsoft Windows.

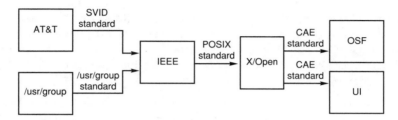

Fig. 12.1. *Various open systems standards.*

MS-DOS

Analysts have been predicting the demise of DOS for years, and all such predictions seem to be premature. Because of its enormous base of existing software, most industry analysts believe that DOS will continue to be the biggest-selling operating system for the foreseeable future. At some point, DOS may come to include multitasking capabilities, blurring the distinction between DOS and other desktop operating systems.

DOS got a sudden, unexpected boost in the late 1980s and early 1990s from Microsoft Windows, a multitasking graphical user interface (GUI) that works in conjunction with DOS and gives DOS many powerful capabilities it normally lacks. By 1994, Windows may control as much as 28 percent of the desktop market, a situation that would hardly have been predicted a few years ago. Microsoft believes that its hottest prospects for the future rest with Windows.

Although Windows provides, at best, a mere bandage for DOS's shortcomings, the combination of DOS's huge base of existing software and Windows' additional capabilities may give DOS the momentum to continue well into the next century.

OS/2

In the mid-1980s, MS-DOS was already beginning to show its age, as machines became more powerful and application programs became more demanding. MS-DOS was unable to provide a multitasking, memory-intensive environment, which new machines were now capable of supporting. IBM and Microsoft began development of what they saw as the next generation of PC operating systems. Initially called DOS 5.0 within Microsoft, the new operating system was later renamed OS/2.

IBM and Microsoft intended OS/2 to fill the gap between DOS and larger operating systems and expected DOS users to jump on the OS/2 bandwagon. They were surprised, however, that many users remained with DOS, switched to Microsoft Windows, or jumped the gap above DOS and opted for UNIX over OS/2. Many analysts believe that this "gap" above DOS never existed, having always been filled by UNIX.

Although some users have chosen OS/2 because of its similarity to DOS—with which they are already familiar—many users began looking at other operating systems after making the decision to abandon DOS. UNIX cost the same as OS/2—or less, in some cases—and provided multiuser capabilities that OS/2 did not.

One of the major advantages of OS/2 over DOS was the introduction of Presentation Manager (PM), OS/2's graphical user interface. Presentation Manager draws on many concepts from the UNIX GUIs based on X Windows, especially Motif, and most users find very little to distinguish one GUI from another.

Another useful OS/2 feature is the capability to run DOS software through the DOS *compatibility box*, which enables OS/2 users to take advantage of DOS's huge base of existing software. UNIX users, however, also can use DOS software with add-on products such as SoftPC from Insignia Solutions and VP/ix from Interactive Systems Corporation.

IBM also sees OS/2 as an integral part of its networking strategy, in which desktop machines are linked together so that data flows easily from one machine to another; however, networking has long been one of UNIX's strengths (see the discussion of networking in Chapter 7, "Understanding Communications and Networking").

The future of OS/2 is still uncertain. Although many predict that it will command a large share of the desktop market in the coming years, others believe that UNIX will control the portion of the market that DOS and Windows leave up for grabs. Robert Kavner, AT&T Group Executive for Data Systems and Federal Systems, describes the situation this way: "OS/2 as a challenger to UNIX in the network server environment is' pretty much history."

UNIX-Like Operating Systems

The popularity of UNIX today and its adaptability to today's problems are a testament to its good design. In the more than 20 years since the birth of UNIX, however, operating system designers have been continually experimenting with new techniques. Programmers tinker with the basic design of UNIX, trying to improve UNIX or, in some cases, produce the next great operating system. Work is underway on new, UNIX-like operating systems that build on more sophisticated techniques than UNIX's.

When UNIX began in the late 1960s, the kernel was a small, relatively simple bit of software. In part, it was small because it had to be—the architecture of the machines that originally ran UNIX, such as the PDP-11, was not capable of supporting a kernel that required more than 64K of memory. Whatever the designers couldn't fit into 64K simply could not go into the kernel.

With the advent of new, more advanced equipment, the 64K limit soon disappeared. Because features usually run more efficiently when built into the kernel, designers had a tendency to build new features into the UNIX kernel instead of implementing them in terms of other features already present in the kernel. The kernel grew in size over the years; today the largest UNIX kernel, belonging to Berkeley UNIX (version 4.3BSD), requires about 400K of memory.

In recent years, one of the clear trends in new experimental, UNIX-like operating systems is a reduction in the size of the kernel. Designers today are building new operating systems with lean kernels, called *microkernels*, containing only the essential set of features that must be in the kernel; all other features are relegated to software libraries. Microkernels usually contain about 100K of code, ironically very close to the size of the older UNIX kernels.

Also common to most new UNIX-like operating systems is a sophisticated multitasking concept called *threads*, with which a process can perform multiple operations simultaneously, sharing information among them. This capability will become increasingly important as computer systems tackle complex, CPU-intensive operations, such as simultaneously displaying graphics and video while playing audio. A program that makes use of graphics, video, and audio at the same time essentially is performing three distinct tasks simultaneously. On an operating system with threads, a programmer probably would write a program such that each of the three tasks—audio, video, and graphics—is a separate thread.

Plan 9

Plan 9 (named after what is sometimes regarded as the worst science fiction movie ever, *Plan 9 From Outer Space*) is an experimental operating system being designed at AT&T Bell Labs in Murray Hill, New Jersey. The Bell Labs facility at Murray Hill is the birthplace of UNIX itself, and in fact many of the same programmers who designed UNIX over two decades ago are lending their expertise to Plan 9, including Ken Thompson, Dennis Ritchie, and Peter Weinberger (who provided the *w* in awk, as discussed in Chapter 8, "Programming Languages and UNIX Software"). Although the folks involved with Plan 9 insist it is only experimental and will never be released as a commercial product, Plan 9 provides a fascinating look into a network environment carried to an extreme.

A system running Plan 9 consists of many computers networked together, but it differs radically from a typical network. Instead of connecting a group of general-purpose computers, as do most networks, Plan 9 connects groups of specialized machines. Each computer is a *server*, which provides one of three services for the system as a whole:

- *File servers* have large disk drives, on which users store their files. These servers are the only computers on a Plan 9 system that have file storage space available.

- *CPU servers* carry out computations. User programs run on these machines.

- *Terminal servers* provide a screen and keyboard at which the user works. These machines accept user input and perform complex display and graphics functions.

Thus, when a user runs a program under Plan 9, the program executes on one machine (a CPU server), accesses data files on one or more other computers (file servers), and displays results on yet another machine (a terminal server).

Many benefits accrue from this arrangement. When building a Plan 9 system, designers might choose one type of machine—a type that processes files especially well—as file servers, a second type of machine as CPU servers, and yet another type of machine—with excellent graphics capabilities—as terminal servers. What's more, designers can easily increase the computing power of the system by adding more CPU servers, or they can add more file storage capability simply by attaching more file servers to the network.

Plan 9 introduces other extreme concepts. Although UNIX enables you to treat all hardware devices as files, Plan 9 enables you to treat *everything* as a file. Even processes—running programs—have file names.

Although Plan 9 may never venture outside Bell Labs, the experience AT&T is gaining from Plan 9 may have far-reaching effects on future UNIX systems.

Chorus

Chorus, written by Chorus Systèmes, S.A., in Paris, has the smallest microkernel of all the UNIX derivatives—only 25K on some computers, although 100K is more typical. Chorus, however, uses a bit of novel terminology: the Chorus kernel is called the *nucleus*. The nucleus contains functions for *real-time* (that is, time-critical) applications, memory management, a process supervisor, and interprocess communication features. The Chorus microkernel also supports threads.

In the fall of 1990, Chorus undertook a joint development project with UNiSYS to create a hybrid Chorus, called Chorus/Mix, which was fully compatible with UNIX System V.

V

The V (pronounced *vee*) operating system—not to be confused with UNIX System V—is a UNIX-like operating system written at Stanford University about 1981. The microkernel included a virtual memory manager and facilities for communication between processes. The latter is V's strong suit; its design is optimized around fast communication. V runs on Sun workstations, the DEC MicroVAX, and DEC's DECstation.

Mach

Mach is a UNIX-like operating system written at Carnegie-Mellon University as part of a job for the Defense Advanced Research Projects Agency (DARPA), and it has been implemented on computers from DEC, Sun, Encore, and Sequent. The operating system for computers by NeXT is a modified version of Mach, and Mach is the basis for OSF/1, the operating system from the Open Software Foundation.

Mach includes a very lean microkernel, which supports threads, virtual memory management, interprocess communication, and very little else. The most current version of Mach—version 2.5—was built from Berkeley's version of UNIX, BSD 4.2, and AT&T UNIX System V; however, the next release of Mach—version 3.0—will be built from scratch.

The Worldwide UNIX Market

UNIX is not confined only to the United States; it enjoys a rapidly growing global market. In fact, UNIX's greatest popularity is not in the United States, but overseas, especially in Europe. In the first half of the 1990s, industry analysts predict a 39 percent growth rate for UNIX in the United States and 46 percent elsewhere. In 1991 alone, more than 1 million UNIX systems are expected to be shipped, bringing the base of UNIX systems to 3.5 million worldwide.

As Eastern Europe and the Soviet Union open up and as new markets and economic systems in Europe become larger and more unified, open systems will become even more important than they are today. Although demand in the early 1990s is still light in Eastern Europe and the Soviet Union—these countries are still more concerned with distributing food than computers— some vendors, mostly Japanese and European, are already selling systems there, and more U.S. vendors are sure to follow.

The largest growth in computers is in the area of PCs and workstations. UNIX has long been a popular desktop system, but DOS has retained the lion's share—for PCs, at least. Only a few years ago, analysts might reasonably have predicted impressive growth for UNIX in the area of desktop computing, but few analysts expected the explosive growth of Microsoft Windows. In 1987, Windows commanded only 2.3 percent of the PC market; by 1994, some 29 percent of desktop machines will run Windows. Meanwhile, the jury is still out on the fate of the other desktop competitor, OS/2. Some analysts believe it will capture a sizable fraction of the market; others expect it to fade away.

UNIX will do best throughout the 1990s in the mid-range area, which includes systems in the $100,000 to $1 million range. International Data Corporation (IDC) predicts that, by 1994, 35.6 percent of all mid-range systems will be based on UNIX.

In the mainframe area, largely dominated by IBM and its proprietary operating systems such as MVS and VM, UNIX will probably continue to have only a small market. By 1994, UNIX may command only 11 percent of the mainframe market in the United States and 6 percent elsewhere.

Chapter Summary

When UNIX began in 1969, it was designed purely as a research vehicle for its designers; Thompson, Kernighan, Ritchie, and the others who contributed to the early UNIX system did not foresee what was in store for their fledgling operating system. A classic description of early UNIX appeared in a humorous article on Usenet some years ago. The article, comparing various operating systems to transportation systems, alluded to UNIX's original lax security and willingness to perform any operation the user requested:

> UNIX is like the maritime transit system in an impover-
> ished country. The ferryboats are dangerous...offer no
> protection from the weather and leak like sieves. Every
> monsoon season a couple of them capsize and drown
> all the passengers, but people still line up for them and
> crowd aboard.

But UNIX has grown up. In fact, in 1990 it turned 21. Since its inception in the late 1960s, UNIX has developed steadily from a research tool used exclusively by computer scientists to a commercial operating system used by businesses of every kind.

Throughout this book, you have been introduced to some of the colorful history of UNIX and have seen how the various pieces of UNIX operate and interrelate. Perhaps you have come to appreciate the unique position of UNIX as an open operating system, embraced by almost every computer vendor worldwide. As the computer market expands and the need to interconnect computers of all kinds increases, the popularity of UNIX will continue to grow, well into the 21st century.

A

Common UNIX Commands

This appendix lists many of the common UNIX commands. Not all of these commands are discussed in this book. For more information on these commands, consult a how-to UNIX book, such as Que's *Using UNIX*, a general UNIX command reference, or your computer's reference guide.

Many commands that may be important to your work may not be listed in this appendix, because they are found only on select machines or within optional software packages. For example, if you work on a UNIX network, you may use rcp often to copy files from one computer to another. Because this command is available on a limited number of systems, however, it is not listed here.

Command	Description
accept	Enable the print spooler to accept print requests for a specific printer
adb	Invoke absolute program debugger
admin	Create and administer an SCCS file
ar	Create or access a program library (archive)
as	Invoke the assembler
asa	Interpret ASA carriage control characters
at	Execute a command or series of commands at a specific time

387

Command	Description
awk	Invoke the awk pattern scanning and processing language
banner	Print a banner in large letters
basename	Extract the name of a file with directory portion stripped off
batch	Execute commands in the background on a low-priority basis (only System V)
bc	A numeric calculator
bfs	(Big file scanner) Scan and edit very large files
cal	Print the calendar for a specific month or year
calendar	Simple reminder service
cancel	Cancel a print request (only System V)
cat	Display the contents of a file or concatenate two or more files
cb	(C beautifier) Reformat C programs to improve readability
cc	Invoke the C compiler
cd	Change current working directory (shell built-in)
cdc	(Change delta commentary) Add additional comments to an SCCS file
cflow	Display a graph showing the flow of a C program
chgrp	Change the group to which a file belongs
chmod	Change the permissions on a file or change one of the other attributes that make up the file's mode
chown	Change a file's ownership
chroot	Cause a directory to seem to be a user's root directory (only some systems; can be executed only by system administrator)
clear	Clear terminal screen (only some systems)
cmp	Compare two files

Command	Description
comb	Decrease the size of an SCCS file by discarding old versions
comm	Find lines that two files have in common
compress	Encode a file so that it occupies less disk space; similar to pack, but more efficient (only some systems)
copy	Copy files or copy a directory and its files and subdirectories (only Berkeley UNIX)
cp	Copy files
cpio	Create a backup or copy files and directories
cpp	Invoke the C preprocessor
crash	Diagnose a system crash
cron	Execute commands on a regular basis according to a specified schedule
crypt	Encrypt or decrypt a file (available only in the United States)
csh	The C Shell
cu	Call another UNIX system and allow the user to log in to that system
cut	Extract selected columns or fields of data
cxref	Generate a cross-reference listing for a C program
date	Print or set the system date
dc	Desk calculator
dcopy	Copy a file system, reorganizing for optimal access
dd	Copy (and possibly convert) data
delta	Insert a new version into an SCCS file
deroff	Remove nroff and troff commands from a document, leaving only raw text
df	Display the amount of free space on each UNIX file system
diff	Display differences between two files

Command	Description
diff3	Compare three files for differences
dircmp	Compare directories (not all versions of UNIX)
dirname	Display the directory portion of a file name
disable	Deactivate a printer (only System V)
du	Show disk usage for selected directories
echo	Display text on-screen (shell built-in)
ed	The original UNIX line-oriented editor
egrep	(Extended grep) Search for a pattern or phrase; like grep, but with additional capabilities
enable	Activate a printer (only System V)
env	Display environment variables
eqn	Invoke the equation formatter
ex	Invoke the line-oriented mode of vi
expr	Evaluate arithmetic expressions (used in shell programs)
factor	Compute the prime factors of a number
false	Do nothing and return a failure return code to the operating system
fgrep	(Fast grep) Search for a phrase within a file; like grep, but faster, with limited capabilities
file	Determine type of file
find	Search directory and subdirectories for files that meet specified criteria
fsck	Check the integrity of a file system and display problems (only system administrator)
fsdb	(File system debugger) Fix a damaged file system (only system administrator)
fuser	Identify users currently using a specific file or device
get	Extract a version from an SCCS file
grep	Search for a pattern or phrase within a file

Command	Description
grpck	Check the /etc/group file for errors
haltsys	Stop the computer's processor (only XENIX systems; only system administrator)
head	Display the first few lines from a file (only Berkeley UNIX)
help	Get help on a command (some versions)
id	Print user's user ID and group ID (some versions)
init	Send a message to the init daemon (only system administrator)
ipcrm	Remove an interprocess communication ID (used by programmers to share data between programs)
ipcs	Display the status of an interprocess communication ID
join	Match lines from two files based on a specified relationship
kill	Send a signal to a process (usually causes the process to terminate)
killall	Kill all active processes in preparation for shutting down the system (some systems; only system administrator)
ld	Invoke the UNIX program linker
lex	Invoke the lex compiler
line	Read one line from standard input and print it to standard output
lint	Check a C program for bugs
ln	Create a link
lp	Submit a print request (only System V)
lpadmin	Configure the print spooling system (only System V)
lpr	Submit a print request (only Berkeley UNIX)

Command	Description
lpshut	Shut down the print spooling system (only System V; only system administrator)
lpstat	Display status of print requests and print spooler system (only System V)
ls	List files and directories
m4	Invoke the m4 macro processor
mail	Send or receive electronic mail
make	Maintain, update, and regenerate groups of programs
mesg	Enable or disable receiving of message from write
mkdir	Make a directory
mkfs	Make a file system
mknod	Create a device file or FIFO
mm	Format documents, using the mm macro package
mmt	Typeset documents, using the mm macro package
more	Display text one screen at a time (only Berkeley UNIX)
mount	Mount a file system
mv	Move or rename a file
ncheck	Display file names associated with specific i-node numbers (only system administrator)
newgrp	Temporarily change user's group ID
news	Read news articles (only System V)
nice	Change a command's priority
nl	Display text with line numbers
nohup	Submit a background program that will not be killed when the user logs off
nroff	Format document using the nroff next formatter

Command	Description
od	Display the contents of a file in octal or hex
pack	Compress a file by encoding its contents
passwd	Change user's password
paste	Merge lines from multiple files
pcat	Display a file that has been compressed by pack
pg	Display the contents of a file one screen at a time (only System V)
pr	Format lines of text, adding headers and page numbers
prof	Display profiling information about a recent program execution
prs	Print information about an SCCS file
ps	Display status of running processes
ptx	Generate a permuted index
pwck	Check the /etc/passwd file for errors
pwd	Print current working directory
read	Read input and assign to one or more variables (shell built-in)
reject	Cause the print spooler to reject print requests for a specific printer
rm	Remove files
rmdel	Remove the most recent version from an SCCS file
rmdir	Remove a directory
sact	Display current SCCS activity
sar	Report on system activity (only some systems; only system administrator)
sccsdiff	Display the differences between two versions of an SCCS file
sdb	Invoke the source program debugger
sed	The UNIX stream editor

Command	Description
setcolor	Set screen colors (only SCO XENIX)
sh	The Bourne Shell
shutdown	Shut down the system
size	Display the amount of memory required by the various parts of a program
sleep	Pause for a specified number of seconds
sort	Collate lines of text in alphabetical or numerical order
spell	Check spelling
split	Divide a file into smaller files
strip	Remove symbol and line number information from an executable program
stty	Set terminal options and parameters
su	Switch user ID
sum	Compute a checksum on a file (only some systems)
sync	Write the superblock and internal buffers to disk
tabs	Set default tabs
tail	Display the last few lines of a file
tar	Create or restore a backup
tbl	Format a table in a document
tee	Copy data within a pipeline to a file
test	Test conditions within a shell program (shell built-in)
time	Report the elapsed time required by a process
touch	Change the modification or access time of a file
tr	Translate selected characters within a file
troff	Typeset a document
true	Do nothing and return a success return code to the shell

Command	Description
tty	Show the name of the current terminal device file
umask	Set or display default permissions
umount	Unmount a file system
uname	Display the name of the current UNIX computer
uncompress	Convert to its original form a file compressed by compress
unget	Undo a previous get of an SCCS file
uniq	Display repeated lines
units	Convert quantities from one unit to another (such as from miles to kilometers or fathoms to feet)
unpack	Convert to its original form a file compressed by pack
uucp	Copy a file from one computer to another using the UNIX UUCP system
uupick	Pick up files sent from another user on another computer
uustat	Display status of UUCP file transfers
uuto	Send files to a user on another computer
Uutry	Try to call another computer or test a UUCP connection
uux	Execute a command on another computer
val	Check the validity of an SCCS file
vi	Standard UNIX full-screen editor
volcopy	Copy a file system (only system administrator)
wait	Wait for a process to complete
wall	Send a message to all users' terminals
wc	Count lines, words, and characters in a file
what	Identify the version of a program
who	Display list of users on the system

Command	Description
whodo	Determine which user is doing what process (only Berkeley UNIX)
write	Write messages to a user's terminal
xargs	Execute a command with a very long argument list
yacc	(Yet another compiler compiler) Invoke the yacc compiler
zcat	Display the contents of a file compressed with compress

B

System Calls

Systems calls form the interface between the UNIX kernel and programs running on a UNIX computer. This appendix lists the system calls common to most UNIX systems: standard system calls and system calls for interprocess communication. The following information is not intended to be sufficient for you to write C programs; consult your system's programmer reference guide for more information.

Standard System Calls

You will find the following system calls on every UNIX computer, regardless of the version of UNIX you are using.

System Call	Description
access	Determine whether or not a file exists and whether your program has permissions to perform certain operations
alarm	Set the "alarm clock" to interrupt your program at a specified time
brk	Change the size of a program's data area (sbrk performs essentially the same function)
chdir	Change current working directory
chmod	Change the permissions on a file or set other attributes associated with a file's mode
chown	Change a file's owner and group ID

System Call	Description
chroot	Cause a directory to seem like the root directory to a program (only system administrator)
close	Close a file
creat	Create a new file or delete all data from an existing file; note the missing final *e*
dup	Duplicate an open file descriptor
exec*	A family of six system calls: execl, execle, execlp, execv, execve, and execvp. All cause the current program to terminate and a new program to begin execution in its place. The six system calls differ in their arrangement of arguments.
exit	Cause a program to terminate, after closing open files (a library routine rather than a system call on some systems)
_exit	Terminate a program, circumventing cleanup such as closing files
fcntl	Change the way in which a file is accessed
fork	Split a process into two processes; fork is used to create new processes
getpid	Get the process ID number associated with the current process
getegid	Get the effective group ID number associated with the current process
geteuid	Get the effective user ID number associated with the current process
getgid	Get the real group ID number associated with the current process
getuid	Get the real user ID number associated with the current process
ioctl	Perform control operations on a device. ioctl is used for operations unique to a specific type of device. It is the only UNIX system call with which you must know whether you are dealing with a disk drive, terminal, tape drive, or other such device.
kill	Send a signal to a process or group of processes
link	Create a link to a file

System Call	Description
lseek	Move to a new location within a file or determine the current location within a file
mknod	Create a directory, device file, or FIFO
mount	Mount a file system (only system administrator)
nice	Change the priority of the current process
open	Open or create a file
pause	Suspend processing until a signal is received
pipe	Create an unnamed (regular) pipe
plock	Lock a process in memory (only system administrator)
profil	Gather profile statistics about a process (primarily used by the UNIX prof tool)
ptrace	Process trace (primarily used by UNIX debuggers such as sdb)
read	Read data from a file or device
sbrk	Change the size of a program's data area (brk performs essentially the same function)
setpgrp	Set process group; sets the current process's process group ID to its process ID
setuid	Change the real user ID and the effective user ID
signal	Specify action to take upon receiving a specific signal
stat	Get information about a file
stime	Set the current system time (only system administrator)
sync	Update all file system superblocks and flush buffers to disk
time	Get current date and time
times	Get accounting statistics, such as amount of CPU time used by this process and its children
ulimit	Set the maximum amount of memory available to this process
umask	Set the default permissions for creating new files
umount	Unmount a file system (only system administrator)
uname	Get information about the current UNIX computer, such as its name and the version of UNIX being used

System Call	Description
unlink	Remove a link to a file or remove the file
utime	Change file access and modification times
wait	Wait for a child process to terminate
write	Write data to a file or device

System Calls for Interprocess Communications

An additional set of system calls control interprocess communication under UNIX System V. The interprocess communication (or IPC) facilities include *semaphores*, *shared memory*, and *message queues*.

System Call	Description
msgctl	Control a message queue
msgget	Get a message queue ID or create a message queue
msgrcv	Receive a message from a message queue
msgsnd	Send a message to another process using a message queue
semctl	Control a semaphore
semget	Get a semaphore ID or create a semaphore
semop	Perform operations on a semaphore
shmat	Attach to a shared memory segment
shmctl	Control shared memory
shmdt	Detach from a shared memory segment
shmget	Get a shared memory ID or create a shared memory segment

Important Files and Directories

This appendix lists some important files and directories found on most UNIX systems. Directories are given as full path names, such as `/usr/lib`. Files are given only by file (such as `uucico`) and indented beneath the directory in which the file is found.

Directories and Files	Description
/	Root directory
unix	The UNIX kernel (called `xenix`, `ultrix`, or another name in some versions of UNIX)
/bin	Contains the most essential UNIX commands
/dev	Contains most of the special device files
console	Computer console
diskette	Diskette drive (only some systems)
kmem	Memory used by the UNIX kernel
mem	Memory used by user programs
null	The UNIX bit bucket
tty	The user's terminal
tty*	Specific terminals, such as `tty24` or `ttya`. Numbering varies by system.

Directories and Files	*Description*
/etc	System administration files and programs
TIMEZONE	Contains information describing the local time zone (name may be different on some systems, such as TZ)
brc	Local commands executed at system startup
checklist	List of file systems checked at system startup
crontab	Table of commands used by cron (only non-System V)
gettydefs	Definition of terminal parameters; used by getty
group	List of user groups
hosts	List of computers on a local network
inittab	List of processes started by init
magic	List of magic numbers that identify various types of files
mnttab	List of mounted file systems
motd	Message of the day
passwd	List of valid system users and related information, including passwords
rc	Contains commands executed upon system boot
termcap	Database of terminal types and capabilities (replaced under UNIX System V by terminfo database, located in /usr/lib/terminfo)
ttys	List of terminals (only Berkeley systems)
ttytype	List of terminals and their types (only Berkeley systems)
utmp	Lists users currently logged in
wtmp	History of logins and other system activity, such as system startups and shutdowns

Directories and Files	Description
/etc/master.d	Computer configuration information (only some systems)
/lib	Various files and commands, used mostly by programmers
comp	The C language compiler
cpp	The C preprocessor
crt0.o	C language startup routines
libC.a	The C++ program library
libc.a	The C program library
libm.a	The math function library
/lost+found	A directory in which to place files whose names have been lost (used by fsck)
/mnt	An empty directory commonly used as a mount point for file systems (such as diskettes) used occasionally
/tmp	Used to store user files created temporarily
/usr	A hierarchy of directories used for storing files commonly associated with or used by ordinary users
/usr/adm	Administrative programs and files, including logs
errlog	Log of system errors
sulog	Log of su commands, in which users have changed to other user IDs
/usr/bin	Programs commonly used by users
/usr/games	Games (only some systems)
/usr/include	Header files used by C programmers
/usr/include/CC	Header files used by C++ programmers
/usr/include/CC/sys	System-specific header files used by C++ programmers
/usr/include/sys	System-specific header files used by C programmers

Directories and Files	Description
/usr/lbin	(*Local bin*) Nonstandard programs, written locally or obtained from friends and associates (only some systems)
/usr/local/bin	Nonstandard programs, written locally or obtained from friends and associates (only some systems; alternate name for /usr/lbin)
/usr/lib	Various data files commonly used by users
libcrypt.a	Encryption library for C programmers
libcurses.a	Curses programming library for C programmers
libl.a	Library used by lex
libtermcap.a	Library of functions allowing C programmers to access the termcap terminal library
liby.a	Library used by yacc
llib-lc	Library of functions known to lint
lpadmin	Program to control the print spooling system
lpsched	Print spooling daemon
lpshut	Program to shut off print spooling system
unittab	Table of conversion units, used by the units program
/usr/lib/cron	Data tables used by cron (only UNIX System V)
at.allow	List of users allowed to use at
at.deny	List of users not allowed to use at
cron.allow	List of users allowed to use cron
cron.deny	List of users not allowed to use cron
log	Log of all cron activity
/usr/lib/macros	Macros used by nroff and troff formatters

Directories and Files	Description
/usr/lib/news	Usenet news data files
/usr/lib/spell	Dictionary and other files used by spell
/usr/lib/terminfo	The terminfo database (only System V; contains many subdirectories, which are not listed here)
/usr/lib/tmac	Macros used by nroff and troff formatters
/usr/lib/uucp	Data files associated with the UUCP system
Devices	List of modems and other communication devices
Dialcodes	List of codes for common area codes
Dialers	List of types of modems
Permissions	Permissions for communications with other systems
Roll	List of computers to be contacted regularly
Systems	List of other computers, with information on how to contact them
remote.unknown	Script describing what to do when an unknown computer calls
/usr/mail	User mailboxes, used by mail
/usr/man	On-line reference manual (only some systems)
/usr/news	News articles, used by the news program
/usr/preserve	Holding location for edit buffers when the system crashes or users are suddenly disconnected while using vi
/usr/pub	Various public data files (only some systems)
/usr/spool/locks	Lock files used to indicate which devices are currently in use
/usr/spool/lp	Data files used by the print spooler system

Directories and Files	*Description*
/usr/spool/news	News articles and some data files associated with Usenet news (contains many subdirectories, which are not listed here)
/usr/spool/uucp	Data files and administrative files associated with UUCP (many subdirectories, not listed here)
/usr/spool/uucppublic	Storage location for files being sent through UUCP
/usr/src	Source code for the UNIX operating system (only some systems)
/usr/tmp	Used to store files created temporarily (similar to /tmp)

Glossary

absolute path name A notation specifying the location of a file, given as a list of directories separated by slashes, starting from the root directory. Absolute path names always start with a slash. Also known as *full path name*. See *relative path name*.

AIX (Advanced Interactive Executive) IBM's UNIX-like operating system.

alias A short command that represents a longer command; used as a typing saver within C Shell and Korn Shell.

ANSI (American National Standards Institute) An organization that prepares standards for use in the United States.

APL (A Programming Language) A programming language well-suited for mathematical and matrix operations. First described in 1962 by Kenneth Iverson.

application program A program or group of programs that solves a problem associated with people's real-world tasks, such as accounting, word processing, or record keeping. Application programs solve the problems or perform the tasks for which people buy computers.

archive Generally, a collection of files that have been combined into a single file with the ar utility; specifically, a collection of program object files that have been combined into a library.

archive site Any of several computer installations that collect public domain programs and data and that make it available to the general public.

ARPANET A network of computers run by the Department of Defense for use by government computers and contractors working on government contracts.

assembly language A programming language that represents the computer's innate machine code. Assembly language is the most efficient language possible; however, each machine has its own assembly language, and programs written in one machine's assembly language cannot be used on a different type of machine.

backbone The high capacity data conduits that link major sections of a network. When distant computers communicate over a network, data flows from the sending computer to the nearest backbone connection, then through the backbone to a location near the other computer, and finally through a local link to the receiving computer.

background execution Running a UNIX program that does not interact with the screen or keyboard. You use background execution to perform tasks that require significant time but that do not interact with you, such as to sort a file.

backup A copy of files, usually stored on diskettes or tape, kept as a safety measure in case the original files are lost due to error or breakdown.

ball bat A common slang UNIX term for the exclamation point (!).

bang A common slang UNIX term for the exclamation point (!).

bang notation A file name or a user name preceded by the name of the computer on which the file or user resides. An exclamation point separates the computer name from the user name or file name, such as `empire!fred`.

BASIC (Beginner's All-Purpose Symbolic Instructional Code) A popular general-purpose programming language that is especially easy to learn. Many people learn BASIC as a first programming language. Designed in 1965 at Dartmouth College by John Kemeny and Thomas Kutz.

Basic Networking Utility See *HoneyDanBer UUCP*.

batch processing A mode of executing programs that do not interact with people. Typically tasks are collected into a group called a *job*, which is submitted to the computer. The computer then runs the job without human intervention.

baud rate The number of electrical impulses transmitted every second over a serial communication line; widely misused as a synonym for *bit transfer rate*. The two terms are the same only if each electrical impulse carries a single bit, which often is not true. For example, a so-called 2400 baud modem transmits 2400 bits per second, but because each electrical impulse carries 4 bits, the correct baud rate is 600.

Berkeley   See *University of California at Berkeley*.

bit bucket   A slang term for a pseudo-device that accepts data and discards it. The UNIX bit bucket is the special device /dev/null.

bit transfer rate   A measure of the number of bits per second transmitted from one serial communication device to another. Typical values range from 300 to 19,600.

boot block   The first block of a UNIX file system, which contains the *boot program*. Only the boot block on the first disk of a UNIX computer is used.

boot program   A relatively simple program, executed when a computer is first turned on, which usually locates and starts a more powerful program to perform the process of getting the computer started. In UNIX, the boot program is stored on the first block of the first disk, and loads the UNIX kernel.

Bourne Shell   The original UNIX shell, written by Steve Bourne of AT&T Bell Labs.

broadcast message   An electronic message sent to all users on a computer, usually warning them of some impending event.

C   A powerful general-purpose programming language used extensively by many UNIX programmers. The UNIX kernel and shell are written almost exclusively in C. Developed in 1971 by Brian Kernighan and Dennis Ritchie at AT&T Bell Labs.

C++   A general-purpose programming language that encourages programmers to use an object-oriented approach to problem solving. Developed in the early 1980s by Bjarne Stroustrup of AT&T Bell Labs.

central processing unit (CPU)   The circuitry within a computer that interprets program instructions and manipulates data.

change management systems   A software system that keeps track of changes made to programs or documents and that can extract any previous version of a program or document. The most common UNIX change management systems are SCCS and RCS.

child   A process that was started by another process. Every UNIX process except init is the child of some other process.

Chorus   An operating system, produced by Chorus Systèmes, S.A., which bears many similarities to UNIX but includes many additional features, such as real-time processing and threads.

client In a networking environment, the computer or software that uses a service provided by another computer or other software. In X Windows, a client is a program that uses X Windows. See *server*.

COBOL The most commonly used computer language in the world, oriented toward business applications. COBOL is based on the work of Dr. Grace Murray Hopper of the U.S. Navy.

Coherent A version of UNIX from Mark Williams Company.

command history A feature of some shells, such as C Shell and Korn Shell, which keeps a record of commands you recently entered, and enables you to recall any recent command for editing or reexecution.

command substitution A shell feature that enables you to use the output from one command as part of another command. You use backquotes (`) to request command substitution.

Common Applications Environment (CAE) A set of standards that defines how application programs interact with an operating system. The term is used by X/Open, which published their CAE in the document *X/Open Portability Guide*.

console A terminal found on all UNIX systems, unique in that system error messages are displayed on it. The console is not physically different from any other terminal, but acquires its unique status by virtue of being plugged in to a special terminal port on the computer.

CPU See *Central Processing Unit*.

cron A UNIX program that starts other programs or executes commands automatically and repeatedly, according to a schedule that you can define.

csh The executable program representing the C Shell.

C Shell A popular UNIX shell, written by Bill Joy at the University of California. C Shell is so called because the built-in C Shell programming language resembles the C programming language. C Shell includes many speed enhancements, typing savers, and safety features.

current directory Also known as *current working directory*. The directory that is the focus of your activities and is the directory from which all relative path names start. You execute a cd command to make a directory the current directory.

curses   A library of programming functions that enables C programs to perform screen and keyboard operations independent of the type of terminal on which the programs run. Many UNIX utilities, such as the vi editor, are based on curses.

daemon   (DEE-muhn) A program that executes in the background and performs tasks independent of human intervention. *Daemon* usually refers to any of several system programs, such as init, cron, or the line printer spooler, that always run in the background and perform important system tasks.

DARPA   (Defense Advanced Research Projects Agency) An agency of the Department of Defense that conducts research, much of which is centered around powerful computer systems.

data block   One of many equal-sized areas of disk used to store data represented by files and directories. Most of a disk's space is used by data blocks. On old UNIX systems, data blocks are 512 bytes; on newer systems they are 1,024 bytes.

DEC Windows   A graphical user interface distributed by Digital Equipment Corporation on many of their computers.

de facto standard   A way of performing a task that becomes a standard by virtue of its widespread use. For example, UNIX is the de facto standard operating system for medium-sized computers, not because a standards organization such as ANSI says so, but because UNIX is already in use by a large number of people and organizations. (The term *de facto* is Latin for *from the fact*.)

device driver   A software module within the UNIX kernel that controls the operation of a specific type of device, such as a disk drive, terminal, or tape drive. A device driver is included for each type of hardware on the system and contains the instructions to perform operations such as reading and writing data.

device file   A UNIX file that represents not an area of disk space, but a hardware device, such as a printer or terminal, or a logical entity, such as the bit bucket null. Device files usually reside in the dev directory and can be identified by a file type b or c at the beginning of the line from an ls -l listing.

device independent   Technique of accessing files and devices in a uniform manner. UNIX enables all files and devices to be accessed in a device-independent manner, because the same commands and features can be used with most files and devices.

directory A file that contains a table of contents for other files. From your perspective, directories serve as a place on-disk in which you can store files. Internally, directories enable the kernel to relate file names to i-node numbers.

display server In the X Windows system, a screen, keyboard, and pointing device (usually a mouse) that enables you to interact with programs.

DOS shell A UNIX shell that enables you to use MS-DOS commands on a UNIX system.

edit buffer An area of disk space used by a text editor to hold a file while you edit the file.

effective user ID The user ID used by the UNIX kernel to determine permissions. When a user runs a program, the effective user ID is usually the same as the real user ID; however, if the program is *set UID*, the program may temporarily assume the permissions of a different user ID, known as the effective user ID. See *set user ID bit*.

encrypted password A version of your password that UNIX stores in an encoded form. You cannot determine the original password by analyzing the encrypted password. Encrypted passwords are always 13 characters long, regardless of the length of the original password.

environment A collection of attributes and information that a program inherits from its parent. The environment includes shell variables, such as PATH.

ESIX A UNIX-like operating system developed by Esix Computer.

Extended FORTRAN Language A dialect of FORTRAN that includes structured programming constructs, which standard FORTRAN lacks. The new statements are based on structured control statements from C. See *FORTRAN*.

extension At the end of a file name, one or more characters that identify the type of data contained within the file. Extensions are separated from the rest of the file name by a period. For example, in the name testprog.c, the extension is c, indicating a C source program. Not all files have extensions. The extension may be meaningful to application programs, people, and UNIX tools, but has no special meaning to the UNIX kernel.

fault tolerant A system or computer in which all components are duplicated so that the system can continue to operate despite the failure of any single component.

feed   The transferring of Usenet files and articles from one computer to another.

FIFO   (First in, first out) A type of special UNIX file that enables two programs to exchange information.

file   A group of related data organized into a single unit and stored on the UNIX file system under a file name.

file generation character   Also known as *wild cards*. Special characters (?, *, and [ ]) that you can use in UNIX file names to indicate that an operation should be performed on many files with similar names. For example, `rm rpt*` removes all files whose names begin with `rpt`.

file system   A disk or disk partition organized into a standard format for storing files. A file system contains a superblock, i-node list, and data block area, and is created by the system administrator with the `mkfs` (make file system) command. Most UNIX files are stored on disks organized into file systems.

foreground execution   The characteristic of a program that can accept input from the keyboard and display data on-screen. By default UNIX programs are run in the foreground. Programs that run in the foreground are also said to be *interactive*.

Forth   A general-purpose programming language, popular on microcomputers, developed by Charles Moore in the late 1960s.

FORTRAN   A general-purpose programming language, especially popular for scientific and engineering work, developed between 1954 and 1957 by an IBM team headed by John W. Backus.

fragmentation   A situation in which related data is stored in separated sections of a disk, rather than in contiguous areas. Fragmentation requires UNIX to do more work to access the data in files. Fragmentation accumulates over time on UNIX disks. Several utilities exist to rearrange a disk to reduce fragmentation.

freeware   Free software distributed by its author. In most cases you legally may copy and distribute freeware to other users, although you may not charge others for the software. In the UNIX environment, the most well-known freeware is that distributed by the Free Software Foundation.

full duplex   An attribute of a communication connection in which data can flow simultaneously in both directions, much the same as a telephone can carry voice in both directions at the same time. For example, UNIX terminals almost always are connected to the computer through full duplex connection; therefore, the computer can display information on-screen at the same time that you type on the keyboard. See *half duplex*.

full path name   See *absolute path name*.

graphical user interface (GUI)   A program that interacts with you by presenting small pictures and symbols that represent operations and by requiring you to use a mouse or other pointing device to make a selection. Most graphical user interfaces in UNIX are based on the X Windows system.

GUI   See *graphical user interface*.

half duplex   An attribute of a communication connection in which data can flow in only one direction at a time. At any time, one device is the sender, the other the receiver. For data to flow in the other direction, the two devices switch roles, a process known as *turning the line around*. Many mid-range and mainframe non-UNIX systems use half duplex terminals. UNIX terminals almost always are *full duplex*. See *full duplex*.

header   A small amount of information that identifies the data that follows. Several UNIX programs use the concept of a header, although the actual contents of the header is unique to each program. In the case of UNIX mail messages, each message is preceded by a header consisting of one or more lines at the beginning of the message that describe who sent the message and when it was sent. Similarly, a Usenet news article begins with a header—a dozen or so lines that describe the origin of the article. On backup tapes or disks, programs such as `cpio` and `tar` write a header before each file, a header that contains the file name and information about the file.

home directory   A directory provided by the system administrator in which you can create and delete files. Your home directory becomes your current directory when you first log in.

HoneyDanBer UUCP   A version of the UUCP software system, developed in 1983 by Peter Honeyman, Dan Nowitz, and Brian E. Redman at AT&T Bell Labs. Also known as AT&T's Basic Networking Utility, or BNU, it is one of the most popular versions of UUCP. Its name derives from the login names of the three key players: `honey`, `dan`, and `ber` (Redman's initials), respectively. See *UUCP*.

HP-UX   A version of UNIX sold by Hewlett-Packard Company.

humidity   A measure of the amount of moisture in the air, usually expressed as a percentage of the maximum amount of moisture that the air can possibly hold at that temperature. For example, 50 percent humidity indicates that the air contains half the moisture it possibly can at its current temperature. Most computers must operate within a specific humidity range.

hygrometer   An instrument for measuring humidity.

icon   A small drawing or symbol displayed on-screen, used within a graphical user interface to represent an operation or function. For example, a small drawing of a trash can might represent the "remove" operation, symbolizing the concept that a file is being discarded.

IEEE   Institute of Electrical and Electronic Engineers.

init   Short for *initialize*. An important UNIX daemon that is the ancestor of all processes. init is the first process started when a UNIX computer boots and is the only process that does not have a true parent. init performs many important functions, the most visible of which is to start a new process on each terminal (called getty), which enables you to log in. init is always running while UNIX is running, and without it UNIX does not function correctly.

i-node   Short for *information node*. A 64-byte area of disk that contains important information about a file, including the file's mode, number of links, user ID of the owner, size of the file, several time and date stamps, and information telling where the data associated with the file or directory is located on-disk.

i-node list   The portion of a UNIX file system that contains the i-nodes.

i-node number   The number by which an i-node is identified, corresponding to its position in the i-node list. The first i-node, 1, is never used. The second i-node, 2, represents the root directory.

interactive   See *foreground execution*.

interface   The point at which a human interacts with a software component or at which two software components interact. The shell is the interface between UNIX and people.

Internet   The supernetwork that connects a large percentage of the UNIX computers throughout the world. The Internet was not formed by—and is not controlled by—any single entity, but instead is made up of the loose interconnection of many smaller TCP/IP networks throughout the world.

Internetworking   The process of connecting networks together to form larger networks.

Internet Worm   A notorious program released in late 1988 by a graduate student at Cornell University—a program that managed to disable an estimated 3,000 UNIX computers for several days. The computers were all DEC VAXes and Sun workstations running versions of Berkeley UNIX and connected to the Internet.

job control   A feature in Berkeley UNIX that enables you to switch programs between the foreground and background and to interrupt programs temporarily and later continue them where they left off.

kernel   The central core of UNIX, in which the computer's activities are coordinated and controlled. The kernel remains in the machine's memory at all times, as long as the computer is running.

Korn Shell   Also *K Shell*. A shell written by David Korn at AT&T Bell Labs in 1982, which attempts to integrate the best features of Bourne Shell and C Shell. Korn Shell is compatible with Bourne Shell and is now included with versions of UNIX from AT&T, Hewlett-Packard, and Apple.

library   A collection of functions, usually provided by a manufacturer or software vendor, which programmers can use as a shortcut for accomplishing common tasks.

link   A file name. UNIX enables a file to have several different file names, and each name is known as a *link*. As a verb, "to link" means to add a new name for an existing file.

LISP   A list processing language especially popular in artificial intelligence applications, developed in 1960 by Professor John McCarthy at the Massachusetts Institute of Technology.

login name   A unique name assigned to you by the system administrator and used as a means of identification. The login name usually is your first name, last name, initials, or some combination, depending on local custom.

loosely linked network   A computer network in which computers are connected to each other only when data is being transferred. Most loosely linked networks use the public telephone network. When one computer needs to contact another, it places a telephone call, identifies itself, and begins the transfer. When the transfer is complete, the computers break the connection.

Mach   A UNIX-like operating system written at Carnegie-Mellon University in conjunction with work for the Defense Advanced Research Projects Agency (DARPA). Mach has been implemented on computers from DEC, Sun, Encore, and Sequent, and is the basis for the operating system for NeXT computers and for OSF/1, the operating system from the Open Software Foundation.

machine dependent   An attribute of software that was written to run on a single machine and that will not run on other machines without extensive modifications.

machine language   The sequence of binary codes that form the instructions that a computer inherently understands. All programs must ultimately be translated into machine code before a computer can execute them. Although all computers understand a machine code, the format of machine code is different for each type of computer.

magic number   At the beginning of certain types of files, a special 2-byte number that identifies the file type.

man   Used with `troff` and `nroff`, a macro package used for formatting manuals.

master   The computer or program that assumes a controlling role when two computers or programs communicate with each other. For example, when one UNIX computer, using UUCP, contacts another, one computer—the master—tells the other computer which files are to be transferred. See *slave*.

me   A general-purpose macro package used with `nroff` and `troff`; available on some Berkeley systems.

memory manager   A portion of the UNIX kernel that controls which processes are given the use of which sections of memory and that keeps track of which parts of memory are unused—so that they can be allocated to new processes—and which parts of memory are in use—so that as processes end, previously used memory can be marked as available. The memory manager also must ensure that one process does not inadvertently attempt to use another process's memory.

microkernel   An operating system kernel intentionally designed to be as small and simple as possible, containing only the essential set of features that must be in the kernel. All other functions are relegated to software libraries. Microkernels tend to contain about 100K, or less, of code.

mm   A large, general-purpose macro package used with `nroff` and `troff`; especially oriented toward letters, memos, proposals, reports, and technical papers.

mode   A set of attributes associated with a file, including the permissions on the file and the type of file.

Modula-2   A general-purpose structured programming language, very similar to Pascal, used for scientific, engineering, and business applications. Modula-2 was implemented in 1979 by Pascal's designer, Niklaus Wirth of the Eidgenossische Technische Hochschule (Federal Institute of Technology) in Zurich, Switzerland.

Motif   A popular graphical user interface based on X Windows, available from the Open Software Foundation, IBM, Hewlett-Packard, and others.

mount   The process of causing the root directory of one disk drive or partition to be superimposed over a directory on the root disk drive or partition. Mounting a disk causes its contents to become accessible through the directory on which it is mounted.

mptx   A special-purpose macro package used for printing a permuted index.

ms   The original macro package for `nroff` and `troff`; developed at Bell Labs but no longer supported by AT&T. Still widely used as a general-purpose macro package and shipped with many Berkeley versions of UNIX.

multitasking   The capability to perform more than one task at a time for each user.

multiuser   An operating system that enables more than one person to use the computer simultaneously.

named pipe   See *FIFO*.

Network File System (NFS)   A computer networking system that enables multiple computers to access each others' files. NFS was developed by Sun Microsystems in 1984 for Sun's version of UNIX, SunOS, and has since been implemented on over 100 different types of computers. NFS runs under many different versions of UNIX.

networking   Connecting computers together so that computers can share data and programs.

newline   A special character that occurs at the end of each line in a text file. All UNIX tools and programs that create text files add a newline to the end of each line, and tools and programs that read text files use the newline to determine where the end of each line occurs. The newline is represented by the ASCII line-feed character (binary value 10).

newsgroup   One of the hundreds of categories into which Usenet articles are organized.

news reader   Any of several public domain programs used to examine Usenet articles. News readers keep track of which newsgroups interest you and which articles in those groups you already have read.

NFS   See *Network File System*.

NonStop-UX   A UNIX-like operating system from Tandem Computers.

NSFNet   A nationwide TCP/IP network, maintained by the National Science Foundation.

object-oriented programming (OOP)   A style of programming that invites the programmer to look at a problem in a way that is different from the traditional approach; an object-oriented programmer focuses on the things that the program must manipulate, called *objects*, and how they interact. Object-oriented programming is based on the cornerstones of encapsulation, inheritance, and polymorphism.

OOP   See *object-oriented programming*.

OPEN LOOK   A popular graphical user interface based on X Windows, available from AT&T and Sun Microsystems.

open systems   Hardware and software not controlled by any single manufacturer and available from a wide variety of suppliers.

operating system   Software that supervises and assists the users and application programs running on the computer. Operating system tasks include coordination of the sequence of events, controlling resources, and enforcing security.

ordinary file   Also known as a *regular file*. A UNIX file used to store user data or programs. *Ordinary file* is one of the basic UNIX file types; the others are *directory*, *device file*, and *FIFO*. The majority of files in a UNIX system are ordinary files.

orphan   A process that continues to run after its parent process has died. The init process becomes the parent for all orphans and assumes the responsibilities of parent for these processes.

OSF/1 A UNIX-like operating system provided by the Open Software Foundation.

page An area of memory, usually 4K in size. On a paging computer, all of the random-access memory is divided into pages.

page fault In a virtual memory system, an attempt to access a page of memory not currently loaded into memory. When a page fault occurs, the program attempting to access the page is temporarily suspended by the memory management hardware while the desired page is retrieved.

paging A technique in which UNIX organizes its memory into equal-sized pages, usually 4,096 bytes in size, and uses disk space in place of main memory when not enough main memory is available. See *swapping*.

paging area The area of disk space used by the UNIX kernel for storing data when not enough main memory is available.

panic A situation in which the UNIX kernel encounters a condition with which it cannot cope. Panics usually involve a severe hardware malfunction or corrupted data within the UNIX kernel.

parent A process that creates another process. The other process is known as a *child*.

parent directory The directory in which another directory is contained; the directory one level higher, or closer to the root, in the file system hierarchy.

parity An error-checking mechanism that sometimes can detect characters that were not received correctly by the computer or terminal.

partition A section of a disk used as though it were a separate, complete disk. Large disks are often partitioned into many partitions, and UNIX treats each partition as though it were a disk.

Pascal A popular, general-purpose structured programming language loosely based on ALGOL and often used by schools and universities as a teaching language. Pascal was developed by Niklaus Wirth of the Eidgenossische Technische Hochschule (Federal Institute of Technology) in Zurich, Switzerland.

pass-through On a network, a computer that serves to pass data from one computer to another. On many networks, each computer is not directly connected to every other computer, and some computers can communicate with certain other computers only by using an intermediary—the pass-through computer.

password   A combination of characters that you enter when logging in. Your password serves to prove your identity.

permissions   The security information that the kernel uses to determine who is allowed to access a particular file and what they are allowed to do.

permuted index   The index near the beginning of most UNIX reference manuals that helps you find information by listing command names and important key words in alphabetical order.

PID   See *process identification number*.

pipe   A communication device that enables the standard output from one command to be sent directly to the standard input of another command. A pipe is symbolized by a vertical bar (¦) on the command line, such as in the command who ¦ sort.

Plan 9   An experimental operating system under development at AT&T Bell Labs in Murray Hill, New Jersey. Plan 9 creates a network of computers, each of which performs a specialized function, such as accessing files or performing computations.

PM/X   A graphical user interface developed by Hewlett-Packard.

POSIX   A series of standards, formally known as IEEE 1003, published by the Institute of Electrical and Electronic Engineers (IEEE). POSIX describes an interface with various aspects of an operating system.

POSIX-compliant   An attribute of an operating system that complies with the standards set forth in the POSIX documents. Any program that runs on one POSIX-compliant computer (and does not make use of any extra features on that computer that are not part of POSIX) should run on any other computer that also is POSIX-compliant.

preprocessor   A program that accepts input data, processes it in some way, and passes it along to another program. When compiling C programs, the C preprocessor, cpp, performs several transformations on the C source code and passes on the result to the C compiler. When processing documents, the tbl preprocessor formats tables, eqn formats equations, and pic handles pictures.

print daemon   A program that runs in the background and handles the details of printing files according to your requests. Under UNIX System V, the print daemon is lpsched.

print request   A request you send to the print daemon to print a file.

process   A program running on the computer.

process identification number (PID)   A unique number assigned to every running process on a UNIX computer; used internally by UNIX to identify processes. Some commands, such as `kill`, require you to supply a process ID number to identify the process you want to affect.

processor unit   The part of the computer in which information is stored and processed. The processor unit may include the central processing unit (CPU), random-access memory (RAM), and one or more disk drives.

process table   A table of information about the processes running on a UNIX computer. The process table is stored in an area of memory controlled by the kernel. The process table stores scheduling information, which the kernel uses when deciding which process to run next, and stores information required to locate the areas of memory that contain the various parts of the process.

program   A series of machine instructions that the computer follows to do useful work. Most programs are written in a high-level language, such as C, FORTRAN, or COBOL, and translated into machine code by a tool called a *compiler*. Programs are usually stored on-disk as a file until they are run. A running program is a *process*.

proprietary   Used to describe software, such as operating systems, which are designed, written, owned, sold, and controlled exclusively by a single manufacturer or vendor. Proprietary systems are usually designed for a single make or model of computer.

protocol   An agreed-upon series of signals and codes by which equipment or programs communicate. In effect, a protocol is the language that computer components speak to communicate. If two components do not understand the same protocol, they cannot communicate effectively. Examples of protocols are TCP/IP and UUCP Protocol g for networks.

prototype   A throwaway version of a program or piece of equipment built to enable its designers to get a feel for what the program or equipment will look like or how it will function.

public domain   Software donated by its author to the public. In most cases, public domain software is freely used and distributed, although in many cases the author prohibits users from selling the software to one another.

RAM   See *random-access memory*.

random-access memory   The computer's primary working memory in which program instructions and data are stored so that they are accessible directly to the central processing unit (CPU).

Rational FORTRAN   A dialect of FORTRAN that includes structured programming constructs, which standard FORTRAN lacks. The new statements are based on structured control statements from C.

RCS   (Revision Control System) A system similar to SCCS that enables software developers to track modifications to software or documents.

redirection   An operation that enables you to specify that standard input, standard output, standard error, or some combination should be connected to a destination other than the terminal, such as to a file.

regular expression   A type of text pattern you can use with many different UNIX tools to specify a search phrase. Regular expressions use special characters in place of unknown words or letters. For example, searching for `c..x` finds any line on which `c` and `x` occur separated by two characters. You can use regular expressions with most tools that perform searching, including `grep`, `awk`, and most UNIX text editors, such as `ed` and `vi`.

regular file   See *ordinary file*.

relative path name   A notation specifying the location of a file; given as a list of directories separated by slashes, starting from the user's current working directory. Relative path names never start with a slash. See *absolute path name*.

Remote File Sharing (RFS)   A computer networking system that enables multiple computers to access each others' files. RFS was developed by AT&T and was introduced with UNIX System V Release 3. Originally you could use it only in conjunction with AT&T's STARLAN network, but it later was modified to work with other networks as well.

resource   Anything in limited supply on a computer, including memory, disk space, and various pieces of hardware.

restore   To retrieve files from a backup disk or tape.

restricted shell   A special version of the Bourne Shell that enables the system administrator to control exactly what you are allowed to do on the computer.

RFS   See *Remote File Sharing*.

root A special login name on all UNIX systems; used by the system administrator. As the system administrator, when you log in as `root`, you bypass all system security and are allowed to perform any valid function.

root directory The highest directory in a UNIX file system; symbolized by a slash (`/`). The root directory is the only directory that has no parent.

rsh See *restricted shell*.

SCCS (Source Code Control System) A series of commands that enables programmers to keep all past versions of software, retrieve any past version, and maintain a narrative history of the changes applied to the software. SCCS also tracks who makes changes to the software and when the changes are made. Although SCCS originally was designed to track program source code, you actually can use it track versions of any text file, including documentation.

scheduler The portion of the kernel that handles the task of starting and stopping the various processes running on the machine. The scheduler maintains a list (the *process table*) of all processes currently running and uses this information to make decisions concerning which processes are allowed to execute, in what order, and for how long.

server In a networking environment, the computer or software that provides a service used by another computer, software, or user. On a computer network, servers provide disk space in which files can be stored, or they provide access to a printer. Database servers act as an intermediary between the database and programs that need to extract or store data. In X Windows, a server is a workstation that provides a keyboard, screen, and mouse (or other pointing device), which can interact with X Windows programs. See *client*.

set user ID (set UID) bit A bit within the program's mode that affects the kernel's method of examining permissions. When you run a program that has the set UID bit turned on, you temporarily gain the privileges afforded to the owner of the program.

sh The Bourne Shell.

shadow password file A protected file in which some UNIX versions store users' passwords so that the encrypted password need not be stored in the `/etc/passwd` file.

shareware A relatively new and popular way of distributing software; the software is distributed without charge and paid for by users who find the software useful. Shareware is usually distributed through bulletin boards or bundled with other software. You are encouraged to try the software and pass it along to colleagues. If you want to use the software regularly, you are supposed to send in a registration fee, for which you often receive free updates and printed documentation. The shareware concept enables individuals or small companies to distribute software widely at very little cost.

shell   A program that serves to link the internal portions of UNIX (the kernel) with you. The shell provides an interface between the kernel and you. You issue commands, which the shell translates into system calls for the kernel, and information returned by the kernel is displayed on-screen by the shell in a form you can use. The shell provides two major functions: it serves as a command interpreter and provides a built-in programming language.

shell built-in   Any of a series of operations that the shell performs by itself, without calling on another program. The cd command is an example of a shell built-in.

shell procedure   See *shell program*.

shell program   A program written in the programming language built into the shell. Most shell programs are written in the language built into Bourne Shell, although C Shell programs are popular in some environments.

shell script   See *shell program*.

signal   An interruption sent to a program by the operating system. A signal may indicate a program error (such as division by zero) or an outside event (such as the user logging off), or it may have been sent by a user using the kill command. Programs can choose to ignore signals, take action when certain signals occur, or terminate.

slave   The computer or program that assumes a submissive role when two computers or programs communicate with each other. For example, when one UNIX computer uses UUCP to contact another, one computer—the slave—performs operations as directed by the other computer—the master. See *master*.

special file   See *device file*.

spooler   A system program that accepts requests to print data on a printer and controls the details of getting the desired data from a file onto paper.

standard   A series of guidelines that suggest how certain operations should be performed. Standards enable programs from many different sources to work together compatibly.

standard error   The default destination for error messages, usually your screen.

standard input   The default source for input, usually your keyboard.

standard output   The default destination for output, usually your screen.

superblock   The small block of data at the beginning of a UNIX file system that maintains important bookkeeping information about the file system.

superuser   A nickname for the login name root, signifying root's ability to accomplish almost any task on a UNIX machine. See *root*.

swapping   A technique that enables the kernel to use disk space instead of memory when memory is in short supply. If programs are competing for too little memory, the memory used by waiting programs is copied to disk so that running programs can temporarily use that memory.

swap space   In old UNIX systems, the area of disk space the UNIX kernel uses for storing data when not enough main memory is available. Most UNIX systems today are paging systems, and the area of disk used in place of main memory is called the *paging area*.

symbolic link   On Berkeley systems, a type of link implemented differently than regular links. Symbolic links can link names on one file system with files stored on another file system, which regular links cannot do.

system administration   Tasks that must be performed as part of owning and operating a computer, but that have nothing to do with the tasks for which the computer was purchased.

system administrator   A person who performs system administration, often as a full-time job.

system call   Operations that the UNIX kernel makes available to application programs to perform tasks such as printing data, displaying characters on-screen, and transferring information to and from disk.

system unit   See *processor unit*.

System V   AT&T's version of UNIX. Since 1983, AT&T has sold and supported System V as their only commercial version of UNIX.

terminal   A device containing a screen and keyboard that enables you to communicate with the computer. Terminals superficially look like computers, but most of them lack a processor.

text   The machine instructions within a program that tell the computer what to do.

thrashing   A condition in which a computer spends most of its time swapping programs in and out of memory and very little time actually doing useful work.

thread   A part of a program that can operate independently from and simultaneously with another part of the same program. Some operating systems enable programs to perform several sequences of operations at the same time; each sequence is known as a thread.

tilde substitution   A typing saver available in C Shell and Korn Shell that enables you to represent your home directory with a tilde (~). A path name beginning with a tilde is taken relative to your own home directory. A tilde followed by a user name is taken relative to that user's home directory.

timesharing   Used by multiuser computers, a technique in which the computer spends only a few milliseconds at a time with you, rapidly switching its attention from one user to the next. This technique gives you the impression that the computer is devoting its full time to you.

tool   Any of a large collection of UNIX programs that perform simple but helpful tasks that help you do your work.

toolkit   Provided by various manufacturers and software organizations, a collection of functions and programming aids that enables programmers to accomplish tasks easily when writing programs for graphical user interfaces.

trusted program   A program that has been cleared by the system administrator as coming from a reliable source and containing no hostile codes, such as viruses or worms.

trusted shell   A high-security shell that enables you to run only trusted programs.

tunables   Any of a large set of parameters that the system administrator can adjust to increase system performance. These parameters are called *tunables* because they enable the system administrator to fine-tune the operating system. Choosing values for the tunables requires a thorough understanding of UNIX and a knowledge of how the computer will be used. Many of the tunables specify how large certain tables within the kernel should be.

Ultrix   A version of UNIX developed and distributed by Digital Equipment Corporation (DEC).

UniForum   An international organization of UNIX users, originally established in 1980 under the name */usr/group*. UniForum is best known for its annual conference of the same name.

Uniplus+   A version of UNIX available from Unisoft.

University of California at Berkeley (UCB)   The site of much early UNIX development. UCB produces a widely used version of UNIX, upon which is based many versions of UNIX from manufacturers such as DEC. The term *Berkeley* is sometimes used to mean the version of UNIX provided by UCB.

unnamed buffer   An internal storage area within the vi editor where data is stored temporarily during copy and move operations.

UPS   (Uninterruptable Power Supply) A battery-operated power supply that supplies your computer with power for a short period of time if you lose electrical-line power.

user block   An area of memory that contains essential bookkeeping information about a process; required by the kernel when the process is running. The user block serves as an index for the rest of the process's memory.

user ID   A unique number assigned to each UNIX user by the system administrator; used by the UNIX kernel for internal accounting purposes. User IDs typically are not used by the users themselves.

/usr/group   See *UniForum*.

UTS   A version of UNIX distributed by Amdahl for its mainframe computers.

UUCP   (UNIX-to-UNIX Copy) A software package that enables UNIX computers to exchange data, programs, and mail, and to execute commands on other computers. Computers using UUCP are connected through networks, data switches, or public telephone lines.

V   (*vee*) An operating system written in 1981 at Stanford University that concentrated on communication. V runs on Sun workstations, the DEC MicroVAX, and DEC's DECstation.

Venix   A UNIX-like operating system from Venturecom.

virtual memory management An arrangement that makes the computer seem to have much more memory than it really does, resulting in the illusion that all programs have all the memory they need, when actually the amount of memory used by all programs far exceeds the amount of memory actually present on the computer.

virus A hostile code fragment that duplicates itself from one computer to another. Viruses depend on floppy disks or communication networks to spread from one computer to another.

visual shell A menu-driven shell, such as XENIX's vsh, in which you perform operations by making selections from the menu or by typing simple commands.

wild card See *file generation character*.

window When using a graphical user interface, the portion of your terminal screen that displays the output from a program.

window manager A component of a graphical user interface that interacts with the display server to enable you to perform various windows operations, such as moving windows, resizing windows, iconifying windows, and so on.

workstation Desktop computer with its own processing capacities, which can access larger computer systems through networks.

worm A program—usually written with malicious intent—that duplicates itself from computer to computer.

Writers Workbench (WWB) A text processing product, developed at Bell Labs, that attempts to analyze and proofread documents.

WWB See *Writers Workbench*.

X Consortium An industry group formed by MIT in January 1988, charged with supporting and continuing the development of X Windows.

XENIX A UNIX look-alike originally developed by Microsoft Corporation, among the most popular versions of UNIX.

Xlib An interface library for C programmers that enables them to express what they want to do, such as to draw a circle or display certain text, with Xlib handling the details of getting the proper message to the display server.

X/Open A nonprofit, international consortium of computer manufacturers that produces operating system standards. X/Open defined a set of standards—*Common Applications Environment* (CAE)—that defines how application programs interact with an operating system. X/Open published a document, *X/Open Portability Guide*, that defines their CAE.

X Windows System A set of functions and programs that form the basis for several graphical user interfaces, including OPEN LOOK and Motif. X Windows was developed in the early 1980s at the Massachusetts Institute of Technology (MIT).

zombie A process that has died, but whose parent has not performed a `wait` system call.

Important UNIX Addresses

This appendix lists the addresses of some of the organizations and magazines discussed in this book.

Free Software Foundation
675 Massachusetts Avenue
Cambridge, MA 02139
(617) 876-3296

National Technical Information Service
Federal Computer Products Center
U.S. Department of Commerce
Springfield, VA 22161
(703) 487-4807

UniForum
2901 Tasman Drive, Suite 201
Santa Clara, CA 95054
(408) 986-8840
(800) 255-5620

UNIX Review
Miller Freeman Publications, Inc.
500 Howard Street
San Francisco, CA 94105

UNIX Today!
CMP Publications, Inc.
600 Community Drive
Manhasset, NY 11030

UNIXWorld
Tech Valley Publishing
444 Castro Street
Mountain View, CA 94041
(415) 940-1500

USENIX Association
2560 Ninth Street, Suite 215
Berkeley, CA 94710
(415) 528-8649

UniForum
Affiliate Groups

T his appendix lists the names and locations of UniForum affiliate
groups.

Domestic

Group	Location
Alabama UNIX /usr/group	Birmingham, Alabama
/cny UNIX User's Group	Syracuse, New York
Hounix, Inc.	Houston, Texas
Michigan!/usr/group	Detroit, Michigan
Southwest!Uniforum	Tempe, Arizona
/usr/group/chicago	Naperville, Illinois
WAUUG	Washington, D.C.
Dallas/Ft. Worth Unix Users Group	Dallas, Texas
Seattle/UNIX Group	Mercer Island, Washington

International

Group	Location
AMIX Israel UNIX Users Group	Ramat Gan, Israel
AUUG Incorporated	North Sydney, Australia
Sociedad Chilena de UNIX	Santiago, Chile
China UNIX User Group	Beijing, PRC
DKUUG	Vedback, Denmark
Italian UNIX Systems Users Group	Milan, Italy
Japan UNIX Society	Tokyo, Japan
UniForum NZ	Hamilton, New Zealand
UniForum Singapore	Singapore
UniForum Kuwait	Kuwait
UniForum Mexico	Mexico City
UNIX Group Argentina	Buenos Aires, Argentina
UNIX User Group Austria	Vienna, Austria
UniForum Canada	Etobicoke, Ontario
UniForum SA	Pinegowrie, South Africa
UniForum UK	Surrey, England
USRNIX HK	Hong Kong

Index

Q-R

Que Gives You The Most Comprehensive Programming Information Available!

Using Borland C++

Lee Atkinson & Mark Atkinson

This essential tutorial and reference for Turbo C++ programmers features sample programs, command references, and practical examples.

Version 1.0

$24.95 USA

0-88022-675-7, 700 pp., 7 3/8 x 9 1/4

More Programming Titles From Que

**Borland C++
Programmer's Reference**

*Latest Versions of Borland C++
and Turbo C++*

$29.95 USA

0-88022-714-1, 900 pp.,

C Programmer's Toolkit

Turbo C, QuickC & ANSI C

$39.95 USA

0-88022-457-6, 350 pp., 7 3/8 x 9 1/4

**Clipper Programmer's
Reference**

Clipper 5.0

$29.95 USA

0-88022-677-3, 800 pp., 7 3/8 x 9 1/4

**DOS Programmer's Reference,
2nd Edition**

Through DOS 4

$29.95 USA

0-88022-458-4, 850 pp., 7 3/8 x 9 1/4

Network Programming in C

Book + 2 Disks!

$49.95 USA

0-88022-569-6, 650 pp., 7 3/8 x 9 1/4

ORACLE Programmer's Guide

Version 5.1A-5.1B

$29.95 USA

0-88022-468-1, 500 pp., 7 3/8 x 9 1/4

Paradox Programmer's Reference

Paradox 3.5

$29.95 USA

0-88022-705-2, 800 pp., 7 3/8 x 9 1/4

QuickC Programmer's Guide

Version 2.5

$29.95 USA

0-88022-534-3, 550 pp., 7 3/8 x 9 1/4

UNIX Programmer's Reference

AT&T UNIX System V

$29.95 USA

0-88022-536-X, 750 pp., 7 3/8 x 9 1/4

**UNIX Programmer's
Quick Reference**

AT&T System V, Release 3

$8.95 USA

0-88022-535-1, 160 pp., 4 3/4 x 8

**UNIX Shell Commands
Quick Reference**

AT&T System V Releases 3 & 4

$8.95 USA

0-88022-572-6, 160 pp., 4 3/4 x 8

**Using Assembly Language,
2nd Edition**

*Microsoft Assembler & Borland's
Turbo Assembler*

$29.95 USA

0-88022-464-9, 850 pp., 7 3/8 x 9 1/4

Using BASIC

GW-BASIC & BASICA

$24.95 USA

0-88022-537-8, 584 pp., 7 3/8 x 9 1/4

Using C

*Microsoft C Version 6, Turbo
C++, and QuickC Version 2.5*

$29.95 USA

0-88022-571-8, 950 pp., 7 3/8 x 9 1/4

Using QuickBASIC 4

Version 4

$24.95 USA

0-88022-378-2, 713 pp., 7 3/8 x 9 1/4

**Using Turbo Pascal 6,
2nd Edition**

Through Version 6

$29.95 USA

0-88022-700-1, 800 pp., 7 3/8 x 9 1/4

To Order, Call:
(800) 428-5331 OR (317) 573-2500

Free Catalog!

Mail us this registration form today, and we'll send you a free catalog featuring Que's complete line of best-selling books.

Name of Book _____

Name _____

Title _____

Phone (___) _____

Company _____

Address _____

City _____

State _____ ZIP _____

Please check the appropriate answers:

1. Where did you buy your Que book?
   ☐ Bookstore (name: _____)
   ☐ Computer store (name: _____)
   ☐ Catalog (name: _____)
   ☐ Direct from Que
   ☐ Other: _____

2. How many computer books do you buy a year?
   ☐ 1 or less
   ☐ 2-5
   ☐ 6-10
   ☐ More than 10

3. How many Que books do you own?
   ☐ 1
   ☐ 2-5
   ☐ 6-10
   ☐ More than 10

4. How long have you been using this software?
   ☐ Less than 6 months
   ☐ 6 months to 1 year
   ☐ 1-3 years
   ☐ More than 3 years

5. What influenced your purchase of this Que book?
   ☐ Personal recommendation
   ☐ Advertisement
   ☐ In-store display
   ☐ Price
   ☐ Que catalog
   ☐ Que mailing
   ☐ Que's reputation
   ☐ Other: _____

6. How would you rate the overall content of the book?
   ☐ Very good
   ☐ Good
   ☐ Satisfactory
   ☐ Poor

7. What do you like *best* about this Que book?
   _____
   _____

8. What do you like *least* about this Que book?
   _____
   _____

9. Did you buy this book with your personal funds?
   ☐ Yes   ☐ No

10. Please feel free to list any other comments you may have about this Que book.
   _____
   _____
   _____

— **Que** —

Order Your Que Books Today!

Name _____

Title _____

Company _____

City _____

State _____ ZIP _____

Phone No. (___) _____

Method of Payment:

Check ☐   (Please enclose in envelope.)

Charge My: VISA ☐   MasterCard ☐

American Express ☐

Charge # _____

Expiration Date _____

Order No.	Title	Qty.	Price	Total

You can **FAX** your order to **1-317-573-2583**. Or call **1-800-428-5331, ext. ORDR** to order direct.
Please add $2.50 per title for shipping and handling.

Subtotal	
Shipping & Handling	
Total	

— **Que** —

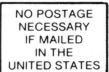